Betty Ford

Betty Ford

*First Lady, Women's Advocate,
Survivor, Trailblazer*

Lisa McCubbin

Foreword by Susan Ford Bales

GALLERY BOOKS

New York   London   Toronto   Sydney   New Delhi

Gallery Books
An Imprint of Simon & Schuster, Inc.
1230 Avenue of the Americas
New York, NY 10020

First Gallery Books hardcover edition September 2018

GALLERY BOOKS and colophon are registered
trademarks of Simon & Schuster, Inc.

For information about special discounts for bulk purchases,
please contact Simon & Schuster Special Sales at
1-866-506-1949 or business@simonandschuster.com.

The Simon & Schuster Speakers Bureau can bring authors to your live event.
For more information or to book an event, contact the Simon & Schuster Speakers
Bureau at 1-866-248-3049 or visit our website at www.simonspeakers.com.

Interior design by Jaime Putorti

Manufactured in the United States of America

10 9 8 7 6 5 4 3 2 1

Library of Congress Cataloging-in-Publication Data

Names: McCubbin, Lisa, author.
Title: Betty Ford : First Lady, Women's Advocate, Survivor, Trailblazer /
    Lisa McCubbin ; foreword by Susan Ford Bales.
Description: New York : Gallery Books, 2018.
Identifiers: LCCN 2018009239 (print) | LCCN 2018025870 (ebook) |
    ISBN 9781501164743 (eBook) | ISBN 9781501164682 (hardback)
Subjects: LCSH: Ford, Betty, 1918–2011. | Presidents' spouses—
    United States—Biography. | BISAC: BIOGRAPHY & AUTOBIOGRAPHY /
    Women. | HISTORY / United States / 20th Century.
Classification: LCC E867 (ebook) | LCC E867 .M43 2018 (print) |
    DDC 973.925092 [B] —dc23
LC record available at https://lccn.loc.gov/2018009239

ISBN 978-1-5011-6468-2
ISBN 978-1-5011-6474-3 (ebook)

To anyone who is facing what seems to be an insurmountable struggle, may you find comfort, strength, and hope in Betty Ford's story.

And to Clint—
Like Betty Ford, your courage and resilience epitomize the capability of the human spirit. I am beyond grateful for your unwavering support, love, and incomparable wisdom. It is truly a blessing to have you by my side throughout this journey.

CONTENTS

FOREWORD

She was known by many names: First Lady, Betty, Gramma, Second Lady, Mrs. Ford, Elizabeth Bloomer; in fact, she even came to be known as a location: *"He went to Betty Ford."* I knew each of those names, but I proudly called her by another: Mom.

Mom has been gone for nearly seven years. Yet the permanence of her various names and their examples for future generations shine today as brightly as ever.

Mom wrote two autobiographical books. The first was a memoir written shortly after we left the White House. The second was the poignant story of her journey to confront (and eventually triumph over) breast cancer, alcoholism, and addiction to painkillers. So when Lisa McCubbin approached me regarding her plans to write a book about Mom, I was skeptical. Surely, I told Lisa, everything that could or should be written about Mom had long since been written and relegated to the history stacks; what relevance could Mom have today, especially to the current generation of young women and girls? Needless to say, and as readers will experience throughout Lisa's narrative, my skepticism has been shattered. Quite simply, Lisa has given voice to what is apparent: this would have been Mom's third book.

There was a time when the notion that "a woman's place is in the home" was commonplace—Mom showed by word and deed the folly of that paradigm. There was a time when the words *breast* and *cancer* were never uttered in public, much less together—but Mom, as first lady, brought both words permanently into the public square by announcing "I have breast cancer." From that moment on, women's health care around the world changed forever. There was a time when alcoholism and addiction to painkillers ravaged our nation, hidden in complete silence and shame—but Mom's very public conquest of those diseases and her creation of the Betty Ford Center erased the silence and shame. There was a time when women's rights and equality of opportunities for women were ignored by policy makers—but Mom's unwavering voice for the Equal Rights Amendment, Title IX, and the rights of women in the workplace and elsewhere forced those issues into the mainstream. And there was a time when the wife of a national leader would never even consider advocating policies diametrically opposite those of her husband and his supporters—but Mom (and Dad) showed America that disagreeing, without being disagreeable, could (and should) be an acceptable norm for such discussions.

Readers will learn about the extraordinary efforts Mom and others made to confront those challenges and the lessons young people today can learn from their efforts.

But if readers think they're about to embark upon nothing more than a journey of continuous personal achievements, White House gossip and intrigue, and stories of an idyllic family and a Midwestern wife's healthy and blissful ninety-three years, they will find those expectations misplaced. With impeccably researched personal and historical details, this book paints a life's tapestry of joy, heartache, accomplishment, and work yet to be done. There are passages that inspire; others that evoke tears of sadness; others that are hilarious; and, yes, even portions that I personally may have preferred to have been omitted.

In short, this is the story of Betty Ford, told with honesty, compassion, and candor. And, in the end, a finer embodiment of what Mom would have expected from such a book there could never be.

I miss her.

Susan Ford Bales
April 2018

PROLOGUE

"We're Doing This Because We Love You"

April 1, 1978. It was a day everyone there would remember with such visceral, painful clarity that talking about it decades later would still trigger tears and a lump in the throat. As they walked past the olive tree and up to the front door, there was a heavy silence in the desert air. Each of them held a piece of paper scrawled with dark secrets none of them had ever dared speak. They knew that what they were about to do would break her to pieces. For all of them, it was the hardest thing they'd ever had to do, but they'd all agreed there was no other choice. They loved her too much to lose her.

Inside, Betty Ford, a week shy of her sixtieth birthday, had no idea what was about to happen. She had risen, gone through her normal morning routine, and was dressed, as usual, in her quilted pink satin robe. She rarely wore makeup these days, and it was almost hard to believe that just fifteen months earlier she'd been first lady of the United States and had appeared on national television with her hair perfectly coiffed, makeup camera ready, wearing a well-coordinated sweater and skirt as she gave ABC News correspondent Barbara Walters a tour of the residential quarters of the White House. Betty had always dressed well—her love of fashion was born out of years as a model and dancer—but somehow her world had spiraled into such despair that these days that pastel robe had become her fashion statement. None of the others would be able to recall what he or she was wearing, but they'd all remember Betty's pink robe.

Outside, Dr. Joseph Pursch looked at his watch and said, "It's time." He made eye contact with each of them—a final reassurance that what they were about to do was absolutely necessary. It was a matter of life or death.

There were twelve of them all together: Betty's devoted husband, Gerald R. "Jerry" Ford, the thirty-eighth president of the United States; two doctors; a nurse; Jerry's executive assistant, Bob Barrett; Betty's personal assistant, Caroline Coventry; Clara Powell, the family's former household helper, who had been like a second mother to the Ford children; oldest son Mike and his wife, Gayle; and the Fords' three other adult children, Jack, Steve, and Susan. For the intervention to work, Dr. Pursch, a psychiatrist, had told them they all had to be there, and it was critical for them to present a strong and united front.

The word *intervention* was a foreign term to most of them just forty-eight hours earlier—for in 1978, it was a relatively new approach—but in the time they'd all gathered in Rancho Mirage from various points across the country, they had been quickly schooled in how it would work.

President Ford had been on the East Coast in the middle of a three-city speaking tour when Susan had called in tears.

"Dad," she pleaded, "you need to come home immediately. Mom is in a bad way."

The former president had been able to get his old friend and one-time secretary of state Henry Kissinger to fill in for him, and had flown in on a private jet from Rochester, New York, just hours earlier.

They had gathered in President Ford's office, which was conveniently located in the house next door to the Fords' new residence at the end of Sand Dune Road.

"This is not going to be pleasant, is it?" President Ford had asked.

"No," Dr. Pursch responded. "It never is. But it's the only thing to do. When it works, it works beautifully and is lifesaving."

Twenty-eight-year-old Mike Ford feared what his mother's reaction might be. Caroline Coventry, also twenty-eight, had fallen into the job as secretary to the former first lady just seven months earlier and had spent more time with Mrs. Ford than any of them during that time. She recalled being "scared to death."

Jack, the second-born son, who was twenty-six at the time, had been the hardest to convince to join in the intervention. He had given up hope that his mother's problem could ever be corrected. "After you've buried somebody three times over," he said, "you're reluctant to start shoveling dirt again." He was afraid they'd just be hurting her gratuitously.

Steve had driven down from Los Angeles that morning, having no idea how this was going to work, but he was in. At twenty-three, he was the youngest of "the boys," and as he'd headed east on Interstate 10, his thoughts went back to all the times he'd been hurt by his mother's behavior. Still, the last thing he wanted to do was hurt her in return.

It was Susan, the youngest member of the family, who had called for this urgent meeting—indeed, she had demanded it. After leaving college the previous year, she had moved to Palm Desert and lived in a condo not far from her parents' new home in Rancho Mirage. Living there, she'd seen her mother's dramatic decline: the way she shuffled when she walked and how her speech was slow and slurred, even in the mornings, well before her usual five o'clock cocktail. None of them understood what was going on, but it had reached the point where something had to be done.

Just two days earlier, Susan and Caroline had confronted Betty, staging their own mini-intervention with the help of their gynecologist, Dr. Joe Cruse, who was himself a recovering alcoholic. They had gone to the house and approached her while she was in her study. At first, Susan tried a gentle approach.

"Mom, you need to stop taking all these pills," she said. "I don't like what it's doing to you."

But they hadn't caught her early enough in the morning—Betty was already under the influence of whatever combination of medications she'd taken with her morning tea—and she immediately became defensive.

"Well, I *am* stopping. I've cut out this pill, and I've cut down on that one . . ."

Dr. Cruse began telling his story: how he had been an alcoholic, and the destruction it had caused in his life until he got sober. And then he told Betty there was no doubt in his mind that she, too, was chemically dependent.

What a bunch of pips they are to have dreamt this up, Betty thought. How dare they gang up on her like this. After a while, she'd had enough.

She stood up, her eyes glaring. "You're all a bunch of monsters!" she screamed. "Now, get out of here! Get out of my house and never come back!"

Just two days later, those words and the bitter anger on her mother's face were still fresh in Susan's mind.

No, it was not going to be pleasant.

Mike and Gayle walked up to the door, as the others stood a few feet away, just out of sight. With a firm hand, Mike knocked. Collectively, the twelve of them held their breath.

Betty was startled by the knocking and wondered who it might be. She wasn't expecting anyone—especially at this hour on a Saturday— and her Secret Service agents hadn't alerted her that anyone was coming. When she opened the door, she could hardly believe her eyes.

"Mike! Gayle! What are you doing here?" She broke into a huge smile and reached out to hug them. "What a wonderful surprise!"

Her first thought was that they'd come because they'd heard she wasn't feeling well. Or maybe it was to celebrate her birthday. Turning sixty was, after all, one of those milestones. And then, out of the corner of her eyes, she saw the others. No one was yelling "Surprise!" They were all stone-faced, somber. Like someone had died.

And there's Jerry. What is Jerry doing home? He was supposed to be giving a speech in—where was it?—New York or North Carolina or someplace? She could never keep his schedule straight. Ever since they'd "retired," he'd been traveling just as much as when he was in Congress. But she knew he wasn't supposed to be home for at least a couple more days.

A sinking feeling started coming over her as they trooped inside. Jerry took her by the hand and led her through the foyer and down the two steps into the expansive sunken living room. There was an uncomfortable silence as everyone else followed.

"Mother," Jerry said gently—ever since they'd had children, he'd always called her "Mother"—"sit down. We've got something we want to talk to you about, and we want you to listen because we love you."

The room had a light, airy feeling and was set up for conversation and entertaining. A large sofa faced the floor-to-ceiling white brick fireplace, with four overstuffed chairs, two on each side, all surrounding a square coffee table in the middle. Two high-backed wicker chairs provided additional seating. Behind the sofa were three sets of sliding glass doors that led to a patio overlooking the thirteenth fairway of the Thunderbird Country Club golf course. Long drapes in a floral fabric of soft green, blue, and white matched the upholstered furniture. The cheerful yet soothing palette had been chosen to complement the enormous painting that hung on the far wall and was the focal point of the room: John Ulbricht's stunning portrait of Betty, dressed in an elegant pale-green silk gown, which had been presented to her at the White House.

The woman in the pink robe barely resembled the first lady in the painting, and as they all took their places, it was as if the woman on the wall was there as a reminder of the mother and wife everyone wanted back so desperately. Jerry guided Betty to the sofa, as the others moved to sit in particular chairs, and it was obvious to Betty that this had all been choreographed without her knowledge.

Anger was building inside her. Who was behind this? Jerry? Susan? Dr. Joe Cruse, who had betrayed her two days earlier?

Jerry was the first to speak. "This is Dr. Joe Pursch and nurse Pat Benedict," he said, nodding toward them. She, of course, knew everyone else. Then he took her hand and said, "Betty, the reason we're here is because we love you." You could tell he was struggling. He had been the most powerful man in the world and had made decisions that affected millions of people. But nothing had prepared him for this.

"We love you, Mother," Jerry repeated, "but we think you are chemically dependent, and the doctors want to talk to you."

Bob Barrett would recall that she looked so small, "almost like a doll, lost in the cushions, confusion written all over her face."

"Mrs. Ford, you don't have to be alarmed," Pursch said. "All these people care for you."

Jerry turned to Mike and said, "Mike, you start."

Mike had his notes in front of him, but he didn't need to look down. "Mom," he said, "being the oldest, I probably saw more clearly the strain on you, having been a wife in Washington with four children, and all the pressures and demands that created in your environment. But, Mom, now you've got to the point where your lifestyle is destructive. It's hurting your relationship with Dad, with all of us, and with your friends. Those relationships are too valuable to lose."

It was hard. It was so hard. "Mom," he continued, "your life is too valuable to let go."

He turned to his wife and, with a glance, passed the baton.

"Mother," Gayle began, "you know we've been married for four years, and we want to start a family." Her voice quivered as she looked at her mother-in-law, sunken forlornly on the sofa. "But we want our children to know their grandmother. Not just to know her, but to know her as a healthy, loving person . . ."

Betty's eyes welled with tears. What was Gayle saying? That she wasn't fit to be a grandmother?

Jack spoke next. "There were so many times, Mother, when we lived at Crown View Drive, when I was a teenager . . . we had the pool, but I didn't like to bring friends home. I was embarrassed. If we'd gone out to the movies or something, I was always peeking around the corner into the family room to see what kind of shape you were in."

Betty still had barely reacted. She didn't know whether she should feel hurt or mad as hell. *How dare they?* She had practically raised these children on her own. God knows Jerry was never around. She'd been the good wife—first, all those years when he was in Congress—and then when he'd suddenly become vice president, she'd stepped right into the limelight. She had never wanted to be first lady, but what choice did she have? And she'd made the most of it. Had they forgotten how popular she was during the 1976 campaign? All those buttons and signs that said "Betty Ford's Husband for President" and even "Betty for President."

Jerry could feel the tension and anger growing in his wife. As each person spoke, he would clutch her hand a little tighter, give it a squeeze, and over and over again, he kept repeating, "Betty, we love you."

Steve spoke next. "Mom, do you remember that weekend I came home? Dad was gone, and I didn't want you to be alone in that rented house. You'd only been in Palm Springs a short while, and I thought you must be lonely. So, I brought my girlfriend and I made dinner. I fixed vegetables, salad, the whole thing. And then when I told you it was ready, you said, 'I really don't feel like eating.'" Steve looked at her and winced. "That hurt me, Mom."

He looked down and continued, "You know, I'd gone to the store, done the shopping, put the silverware on the proper sides of the plates, like you'd taught me, and you wouldn't even come and sit down. You just went and got another drink."

Betty was reeling. *He's got some nerve,* she thought. *I'm used to having one or two drinks before dinner. I don't have a problem with alcohol.* And yet she couldn't quite recall the incident to which he was referring.

Finally, it was Susan's turn. The twenty-year-old was shaking. She wasn't sure she could say what she'd written down. Her mouth opened, and before she could get the words out, tears started streaming down her cheeks. She turned to Clara—sitting next to her—and crumpled.

Clara put her arm around Susan and stroked her, just like she had so many times when Susan was a little girl. Through her tears, Susan began to speak. She realized she had to say what had been building up inside her for so long.

"Mom, when I was little, and even as I grew up, I always admired you for being a dancer. I wanted to be just like you. But now . . ."

She began sobbing, and everyone was starting to lose it. They'd all held their composure up to this point, but now, Susan was killing them.

"These days," Susan continued, "you're falling and clumsy. You're just not the same person. And I've talked to you about things—things that were important to me, and the next day, you didn't even remember."

Seeing her daughter fall apart was what finally cut through Betty's iron will. She had been blindsided, and now, all these stories. They were mean and cruel. And true.

What had happened? How did she go from being that woman in the painting on the wall, so regal and proud, to the woman her family was describing? And what was going to happen next?

It was all a blur. Dr. Pursch was talking about treatment and detox, and Betty was sobbing, and Jerry was holding her hand and saying over and over and over, "We love you, Betty. We're doing this because we love you."

Sitting there, in her pink robe, all Betty could think was, *This isn't the way it was supposed to be.*

PART ONE

◆

BETTY FORD, DANCER

In 1974, in the most extraordinary and unpredictable of circumstances, Betty Ford went from being a housewife in Alexandria, Virginia, to first lady of the United States in the span of ten months. She was thrust onto the world stage, and while the position was not one she had ever desired or expected—and most certainly wasn't one she was happy about—she slipped into the role as if she'd been preparing for it her entire life.

Betty's poise, grace, and indomitable spirit can all be traced back to her childhood in Grand Rapids, Michigan. It was there she developed a toughness as the younger sister of two brothers and the only daughter of a strong-willed mother; it was there she fell in love with dancing; and ultimately, it was there she met the man whose own journey would intertwine with hers.

As much as Betty Ford's story is that of an ordinary girl who would become one of the most admired and influential women of the twentieth century, it is also one of the great love stories of all time.

1

—

The Bloomer Girl

"Mother always said I'd popped out of a bottle of champagne," Betty was fond of telling people. She would break into one of her contagious smiles, and with a glint of mischief in her eyes, she'd add, "I think I was an accident; the result of an unplanned party."

Actually, Elizabeth Anne Bloomer came into the world at Lake View Hospital in Chicago on April 8, 1918, the third child born to Hortense Neahr Bloomer and William Stephenson Bloomer. Her two brothers, Bill and Bob, were seven and five, respectively, at the time of her birth, and it was that five-year spread, along with the fact that her mother was in her early thirties, that had her wondering whether she was a surprise addition to the family. Whatever the circumstances of her conception, the round-faced baby girl with sparkling blue eyes made the family complete.

Elizabeth was her given name, but perhaps it was just too formal for the bubbly personality that developed—or perhaps her mother always intended to shorten it to match the *B* names of her brothers— but as far back as she could remember, everyone called her "Betty" or "Bets."

A few months after Betty was born, the Bloomers moved from Chicago to Denver, Colorado, where William Bloomer had accepted a job as district sales manager for the Republic Rubber Corporation. After

more than twenty years in the rubber industry, William had earned
a good reputation selling conveyor belts—previously for the B. F.
Goodrich Company—and by this point, he was earning a comfortable
living.

The Bloomers rented a large house in the prestigious Capitol
Heights neighborhood and hired a live-in maid, a German woman,
to help Hortense manage the household. The house at 1410 Josephine
Street was nestled in a row of similarly grand homes owned or rented by
families of comparable status, all with sprawling front porches facing a
tree-lined sidewalk.

While Hortense appeared to enjoy life in Denver, just before Betty
turned two, William switched jobs again, this time taking a position at
the Quaker City Rubber Company, which was based in Chicago. This
would be the fourth move in less than four years—they'd been in Seattle
prior to the short stint in Chicago when Betty was born—and since William would be traveling all over the Midwest, a decision was made to
settle in Grand Rapids, Michigan, where Hortense had a cousin. This
would be the last move, and for Betty, Grand Rapids would be where her
childhood memories began.

The city of Grand Rapids lies along the Grand River, some thirty miles
east of Lake Michigan, and by the time the Bloomers arrived in the winter of 1920, the city was home to a booming furniture industry, with a
variety of immigrants making up the population. Known as "Furniture
City," Grand Rapids was one of the country's major manufacturing hubs:
a bustling midsize city with a state-of-the-art electric trolley system. For
a nickel, you could ride the electric streetcars throughout the downtown area or out to Ramona Park—an amusement park on Reeds Lake
that was famous for its double-track wooden roller coaster and outdoor
entertainment pavilion.

The Grand River flowed from north to south, dividing Grand Rapids in half, and in the 1920s, it segregated the city by income levels and,
to some extent, ethnicity. The furniture factories stood along the river,
and the men who worked in them tended to live in the small homes that
had been built in residential neighborhoods on the west side, while the
mill owners and businessmen lived on the east side in grand neighbor-

hoods with ornate mansions. The citizens of Grand Rapids held tight to traditional values, were largely churchgoers—in 1920 there were 134 churches in the city—and had overwhelmingly embraced prohibition of alcohol, banning all bars, saloons, and taverns nearly two years before it was required by the Eighteenth Amendment.

The Bloomers moved into a two-story wood-frame house at 717 Fountain Street in an affluent, predominantly Dutch east-side neighborhood where people took pride in their homes and yards. It wasn't a large house—not nearly as big as the one in Denver—but it had enough bedrooms and a separate one-car garage in back that was accessible by an alleyway. Betty would remember the house as being "filled with light" and that she was happy there.

Hortense's cousin Charlotte Neahr Irwin and her husband, Earle, lived nearby with their two children: a son named Bill and a daughter named Charlotte, whom everyone called "Shine." With William Bloomer traveling so much, it was nice for Hortense to have family close by and for her children to grow up around cousins.

Because the Grand Rapids winters were so long and cold, by the time spring came around, many well-to-do families flocked to the lakes, eager to make the most of the few months of warmth and sunshine. The Bloomers found a place called Hartt's Resort on Whitefish Lake, in Pierson, Michigan, about thirty miles due north of Grand Rapids, where you could rent a lakeside cottage for $10 a week. It was a tight-knit community in which the same families came back year after year, the kind of place where children made lifelong friends with shared memories of carefree days. The day after school let out, the Bloomers would pack up the family's Cole Eight touring car, and Hortense and the children would stay for the entire summer, with William joining them when he could take time off.

Betty had a Dutch-boy bob haircut that was popular at the time and a happy personality that attracted people to her. The first summer at the lake, she realized she could wander around the picnic grounds, and if she stopped at each table, someone would invariably offer a cookie or piece of cake. It became such a habit that she was growing chubbier by the week, prompting Hortense to hang a sign on her back that said "Please do not feed this child."

The resort had a safe bathing beach with a long L-shaped dock down the middle, and cool, clear water that was shallow enough so even the younger children could wade in up to their knees for a good distance before it got too deep. Boys and girls of varying ages romped around together, spending hours and hours in and out of the water, making up games and competitions—swimming, sailing, canoeing, and fishing from the dock with bamboo poles—their fair skin turning browner and browner as the summer days seemingly went on forever.

When Betty's father joined the family at the lake, he would take out a rowboat and fish for hours. "He was a great fisherman," she recalled. "He spent his entire vacation fishing, and we were served fish and fish and fish until I hoped I would never see fish again."

It was a simpler time, when children would leave the house in the morning and run around the neighborhood inventing games and finding ways to entertain themselves. Betty adored her two older brothers, and she trailed after them, constantly trying to be part of whatever activity they were doing. By her own admission, she was a "terrible tomboy," and it was thanks to her brothers that she learned how to properly throw a football and play ice hockey. When the two of them would get into fights—as brothers do—she'd get right down on the floor with them, trying to pull off the one who was on top. It didn't make any difference which one was on top, she was always rooting for the guy on the bottom, and she had no qualms about getting right there in the thick of things.

As soon as she was old enough, Betty walked with her brothers to Fountain Street Elementary School. On one of her first days in kindergarten, someone noticed a blemish on her left hand and began teasing her about it. It was a birthmark that she'd never paid any attention to, but soon a whole group of kids were making fun of her. She was mortified to be made to feel such an outcast, and when she got home and saw her mother, she burst into tears.

Through the sobs, Betty explained how the other children had been so cruel and how embarrassed she was to have this mark on her hand.

"Oh, dear Betty," Hortense said, as she swept her daughter into her arms, "don't you realize? You are the only little girl in the world with a birthmark like that. It makes you special, and most importantly, because of that mark, no matter where you go, I will never lose you." The next day, Betty returned to school filled with pride and a newfound sense of confidence.

Even though Betty loved sports and could hold her own with her brothers, Hortense was determined to make a young lady out of her. From the time Betty could walk, her mother insisted she wear a hat and gloves whenever they went downtown, and she was a stickler for proper manners. She was particular about table manners: napkin in the lap, using the proper utensils, and chewing with your mouth closed. "You sound just like a horse," she'd say if Betty was chomping on an apple. "Go into the kitchen or go to your room. I don't want to hear it."

As a traveling salesman, William Bloomer would be gone weeks at a time, but Hortense kept him apprised of what was going on in the family through daily letters. Every evening, Betty would come downstairs after finishing her homework and see her mother sitting at the desk writing to her father. When he came home after a long trip, he'd always bring something for Betty, and over the years of her childhood, she amassed a cornucopia of stuffed animals. Her favorite was a teddy bear that she dragged everywhere as a little girl, but the gifts didn't make up for her dad being gone so often, and she vowed to herself that she'd never marry a man who traveled.

With William gone so much of the time, Hortense basically raised Betty and her brothers as a single mother. She was warm and loving, but she taught her children to know right from wrong, tending to teach through humor rather than pressure. Spankings in the household were rare, but the threat of a hairbrush on the bottom was always there.

When Betty was eight years old, her mother enrolled her in dance lessons.

About five blocks away from the Bloomer house, an unmarried woman named Calla Travis had transformed her home at 220 Fulton Street into the Miss Calla Travis School of Dancing. It was a big Victorian house with high ceilings, beautiful wood floors, and large rooms that were empty except for dozens of wood-slat folding chairs backed up against the walls. Miss Travis held classes upstairs and downstairs for "every phase of dance art"—ballroom, ballet, tap, Latin dancing, and even acrobatic—and while she taught many of the lessons herself, she also used previous graduates as instructors. Betty's first class was social ballroom dancing, with the boys, in jackets and ties, sitting on one side of the room, and the girls, in white socks, black patent leather Mary Janes, and white gloves, sitting on the other.

"Ladies!" Calla Travis would call out as she clapped her hands, "You sit with your legs crossed!"

The boys would stride across the room to ask a girl to be their partner, and they'd dance the waltz and fox-trot in time to Calla's clattering castanets. Betty loved it so much, she persuaded her mother to send her to Calla's studio for more classes.

"I signed up for everything," Betty wrote in her memoir. "I adored it all. Dance was my happiness."

It was on her very first day at Miss Calla's that she met Lilian Fisher, another eight-year-old, who lived a few miles out of town. Their birthdays were just two months apart, and the girls became instant friends. It was a friendship that would last their entire lives.

"She was pretty," Lilian said. "Just pretty . . . and she wasn't too tall, and she could kick. She could pirouette and do all these crazy things."

Each spring, Miss Calla put on a show featuring all her students. It was an impressive production with elaborate sets, props, and costumes, held in the St. Cecilia's Society building, which had a big stage and plenty of auditorium seating for the parents and families of the aspiring young dancers. In her debut performance, Betty was skipping around the stage with a group of girls, each of them holding tin buckets meant to look like flower baskets. Betty lost her grip, the bucket went rattling down toward the footlights, making a terrible racket, and the audience roared with laughter. For someone with less confidence, such an incident might have put them off performing for good, but not Betty. She loved being onstage. More important, she just loved to dance.

Every afternoon, right after school, Betty would head straight to the dance studio. Her report cards from middle school and high school show that she struggled to get average grades in the standard subjects, but when it came to dance, she was a perfectionist. She never tired of practicing and read voraciously about different methods and prominent dancers from around the world. She took every class Miss Travis offered, with the goal of becoming a dance instructor herself.

"There was no kind of dance that didn't fascinate me," Betty wrote. "I'd hear about some boy who'd been out west among the Indians and learned a rain dance, and I'd go to him and make him teach it to me. I was insatiable."

Calla Travis had developed a rigorous and specific "Graded System of Dance Instruction," and you had to be able to perform every move perfectly to progress to the next level. At first, it was ballet that Betty adored most of all, and she dreamt of going to New York City to become a ballerina. But the movements and positions were so precise, and she couldn't seem to get her knees straight enough to appease Miss Travis. To pass the ballet course, Betty cleverly realized that if she designed her own costume, she could wear a flowy skirt made with scarves hanging down to camouflage whether her knees were straight or bent.

A few years into Betty's dance instruction, Miss Calla returned from a visit to the University of Wisconsin, where she had learned about something new called the Dalcroze method. This method taught concepts of rhythm, structure, and musical expression using movement, which came to be known as eurythmics. It was Betty's first introduction to modern dance, and she loved the idea of experiencing music through the body as a means of self-expression. Gone were her dreams of being a prima ballerina—her new passion was modern dance.

Hortense encouraged Betty's interest in dance, but she also strived to teach her daughter humility and charity. Mrs. Bloomer had become active in the Grand Rapids community, joining Junior League—the educational and charitable women's group; and volunteering with the Mary Free Bed Guild—a women's organization that raised money to provide facilities and care for handicapped and crippled children. From a young age, Betty accompanied her mother to the Mary Free Bed convalescent home, where she'd see children her own age who were confined to wheelchairs, or had legs in braces, their disabilities due to polio or malnutrition.

By the time Betty was a teenager, Hortense was guild president, and Betty realized that she could entertain the children by creating a dance party. She would bring in a phonograph, and with the children all gathered together in a big room, she taught them how to move their bodies to the beats and rhythm of the music, using the methods she'd learned in modern dance. It delighted her to see wheelchair-bound children, with both legs in casts, clapping with their free hands and moving their upper

body, while those whose arms were crippled tapped their feet in time
to the music. With Betty's encouragement, the children escaped their
confinement for a short while, laughing and feeling the joy of music
and the pleasure of moving their bodies in whatever way they could.
This sense of compassion and connection to children with disabilities
or illnesses, or those who were victims of unfortunate circumstances,
became ingrained in her.

There were few shadows over Betty's childhood, but when the stock
market crashed in October 1929, it affected everyone. In Grand Rapids,
the furniture business collapsed. Fathers lost their jobs. Some committed suicide. Betty was just eleven years old, and suddenly things changed.
It's unclear whether William Bloomer lost his job, but Betty knew he lost
a lot of money, and as a traveling salesman whose livelihood depended
on a strong economy, his wages undoubtedly took a dramatic decline.
There would be no more household help, no more summers at Whitefish Lake, and no more store-bought dresses. For the next several years,
almost all of Betty's clothing was sewn by her mother.

As America fell into the Great Depression, the Bloomers were still
more fortunate than most, as there was always food on the table, and
Betty was even able to continue dance lessons.

Along with dance, she still loved sports, especially playing football,
and when she was in seventh and eighth grade, she was part of an all-
girl football team that played the boys in neighborhood sandlot games.
Having grown up alongside two older brothers, Betty played to win. It
never occurred to her that the girls couldn't beat the boys—and often
they did.

The year she turned fourteen, Betty began teaching ballroom dance
classes to younger children for fifty cents each, to help contribute to
her upkeep. It was half the price Calla Travis charged—she was only
fourteen, after all—but the money she made allowed her to continue
her own lessons with Miss Travis. The Bloomer house at 717 Fountain
Street didn't have a space big enough, so Betty rented the basement in
her friend Mary Adelaide Jones's house for $1. Her buddy Wally Hook
would come and play the piano—she paid him $1 too—and sometimes
Mary Adelaide's brother, Walt, would join in with his saxophone or

drums, providing the background music as Betty taught her young students how to fox-trot, waltz, and tango. Word got around, and the Betty Bloomer Dance School flourished.

That same year, she got a part-time job at Herpolsheimer's Department Store as a clothing model. "Herp's," as everyone called it, was a fixture in downtown Grand Rapids at the corner of Monroe and Ottawa Streets, with ten floors of home furnishings, housewares, jewelry, and clothing. As a teen fashion model, Betty's job was to stroll through the tearoom on Saturdays at lunchtime, wearing one of the latest ensembles. With her dancer's training, Betty was a natural model. She'd stop at each table, allowing the ladies to feel the fabric and observe the stitching.

"Twenty-five ninety-five. Third-floor sportswear," she'd say, spinning around.

"Talk about personality; she had it," recalled one of her first supervisors at Herpolsheimer's. "Everyone liked her. She was one hell of a gal."

Betty earned $3 a week and developed a real sense for fashion. Her friends admired her knack for turning something simple into something fabulous. One friend recalled how "she could come down the stairs in a basic blue dress that she had dressed up with a bit of green grosgrain and look like a million dollars."

When she entered the ninth grade, Betty attended Central High School, which was just a few blocks from her home. She participated in all sorts of extracurricular activities, such as the Sock and Buskin theater group, the vaudeville ensemble, the high school yearbook, and Gamma Delta Tau sorority—a social club whose members were known as the "Good Cheers." Given the choice between studying and socializing, though, Betty preferred the latter.

She had a large circle of friends—the girls liked her, the boys liked her—and she was just plain fun to be around. "She was very popular with the boys," Lilian Fisher recalled. "There'd be several of us who would sort of wait and see who was asking her for the Friday and Saturday night dates, and then see who was going to be left over for us."

Betty loved the attention, but she wasn't one to settle down in a long relationship with any one boy. She admitted that, for her, it was all about the pursuit.

"I would set my cap for somebody and work at it until I got his fraternity pin," she wrote. "As soon as I'd got it, I was satisfied, and I moved on to the next victim. I was scrupulous about giving the last fellow's pin back, that's the only good thing I can say for myself."

She also expected boys to be courteous and respectful, and wouldn't put up with boorish behavior. One night she went to a dance with a boy named Bill Warren. He was three years older, good-looking, with curly blond hair and a fun personality. At one point during the evening, though, he left her to go out in the parking lot and have a beer with some other boys. When he returned, Betty was fuming. As he held out his hand for her to dance, she slapped him in the face.

"You're no gentleman," she scoffed. "Don't ever bother to call me again."

Every so often, Betty and some friends would drive two and a half hours east to Ann Arbor to attend a University of Michigan football game, where one of the star players was a young man named Gerald Ford Jr. from Grand Rapids. Jerry Ford, five years older than Betty, had grown up on the west side of town in more of a working-class area than where Betty lived, and while she had never met him, she knew *of* him. Everybody in Grand Rapids knew the name Jerry Ford.

In 1930, when Betty was still in junior high school, he was a senior at South High School, and captain of the football team. That year, Jerry made the all-city and all-state teams, and his name appeared often in the sports pages of the *Grand Rapids Herald*.

Ford went on to play center for the University of Michigan, with number 48 on his blue-and-maize jersey. In 1932 and 1933, the Michigan Wolverines went undefeated with back-to-back national titles, and the following year, senior Jerry Ford was named the team's Most Valuable Player.

In 1934 Betty was sixteen years old, and one afternoon, she and some of her girlfriends went to a gypsy tea-leaf reader, just for fun. The fortune teller went around and looked into each girl's cup, supposedly able to see how their lives were going to turn out. "You'll meet a tall, dark stranger," she said to one. "Many children are in your future," she proclaimed for another. When it came Betty's turn, the gypsy peered into Betty's teacup and then made a statement that was so different from all the others, and so striking, it took Betty by surprise.

"You will be meeting kings and queens and people of great prominence," the fortune teller said with conviction. Then she looked into Betty's eyes and added, "You will have an extraordinary life."

With dreams of becoming a professional dancer, Betty took the gypsy's words to heart, and envisioned herself performing in London and Vienna, Austria. She could never have imagined in her sixteen-year-old mind that yes, she would meet kings and queens, and people of great prominence, but it would be on the world stage, and the partner by her side would not be a dancer but a tall, blond, former football player from, of all places, the west side of Grand Rapids. While that would be decades later, something the tea leaves did not predict—a sudden tragedy—was just around the corner.

It was a hot, hot day in July 1934—one of those hazy summer days when the humidity made everything feel heavy. Betty and her girlfriend Ev Thompson had been out driving around town in Ev's convertible with the top down. As they came wheeling up to Betty's house, Ev was honking the horn, and they were both "waving and yelling and showing off the way sixteen-year-olds do," she wrote.

As the car pulled to a stop, the front door of the house swung open, and Betty's twenty-year-old cousin Shine came running outside.

"Shh!" Shine said, waving her hands. "Just calm down."

Betty could tell by the look on her face that something was wrong. "What's happened?" she asked.

Shine hesitated and then said, "They had to take your father to the hospital."

As the details came pouring out, Betty could hardly believe what she was hearing. A couple of her parents' friends from Detroit had stopped by the house a few hours earlier to visit her mother and dad. Hortense invited them in and went to find William. He had gone out back to the garage to work on the car. And that's where she found him.

In the stifling heat, one can only imagine the horror Hortense felt when she found her husband's lifeless body and saw the key in the ignition, the car emptied of gas.

A police ambulance took William to nearby Butterworth Hospital, but "efforts to revive him were of no avail." The official cause of death was carbon monoxide poisoning, and it was ruled accidental. The next day, on what would have been William S. Bloomer's fifty-eighth birthday, a front-page article in the *Grand Rapids Press* noted that he had been unemployed for several months after losing his job at the Corduroy Tire Company plant.

"He'd gone through the Depression and lost everything," Betty's brother Bill recalled. "I can remember vividly the pain that he showed from not being able to do everything."

Still, Betty's brothers would never admit what others speculated—pointing to the fact that the insurance claim was paid and no inquest was made by the coroner—and it wouldn't be until many years later, after the pain had dulled, that Betty herself would acknowledge it was likely her father took his own life.

Friends and family members came by to pay their respects, and when the funeral was held a couple of days later in the Bloomers' living room, Betty overheard hushed voices discussing something she had never known or even suspected: her father had been an alcoholic. Her mother had kept it a secret from her, and Betty never witnessed it, for he drank only when he was traveling. But now, all those job changes, and moving the family from city to city made more sense. It's likely that William Bloomer had trouble holding down a job, and that's the reason Hortense insisted on settling in Grand Rapids, near family.

In 1934 alcoholism was far less understood, and the word *alcoholic* conjured up images of a destitute man, lying filthy in the street, drinking straight from a bottle in a brown paper bag. To learn that her father had been an alcoholic would have added a feeling of shame on top of the devastation of his sudden death. There was no counseling; no one dared broach such subjects. It was a lot for a sixteen-year-old girl to handle.

"It was rougher for everybody after that," Betty wrote. "Because he was gone, and we'd loved him."

Financially, there was insurance money to help the family get by, and her brothers, who were already in their twenties, had jobs, but eventually Hortense, too, needed to go to work. She got a real estate license, and just went out and did it. Betty would recall what an impression that made on her—an example of "how independent a woman can be if she needs to be."

After William's death, the bond between Betty and her mother grew even stronger—they depended on each other and had a very open dialogue about everything, including sex. Hortense explained to Betty that sex was "beautiful," but instilled in her that it was something to be experienced only after marriage. Whenever Betty went out to a party or a dance, her mother used to wait up for her to come home, and Betty would tell her all about the evening—who she danced with and what the girls were wearing. In an interview later in life, though, Betty admitted that she didn't always tell her mother everything. "I told her what I wanted to," she said with a grin.

In high school, she didn't smoke or drink like some of the girls—although she would ask her dates to light a cigarette so she could just hold it and look as though she were smoking like Bette Davis—and if anyone handed her a cocktail at a fraternity party, she'd simply pour it into the nearest potted plant.

Hortense continually pushed Betty to do her best and was quick to point out when she knew she hadn't. One night, after a performance in the high school follies, in which Betty admitted she "did sort of a sloppy job," her mother sat her down and said, "If you don't do it well, don't do it at all." That consistent message, expressed with love and encouragement, inspired Betty to strive for perfection in everything she did. Now with her father gone, it was especially important for Betty to make her mother proud.

In the spring of 1935, the year before her senior year in high school, Betty graduated from the Miss Calla Travis School of Dancing, with top marks across the board for attendance, technical terms, original waltz, examination, and senior dance composition, and now she was qualified to be an instructor herself.

That year, a curly haired little actress named Shirley Temple became a sensation as she sang and tap-danced her way into the hearts of moviegoers, appearing in uplifting films such as *Curly Top* and *Bright Eyes*. She was a breath of fresh air to a people beaten down by economic woes, and every little girl under the age of ten suddenly wanted to be just like her. With Shirley Temple dolls, Shirley Temple dresses, and Shirley Temple look-alike contests across the country, there was an influx of girls signing up for dance lessons at Calla Travis's school. Betty became the main instructor and the girls idolized her.

Lilian Fisher's younger sister Edith, whom everyone called Toto, was one of Betty's students at that time. "We had black patent tap shoes with grosgrain ribbons to tie them, and velvet dresses," Toto remembered. Betty would get out and demonstrate what it was like to dance with a boy, and "she was so beautiful, so graceful, and so nice. That lovely smile, that soft manner. You wanted to be just like her."

Betty loved teaching the youngsters, but her dreams went beyond being a dance instructor in Grand Rapids. She was desperate to pursue a professional career in New York and begged her mother to let her go as soon as she graduated high school. Hortense wasn't about to allow her only daughter to move to New York City at such a tender age, but eventually she promised that Betty could go once she turned twenty. It wasn't what the teenager wanted to hear, but she respected her mother's decision and continued teaching dance and working at Herpolsheimer's through her final year of high school.

That year, Miss Travis invited an official from a program at Bennington College to visit the studio and evaluate the senior dancers. A short while later, she informed Betty that out of everyone at the school, Betty and her friend Mary Snapp had been chosen to attend the elite Bennington School of the Dance in Vermont that summer. It was the chance of a lifetime, and Betty was thrilled when her mother agreed that she could go. At eighteen, it would be her first trip far from home, and an opportunity she believed could change the course of her life.

2
—

The Martha Graham
of Grand Rapids

When Betty arrived in Bennington, it was like she'd entered a whole new world. Nestled in the southwest corner of Vermont, with the Green Mountains on one side and the Taconics on the other, the Bennington College campus was made up of a dozen or so stately brick Georgian buildings surrounding a vast swath of lawn, from which you could see for miles and miles across rolling, wooded hills. It was serene, and yet a creative energy permeated the campus.

The Bennington School of the Dance had been in operation only for a few years and was the first program of its kind. By being associated with a college, the school offered a legitimacy to modern dance—which was considered avant-garde, if not downright bizarre, to many—and strived to have its students pursue dance as an art form rather than as a component of physical education. The school's instructors were top names in the dance world—Martha Hill, Doris Humphrey, Louis Horst, Charles Weidman, Hanya Holm, and Martha Graham—people Betty had been reading about in dance magazines for as long as she could remember. Being able to learn from the masters was a dream come true.

Betty felt like she had been "born to dance," and at Bennington, she found herself among girls from all over the country who shared the same passion. Her roommate was a bubbly girl from Connecticut named Natalie Harris, whom everyone called Nat, and who would remain a lifelong friend. All the girls had nicknames: Mary Snapp was Snappie, and Betty, who flounced around in a favorite nautical cap, became Skipper. For six weeks, "We breathed, we ate, we slept—nothing but dance," Betty would recall forty years later when she returned to Bennington as first lady. "Oh, what a glorious feeling!"

The modern dance students were divided into three groups according to previous experience, with group three being the most advanced. Betty, despite having ten years of dance experience, landed in group one. There was still so much to learn.

Breakfast was at seven fifteen, and then, beginning at eight, the morning session included Dance History and Criticism, Elements of Music, Basis of Dramatic Movement, and Dance Composition. After a break for lunch at one, the afternoon sessions included Percussion Accompaniment, Techniques of Modern Dance, and Modern Dance Movement. Betty soaked in the information like it was water, scrawling detailed notes in a stack of spiral memo books—one for each class. But it was Martha Graham, who taught for two weeks in the middle of the program, who made the biggest impression on Betty. A pioneer in the establishment of American modern dance, Graham was well on her way to becoming one of the principal choreographers of the twentieth century, and Betty hung on Martha's every word. Betty memorized her meticulous notes and practiced until the movements became automatic.

"Martha Graham Technique: Most important point stressed by Miss Graham is pulling up straight of the body between the pelvis and the bust," she wrote in her notes.

There was a precise way to do everything. Stretches: "Sit on floor up straight. Place bottoms of feet together in front of you. Hang on to ankles and for 16 counts bend forward and touch head to feet with a bouncing movement." Swings: "Stand on left foot, starting with right foot back, swing right foot forward and back from hip, swing arms in opposition to leg. Swing hard enough to pull yourself off the floor by the pendulum swing of your leg. Hip does not open for the swing."

In between classes, the girls bounced around the lawn trying to pick up as much grass as possible with their toes—an exercise ordered by Graham—and which prompted a local newspaper article entitled: "Bennington Campus Seethes with Women Who Jump in Odd Fashion." In the evenings, there were rehearsals and tryouts for special groups, and often they'd stay up all night to perfect a movement. The days were so strenuous that at times Betty's thigh muscles knotted up so much that she couldn't flex her knees, the pain so bad that to go down a flight of stairs, she had to sit on her bottom and slide down, step by step. But still, being able to dance eight hours a day was "ecstasy."

Martha Graham was in her forties at that time, and Betty "worshipped her as a goddess." Her mere presence was riveting. She saw Martha's body as "a beautiful instrument" that she used with remarkable strength. When she did an extension, she'd be up on the ball of one foot, and the other leg would be straight up behind her head.

To have that kind of presence—to be able to twist your body effortlessly into unnatural positions—required a tremendous amount of discipline, and Martha demanded it. If you weren't sitting up straight enough during an exercise, you'd feel the sharp punch of Martha's bony knee in your back. It required discipline not only of the body but also of the mind. It was a life-changing experience for Betty, and when the six weeks came to an end, she had a renewed sense of who she was and what she needed to do to become the dancer she wanted to be.

Back in Grand Rapids, Betty felt like she was simply biding her time until she could return to Bennington the following summer. She became an official member of the faculty at the Miss Calla Travis School of Dancing as the director of modern dance, teaching students the techniques she'd learned at Bennington and designing costumes for the annual spring production. In addition, she earned extra money modeling for Herpolsheimer's, appearing in its newspaper and magazine advertisements. Still, Betty made time to work with the children at the Mary Free Bed Guild and joined her mother in the Junior League.

When she returned to Bennington the summer of 1937, she was better prepared for the rigorous training and had progressed to the next level. Once again it was Martha Graham who captivated her, and by the end of the session, Betty was more determined than ever to go to New York City, with the ultimate goal of dancing in Martha's company.

The opportunity would come in late March the following year, when Martha and her traveling troupe held a performance in Ann Arbor. The program was presented by the University of Michigan Department of

Physical Education for Women, as dance still wasn't viewed as an art form but more as an appropriate physical activity for women. No matter what you called it, Betty knew she had to seize this opportunity. After the performance, she ran backstage, "grabbed Martha's hand, and blurted out, 'If I come to New York, can I be at your school?'"

When Martha said yes, Betty was ecstatic. With her twentieth birthday less than two weeks away, Hortense gave her blessing, and soon Betty was on her way.

Betty had contacted Natalie Harris, her former roommate from Bennington, and the two agreed to rent an apartment together as they pursued their dreams of dancing with Martha Graham. Naturally, Hortense was concerned about her only daughter setting out on her own, and insisted on driving her to New York and helping her get settled. She was very suspicious of New York men and warned Betty about what could happen if she wasn't careful.

The girls wanted to live in artsy Greenwich Village, but Hortense vetoed that idea after observing some "colorful" activity in the area; she preferred they live on the Upper East Side. They finally compromised on a one-bedroom apartment on Sixth Avenue, near Washington Square, which was within walking distance of Graham's studio at 66 Fifth Avenue.

Hortense returned to Grand Rapids, and suddenly Betty was on her own. It was her first taste of real independence, and she thrived on it. Her first session at the studio ran for four weeks, and it was intense. The schedule was Monday through Saturday: first, a ninety-minute class in dance technique with Martha every morning, followed by an hour practice class with Martha's assistant. Then, each afternoon, a ninety-minute class in technique of dance composition with Louis Horst, followed by an hour practice with his assistant.

Her mother was helping financially, but Betty had to find a way to earn a living if she wanted to continue taking dance classes. The only real work experience she had, other than teaching at Calla Travis's studio, was modeling at Herpolsheimer's, so she decided to try to get signed on with a modeling agency. She traipsed into a few agencies dressed in a long, slinky gown and a silver fox cape, thinking she looked chic, but when she was turned away, she looked around at what the other girls were wearing and realized they could probably tell she was "straight from the sticks."

Her confidence had taken a blow, but Betty persisted—the next time with a whole different look. She walked into the John Robert Powers Agency, one of the leading agencies at the time, wearing a tailored Chesterfield coat with a brown velvet collar and a large-brimmed brown felt hat that she'd placed at an angle on her head, pulled down over one eye. The waiting room was filled with beautiful girls, and she thought immediately, "This is a waste of time, I'm not going to make it."

She was about to leave, when a man came in and walked around, looking each girl up and down. He stopped in front of Betty.

"I'll see you," he said. "Come into my office."

It was John Robert Powers himself, and although he told her that her muscular dancing legs were "pretty heavy," he signed her on.

The few modeling assignments Betty got didn't provide steady income, though, so she had to settle for a job working in the showroom of a clothing manufacturer to make ends meet. Working, dancing, riding the subway, going out with friends, and dinner dates with attractive young men—Betty thrived on the energy of New York City. Every Sunday, she'd buy a copy of the *New York Times* and flip immediately to the Arts section to dance critic John Martin's column "The Dance," which reported everything going on in the world of dance. Mr. Martin had been her Dance History and Criticism instructor at Bennington, and what a thrill it was to see his name in print in the *Times*! She cut out all his columns and carefully pasted them in a big, square leather scrapbook, along with programs and other mementoes. She didn't care about movie stars—in one clipping, there were photos of Bette Davis, Katharine Hepburn, and Vivien Leigh, the actresses being considered to play Scarlett O'Hara in *Gone with the Wind*—but Betty had saved it only because on the same page was an article about Martha Graham.

At the dance school, Graham was impressed by how hard Betty worked. "You've got ability," she once told her, "a nice animal-like movement that's appealing." But the competition was fierce, and there were others who were even more committed.

One day Martha confronted her. "Betty," she said, "to have a future, you've got to give up everything else."

Martha knew—like a mother with eyes in the back of her head—
that Betty liked to go out on dates and have fun with her friends. But
serious dancing and a social life didn't mix. "You can't carouse and be a
dancer too," Martha told her.

It was a reality check for Betty. Ultimately, her roommate, Nat, got
picked to be one of Martha's main dancers, and Betty wound up in the
auxiliary group. She would appear in Graham's New York performances,
but she wouldn't have the opportunity to be part of the main group that
traveled. Still, it was an accomplishment, one for which she had worked
very hard, and just a few months after arriving in New York, Betty was
dancing on the stage in Carnegie Hall. It was a Sunday evening performance, on October 9, and the iconic theater was packed. For a twenty-
year-old from Grand Rapids, Michigan, it was a tremendous thrill, and
Betty felt like she "had arrived."

She performed with the group in a special Christmas evening concert at the Alvin Theatre, but then, in the first few months of 1939, it
must have been bittersweet as she watched her roommate pack a suitcase and head off with Martha to Los Angeles, Atlanta, and Philadelphia.

Meanwhile, back in Grand Rapids, Betty's widowed mother had
gone on with her life, too, and had fallen in love. It had been nearly five
years since William Bloomer's sudden death, and Betty was thrilled to
learn that Hortense was planning to marry Arthur Meigs Godwin, a
longtime family friend whose wife had died years earlier in a tragic car
accident. Betty adored Mr. Godwin and was tickled to hear her mother
acting like a "sixteen-year-old girl with her first beau." But with each letter or phone call, Hortense was also subtly, and sometimes not so subtly,
pressuring Betty to come home.

After more than a year had gone by, Hortense came for a visit, and
that's when she really applied the pressure. She talked endlessly about
Betty's friends back in Grand Rapids—who was getting married; all the
parties she was missing—hoping to make her daughter homesick. Betty
didn't want to hear any of it. She loved the fast pace of New York and
dancing with Martha Graham. She had no intentions of returning to
Michigan. Finally, at the end of her two-week visit, Hortense made one
last impassioned appeal.

"Betty, darling, come home for six months, just to humor me," she pleaded. "At the end of that six months, if you find you still want to come back here and go on with your dancing, I will never say another word against it."

Betty was torn. It was the most difficult decision she had ever had to make, but in the end, she couldn't turn down her mother. Harder still was telling Martha Graham.

Martha stressed consistently to the young girls in her troupe that "part of a training of a dancer is to meet a situation with courage and the necessity of complete honesty," and Betty knew she had to tell her mentor face-to-face.

One day before practice, Betty went in to see Martha. "I'm going home for six months," she said. Six months to appease her mother, and then she'd be back. She was trying to sound confident, and yet, as the words came out of her mouth, she felt utterly sick.

Martha listened, nodded, and said finally, "I think it's a wise thing for you to do." More than ten years into her own career, she knew this life wasn't for everyone, and she'd seen enough girls come and go to know that Betty probably wasn't going to return.

With the prestigious credentials of having been a professional dancer in New York City, Calla Travis immediately hired Betty back at the dance school, and just as Hortense had hoped, it wasn't long before her daughter slipped right back into life in Grand Rapids.

Kay DeFreest was an associate director for Calla Travis and for the previous several summers had been the dance instructor at Camp Bryn Afon, an exclusive girls' camp in Wisconsin. She'd been looking for someone to take over and offered Betty the job.

Always ready for a new adventure, Betty accepted eagerly, packed up a summer's worth of clothing in a large steamer trunk, and headed up to northern Wisconsin. A newspaper article about the many camps in Oneida County touted them as "Where Fortunate Children Spend Summer at Play." Located in Rhinelander, on the banks of Snowden Lake, Camp Bryn Afon offered "a happy and safe out-of-doors vacation for the growing girl." Girls came from all over the Midwest to "gain the glowing health that comes from exercise in the pure outdoor air," to learn "poise and calmness of spirit," and "the meaning of real friendship of a sort that a girl can never know under the artificial conditions of conventional society."

Ann Lewis was one of the young girls from Grand Rapids who attended the camp when Betty was a counselor and dance instructor. "You took the train, picked it up in Kalamazoo, transferred in Chicago, and then up to Rhinelander," she recalled. "Your parents would put you on the train, wave goodbye, and off you went for seven or eight weeks."

The summer of 1941, Betty and another girl named Nancy Keeler, from Atlanta, oversaw the dance program. Working as a counselor to the young girls at Camp Bryn Afon brought back fond memories for Betty of her summers at Whitefish Lake. Photos from her scrapbook show her playing tennis, swimming, and sailing, and often wearing the same "Skipper" cap she'd worn at Bennington.

Ann Lewis remembered what a thrill it was as a thirteen-year-old who loved to dance to have Betty Bloomer as her instructor. "She was fun. She strongly believed in dance and loved it so much. We looked up to her and wanted to emulate her. You couldn't help but like her."

There was a boys' camp on the other side of the lake, and every couple of weeks there'd be a coed mixer or recital, to which the boys would be invited. Betty would dance with a partner, and she was so lovely on the dance floor that all the boys—even the ones that were five or six years younger than she was—wanted to go see her dance.

Once the eight-week summer camp finished, Betty returned to Grand Rapids and, along with Kay DeFreest, started the Grand Rapids Concert Dance Group, which performed for charities and fund-raising galas. Betty did all the choreography and also designed the costumes. She'd get an idea and sketch out the designs on scrap paper, and then search for reasonably priced fabric so the dresses would be affordable. The group became so popular that it had to hold auditions and turn away some dancers. As it turned out, while she hadn't made the first string in New York, Betty Bloomer became known as the "Martha Graham of Grand Rapids."

At twenty-three, she was of the age when all her friends were getting married, or were already married with a baby or two, and her mother had begun making comments, wondering when Betty was going to find a suitable mate. A couple of years earlier, Betty's brother Bill had gotten married—to a woman also named Betty, which caused some confusion with two Betty Bloomers around—and was living a few hours away in Petoskey, Michigan. Betty became godmother to their firstborn daughter, Bonnie, and on one trip when she went up to visit, Bill and Betty introduced her to a lawyer friend of theirs. Like many of the men who dated Betty, this one fell head over heels. Before Betty knew what was happening, he had bought an engagement ring, and she'd accepted.

It didn't last long. The fellow came to visit her in Grand Rapids one weekend, and Betty took him out with a group of her "wild friends." When they got home, after partying until four in the morning, it was clear her fiancé did not approve of this kind of behavior.

"I won't talk to you now," he said. "I'll talk to you in the morning."

Betty may have had a few drinks during the evening, but her head was clear enough to realize that she didn't like his tone or attitude. She knew he was going to tell her she had to change her ways, and she wasn't about to change who she was. There was no need to wait until the morning.

"That's all right," she said. "You don't have to talk to me." She pulled the ring off her finger and handed it to him. "Here's your ring."

It was terribly embarrassing—he was a good friend of her brother's—but it was the right thing to do. Betty wasn't in love with him. She realized she'd agreed to marry him only because that's what everyone else was doing. She swore to herself she wouldn't make that mistake again.

On September 23, 1940, Hortense married Arthur Godwin, and Betty was thrilled to have a stepfather. She adored him so much, she asked if she could call him Dad, and, of course, that delighted him. Arthur had always loved to travel, and having retired as a successful banker, he had the means to take his new wife on a yearlong honeymoon around the world.

Hortense would be moving into Arthur's house after the trip, so while they were gone, she put Betty in charge of selling the house at 717 Fountain Street and getting rid of everything in it. It was a cleansing of sorts, as Betty packed up the remnants of her childhood, sold off the china, the crystal, the furniture, and the rugs. Once the house sold, she said goodbye to the home where she'd gone from girl to woman and took one last look at the garage in the backyard.

She lived temporarily in a one-bedroom apartment until her mother and stepfather came home, and then joined them in Arthur's house, just one block down, at 636 Fountain Street. For as much as Betty liked her independence, she wasn't much of a cook and wasn't keen on housework.

She'd gone back to Herpolsheimer's and got a job as assistant to the fashion coordinator, training models to show clothes. She still taught dance in the evenings, including one night a week at an all-black school in a district where there weren't any other dance teachers. It was a new experience for her, and she loved it. The kids were talented and enthusiastic, but it caused a few problems for Betty at home. Her stepfather didn't approve, and while Betty described him as "typically a generous-natured man," every Tuesday night, when Arthur knew she was heading over to the other side of town, it was always very quiet at the dinner table.

At twenty-three, Betty had matured into a beautiful woman, and her brother Bill would recall that "there were always boys lined up for her." She enjoyed being "wined and dined by the local bachelors," and ultimately, she began falling for one she'd dated in high school: the curly blond fellow she'd slapped and told never to call again.

Bill Warren had matured and was now working with his father in the insurance business. While many other young men Betty's age had been drafted to serve in World War II, Bill was exempt because he was diabetic. As it turned out, he and Betty had a lot in common. He loved to dance, he was athletic, a good tennis player, and enjoyed going out with other couples. There was something about him, though, that Betty's mother and stepfather didn't like, and they made it known. To Betty, that just made Bill even more alluring.

She continued dating him without their knowledge—going to such lengths as to have another man come to the door to pick her up, and then go out to the car, where Bill would be waiting. The relationship grew more and more serious, and after a few months, they were talking marriage. Bill was so different from that stuffy lawyer to whom she'd previously been engaged—he enjoyed a good party as much as Betty did—so when he eventually proposed, she said yes.

She fully expected a blowup when she told her parents, but they were smart enough to know that Betty was going to do what she wanted to do, with or without their approval, and they gave their blessing.

And so it was that Elizabeth Ann Bloomer married William Cornelius Warren on the twenty-third of May 1942. It was a small family wedding held at four o'clock on a Saturday in the living room at 636 Fountain Street. Betty's brothers had come—Bill from Petoskey and Bob from Detroit—with their wives, as well as the groom's immediate relatives. The living room was decorated with white peonies and snapdragons, and as Betty glided down the stairs, dressed in an elegant off-the-shoulder white satin gown, a pianist played the traditional wedding march.

As Betty vowed to have and to hold, for better or for worse, in sickness and in health, she could not have imagined how those words would hang heavy just a few years later. For she had just begun what she would refer to later as "the five-year misunderstanding."

3

The Five-Year Misunderstanding

Shortly after they got married, Bill Warren left his father's insurance company and took a position as an agent with the Northwestern National Insurance Company. The job required them to move to Maumee, Ohio, a suburb of Toledo, which meant Betty had to give up her job and the dance company she'd developed. She hated to leave her mother, stepfather, and her dancing, but she was married now, and her husband's career came first.

In Maumee, she and Bill rented an apartment in a house right along the river, and Betty quickly found a job as a "demonstrator" at LaSalle's department store. Much like what she'd done at Herpolsheimer's, she modeled, worked in the fashion office, and sold merchandise. Bill would often go up to LaSalle's during his lunch hour with a friend or some workmates to watch Betty model in the dining room. "She was spectacular looking," recalled a friend.

After just ten months, Bill decided he didn't want to be in the insurance business any longer, so they left and moved back to Grand Rapids until he found another job. That became the story of their marriage. "We moved around, pillar to post," Betty wrote.

The next move was to Syracuse, New York, where Bill took a sales job with the Continental Can Company. The commissions didn't start right away, so Betty found a job on the production line at the Birds Eye frozen food processing plant in nearby Fulton to supplement their income. She worked four-hour shifts at a conveyor belt, sorting various vegetables and putting them into boxes. One time, while picking through some spinach, she found a worm, and from that day forward, whenever she ate spinach, she checked it very carefully.

Betty liked living in New York State, but Bill lost his job with Continental Can, and they again moved back to Grand Rapids, where his next venture was as a salesman for the Widdicomb Furniture Company. With a territory that covered the entire East Coast, from Maine to Florida, Bill began traveling constantly.

Betty's friend Kay DeFreest sensed that there was trouble in the marriage. "Bill Warren was very ambitious, and the sky was the limit as far as he was concerned," she said. "But not having the sky left Betty a great deal to do in order to support this ambition of his."

Betty wanted a family, but without a steady paycheck coming, it was up to her to make ends meet. She went back to Herpolsheimer's Department Store and got hired as the head fashion coordinator—working with buyers, dealing with the advertising department, training models, and directing monthly fashion shows. It was a great boost to her confidence, and she loved it.

In addition to her full-time job, she remained devoted to the Mary Free Bed Guild, working with crippled children, and several mornings a week, she taught modern dance classes at the YWCA. Many of her old friends already had a child or two, so she'd put out mats where the toddlers could play while she conducted the classes for the young mothers.

Betty became very active in the Junior League, and the seriousness with which she took her involvement is evident in the detailed notes she kept. She wrote pages and pages about the way the Junior League operated: the proper protocol at meetings, the various welfare organizations the group helped, and the difference between public and private agencies. Publicly, Betty was known for her role with the musical productions and dinner dances that raised money for the Junior League, but behind the scenes, with no fanfare, she worked with counselors and her church to provide emotional assistance to children who were living in abusive or otherwise dysfunctional households.

By age twenty-seven, Betty was ready for a house and children of her own, but Bill was not the staid, dependable husband she thought he would be. Ironically, she'd married someone just like her father.

Betty tried her best to be a supportive wife, emulating what she'd learned from her mother. When Bill was in town, she'd rush home from work to prepare a nice dinner for the two of them, but more often than not, the meal would get cold as Betty waited for him to come home. It might be ten o'clock before he'd call—from a bar where he'd been drinking with the guys from the showroom—and say, "Why don't you come down here, and we'll go somewhere to eat?"

There were indeed difficulties, and a few times, she asked her friend Kay DeFreest to be present for "a little backup" when she confronted Bill about his behavior, seemingly concerned about what his reaction might be.

In her memoir, Betty stops short of saying that Bill Warren had a drinking problem or was abusive, but she acknowledged that "the things that made our dating so amusing, made the marriage difficult," and "even when Bill was home, I wasn't happy."

Three years into the marriage, Betty had finally had enough. "He can do what he wants with his life," she thought, "but, damn it all, this is not for me."

It was a difficult decision to make. In the 1940s, divorce was uncommon and highly frowned upon. She knew that to be a divorcée was akin to wearing a scarlet letter, but the marriage was so bad, Betty was willing to walk that path. One evening, she was sitting home alone while Bill was on yet another business trip, when she decided to write him a letter telling him she didn't want him to come back. "I'm sending your things to your family's house," she wrote. She hadn't quite finished the letter, when the phone rang.

It was Bill's boss, calling from Boston.

"Betty," he said, "Bill has taken ill. He's in a diabetic coma. It's very serious." So serious, the doctors didn't think he would live.

Betty got on the next available flight to Boston. Bill was alive, but one side of his face was paralyzed, he was unable to move on his own, and he required round-the-clock care. Her intention had been to leave him, but now, how could she leave under these circumstances? For six weeks, she stayed with friends in Boston, spending her days at the hospital learning how to give insulin shots and provide Bill the care he would need upon release from the hospital.

What am I doing here when I no longer love this man? she kept thinking. But to divorce him at that point was, in her mind, unconscionable.

Eventually Bill was able to be transported back to Grand Rapids by train, on a stretcher. But now, since he was unable to work, earning a living was solely up to Betty. At twenty-seven, she felt like her life was over. It was devastating. *This must be my cross*, she thought. Her dreams of having a family were gone, as her life turned into a blur of days that went from work to the hospital, and returning to her apartment to sleep. Then she'd wake up and start the whole cycle over again.

Two years went by, and then, miraculously, Bill began to recover. Had God heard her prayers? She waited until he was well enough to return to work, and then she went straight to a lawyer and filed for divorce. Now twenty-nine years old, on her way to becoming free from her disastrous marriage, Betty Bloomer Warren was ready to spread her wings. As she waited for the divorce proceedings to become final, she began envisioning what she'd do next. Perhaps she'd go to Rio de Janeiro and work in the fashion industry. There was a whole world out there, and while thus far not much in her life had gone as planned, she wasn't one to look back.

To divorce her husband was an incredibly difficult decision, and one she didn't take lightly. For a while, her whole demeanor changed. The models she worked with at Herpolsheimer's could tell how upsetting it was for her. The five-year marriage to Bill Warren had so shattered her image of "happily ever after" that Betty made a commitment to herself that she'd never consider marrying again.

And that's when Jerry Ford showed up.

Gerald Rudolph Ford Jr. was well known in Grand Rapids. He'd been a star football player at South High, and then had gone on to play for the University of Michigan Wolverines. He had garnered the attention of some professional football scouts, and upon graduation from Michigan in 1935, he was offered positions with both the Green Bay Packers and the Detroit Lions of the National Football League. But Ford declined the offers. He had his sights set on law school, and playing pro football was not going to get him there.

Throughout school, he was registered and known as Gerald R. Ford Jr., the son of Dorothy and Gerald R. Ford. The truth was a bit more complicated. In those days, especially in a conservative city such as Grand Rapids, if your family didn't conform to societal norms, some things were better left vague. The reality—which Jerry wouldn't learn until he was a teenager—was that his mother had been married before, to a man named Leslie Lynch King. On July 14, 1913, in Omaha, Nebraska, Dorothy gave birth to a son, and the name on his birth certificate was Leslie Lynch King Jr.

Dorothy was just twenty-one years old and had been married less than a year to Leslie King, who was ten years her senior. They'd had a whirlwind courtship, but weeks into the marriage, Dorothy discovered her husband had a violent side. He was physically and emotionally abusive to her, to the point that when she was still in the hospital after having given birth, a nurse called the police. Leslie King had shown up with a butcher knife threatening to kill his wife and son.

When her newborn baby was just sixteen days old, Dorothy fled Omaha with her son and returned to her parents in Harvard, Illinois, where she filed for divorce. It took great courage and determination, because to be a divorced single mother in 1913 often elicited whispers of scandal. To avoid embarrassment in her hometown, Dorothy's parents helped their daughter and her baby son relocate to Grand Rapids, where the young woman's father had some business interests. She began a new life, determined to put the past behind her and raise her son as best she could in a positive environment. Her fifteen-month marriage had been painful, and Dorothy couldn't bear to call her son by her ex-husband's name, so instead she called him Junior, or Junie.

She was in no hurry to marry again, but just a few months after moving to Grand Rapids, she met a ruggedly handsome bachelor named Gerald R. Ford at an Episcopal church social. Ford was everything Leslie Lynch King was not—kind, thoughtful, and devoted—both to Dorothy and her infant son. He was hardworking, scrupulously honest, and well respected in the community. They dated for a year, and on February 1, 1916, Dorothy and Gerald Ford got married in the church where they'd met.

Junior was just eighteen months old, and from that point on, he was called Jerry and grew up believing Gerald R. Ford was his father. Gerald and Dorothy would have three more children together—all boys—providing Jerry with three younger brothers: Thomas, Richard, and James. There were times they barely had enough money to get by, moving from one rented house to another, but they had a strong faith and were active in both church and community. Gerald would take the boys camping and fishing, and he spent many a summer evening tossing baseballs and footballs. He was a man of impeccable integrity, and while he drilled into his sons the importance of honesty, Dorothy instilled in them the importance of helping others who were less fortunate. Both parents were strict disciplinarians and didn't tolerate any backtalk. There were three house rules: tell the truth, work hard, come to dinner on time—and woe unto any who violated those rules.

At twelve, Jerry joined the Boy Scouts, and within three years earned the rank of Eagle Scout. On top of scouting, school, and sports, he worked several part-time jobs. When he was sixteen, he was working the lunch counter at a restaurant directly across the street from school. One day a man came in, and, after standing around for about fifteen minutes, he approached Jerry and said, "I'm Leslie King, your father."

A few years earlier, Jerry's mother had told him that she had been married once before, and that he was born before she married Gerald Ford. It hadn't really registered with him, but now, to have his real father show up, unannounced, was a tremendous shock. King had arrived with his wife in a brand-new Lincoln, and he wanted to take Jerry out to lunch. Jerry got approval from his boss, and off they went to a nearby restaurant. The conversation was mostly superficial, but Jerry quickly surmised that Leslie King was much more well off financially than his stepfather and mother were. In the fifteen years of his life, his birth father had never sought to find him, until now, and had never contributed a dime for his upbringing. After lunch, King dropped off Jerry back at work and handed him $25.

"Now, you buy yourself something—something you want that you can't afford otherwise," he said. With that, he turned, waved, and drove away.

That evening, after his younger brothers had gone to bed, Jerry told his parents what had happened. It was so deeply emotional for him that years later—after experiencing war, witnessing death, and the loss of a presidential election—he would still recall it as one of the most difficult nights of his life. His mother and stepfather consoled him as he struggled to come to terms with what had happened that day. He didn't doubt that his stepfather loved him as much as he loved his three biological sons. What hurt, he wrote in his memoir, was the indelible image he now had of his birth father: "a carefree, well-to-do man who didn't really give a damn about the hopes and dreams of his firstborn son."

That night, Jerry lay in bed, sobbing, turning to prayer for comfort and guidance. Over and over, he repeated his mother's favorite prayer from Proverbs:

> *Trust in the Lord with all thine heart; and lean not unto thine own understanding.*
> *In all thy ways acknowledge Him; and He shall direct thy paths.*

Even though Jerry Ford and Betty Bloomer grew up in Grand Rapids at the same time, albeit on different sides of the city, their lives took such separate and diverse routes, it is somewhat surprising they ever managed to get together. But there were times their paths may have crossed; when they may have been in the same place at the same time and never realized it. It seemed that no matter which way they turned, no matter the choices they made, they were destined to be together.

When Betty was modeling and dancing in New York City, Jerry Ford was attending law school at Yale University in New Haven, Connecticut. A friend from Grand Rapids introduced him to a beautiful young woman named Phyllis Brown, who was attending Connecticut College, in New London, less than fifty miles away, and the two fell in love.

Jerry's family owned a small cottage at Ottawa Beach on the western shore of Lake Michigan, where he'd grown up swimming and boating with his brothers each summer. In August 1938 Jerry brought Phyllis there for a few weeks to get to know his family and to share his love of Michigan with her.

Phyllis introduced Jerry to downhill skiing, and in the winter of 1939, they were on a slope in New Hampshire when Phyllis collided with a man who happened to be a magazine cover artist in New York City.

"Have you ever been a model?" he asked. He gave her his card, and the next time she was in New York City, he sent her to John Robert Powers—the same modeling agency that had signed Betty Bloomer. Blonde, blue eyed, tall, sleek, and slim, Phyllis was striking yet at the same time wholesome looking, and Powers signed her immediately. While Betty had only sporadic work, Brown became one of Powers's most requested models. She quit college, moved to New York, and, for a while, she was the preferred model for *Cosmopolitan* magazine, her face painted each month by the artist who had discovered her on the ski slope.

Jerry Ford would visit Phyllis in New York City, and she introduced him to big-city life: going to the theater, dining in inexpensive neighborhood restaurants with an occasional splurge for dinner and dancing at the Rainbow Room on top of Rockefeller Center.

The winter of 1939–40, Phyllis received an offer from *Look* magazine to do a photo shoot for a story about the popularity of weekend trips for twentysomethings by train from New York City to the ski slopes of Stowe, Vermont. She asked Jerry to join her, and the two of them appeared in a six-page spread in the March issue.

It was a passionate romance, the first for both. "After his mother, I was the first important woman in his life," Phyllis said. "And he was the first important man in my life, my first love affair, the first man I ever slept with—you never forget that, not ever, ever, ever."

A year later, in 1941, Jerry graduated from Yale Law School. He was twenty-eight, and, already with an eye toward politics, he decided to return home to Grand Rapids to begin his own law practice. He and Phyllis had talked about getting married as soon as he received his law degree, but by this point, her career was going strong, and she wasn't willing to leave New York City. Reluctantly, the two decided to end their relationship.

"The end of our relationship caused me real anguish," Jerry Ford wrote in his autobiography, "and I wondered if I'd ever meet anyone like her again."

Upon returning to Grand Rapids, Jerry got together with Phil Buchen, a fraternity brother from the University of Michigan, and each put up

$1,000 to open the law partnership of Ford and Buchen. They'd barely gotten the practice off the ground when, just a few months later, on December 7, 1941, the Japanese attacked Pearl Harbor. Suddenly the United States was at war, and Jerry Ford wanted desperately to be a part of it.

In April 1942, as Betty Bloomer was making arrangements for her upcoming wedding to Bill Warren, Jerry was commissioned into the US Navy. Originally assigned to be a physical fitness trainer at the navy's preflight school in Chapel Hill, North Carolina, he wrote letters to everyone he knew, pleading for a billet on a ship. It worked, and finally, in the spring of 1943, he received orders to report to the USS *Monterey*, a light aircraft carrier that was about to be commissioned and then head for battle in the Pacific.

Jerry Ford saw plenty of action aboard the *Monterey*—"as much action as I'd ever hoped to see," he recalled. As a gunnery officer, it was his job to direct the crew firing the 40-millimeter antiaircraft gun as Japanese warplanes tried to destroy them. Not only were there months of fierce battles, but one night Ford was nearly swept off the flight deck during a vicious typhoon in the Philippine Sea. The seas were so violent that three destroyers rolled and capsized, drowning everyone aboard. When a fire broke out in the *Monterey*'s hangar deck during the storm, and three out of the four boilers stopped functioning, it seemed the crew was doomed. They were preparing to abandon ship, but the captain came up with a plan that got the boilers working, allowing the men to extinguish the flames and make it safely to the island of Saipan. It was a lesson in courage, resourcefulness, and leadership that Ford would never forget.

When Jerry Ford returned to Grand Rapids in February 1946 after being honorably discharged from the navy as a lieutenant commander, he was a much-changed man.

4

A Courtship and a Campaign

Ford's former partner, Phil Buchen, had by this point joined another law firm, Butterfield, Keeney, and Amberg, and when Jerry returned, the senior partners there invited him into their practice too. Jerry flung himself into work, happy to be back in the career for which he'd studied and worked so hard. At the same time, he became active in numerous civic organizations around the county.

A year and a half later, Jerry was thirty-four years old, and most of the women he'd known before the war were already married. After Phyllis Brown, after seeing the world and war from the deck of an aircraft carrier, Jerry Ford wasn't going to settle for just any woman. He needed someone special. One night in August 1947, he was at the home of friends Frank and Peg Neuman for a cancer drive planning meeting. When everyone else had gone, he mentioned that his mother had been pestering him about when he was going to settle down.

"Who's around that a bachelor my age can date?" he asked. "You have any ideas?"

Peg Neuman immediately thought of her good friend Betty. The two had been friends since high school, and they saw each other frequently through their work with the Mary Free Bed Guild.

"How about Betty Warren?" Peg suggested.

Jerry knew the name. He recalled meeting her briefly at one of the

Kent Country Club Saturday night dances, and what stuck in his mind was how very attractive she was—and that she was married.

"She's getting a divorce," Peg added with a glint in her eye.

Jerry's interest was sparked. "Well, would you give her a call?" he asked. "I'll get on the phone and see if I can convince her to have a drink."

Betty was at her apartment with a stack of notecards, writing out the script for a fashion show she was hosting at Herpolsheimer's the next day. It was past dinnertime and surprising to hear the phone ring at such a late hour.

"Hello, Betty," Peg said on the other end of the line. "We're here working on the cancer drive, and Jerry Ford's here. He wants to know if you'll have a drink with him."

Jerry was standing close to Peg, and she held the phone to his ear so he could hear Betty's reply.

"Oh no, I couldn't possibly. I'm working on a style show for tomorrow, and I expect I'll be working until two in the morning," she said.

Jerry grabbed the phone and said, "Hi, Betty, this is Jerry Ford. You know, it would do you good to take a break for a few minutes. I'd really like to take you out for a drink."

"Oh no, I couldn't possibly," Betty repeated. Her divorce wasn't yet final—it was a sixty-day process—and even though Bill Warren wasn't contesting, she didn't want to take any chances. Besides, it just wasn't proper.

Jerry persisted. "I'll just come by and get you, and we can go around to a place I know and have a beer. You'll feel refreshed."

"Jerry, you know, I'm in the process of getting a divorce." She thought that would stop him, but he wasn't ready to give up.

"We'll just go to some quiet little spot where nobody will know us," he said.

"I don't think that's quite cricket," she said. "You're a lawyer; you ought to know better," she teased. Truth be told, she was intrigued.

"Just for an hour or so," Ford promised.

Finally, she agreed. "All right. But I can only be gone twenty minutes."

A short while later, Jerry knocked on her apartment door. He had expected she might be standoffish or distant, but she greeted him with enthusiasm and a warm smile. They drove to an out-of-the-way bar on the corner of Hall Street and Division Avenue, and settled into a quiet booth in the back. The conversation flowed, and the next time Betty looked at her watch, an hour had passed.

"I can't say love at first sight," Betty would say later, "but it certainly was 'I wonder if maybe it wouldn't work if we got together.'"

There was attraction on both sides, but because of the circumstances, neither of them was ready to jump into anything serious. The next day at work, Betty found herself thinking about Jerry and wondering if he'd call again. He left her hanging for a few days, but then he did call and ask her out again. They were both busy with work, and cautious about being seen, but over the course of the next several weeks, they began to go out to dinner and an occasional movie. One night, they were waiting in line to buy tickets for a nine o'clock movie when Betty's mother and stepfather came walking out of the theater, having just seen the earlier show. Betty could tell that her mother was "quite shocked," to see her with a man, obviously on a date. Betty shrugged it off, acted casual, and introduced Jerry to her parents.

On September 22, 1947, Betty was officially and legally divorced from Bill Warren, based on grounds of incompatibility. She was given a token settlement of $1 and the furnishings of their Grand Rapids apartment. Finally, she was once again a free and independent woman.

Over the next few months, Betty and Jerry began spending more time together, but not exclusively. She had told him marriage was the last thing on her mind, and he had assured her that he wasn't interested in getting serious either. Admittedly, Betty had always liked handsome blond men, and she found Jerry physically attractive, but after experiencing such disappointment in her marriage, she was interested only in having a male companion with whom she could relax and go out.

One night, Jerry stopped by Betty's Washington Street apartment and found three other young men sitting with her in the living room drinking beer and hanging out. Betty invited Jerry in, but immediately it became clear that he wasn't happy about the situation. He "plunked himself down on the couch and opened up the evening paper—like a stern father," she recalled.

Eventually two of the three men got up and left, but the other one stayed. He and Jerry were both vying for Betty's attention, and, finally, Betty said, "I don't know about you guys, but I've got to work in the morning, so I'm going to bed."

Betty's apartment was on the ground floor, and with her bedroom window open, she heard them talking outside.

"What are your intentions with Betty?" Jerry asked pointedly.

"I'm very interested," the other young man said.

"Fine," Jerry replied. "I just wanted to find out."

Betty never let on that she had overheard the conversation, and at the time, she felt it was "pretty nervy" of Jerry to be asking about the other's intentions. He had told her about his four-year relationship with Phyllis, and Betty wasn't so sure that he didn't still hold a torch for her.

That fall, they went to Michigan football games in Ann Arbor, and when Thanksgiving came, Jerry invited her to dinner with his parents, brothers, and their families. Betty felt immediately at ease, charming them with her quick wit and sparkling smile as she bounced his brothers' babies on her knee. They were still uncommitted, but Betty was beginning to realize she felt something more than just a friendship with Jerry.

"I wondered if I was going to ruin everything by falling in love with a man who didn't want me to love him," she wrote.

Jerry wasn't very demonstrative, which wasn't unusual—in those days, people didn't show a lot of open affection—but he was falling in love too. "Betty just lit me up," Jerry would later say. "She touched me in a way no other woman ever could. She made me laugh and also feel protective of her." Still, they were each afraid to admit to the other what they were feeling.

At Christmastime, Jerry had planned a two-week ski vacation in Sun Valley, Idaho, with some friends. The separation would put their relationship to the test.

Jerry Ford was the most eligible bachelor in Grand Rapids, and Betty had seen how ladies followed him wherever he went. She "knew darn well he would have a good time" out there in Sun Valley, and, admittedly, she was jealous. She had to find a way to subtly let him know that her feelings had deepened, with the hopes that he'd think of her while he was gone. So before Jerry left, Betty had one of the Herpolsheimer's seamstresses make up an elegant red corduroy Christmas stocking with a black velvet cuff, and she filled it with "silly" presents that each sent a message: a pair of argyle socks she'd knitted, to keep him warm; a pair of sunglasses to which she'd fastened blinders on the sides, to keep his eyes from wandering; and the most daring gift of all: a gold lighter for his pipe onto which she had engraved "To the light of my life." She gave him the stocking to take with him, and off he went.

As part of her job at Herpolsheimer's, Betty was scheduled to go to New York City for a buying trip on January 2. She'd gone out New Year's Eve with another man, celebrating with a group of friends at the Blythefield Country Club, but all she could think about was Jerry. She got home around four in the morning and decided to call him at his hotel in Sun Valley to wish him a Happy New Year. The phone rang and rang with no answer. She left a message with the operator and promptly fell asleep.

A few hours later, he called her back. It turned out that Jerry was missing her just as much as she was missing him. He had written her letters every day. With her about to leave for New York, he suggested she get together with Bradshaw Crandell, a friend of his. Crandell was somewhat of a celebrity, as the artist who painted models for magazine covers, and Betty knew that he and his wife had been close friends with Jerry's former girlfriend Phyllis Brown.

"If you think I'm going to call him up, you're crazy," she said. "If you want me to meet him, you can call him yourself."

When she arrived in New York—she was staying at the Waldorf Towers, where the Junior League offered discounted rooms to its members—there were already several messages from Brad Crandell. Jerry had indeed called him, and Brad invited Betty over to his apartment for cocktails one evening.

As it turned out, Betty's childhood friend Mary Adelaide's brother, Walt Jones, was living in New York, so she asked him to accompany her to Crandell's apartment. She was feeling quite chic, wearing a maroon-colored suit with a matching blouse and taffeta petticoat, and a hat perched at an angle on her head. Crandell was very cordial as he invited them in and offered drinks in the living room. They hadn't been there more than fifteen minutes, when the doorbell rang.

"Darling, what a surprise!" Crandell said as he opened the door. And there she was—"gorgeous, blonde, skinny as a rail"—Phyllis Brown.

Betty was fuming. Phyllis and Brad Crandell made it seem as if Phyllis's dropping by was a surprise visit, but Betty knew Crandell must have told her that Jerry Ford's new girlfriend was in town, and Phyllis wanted to check her out. Phyllis slinked in wearing a mink coat, which she casually slung onto a chair, revealing a low-cut, black satin dress that left nothing to the imagination. She proceeded to interrogate Betty about Jerry's friends and family in Grand Rapids, making it clear how close to all of them she had once been.

"How is his mother? Do they still have barbecues up at the cottage?"

"At the same time she was staking out a prior claim to Jerry," Betty noted, "she was somehow managing to vamp Walt Jones." The evening was a total disaster. The final humiliating blow was when Walt invited Phyllis out to dinner—he said he'd come back and pick her up after he dropped off Betty at the Waldorf.

Betty and Jerry had been writing to each other daily, and when Betty got back to her room, she sat down and wrote him a scathing letter. She didn't think he was behind Phyllis's surprise visit, but she had been so put off by Brad's and Phyllis's phoniness that she told Jerry if he wanted to associate with these kinds of people, he could count her out. As soon as she finished, she folded up the letter, sealed and stamped the envelope, marched down the hall, and dropped it in the mail chute.

When she awoke the next morning, she was filled with regret. She wished she could take back her words, but there was no way to retrieve the letter. She'd just have to wait and see how Jerry reacted. Hopefully, she hadn't ruined everything.

When she returned to Grand Rapids, Jerry greeted her warmly. He'd brought her a present—a hand-tooled leather belt with a silver buckle—and chatted amiably about his vacation. Not one word about the letter. Finally, Betty couldn't stand it any longer. "Listen," she said, "did you by any chance get a letter from me that mentioned your artist friend and the model?"

"Yes, I did," he said. Betty held her breath. *Oh no.*

"I gather you didn't care much for them," he said with a smile. The subject never came up again, and "everything moved very fast after that."

There were ski weekends in northern Michigan at Caberfae Peaks, with friends Phoebe and Jack Stiles, and two other couples, where they stayed in a primitive cabin that had eight cots, a potbelly stove, and a one-hole outhouse. They'd ski all day and then go out to dinner at a nearby tavern, dancing to the music on the jukebox until the place closed.

"It was our big Saturday bash," Betty recalled, "and we reveled in it."

After six months of dating, Jerry Ford had no doubt that Betty Bloomer Warren was the woman with whom he wanted to spend the rest of his life. She was beautiful, intelligent, adventurous; she had a great sense of humor, was fun to be around, and unafraid to speak her mind. They'd both been in previous relationships from which they'd learned and matured, and now Jerry, at age thirty-five, and Betty, nearly thirty, knew what they wanted in a lifetime partner.

One cold February night, they were sitting together on the couch in Betty's apartment, when Jerry looked into Betty's eyes and said, "I'd like to marry you."

"He didn't tell me he loved me," Betty said. "He just told me he'd like to marry me." That was enough for her. "I took him up on it instantly," she recalled, "before he could change his mind."

But there was one more thing. "We can't get married until next fall," Jerry added. "And I can't tell you why."

"A fall wedding will be fine," Betty said. She trusted him with all her heart. She knew if he told her they needed to wait, there must be a good reason. She loved him, and she knew he loved her, even if he couldn't say it out loud.

And that letter? It may well have been that letter she'd written in a moment of anger that cemented it for him. He knew Betty would always tell him the truth; would always speak her mind. And just as a reminder—perhaps a reminder not ever to take her love for granted—Jerry put the letter in a safe-deposit box.

The secret he was keeping from her—the reason they couldn't marry until the fall—would set a course for their lives that neither of them could have imagined.

You will be meeting kings and queens. Trust in the Lord with all thine heart.

Betty's mother and stepfather were fixing up a lake house in Wabaningo on Lake Michigan, getting it ready for summer visitors, and at that time, before texts and emails, when long distance phone calls were a luxury expense reserved for emergencies, Betty and Hortense stayed in touch with frequent letters back and forth. Shortly after Betty's thirtieth birthday, Hortense wrote:

> *Bets darling,*
>
> *Your letter just arrived, and we do so hope the package arrived for your birthday . . . it was grand to hear how well you do your job . . . how proud I would have been to be at the show—you are a great gal—and I can't wait to get home to see you.*

She wrote about all the goings-on, the various visitors at the house, and clearly, she was happy about Betty's fiancé:

> *We do wish you* two *could run in and see us—we can always tuck you in. And tell Jerry we want him to think of this as his home too.*
>
> *Bye my little darling. Must get this in the mail—all our love,*
> *Mother*

For two months, Betty had wondered what the secret could possibly be that Jerry was keeping from her. Those close to Jerry at the time have said it wasn't that he didn't trust her to keep his secret; it was only that he hadn't completely made up his mind yet, and it was just his nature to keep his thoughts to himself until he had reached a decision.

Finally, in late April, Jerry was ready to reveal what he'd been holding inside. Betty could tell it was something very serious by the look in his eyes as he asked her to sit down.

"Betty," he said, "I've decided I'm going to run for Congress."

"Okay," Betty replied. She didn't know what running for Congress meant, but if Jerry wanted to do it, that was fine with her.

He explained that he was going to run against incumbent representative Bartel "Barney" J. Jonkman for the Fifth Congressional District seat in Michigan's September primary elections. Jonkman, a senior Republican on the US House Committee on Foreign Affairs, was an ardent isolationist and was opposed to helping the nations of Europe rebuild. Jerry had seen firsthand how critical it was for America to maintain strong relationships with our allies, and he felt so fervently that Jonkman's views were bad for the country, he couldn't stand by and do nothing, even though the odds were heavily stacked against him.

In Grand Rapids's conservative, largely Dutch community, Jonkman, himself Dutch, was enormously popular. In 1946 he faced no Republican opposition at all and had swamped the Democrat for his fourth consecutive term. Jerry had been discussing his plans with close friends Phil Buchen and Jack Stiles, and while they were enthusiastically supportive of his decision to run, they stressed that it was important to keep it under wraps until the last possible moment, largely because his engagement to Betty was potentially a problem. While it would be beneficial for voters to know that he was planning to marry, some might not approve if they knew his wife-to-be was a divorcée—and there was a good possibility that Betty's past could cost him the election. Jerry's biggest advantage would be to catch his opponent off guard, declaring his candidacy just before the filing deadline.

Betty wasn't too concerned because, honestly, she didn't think Jerry had a chance of winning. *Only old men go to Congress*, she thought. Still, she saw how much this meant to him, and she wanted to do everything she could to be supportive.

In June 1948, just before the filing deadline, Jerry announced both his candidacy and his engagement to Betty Bloomer Warren. From that point on, Betty recalled, "it was wild." People were throwing engagement parties, Betty was working at Herpolsheimer's and helping with the campaign, while Jerry was "campaigning furiously."

"He took to campaigning like a starving man to a roast-beef dinner," she wrote. He was on the trail from early morning until late at night, up and down the two counties of Michigan's Fifth District. Betty found herself getting caught up in the excitement—she liked the challenge of being the underdog—and every evening after work, she would dash down to the "Ford for Congress" headquarters and join the volunteers making phone calls, stuffing envelopes, or doing anything else to make herself useful. She recruited models and dancing friends to help with the campaign, and when they'd say, "I've never been in politics," Betty would reply, "I don't know anything about politics, either, but you can lick stamps and stuff envelopes, can't you?"

She asked her friend Kay DeFreest to head the women's division of the campaign, and Kay promptly set out to coerce as many females as she could to work on behalf of Jerry. They'd write letters to ten friends supporting Jerry and then ask each of them to write ten more letters—a political chain letter campaign targeting women voters. Kay recalled that everyone who knew Jerry Ford was willing to help, "most particularly because of Jerry's character. There wasn't any way that you could look at that young man and not know that every word he said came right from the heart. There was no falsifying or no putting on of any false front. Anything he talked on, he knew about. It was either through personal contact or through extensive reading and studying all angles of government."

Everyone who worked for him felt the same way. "There was no pretense there. We were most pleased to do anything we could to further his career, and we did," Kay added.

From June until September, it was nonstop. Jerry went door-to-door in Grand Rapids, gave speeches at county fairs, tromped into the fields to speak with farmers, and shook hands with factory workers as they finished their shifts, while Betty ran around asking storekeepers to put up posters. "It was exhilarating to be in a race like that," she remembered. And, although she had no idea what being a political wife would entail, somewhere along the line she found herself wanting him to win.

"We worked our tails off," Jerry said. "We had the organization, and we developed the momentum."

Throughout the frenzy of the campaign, Jerry's good friend Jack Stiles was concerned that this upcoming marriage might not work. "Like fire and water," he told Jerry, "sometimes politics and marriage don't mix."

Late one night, Jerry and Jack were sitting in Jack's car after another frantic day, and Jerry said, "What do you think about me marrying Betty?"

"Well, I've known Betty since she was a teenager," Jack said, "and she's a terrific gal. But I don't know if she can put up with your damn political ambitions."

About ten days later, Betty had a similar conversation with Jack.

"What do you think about Jerry and me?"

"Well, Betty," Jack said, "if you can accept the idea that politics will come first and your marriage second, if you can live with that, then I think you'll have a good marriage. You'll make a good team in Washington."

Washington. That's when it hit her. When Betty had said she'd marry Jerry, she thought she'd be marrying a Grand Rapids lawyer; they'd buy a house and raise a family right in their hometown. But if Jerry won the primary, it was almost guaranteed he'd be going to Congress: the Fifth District hadn't elected a Democrat to the House since 1910.

Their hard work paid off, and on September 14, 1948, Jerry Ford won the Republican primary in a huge upset, defeating incumbent Barney Jonkman by nearly two to one. Betty's previous marriage hadn't been an issue at all, and now, finally, they could set a wedding date. Jerry had just one stipulation: the wedding couldn't interfere with a Michigan football game.

Over the next few weeks, Betty didn't fully realize it, but she was already getting a taste of what life with Congressman Jerry Ford would be like. While she designed her wedding dress, chose flowers, and sent invitations, Jerry was still spending every waking hour campaigning.

Betty became close with Janet Ford, the wife of Jerry's brother Tom, and at one point, Betty complained to her future sister-in-law about Jerry's single-minded focus on politics.

"You won't have to worry about other women," Janet warned her. "Jerry's work will be the other woman."

Indeed, one of the things Betty admired about her husband-to-be was that he was a hard worker. "I loved him for that," she said. There were so many qualities she loved about him: his strength, his goodness. He was one of the most honest, fair, caring people she had ever known.

The wedding was set for October 15—eighteen days before the general election, and on a Friday, "because it was fall, and in the fall, we couldn't miss a Saturday football game." Especially when Michigan was playing rival Northwestern University at home.

The night before the wedding, Jerry's parents held a rehearsal dinner at the Peninsular Club: a swanky private club in Grand Rapids for prominent businessmen and of which Jerry's father was a member. As it turned out, both of Michigan's senators—Republicans Arthur H. Vandenberg and Homer Ferguson—were appearing at a GOP dinner at the same time, just five blocks away, and Jerry figured he could time it to make both events. He showed up for the cocktail reception at the Peninsular, had a drink, and then just as the meal was being served during his own wedding rehearsal dinner, he ducked out, promising to make it back in time for dessert.

While most brides would have been fuming, Betty took it in stride. Jerry returned as promised, and the photos Betty saved in an album show the two of them laughing and looking at each other with adoration.

The following afternoon, families and friends of Betty Bloomer Warren and Gerald R. Ford Jr. filed into the floral-decorated pews at Grace Episcopal Church as the organist played in the background. For this second marriage, Betty had chosen an elegant two-piece blue satin suit with a fitted jacket that accentuated her tiny waist, and instead of a veil, she wore a matching hat affixed with a long piece of rose-colored lace that had come off a parasol belonging to Jerry's grandmother. She looked ravishing. The only thing missing was the groom.

It was four o'clock, and Jerry had yet to appear. Betty was "growing more livid by the moment," when suddenly Jerry came rushing in. He had been campaigning all day, pushing it to the last possible moment, and while he'd managed to change into a suit and tie, he'd completely neglected to notice that his shoes were covered in mud. Betty pretended not to notice, but Jerry's mother was furious. As soon as they got to the reception at the Kent Country Club, Dorothy "gave him the devil," Betty recalled. It was something they'd laugh about for years to come.

There were toasts, and cake, and after a couple of hours, the new Mr. and Mrs. Ford, delirious with joy, set off for Ann Arbor, chauffeured by best man Jack Beckwith—the three of them piled into the front seat of Jack's car. The celebration continued with dinner and champagne at the Town Club, a private club in the Allenel Hotel, "whooping it up" with friends until the wee hours, when the newlyweds finally went up to their room.

Their honeymoon began sitting in bleacher seats watching the Michigan-Northwestern football game on Saturday afternoon (Michigan won, 28–0), followed by a seventy-mile drive to Owosso, where they sat in the bleachers at another football field to hear Republican presidential candidate Thomas E. Dewey speak at a rally. "The thing wasn't over 'til midnight," Betty recalled, "and of course my new husband and I stayed to the bitter end."

They'd booked a hotel in Detroit but didn't arrive until three o'clock Sunday morning. Jerry spent the day reading every newspaper he could find, and Monday, after a stop in Ann Arbor, where Jerry had a meeting, they headed back to Grand Rapids. On the return drive, Betty was looking forward to finally having a relaxing evening at home with her new husband, and mentioned she might cook a roast for dinner.

"Oh, Betty," Jerry said, "I won't be home for dinner tonight. There's a meeting that I just have to attend. Can you just make me a sandwich?"

"Of course, dear," Betty said without complaint.

During the months that Betty and Jerry had been courting, she'd rarely seen him before ten thirty or eleven o'clock at night, when he'd stop by her apartment after whatever civic group or community meeting he'd attended. She found it natural while they were dating—and, of course, during those wild weeks of the campaign, it was understandable—but she didn't expect it to be that way once they were married.

"Like every woman," she said, "I thought that when you sign that certificate and walk down the aisle, all of a sudden everything changes, and you have all his attention and regular hours. Well, that wasn't meant to be."

Still, she couldn't be mad. She adored Jerry and was so proud. She heated up a can of tomato soup, grilled a couple of cheese sandwiches, and off he went.

The next two weeks were a whirlwind as Jerry continued campaigning nonstop until election day. On November 2, 1948, Democrat incumbent Harry S. Truman narrowly held on to the White House, and Gerald R. Ford Jr. was elected to a two-year term in Congress, winning nearly 61 percent of the vote.

Shortly thereafter, saddled with $7,000 in campaign debt, Jerry and Betty headed to Washington, DC, to begin their new adventure together, filled with hope, excitement, and newlywed passion.

PART TWO

·◆·

BETTY FORD, WASHINGTON WOMAN

Like so many women at the time, Betty set aside her own dreams to support those of her husband. She wanted Jerry to be proud of her, and as with everything she did, Betty gave being a congressman's wife 100 percent. What began as a two-year term in Washington turned into four years, then six, then eight, as Jerry continually got reelected. As he gained seniority in Congress, and traveled frequently, Betty was expected to be active in Congressional wives' groups; a consummate hostess; travel guide to Michigan constituents visiting Washington; while simultaneously managing a busy household that grew to include four children.

On the outside it looked like she had it all: the former model and dancer, the beautiful congressman's wife with the picture-perfect family.

But inside, Betty was struggling to find her own identity.

5

A Congressman's Wife

The first order of events was for Jerry and Betty to find a place to live. They quickly discovered that the political community on Capitol Hill was small, and people were eager to help. Senator and Mrs. Homer Ferguson from Michigan graciously allowed them to stay in their apartment while they looked for a place of their own.

Meanwhile, Hortense and Arthur Godwin were wintering in Hollywood, Florida. On November 18, Arthur wrote Betty a letter on Hortense's personalized stationery:

Dear Betty:
  Your mother is sick in the hospital. She had an attack of [food] poisoning about two o'clock in the morning on November 10th.
  I telephoned Dr. Snow, and he was at the apartment in about 15 minutes. He gave Horty an injection which put her to sleep in a short time. We phoned for a trained nurse and took her to the hospital in the morning and secured three trained nurses in eight hour shifts so that she is never alone, and she is feeling much better.

The letter went on to say that tests showed blood in Hortense's spinal fluid; the doctor thought a vein in her neck might have ruptured, but, fortunately, no paralysis. They were hopeful she'd be well enough to be released from the hospital in a couple of weeks.

I didn't write before because I didn't want to worry you, but feel now that there is nothing to worry about . . . We were both delighted to receive your nice letter.

The letter was signed: "Your Loving Dad, Arthur."

Unfortunately, Arthur sent the letter to Betty in Grand Rapids, after she and Jerry had already left for Washington. Late on the evening of November 19, Arthur called Jerry's family in Grand Rapids and told them that Hortense had taken a turn for the worse. By the time they were able to reach Betty in Washington, it was ten o'clock.

Jerry booked Betty on the next available flight, and after hours of frustrating mechanical delays, she finally arrived in Florida at nine the next morning. Arthur was waiting for her when she got off the plane, and as soon as she saw his face, she knew it was too late.

"She's gone, honey," he said. Her mother had died just three hours earlier. Betty and her stepfather stood there "holding on to one another, numb with cold, in the hot glare of the sun."

It was a devastating blow. Hortense was just sixty-four years old. She wouldn't see Jerry take his oath in Congress; she wouldn't know her grandchildren; and Betty had suddenly lost her role model—the woman she had looked up to her entire life.

Through the tears, Betty tried to comfort her stepfather, and herself. "She would not have wanted to live a restricted life—mentally or physically," Betty said. "It was probably a blessing God took her."

In her autobiography, Betty wrote: "I believe there's a meaning for everyone's coming into this world, that we're put here for a purpose and when we've achieved that and it's time for us to go, the Lord takes us, and nothing can make it otherwise."

Like so many other times in her life, Betty found inner strength through her faith and relationship with God. Her heart was breaking, but she knew her mother would want her to keep her chin up and move forward.

* * *

On January 3, 1949, Betty was filled with pride as she sat with Jerry's parents in a corner of the gallery, overlooking the chamber of the US House of Representatives as her husband was sworn in as a new member of the Eighty-First Congress.

Jerry and Betty had moved into a one-bedroom apartment at 2500 Q Street NW at the edge of Georgetown, just west of Rock Creek Parkway. It was a quick drive into the heart of downtown DC, and while Jerry was at work, Betty quickly learned her way around. On drizzly spring days, she'd walk down Pennsylvania Avenue, peering in the gates surrounding the White House, never imagining that one day she'd be living inside those historic walls. Before meeting Jerry, Betty hadn't followed politics, but now that she was the wife of a congressman, she figured she'd better learn how things worked. She'd go downtown and watch the US Supreme Court in session, or head over to the Capitol and sit in the galleries of Congress, paying attention to the protocol, trying to understand the way bills and legislation got passed. She'd talk to Jerry about what she'd learned and ask all kinds of questions. He was passionate about being a public servant, furthering the causes of his constituents, and she wanted to speak the same language. It was all new and very exciting.

"I was not a political animal," she noted in her memoir. "I had to really bone up on our government."

It didn't take long for Betty to discover that her sister-in-law Janet had meant it when she warned Betty about work being Jerry's mistress. Even on the weekends, he'd go into the office. With no staff there, Betty would accompany him to help with the filing and whatever else she could do—just so she could be with her husband.

The election of 1948, which returned Harry Truman to the White House, was a landslide for the Democratic Party. In a complete turnaround, the Republicans lost seventy-five seats, giving the opposing party control of the House, the Senate, and the executive branch. It might not have been the most welcoming time to come to Washington as a Republican, but Betty quickly found a camaraderie with other politicians' wives—both Republican and Democrat. She developed warm friendships with Muriel Humphrey, wife of Senator Hubert H. Humphrey, from Minnesota; Abigail McCarthy, Representative Eugene

McCarthy's wife, also from Minnesota; and Pat Nixon, wife of California congressman Richard M. Nixon.

"We were all new together," Betty recalled. It was a time when politics was more civil, and differing political views were left at the Capitol. Men could "berate each other up one side and down the other on the floor of the House," and yet later they'd be at a cocktail party patting each other on the back, saying, "You did a damn good job arguing that point."

Lady Bird Johnson was another woman who befriended Betty and made a special effort to include her. Her husband, Lyndon B. Johnson, had just been elected junior senator of Texas, and after ten years in Congress, was a rising power in the Democratic Party. At one of the first parties Jerry and Betty attended, Lady Bird made a point to introduce the Fords to her husband. "Lyndon," she said, pulling him from across the room, "I want you to meet this young couple. They've just come to Washington."

There was a strict protocol to everything in Washington, especially when it came to who made the guest list to various social events. At first, the invitations came to "Representative Gerald R. Ford," with no "Mrs." attached. So, Jerry would go off to the event, leaving Betty home alone. The next day, she'd run into some of the other wives who had been to the same function.

"Where were you last night?" they'd ask. "We saw Jerry, but we didn't see you."

"I wasn't invited," Betty said matter-of-factly. Years earlier, before her wedding to Bill Warren, Betty had bought, and studied, Emily Post's book of etiquette. She knew that you wore gloves to a tea but took them off during a receiving line, and she knew that if your name wasn't on the invitation, you simply were not on the guest list.

After this happened a few times, she had a chat with Jerry about it. Apparently, word hadn't spread that the handsome new congressman was no longer a bachelor. It wasn't long before all the invitations were addressed to "Mr. and Mrs. Gerald R. Ford Jr."

One subject on which Jerry and Betty were totally in sync was that both wanted to start a family as soon as possible. After six months of earnest trying, and still no sign that Betty was pregnant, they both underwent fertility testing. It turned out Betty had a tipped uterus, which, in 1949, was commonly but incorrectly thought to be a cause of infertility.

She had a surgical "adjustment," and by summertime, she was thrilled to be able to tell Jerry they were expecting a baby.

This being their first summer in Washington, Betty and Jerry were not used to the oppressive heat and humidity, and without air conditioning in their apartment, it was almost unbearable for Betty. Her stepfather had been begging her to visit him at the house on Lake Michigan, and now that seemed like the perfect solution. She stayed with Dad Godwin at his beach cottage through the fall, with Jerry visiting her on weekends. It worked out well because he could focus on his new job during the week without worrying about Betty, and it was just long enough for them to miss each other for happy reunions on the weekends. After spending Christmas in Grand Rapids, Betty and Jerry returned to Washington in January when Congress went back in session.

With the baby due at the end of February, Betty didn't venture out as much as she had when she'd first arrived in Washington, saving her energy for only the most important events. During this time, the White House was undergoing much-needed renovations, so President and Mrs. Truman had moved into the president's official guesthouse across the street, Blair House. First Lady Bess Truman was holding a series of teas for the congressional wives, inviting the ladies in small groups due to the limited space at the temporary residence. At the time, Betty wasn't crazy about President Truman—his politics were often in sharp contrast to her views—but being invited to have tea with the first lady was one of those events you don't pass up.

Betty was nearly eight months pregnant, and as luck would have it, the day of the tea party, the weather was miserable. Rainy, cold—the kind of weather in which she would have preferred to stay home reading a good book. But having never met Mrs. Truman before, and not knowing if there would ever be another opportunity, Betty was determined to go. There was no parking available at Blair House, and to take a taxi the entire way would have been far too expensive, so Betty drove downtown, parked her car in a garage, and hailed a taxi to take her the last few blocks to Pennsylvania Avenue.

Once inside, Betty got into the receiving line, waiting her turn to be introduced. As she approached the first lady, Betty said, "Oh, Mrs. Truman, it's so nice of you to have us. I can't tell you how much I appreciate the opportunity to be here this afternoon."

Looking at Betty's protruding belly, her hair damp and flattened by the rain, Mrs. Truman said, "Heavens, it's you who are nice to come out in such terrible weather."

Her reaction so surprised Betty—that a first lady could stay so humble—and "with that, she went straight to my heart," Betty would later recall. It was a fond memory, and a lesson in grace and sincerity, that would stay with her.

Not long thereafter, on March 14, 1950, several weeks overdue, Betty delivered a healthy, seven-pound, six-ounce baby boy. "He was nice and fat," Betty wrote. Both she and Jerry were ecstatic with their firstborn child.

They had discussed names beforehand, and while Betty wanted another Gerald Ford, Jerry didn't like the idea of having a "junior," remembering the embarrassment he'd felt when his mother called him Junie, so they compromised and named their son Michael Gerald Ford.

A couple of weeks after Mike's birth, Betty received a letter from her brother Bill. Word of the baby was "the most wonderful news of all," he wrote. "Even the children are thrilled to pieces as we are over the thought of Mike." Bill wrote that his children, Bonnie and Stevie, "talk about him as if they were three old pals. Stevie asked this morning, 'When will Mike get to be president?'

"I asked why, and he replied, 'Well, he lives in Washington, and his dad's a congressman.' So," the letter went on, "I'm passing that question along to you, Betty and Jerry, for an answer to Steve's question. I'm sure with two such fine parents, Stevie is not far from the right in presuming that your son will be president someday."

Betty saved the letter to show Mike when he got older, just in case his cousin's prediction came true.

Shortly after moving to the apartment on Q Street, the Fords had hired a woman named Ida to help with the housekeeping. She came in once a week to clean and iron, but while Betty was away in Michigan, Ida found a full-time job at a school and asked Jerry if her daughter-in-law Clara could take her place.

"Clara was like an angel that came into our lives," Betty would say.

With the baby imminent, and not wanting to risk losing Clara, the Fords offered her a full-time position working eight to five, Monday through Friday.

Clara Boswell Powell was forty-one years old when she first began working for the Fords. She and her husband, Raymond, had no children of their own, and when Mike was born, Clara was just as crazy about the baby as his parents were. She came to work wearing a uniform of a white dress, always freshly cleaned and pressed, and always with a smile that shined as bright as her heart. Nothing seemed to rattle her—like the time she was spoon-feeding Mike, and he spewed a mouthful of mashed red baby food beets all over her white dress; she just laughed and told Betty there was no need to buy beets for this one anymore. She knew instinctively what babies needed, and she treated Mike just like he was her own. Before you knew it, Clara was part of the family.

She talked to little Mike as she bathed, fed, and changed him, and one day, when the baby was "just beginning to giggle and grr," Jerry walked in. Clara held up the baby, and as Mike turned to his father, recognizing him with wide eyes and a happy gurgle, Clara said, "That's right, talk to your dad, because some of these days he's going to be president."

Jerry laughed. He had absolutely no drive or desire to be president. It was such a peculiar thing for her to say.

Having Clara to help with the baby and the housework allowed Betty to continue with the social activities that were required of her as a congressman's wife. She became very active with the Congressional Club, an exclusive club for the spouses of House and Senate members, Supreme Court justices, and Cabinet members. In 1950, 98 percent of those positions were held by men, so the Congressional Club was made up purely of wives. There were bridge groups and book clubs, and on Tuesdays, they went to the Red Cross to roll bandages and assemble care packages.

At the book club meetings, someone would stand before the group and give a review of a book she'd read. When it came Betty's turn, she was petrified. First, she didn't know what book to choose, so she called a friend in Grand Rapids for advice.

"What's new?" she asked. "What book should I read?"

Her friend suggested a popular book at the time, *Popcorn on the Ginza*, by Lucy Herndon Crockett. Written by an American woman who had spent eighteen months working with the Red Cross in postwar Japan, the book explored many topical subjects, including the emancipation of Japanese women. It was perfect. But when Betty had to stand up in front of the group and present her review, she was terrified. So many of the other wives were well educated, and now Betty regretted that she hadn't gone to college.

To overcome her self-consciousness, she rationalized, "If I acted smart, and looked smart, maybe strangers would think I was smart."

John Milanowski, an attorney friend from Grand Rapids whom Jerry had hired to be his administrative assistant, recalled rehearsing with Mrs. Ford before her presentation.

"She was terribly nervous, as she wanted to make a good impression for her husband's sake. I told her not to worry about it and that her biggest asset to Jerry was being a good wife and mother. Other things were secondary."

"Just articulate what you are yourself, and you'll be effective," Milanowski told her.

Scared as she was, Betty got up in front of the group and gave her report. It was a big step for her, one she would remember as "a small act of courage." Hoping to quell her fears and improve her confidence, when the Congressional Club offered a public speaking course, she signed right up. The techniques and information she learned would turn out to be very useful.

Jerry and Betty were eager to add to their family, and soon Betty was pregnant again. Their joy turned to sadness and worry when she miscarried around the time Mike was seven months old. The miscarriage prompted them to find a new apartment: one on the ground floor, to avoid Betty's having to go up and down stairs, and with an outdoor space for Michael to play.

Several congressmen and their families, including Dick and Pat Nixon—who would become close friends of the Fords—lived in a large planned development called Parkfairfax, just across the Potomac River in Alexandria, Virginia. Parkfairfax was a series of two- and three-story red brick colonial apartment buildings scattered among nearly 150 beautifully landscaped acres of winding roads, walking paths, and gently sloping hills. The buildings were designed in a U shape to create a sense of community and open space for the residents, and being in the "suburbs," the rents were more affordable than those in the District of Columbia. There were strict rules for residents: only married couples and families were allowed, no dogs or cats permitted, and tenants could grow only flowers, not vegetables. In June 1951 a garden-level apartment at 1521 Mount Eagle Place became available, and the Fords moved in.

The two-bedroom, one-bath apartment was situated at the end of the building, and not only did it have nearly twice the space as their last apartment, but also it opened to an enormous patio where Mike could play and they could host friends for backyard barbecues. On clear days, you could see the Washington Monument off in the distance.

No sooner had the curtains been hung and the boxes unpacked than Betty discovered she was pregnant again. Fearful of another miscarriage, she was careful with her activities. In those days, it was believed that overexertion and even mild exercise could be dangerous for pregnant women.

At Christmas, Jerry, Betty—who was about seven months pregnant—and fifteen-month-old Mike went "home" to Grand Rapids. As often happens when families get together around the holidays, one person gets sick and passes it around. Just as they were getting ready to return to Washington, Mike came down with a cold and a bad ear infection. The night before they were to leave, he was in such pain, he wouldn't stop crying. Jerry and Betty stayed up all night, taking turns walking with him. By morning, everyone was exhausted, and the thought of driving fifteen hours with a miserable baby was almost unbearable. They called the doctor, who gave them some medicine for Mike and confirmed that it would be all right if Betty flew home with him.

So, they booked a flight for Betty and Mike, while Jerry piled all the luggage, toys, and presents into the car and headed east, planning to pick them up at the airport when they arrived that night. It all worked out, but by the time they finally got back to their apartment in Alexandria, it was ten o'clock. Jerry, having driven over six hundred miles straight through, was bleary eyed, and Betty, seven months pregnant, having traveled alone with a sick baby, was completely frazzled. She tucked Mike into his crib, set up a vaporizer with hot water and a dollop of Vicks VapoRub, and then collapsed onto the living room sofa.

"Let me fix you something to eat," Jerry offered.

"All I want," she said, "is a martini and a sandwich. Give me peanut butter, anything; I don't care."

Jerry made her a drink—this was prior to the known health risks of drinking alcohol during pregnancy—and then fixed her a peanut butter sandwich. There was an unusual taste to the sandwich, a sort of menthol flavor, but Betty was so tired, she ate it and didn't say anything. Just before she went to bed, she took her empty glass and plate into the kitchen. Laying on the counter was a knife, the peanut butter, and the jar of Vicks VapoRub.

The baby was due ten days before Mike's second birthday, but this one, too, was reluctant to arrive as scheduled. Finally, two days after Mike's birthday, on March 16, 1952, the Fords welcomed another boy to the family. They named him John Gardner Ford—Gardner to honor Jerry's mother Dorothy's maiden name—and they would call him Jack.

With two boys exactly two years apart, those early days were often chaotic. Mike was a climber—"Once I took him to visit somebody and turned around, and there he was on top of the piano," Betty recalled—and, much to her dismay, gave up his naps at an early age. She'd be changing Jack's diapers and hear loud clanging from the kitchen one minute as Mike hauled out all the pots and pans, and then the next minute it would be dead silent. That's when she knew there was trouble. One day he'd gotten into her makeup and fur scarves, and she came in to see that he'd painted lipstick on all the little mouths of the foxes and minks.

Meanwhile, her husband had to run for reelection every two years. He easily won his first reelection campaign in 1950 with 66 percent of the vote, and in the short time he'd been in Washington, Jerry Ford had gained popularity and influence in the House of Representatives. In 1952 he was one of eighteen young Republican congressmen who urged General Dwight D. Eisenhower to run for president. With two small children at home, Betty couldn't possibly travel back and forth to Michi-

gan with Jerry to campaign on a regular basis, but when Dwight and
Mamie Eisenhower made a stop in Grand Rapids that October, Betty
flew back to join Jerry in welcoming the popular presidential candidate.

It was a heady experience for Betty as she and Jerry rode with the
Eisenhowers in a convertible through their hometown, with thousands
of people lining the streets, cheering. A month later, Jerry again won his
district with 66 percent of the vote, and Dwight D. Eisenhower crushed
Democrat Adlai Stevenson II, the governor of Illinois, to become the
thirty-fourth president of the United States.

After Jerry had won his third election, Betty came to the realization
that her husband planned to stay in Congress, and they were not going
back to Michigan.

When they'd first arrived in Washington, Betty was prepared to be
there for the two-year term, but now, six years later, she was "wall to wall
with tricycles and wagons and toys" and no place for anyone to move.
She and Jerry had lawyer friends back in Grand Rapids who were doing
far better financially, and while there may have been some envy, by this
point, Betty realized politics was in Jerry's blood. He loved every minute
of it, and she wasn't going to stop him.

When it came to the household, however, she held the power, and
she put her foot down. "If you are going to run for Congress again,"
Betty said, "we have got to buy or build or rent a house."

Just two and a half miles away from Parkfairfax sat a tract of land
that was being developed with brand-new homes. Not only would it be
an easy commute for Jerry, but it was close to their church, Immanuel
Church-on-the-Hill, and Douglas MacArthur Elementary School, one
of the best in the district, was nearby. They bought a plot for a token
$10 and signed a deal with the developer to build a house for $34,000.
The mortgage payment of $138.60 a month, plus taxes, was within their
means on Jerry's $15,000 annual salary, but Betty would have to keep to
a tight budget. By getting in pre-construction, Betty could add personal
touches and, after so many years of moving from one apartment to the
next, she was filled with excitement to finally have a home in which to
raise their family.

By this point, with two little boys scampering underfoot, Betty's dreams of becoming a dancer were long gone, and the fortune teller's prediction about meeting kings and queens was all but forgotten. Just eight miles away, however, was a house that was indeed frequented by royal guests from all over the world, and to the Secret Service who protected the ever-changing occupants, the house was codenamed "Crown."

No one could predict what would happen nearly two decades later—it was beyond foresight or comprehension—but it is ironic that the home the Fords built in Alexandria was number 514 on a street named Crown View Drive.

Betty and Jerry worked with the developer to design the split-level, four-bedroom brick house so it would suit their family's casual lifestyle. The front door opened to a foyer that branched out to the rest of the house, with beautiful hardwood flooring connecting all the rooms. Just off the entry hall was a large, sunny living room that had a brick fireplace and two tall windows affording a clear view of the street. The kitchen faced the back of the house, with a window over the sink so Betty could keep an eye on the children, and a back door that made for easy access to the large yard. The kitchen was the heart of the home, and in a nod to their Michigan roots, they had the cabinets and wood paneling custom-made in dark knotty pine from Grand Rapids. There was no formal dining room—Betty did not anticipate entertaining guests for formal sit-down dinners—instead, they had a small breakfast room adjacent to the kitchen with a round table and chairs for the family to share meals together.

A hallway off the kitchen led to a powder room on one side and the two-car garage on the other, with a staircase that led upstairs to four bedrooms. The master bedroom was located over the garage, with big picture windows looking out over the backyard. It had its own small bathroom, and then down the hall was another bathroom shared by three additional bedrooms. A laundry chute made it easy for Betty to toss the never-ending dirty clothes straight to the basement where the washing machine and dryer were installed. It was a good-sized house—it seemed like a mansion compared with the cramped apartment in which they'd been living—and Betty slowly filled it with comfortable but pretty furnishings in her favorite colors of blue and green.

When the Fords moved into their new house in late 1955, it was only the second home on the block, "surrounded by empty lots and mounds of red Virginia clay," Betty recalled. It was the perfect playground for two little boys "to go out in cowboy hats and discover snakes."

Betty and Jerry had been trying—without success—to have another baby, but no sooner had they moved into the new house, then Betty discovered she was pregnant again.

This time she longed for a girl. She went through her entire pregnancy imagining, and really expecting, that this next baby would be a "dear little pink-wrapped bundle," whom she intended to name Sally Meigs Ford: Sally, in honor of her favorite neighbor back in Grand Rapids; and Meigs, to honor her stepfather, Arthur Meigs Godwin, who had just passed away the previous December. But when the little bundle arrived on May 19, 1956, it was another boy. Of course they were happy to have another healthy child, but Betty had been so certain that she was having a girl, she and Jerry hadn't even discussed names for a boy. So, the baby remained nameless for a couple of days until Betty and Jerry finally decided to call their third son Steven Meigs Ford.

Nineteen fifty-six was a presidential election year, and Jerry was running for his fifth term. He loved the legislative life, and in his memoir, he wrote, "My seat in the House seemed safe; every time I ran for reelection, the percentage of my winning margin was larger than in my first race." Continually earning the respect of his peers, he was given additional responsibilities by being appointed to influential subcommittees. When he envisioned what his future held, he wrote in hindsight, "I dreamed of becoming Speaker of the House." On the personal side, "Betty and I were as happy as we could possibly be."

What he didn't recognize was that his wife wasn't nearly as happy as he thought. While Jerry was flourishing in his career, Betty was struggling. She had what she thought she'd always wanted—a house and children, and a husband who adored her—but when a bunch of their friends went off on a trip to Hawaii, she was filled with envy. With three children under the age of six and house payments on a congressman's salary, the Fords couldn't afford lavish vacations. Perhaps it was post-partum depression, or something else, but Betty recalled that several months after Steve came along, she began to feel "the tiniest bit sorry for herself."

During the fall of 1956, Jerry spent weeks in Michigan campaigning while Betty was home with the children. A few months earlier, she learned that her stepfather had left her some money in his will, and while the prudent decision would have been to use the money to pay off the house, Betty and Jerry decided they'd splurge on a much-needed vacation once the election was over. Clara would move into the house while they were gone, and even though Steve was only six months old, she assured Betty it was no problem for her to handle all three boys.

On November 6, 1956, the country voted overwhelmingly to give President Eisenhower another term in office—sending Adlai Stevenson to defeat a second time—and Michigan's Fifth District kept Jerry Ford in his seat as its congressman. Shortly thereafter, Jerry and Betty set off for a three-week European vacation along with their good friends Jack and Phoebe Stiles.

It was Betty's first trip to Europe, and the first real vacation she and Jerry had ever taken together. They drove all over Spain, stopping in Madrid, Mallorca, and Barcelona, and then into Italy, traveling from Naples up to Venice. Betty marveled at the arts, the architecture, and the shopping—she took up collecting demitasse spoons from each locale—but everywhere they went, she had a problem with turista. At least, that's what she thought it was. She just couldn't stomach any of the Spanish or Italian delicacies. By the time they arrived at their final destination—Vienna, Austria—however, she had come to the conclusion that perhaps it wasn't the food that was causing her daily nausea.

When they got home, Betty went straight to the doctor. Sure enough: she was pregnant.

Throughout this pregnancy, Betty didn't dare allow herself to dream of a girl. Jerry's mother had given birth to four boys, and that was probably her destiny as well. Like her first three children, this fourth baby was in no hurry to come into the world. It was a typically hot and humid Washington summer, and by July 6, 1957, Betty woke up "so swollen and sweaty," she thought she could not stand it another day. "I started to cry," she said. "I cried so hard I went into labor."

It was a Saturday, and, fortunately, Jerry was home, but he had promised to take Mike and Jack to a ball game. It wasn't just any ball game. The perennial cellar-dwelling Washington Senators were playing the visiting first-place New York Yankees, starring the boys' idol, Mickey Mantle, and the center fielder was on a streak. The night before, he'd just made his thousandth career hit.

When Betty realized she was in labor, Jerry rushed her to the hospital, "not because the birth was so imminent," she recalled, "but because the ball game started at one o'clock." He had her admitted and then rushed back home to pick up the boys and take them to the game.

The Yankees won, 10–6, and by the time Jerry returned to the hospital, Betty had delivered a healthy, blue-eyed baby girl. "She was born in the seventh-inning stretch, so we didn't disturb anybody," Betty quipped. They named her Susan Elizabeth Ford, and now, finally, their family was complete.

6

Wife and Mother

In Congress, Gerald R. Ford Jr. took on more and more responsibility and continued to earn the respect of his peers. He had a small staff at the office, but there were certain things that a congressman's wife was expected to do. Whenever constituents visited the nation's capital, they'd inevitably want to stop in and say hello to their congressman, and because Jerry represented such a small district, he'd met many of the voters over the years, and they felt like he was a friend. They'd expect Jerry to get them tickets to tour the White House—which back then he could easily do—and then Jerry would give Betty a call to ask if she'd take them around town.

"I don't know how many times I went to Mount Vernon," Betty said. "After a while, I just drove the people out there and sat in the parking lot reading a book while they trudged through George Washington's front parlor and back bedrooms."

Many of the wives did the same things to support their husbands in Congress, and it had become a common practice for members to add their wives and other relatives to their payroll. At one point, Betty was doing so much on his behalf that Jerry considered adding her to his paid staff. His trusted administrative assistant, John Milanowski, advised against it.

"I know it's legal," John said, "and I know that other members are doing it." But not only would it be misunderstood in his conservative district, Milanowski added, "It's contrary to your whole philosophy of public service." Jerry agreed, and Betty never received a nickel for the countless hours she acted as chauffeur and gracious tour guide.

As Jerry's prominence increased, Betty took on greater responsibilities—not because her husband requested it, but because she realized there was a choice to be made.

"I saw that I would have to grow with Jerry or be left behind," she said. "And I had *no* intention of being left behind."

She became the program chairman for the Congressional Club, which entailed putting on cultural programs without any budget. Her experience organizing dance recitals on a shoestring all those years ago became very useful, but Betty also learned she could raise funds by "begging and borrowing from museums and friends."

When she realized that the Democratic wives were more effective in raising money, Betty took it upon herself to "shake up the Republican wives."

"If anybody asks you to do anything," she'd tell them, "say yes. Get off your duffs." She coerced a lot of her Republican counterparts into modeling in fashion shows that raised money for various charities. She'd show them how to walk up and down the runway with their backs straight, one hand on a hip, and they got so they enjoyed it.

Betty's great sense of style and fashion was talked about around town, and at one point, a reporter from *Ladies' Home Journal* pitched the idea for a story on the secrets of this fashionable congressman's wife. Photos were taken of Betty and three-year-old Susan to appear in the magazine a few months later.

Meanwhile, Americans had just elected a new president. It was a stark change, going from the seventy-year-old Dwight D. Eisenhower and his matronly wife, to John F. Kennedy and his wife, Jacqueline, who brought youth and glamour to the nation's capital. When JFK and Jackie moved into the White House in 1961, the country was fascinated by them, and the press couldn't get enough.

The cover article for the April 1961 edition of *Ladies' Home Journal* was "Jacqueline Kennedy: From Wedding to White House, a Look

Inside Her Private Picture Albums." The magazine printed a captivating head shot of the new first lady on the cover with a banner proclaiming: "This Is the President's Favorite Photograph of His Wife."

The edition flew off the shelves. As it happened, inside was a two-page spread about the little-known wife of the representative from Michigan's Fifth District. The headline read: "How Does She Dress So Well and Not Spend a Fortune?"

Presented as "the busy wife of a congressman and four young children who stair-step from three and a half to eleven years old," the article detailed Betty's "expert wardrobe management" secrets on a budget amid an array of stunning photos that proved the point. There was Betty modeling "an irresistible pink suit" purchased for $49.95 to wear to her frequent meetings and luncheons; and another photo of her looking glamorous in a white chiffon evening dress—"just $40.00 on sale"—accessorized with matching turquoise stole and shoes. There was a full-length photo of Betty and her adorable towheaded daughter, Susan, in matching lavender dresses. Betty's secrets included buying a few new pieces each season in classic neutrals and changing the look with colorful shoes, stoles, and jewelry. She confided that she buys expensive long evening dresses only when they're on sale. For daytime, her usual attire was a good suit or a casual dress and sweater. "Slacks are fine to wear around the house," she was quoted as saying, "but for all outside activities, taking the children to the dentist, and so on, I wear a dress."

It was Betty's first appearance in a national women's magazine. She thought it was fun—a one-off experience—never imagining that thirteen years later, every national publication in America would be clamoring to have her on its cover.

During the Eisenhower administration, Jerry and Betty received few invitations to the White House because, as Betty recalled, "the party in power doesn't do as much entertaining of its own people as they do of the opposite party; it's the opposition you have to convince on legislation." But with the election of JFK, a Democrat, the tables turned.

When Jerry first arrived in Washington in 1949, he was assigned an office in the Old House Office Building, on the southwest side of the Capitol. His office happened to be across the hall from John F. Kennedy's. At that time, Kennedy was a junior congressman from Massachusetts, and they often walked together to sessions. Even though they represented different parties, the two found common ground. They had a great deal of respect for each other and became friends.

"The Kennedy White House was much more sophisticated than the Eisenhower White House had been," Betty wrote. With Jacqueline Kennedy as first lady, the parties were more lavish, more lively, and invitations to state dinners were coveted. In July 1961 President and Mrs. Kennedy hosted Pakistan's president, Ayub Khan, in what would be one of the most memorable state dinners of all time, and Jerry and Betty were lucky enough to be among the mere 137 guests.

The dinner was held at Mount Vernon, something Betty noted was an achievement in and of itself. "I don't know how Mrs. Kennedy ever got the ladies of the Mount Vernon Association to let her give a dinner there," she wrote. "They're a very elite, very closed society; in order to belong, your heritage probably has to go back to George Washington, or one of those soldiers who was in that boat with him when he crossed the Delaware." Indeed, it was the first time the mansion had been used for a social function since the 1920s.

The elaborate event began with the guests being transported up the Potomac split among four different US Navy yachts used by the White House: the *Honey Fitz, Sequoia, Patrick J.,* and the *Guardian.* Live music played aboard each yacht—an accordionist on one, a Marine Corps trio on another—as waiters served drinks and hors d'oeuvres during the hour-long cruise to George Washington's historic home. When the flotilla arrived at Mount Vernon, dozens of limousines were waiting at the boat landing to take the guests up the hill to the mansion.

For all the times Betty had visited Mount Vernon, this occasion was unlike any other. Mrs. Kennedy had gone to great lengths to create the colonial atmosphere of the eighteenth century, with soldiers in Revolutionary War battle dress firing musket salutes, a fife and drum corps, and waiters in period tailcoats and white gloves serving mint juleps.

"It took you back in time," Betty recalled. "You could just imagine what it would have been like on a southern plantation long ago."

The plated three-course dinner was served outdoors under a large green tent on the lawn, with the guests seated at round tables. Twinkling white lights adorned the trees, and once the sun set, the atmosphere was magical. After dessert, everyone moved across the lawn to a natural amphitheater to listen to a performance by the National Symphony Orchestra.

Betty shined at these types of social events, mingling confidently among old friends and introducing herself to those she hadn't met before. At one point during the evening, she and Jerry were talking with their longtime friends Lyndon and Lady Bird Johnson, who were now vice president and second lady. They were having such a good time that the Johnsons invited Jerry and Betty to ride with them on their boat for the return trip. Naturally, the Fords accepted.

But just as the guests were getting ready to leave, Jerry and Betty received a message that President and Mrs. Kennedy wanted them to go back on *their* boat.

"Of course, they outranked the Johnsons, so it was the *Honey Fitz* for us," Betty recalled. "I have no idea why we were so sought after, but I had a ball and danced all the way home."

Glamorous Washington soirees like the night at Mount Vernon were in stark contrast to Betty's daytime activities shuttling between Congressional Club meetings, Parent-Teacher Association meetings, car pools, and Cub Scouts.

"Being a housewife seems to me a much tougher job than going to the office and getting paid for it," Betty was known to say.

Muriel Humphrey, wife of then senator and future vice president Hubert Humphrey, recalled that Betty was willing to take on any job. There seemed to be a luncheon, a fashion show, an organizational meeting, or any number of obligations almost every day.

"All of us were always rushing away from meetings to pick up children at school and get home in time to start dinner," Mrs. Humphrey recalled.

For Susan, the memories of her mother not being around began early. "I remember her clothes, the blue linen suits and the yellow linen suits, and her trying to get dressed in the morning, with Steve and me screaming at her ankles." Betty's obligatory outings were so frequent that the two youngest children would sometimes pretend they were sick, hoping their mother would stay home instead. It was especially difficult for the two youngsters because their father was gone so much too.

Even as a junior member of the House, Jerry was constantly on the road. No matter where he was, though, he made it a rule to fly back and spend Sunday with the family. Growing up, Susan recalled that church on Sunday was expected. "You got up, you got dressed, and we went to church on Sunday." Afterward, they'd come home, and Betty would cook up a big brunch of bacon and pancakes, or waffles with strawberries and sour cream. The Sunday evening meal was a big deal too.

"Dad was always home for Sunday-night dinner," Susan said. "It was taken very seriously." During the week, it wasn't unusual for the kids to invite one or two friends over for dinner—and Betty always cooked extra just in case—but Sundays were strictly family time.

Betty usually made a roast beef and mashed potatoes with gravy, served as the family sat around the table sharing the news of the week with one another. "I know that the children looked forward to those Sunday meals as much as I did," Jerry remembered.

If Sundays at 514 Crown View Drive were like a Norman Rockwell painting, the days in between were much more unpredictable. "Our house was chaos," Susan recalled. "It was total chaos."

Somebody was always getting into trouble or doing something he or she shouldn't, and when Susan was little, if the boys found out she'd tattled on them, they'd put her through the "truth test." They'd grab her and hold her at the top of the laundry chute, her feet dangling as she kicked and screamed, threatening to let go if she didn't confess.

When Betty first became a mother at age thirty, she worried about every little scratch on the furniture, but by the time there were four children in the household, "you can forget about order," she wrote. "You just have to hope you don't crack your ankles stumbling over three bags of marbles and a Tinkertoy."

Like every mother, she had to be resourceful. One Christmas, they had been visiting relatives in Michigan, and Jack had received a terrific Roman gladiator's outfit. They were having so much fun at Grandma and Grandpa Ford's house that they were late leaving for the airport to catch the flight back to Washington. Jerry was racing to get there on time, and on the windy Michigan roads, Mike was getting carsick. They didn't have time to stop, so Betty had to make a quick decision.

"Jack, give Mike your gladiator helmet!"

"He filled it up," Jack recalled, "and I could never wear that helmet again."

There was a joke in the Alexandria emergency room that if Mrs. Ford wasn't there with one of the boys at least once a week, there was something wrong at the Ford household. Whether it was stitches or cuts or a broken bone, "Mom was able to deal with the blood," Steve recalled. "She was not squeamish. Probably because she grew up with two older brothers."

All three boys played football, baseball, and basketball, wrestled, and did crew. And back before you could buy a skateboard, the boys made their own. "They'd take my roller skates," Susan remembered, "and strap them to a board. That was their skateboard."

Betty took on the role of Cub Scout den mother, guiding a pack of ten little boys working on their merit badges. "I put in three years' hard time," she quipped. They'd meet once a week at the Ford house, tiling ashtrays, making leather belts, and concocting crafts from milk cartons and a messy mixture of flour and water. When the weather was good, Betty would herd them outside and try to teach them how to do cartwheels.

"I got a modicum of respect for this minor talent," she recalled.

And while the three boys were, well, doing boy things, Betty could hardly wait until Susan was old enough for dance lessons. Modern dance lessons, of course. For most little girls, their first introduction to dance was ballet, but Betty was firmly against it for her daughter.

"Their bodies aren't made to do that at that age," she'd explain. She had nothing against ballet, it was just that she firmly believed children needed free form.

"Be a giraffe or be an elephant," she'd encourage Susan as they danced together around the living room. There was no "point your toe" and "straighten your knee."

Susan loved to dance, and happily took lessons year after year. She idolized her mother, and knowing that her mother had been a dancer in New York City, Susan wanted to be just like her.

* * *

The year Susan turned five, and the boys were twelve, ten, and six, the Fords had a twenty-by-forty-foot swimming pool built in the backyard. It was sixteen feet deep at one end—deep enough so the kids could jump and dive off the diving board without fear of hitting bottom—and long enough for Jerry to swim laps. Betty had handpicked some Japanese-style fish-shaped tiles in two shades of blue that wrapped around the top of the water line, which made the water sparkle an inviting turquoise color, and they'd added a cement patio between the pool and the house, just big enough for an outdoor dining table and a couple of lounge chairs. The pool was heated, so Jerry could use it practically year-round, and from May to October, it was the gathering point for the neighborhood.

"When you have a pool in your backyard, all the kids end up in your backyard," Susan noted. Betty loved having all the children around, but she also didn't want to be roped into sitting out there all summer long as a lifeguard. If a child was going to swim in their pool, Jerry and Betty required the child's parents to sign a release that stated: "We are not lifeguards. If your son or daughter is coming to swim, they need to be able to swim, and you will not hold us liable if anything happens to your child."

Of course, there were incidents. There was the time Jerry and Betty had gone to the Greenbrier—a favorite resort for members of Congress, just four hours from Washington in White Sulphur Springs, West Virginia—for a weekend getaway and came home to find Susan's face bandaged from chin to ears. She'd slipped into the pool—most likely while being chased—and her chin had caught the edge as she slipped underwater. Another time, a neighbor girl, who was babysitting the Ford kids, tried to jump from one corner to the other, fell and scraped her shins, and wound up in the emergency room.

Despite the minor injuries over the years, the pool provided endless hours of fun for the family, and created a beautiful backyard setting in which Betty and Jerry could entertain their friends.

Every so often, however, they'd find things in the pool that weren't supposed to be there.

"One of my strongest memories," Steve Ford recalled with a laugh, "is of Mother dealing with all the childhood pets we brought home." There were fish tanks and aquariums for snakes, chameleons, and turtles.

"We had rabbits, hamsters, gerbils—you name it, we had it," Susan added. And one day Steve convinced his mother to let him get an alligator.

"At the time, I guess it was legal," he said. "You could go down to the pet store and get a small alligator." It started out being just a few inches in length, like a gecko, but it grew and grew until it got to be a couple of feet long. The boys would catch live crickets, and an occasional mouse for it to eat, but mostly they'd feed it store-bought ground beef. As the gator got bigger, it required *a lot* of ground beef. On top of that, "It would bite you every time you got near it," Steve recalled.

Finally, the pet alligator grew so large, Betty insisted it had to be kept outside, so the boys built a box for it in the backyard. One day it got out and decided to take a swim.

"I'll never forget; Mom and Dad were just beside themselves," Steve remembered. "The alligator had gotten loose and was swimming in the pool." It was his pet and his responsibility to get it out. So he piled on layers of clothes in case it bit him, jumped in the pool, and roped him out. It was just a question of time. Something had to be done about the alligator.

As the nights started getting colder, Steve would bring the alligator into a pen in the basement each night. "But Mother ended up doing it most of the time," Susan recalled, "like most mothers do." And one night, Betty decided to let nature take its course.

The next morning, Steve realized he'd forgotten to bring his reptile inside the night before, and when he went to check on it, the alligator was stiff as could be. There had been a frost overnight, and the poor creature had succumbed to the cold. Betty wrote, "Clara helped dig the grave in the backyard, and the horrid pet was buried with all due ceremony, a cross planted over its head." There would be many more pets in the Ford household, but never another alligator.

When Jerry was traveling, he made it a point to call home every night after dinner. Betty would line up the four children, and each one would spend about five minutes talking to Dad, telling him about his or her day.

"He called to say that he was sorry he was gone; he missed us," Mike Ford recalled. "Checking how the football was going or the schoolwork. And then he'd say, 'Take care of Mom. Do what Mom says. Be good for Mom.' He counted on us to be as helpful as we could." Once the kids were all in bed, Jerry would call again and talk to Betty. That time was just for the two of them. By then, Betty would have poured herself a nightcap—her way to unwind after catering to everyone else's needs all day long.

When he returned home on the weekends, Jerry would inevitably need to go to his office at the US Capitol to catch up on mail and other issues that had accumulated in his absence. To give Betty a break from being with the kids all week, he'd bring them up to the Capitol with him.

"The first thing he would make us do was sit down and type a note to our mother," the Ford children recalled. One by one, they'd sit on Dad's leather chair behind the desk, sitting up on their knees when they were too small to reach, and slip a blank sheet of paper behind the roller of the black Royal typewriter. They'd hunt and peck for the letters and tap away a short note that told their mother how much they appreciated her, and often, at their father's suggestion, adding a line about how hard Dad was working.

"Dear Mom, you're the greatest Mom. We love you, stuff like that," Steve remembered.

Jerry would proofread the letters, offering suggestions, and then they'd sign them, fold them up, and put them in an envelope to take home to Mother. Once that task was finished, Jerry would say, "Okay. You're free to go. Be back by three o'clock."

For the next couple of hours, the hallowed halls of the US Capitol became their playground. They'd play hide-and-seek in Statuary Hall, sneaking behind the towering figures of Daniel Webster, Ethan Allen, and Jefferson Davis. They'd run up and down the endless marble staircases and find their way to the underground subways with the wicker carts that led to the office buildings. "We'd ride them back and forth," Susan recalled with a smile, her eyes twinkling with the memory. "But we'd always get lost, and we'd have to ask a Capitol policeman. 'I'm Jerry Ford's daughter, and I can't find my way back to his office, and I don't know what dome I'm under.'" The Capitol policemen were always kind and helpful, happy to guide them back to Congressman Ford's office.

Jerry's staff would always know when the kids had been there.

"They would take all the things off the top of our desks and hide them, or exchange names," Jerry's longtime assistant Anne Holkeboer recalled. "We had name plates on each desk, so my name might be in somebody else's desk, and all the little items that you just kind of keep on your desk—they were gone." Eventually the staff learned to clear their desks on Friday afternoons, just in case.

Later, when Jerry and the children returned home and presented Betty with the letters, she'd open them one by one, always as if it were the first time and she was getting some great surprise. She'd read the letters aloud with a big smile on her face.

"How grown up you are to have typed such a letter," she'd say. "I'll treasure this beautiful note from you."

And she did. Betty tucked them away in a drawer and kept every single one. Of course, she knew Jerry had put them up to it, and after reading the letters, she'd always give him that look—that special look they had between each other when no words were necessary. Even though the letters were from the kids, it was Jerry's way of telling her how much he appreciated and loved her. He knew she carried the load of raising the children—managing the day-to-day activities, being the disciplinarian—and he knew it wasn't easy.

"She ran our house because Dad was gone so much," Susan said. "She was strict about things like homework and bedtime and respect. Respect your elders." If someone got out of line, she'd send them to their room or take away television privileges. Betty wasn't any easier on Susan just because she was the only girl and the youngest. If Susan started a fight with the boys, and it turned into a wrestling match on the floor— which happened a lot—Susan would cry out, "Mom! Mom! Mom!"

Betty wouldn't fall for it. "Don't expect me to bail you out of this," she'd say to Susan. "You picked your fight, now fight your fight."

"They were not rescuers," Susan said of her parents' disciplinary style. They were intent on making sure their children understood there were consequences for what they did—whether it was lying or stealing or not being on time. "With three boys and a girl, and with Dad gone so much of the time, Mom had no choice but to be strict," Susan said. "It was the only way she could survive."

There was no "Wait until your father gets home" for a decision about discipline. "When they misbehaved, I made the decision right then and there," Betty recalled.

When Jerry wasn't traveling, he tried to spend as much time as possible with the kids. Once they started playing Little League baseball and youth football, Betty would drive the boys out to the field, but Jerry would show up as soon as he could get away from work. At home, everyone in the family, including Betty, fought to have time alone with him.

"Dad would always come home and take a swim," Susan remembered. "That was his way of unwinding." He'd swim for fifteen or twenty minutes, go upstairs and change clothes, and when he came downstairs, Betty would have a martini waiting for him.

"They would go sit in the den, or sometimes it was out on the patio if it was a nice evening, and we pretty much knew we were not to be there. That was their time."

Nothing had to be said: there'd be a look, and the kids knew that meant they needed to be upstairs doing homework or feeding the dogs, taking care of other things. It was a special time for Betty and Jerry to relax together before dinner.

Most of the time, though, Jerry wasn't there.

"It put a strain on the marriage," Jerry admitted. Even though he called every night, he was all over the country, sometimes overseas, and "with four active children," he acknowledged, "Betty had a tough obligation. She had to be not only the mother but the father."

At times, it was overwhelming. As the children grew, and as Jerry became more powerful in Congress, Betty began to feel like the more important her husband became, the less important she was. As he was getting all the headlines and applause, she would think: *But what about me? Who do they think is making it possible for him to travel all over the United States giving speeches?* And yet, for a woman who appeared on the outside to have everything, she couldn't understand why she wasn't perfectly happy. Like so many women, not only at that time but still today, Betty tried to find ways to cope.

"I'd have my five o'clock drink at a neighbor's house," Betty wrote in her memoir. "Or even by myself, while talking on the phone with a neighbor. I'd have another while I was fixing dinner, and then, after the kids were in bed, I'd build myself a nightcap and unwind by watching television."

Mike, the oldest of the Ford children, didn't think anything of it at the time. "Dad and Mom would always have an evening drink together. And they would go to cocktail parties a lot," he recalled.

Jerry could have a drink or two and have no problem. Meanwhile, Betty's addiction to alcohol was in its sly infancy, its insidious effects already taking hold. Through it all, there was one member of the household who saw what was happening. She was the keeper of all their secrets and was the glue that held them all together: Clara Powell.

7

A Second Mother

Years later, when asked about Clara, Susan Ford's voice cracked, and tears welled in her eyes. "She was my mom when my mom wasn't home," she reflected.

Indeed, all four of the Ford children regarded Clara as their second mother. "We embraced her that way," Steve said. The kids didn't know a time when Clara wasn't part of their household, since she had started working for the family just before Mike's birth.

As a young girl, growing up in Arlington, Virginia, Clara had dreamt of becoming a nurse. But like so many black girls who grew up during segregation and came from broken homes, dreams rarely turned into reality. Raised by her grandmother, Clara dropped out of high school to go to work and married Raymond at seventeen. "I really didn't have a chance to nurse," she said, in Betty's 1978 memoir, "but I've been nursin' ever since."

Whether it was the flu or chickenpox, being sick meant you got one-on-one time with Clara. "You loved it," Susan said, "because Clara wouldn't clean the house. She stopped. She'd make chicken soup and then cuddle up with a book and read to you. She made you feel special."

Every weekday morning at nine o'clock prompt, Clara would arrive at 514 Crown View Drive. For many years, she didn't have a driver's license, so Raymond would drive her from their home in Bailey's Cross-roads, drop her off, and return to pick her up at five.

Betty and Clara worked together to keep the busy household running as smoothly as possible, and over the years, the two women developed a close bond.

"She and I used to laugh about everything and nothing," Betty recalled. At times, they'd be working alongside each other, Clara scrubbing the floor in one room, and Betty on her hands and knees in another. Betty would put on a record, and they'd be singing at the tops of their lungs. One time, they were both literally on their hands and knees singing along to the spiritual "Get Down on Your Knees and Pray." They looked at each other and doubled over with laughter.

"She was wonderful," Mike Ford recalled. But she was also a disciplinarian. "My parents gave Clara permission to actually use her slipper on us, and she did when it was justified. She had to use it only once or twice, and from then on she would just grab her slipper, and we would comply."

With four kids in the house, there were always meals to make, dishes to wash, and endless loads of laundry. Every morning there'd be a fresh pile of dirty clothes at the bottom of the chute in the basement, and by afternoon, they'd be cleaned, pressed, folded, and back in the drawers upstairs. Most afternoons, you could find Clara in the basement doing the ironing. When Steve was beginning to outgrow his naps, he would sneak out of his room and slide down the two flights of stairs on his behind, trying to be as quiet as possible so Clara wouldn't notice him.

But you couldn't put anything past her. Like all mothers, she had eyes in the back of her head.

"Now, Steve Ford," Clara would say—"She always called me Steve Ford," Steve recalled with a laugh—"Now, Steve Ford, if you're not going to take a nap, you're going to go to work."

"She taught me how to iron," he said. "She started me on Dad's handkerchiefs, and eventually I moved up to other things."

Ironing the handkerchiefs was a rite of passage for all the Ford children, but Clara made each one of them feel like it was his or her special thing.

When the kids got home from school, Clara was always there, often pulling a freshly baked batch of cookies out of the oven or prepping dinner so that all Betty had to do when she got home after driving kids from practice or dance class or the orthodontist was heat and serve.

"My mom made the best meatloaf," Susan said, "but because Mother was always at luncheons and stuff all the time, Clara was the one who taught me how to cook and keep a house."

"Clara was a mainstay in raising the children," Jerry Ford wrote in his memoir. He often said, "If Clara leaves us, I'll have to quit Congress."

On the occasions when Betty would join Jerry on a trip somewhere, Clara would stay with the children at Crown View Drive. At night, the Ford kids recalled, "we'd all pile into Mom and Dad's bed because everyone wanted to sleep with Clara."

They'd sit in bed watching Cassius Clay boxing matches—back before he was Muhammad Ali—and "wrasslin'" on television. "It was 'wrasslin'," Susan recalled with a laugh, "not wrestling.'" When it was time to go to sleep, Clara would get them calmed down, and as they all cuddled up together, she'd begin to sing:

"Swing low, sweet chariot, comin' for to carry me home . . ."

"She was an incredible woman," Susan recalled. "My goal in life was always to be more like Clara."

Neither Betty nor Jerry was demonstrably affectionate with the children. "You'd get a hug and a squeeze," Susan recalled, "but Clara was very affectionate. Mom was always so busy, but Clara always made time."

"Whatever void needed to be filled, that's what she did," Clara's goddaughter, Lynette Williams Thomas, said. And while Clara didn't talk to her own family about the Fords' personal issues—"She respected their privacy," Lynette said—as the years went on, it was clear there was a growing problem. It wasn't Clara's place to say anything, but she'd see an empty vodka bottle in the trash bin, knowing there'd been no party the night before, and she couldn't help but feel compassion for both Betty and the children.

"Clara recognized that there were times Betty wasn't emotionally available to the children, and she stepped right in," Lynette said. "She pretty much raised those kids, and they embraced her."

Because of the age difference between the two older boys and Susan and Steve, it was almost like the Fords had two sets of children. As soon as Mike and Jack were old enough, Jerry and Betty wanted to take them to Boyne Mountain in Michigan to learn to ski. Between the school calendar and Congress's schedule, the only time available was Christmas. So Betty and Jerry would take Mike and Jack skiing, leaving Steve and Susan to stay with Clara and Raymond at their home in Bailey's Crossroads.

"It wasn't punishment," Susan said, as she remembered the pictures of her and Steve sitting in front of the Christmas tree at Clara's house. "We loved Clara. It was fun!"

Because Clara didn't have children of her own, she kept scrapbooks of the Ford children as they were growing up, and every memento they gave her. "And she knew everything," Steve Ford recalled. "Clara knew when you hid anything in your room when you were a kid."

One Christmas, when he was about nine years old, Steve had saved about $25, which was a lot of money for a young boy in the 1960s.

"I took my money, and I snuck down in the basement where she kept her purse, and I put the money in her purse and didn't tell her," he said. "I just wanted her to have a little money at Christmas."

The next day, Clara confronted him. "Steve Ford, I know where you keep your money, and I had an extra twenty-five dollars in my purse, and your money wasn't under your bed."

"She got really mad at me," Steve said. She refused to take the money. "The heart of her was just beautiful."

Betty joked that she stayed home most of the times when Jerry traveled to Michigan because she didn't want the children to think Clara was their mother. "But," she wrote, "in a way, she was their mother. In a way, she was my mother."

Without judgment, and with unconditional love, Clara quietly wrapped her arms around each member of the family, providing comfort and security, like a child's favorite blanket.

"All of us loved her as one of us because she was one of us," Jerry Ford wrote. "She was always there to help when a family crisis arose." One such crisis—a turning point in Betty's life—would happen in the wake of a national tragedy.

In the fall of 1963, Jack Ford was in the fifth grade and appeared to be struggling in school. "He seemed so much brighter than his marks indicated," Betty said. They had him tested, and, as it turned out, he had a "terrifically high IQ, but he was always reading *Time* or *Newsweek* or *Sports Illustrated* when he should have been cracking his school books."

To figure out how best to support their second oldest son, Betty and Jerry set an appointment to meet with an education counselor in the district. It was a Friday afternoon, November 22, a date that would forever stick in their minds, as it would for everyone who was alive at the time. When they came out of the meeting and got into their car, Jerry automatically turned on the radio. And that's when they learned that President John F. Kennedy had just been assassinated in Dallas.

"The news was crushing," Betty said. "It was inconceivable to every one of us that this could happen in our country, to our president." Jerry was shocked. It affected him not only because of his personal friendship with President Kennedy but also because he just "couldn't believe that somebody would assassinate an American president."

Over the next three days, Betty recalled, they "seemed to move through a haze of pomp."

On Saturday they drove to the White House in the drizzling rain and met privately with members of the Kennedy family before kneeling to pray beside the president's flag-draped casket in the East Room. When the body was moved to the Capitol on Sunday, November 24, Betty remembered the haunting sound of the muffled drums, the vision of the six gray horses pulling the artillery caisson that held the casket, and the eerie silence of the crowds along Pennsylvania Avenue.

"There weren't many tears," Betty recalled. "Faces were blank. I think most people must have been like me, too deep in shock to cry."

For the funeral on Monday, November 25, buses were arranged to transport members of Congress and their spouses to Arlington National Cemetery. Jerry attended the Mass at St. Matthew's Cathedral, while Betty went directly to Arlington with two close friends, the wives of Congressmen John Byrnes and Walter Norblad. From a vantage point up on a hill, they witnessed the somber ceremony: the massive collection of kings and queens and heads of state from more than one hundred countries standing alongside the black-veiled Jacqueline Kennedy, as the Scottish Black Watch bagpipes wailed, and fifty jet aircraft flew overhead, with the final team in the missing-man formation. There was the roar of Air Force One flying low, and when the pilot dipped one wing in salute to the fallen commander in chief, it was a sight no one there would ever forget. Betty watched as Jackie Kennedy, just thirty-four years old, now a widow, took a candle and lit what would be an eternal flame. But it wasn't until Betty witnessed the president's casket being lowered into the ground that she truly realized he was dead. "Up until that moment, it had been a nightmare," she wrote. "Now it was real."

Because of the uncertainty of the circumstances surrounding the assassination, the new president, Lyndon Johnson, swiftly appointed a commission to conduct a thorough investigation. The official title was the Presidential Commission on the Assassination of President Kennedy, but it became known unofficially as the Warren Commission, led by Earl Warren, chief justice of the US Supreme Court. Johnson chose six other members—all men he felt that both he and the American people could trust without reservation. One of those men was Congressman Jerry Ford. For the next nine months, Betty recalled, "Jerry attended meetings religiously, trying to digest hours of testimony and stacks of research produced by the commission's lawyers." This was on top of his increasingly demanding schedule as a senior member of the House Appropriations Committee and chairman of the House Republican Conference—the primary forum for communicating the party's message with its members. Betty was proud that her husband had been entrusted with such an important task, but it meant that he was home less than ever before.

When the 888-page report was released in September 1964, Jerry was confident in the commission's findings that Lee Harvey Oswald alone had fired the shots that killed President Kennedy, as well as Dallas police officer J. D. Tippit, and there was no evidence of a conspiracy. "Beyond a reasonable doubt, I felt Oswald killed both President Kennedy and Officer Tippit," he wrote.

Betty was immensely proud of Jerry's contribution. "I would imagine that Jerry knows as much as anybody in the country about that assassination," she wrote. Of course, the *Warren Report* would be criticized for decades to come, and it irked her that "people who have no facts whatsoever are always coming around and saying Oswald never shot Kennedy at all, or it was a conspiracy."

* * *

Every summer, the Fords returned to Michigan to see family and spend time on Lake Michigan. During the summer of 1956, Jerry and his three brothers had built a log-sided, one-story cottage on a lot that had been purchased by their parents. It was a simple house, but the focal point—the pure white sand beach that stretched for miles—was just steps away. Each of the brothers took turns using the cottage with their families; Jerry's turn was always in August to coincide with the congressional recess.

The entire family always looked forward to these annual vacations. Just as Jerry and Betty had spent carefree summer days at various lakes throughout their childhoods, they loved being able to provide their own children the same experiences and memories. Betty would sit in a low folding chair on the beach, a wide-brimmed hat shielding her face from the sun, while Jerry joined the kids in swimming and sailing races, throwing Frisbees and balls on the beach until the sun set along the water's edge.

Decades later, Jack Ford would say, "Some of my fondest memories were spending summers at Ottawa Beach."

Nineteen sixty-four was a presidential election year—President Lyndon B. Johnson was running against Barry Goldwater, the conservative senator from Arizona—and Jerry would be spending most of his time up until November in Michigan. Still, he had set aside two weeks in August to spend with the family, and that year, for the first time, instead of returning to Ottawa Beach, they rented a cottage at Bethany Beach in Delaware.

Two days before they were to leave, Betty woke up in the middle of the night in excruciating pain.

It came on suddenly: a stabbing pain that ran from her neck all the way down her left arm. She'd had pain before—plenty of strained muscles and cramps when she was dancing eight hours a day at Bennington and in New York—but never had Betty felt anything like this, and it scared her. She didn't want to disturb Jerry, so she made her way downstairs, hoping some stretches would make the pain go away. The next morning, however, Jerry found his wife frozen in agony on the living room couch. By that point, Betty's hand had swollen up, and the pain was unbearable.

"I'm taking you to the emergency room," Jerry said. He managed to get her in the car and drove straight to the hospital.

The doctors told her she had a pinched nerve in her neck, and that's what was causing the severe pain. The only thing Betty could attribute to having caused it was when, the day before, she'd reached across the four-foot-wide kitchen counter to raise the window over the sink, and when it wouldn't budge, she gave it all she had.

Her friend Kay DeFreest said, "I knew exactly how that happened—in a moment of anger, probably—heaven knows what had gotten in there at that point to make her angry. But all dancers feel that they can conquer anything. Nothing is too much for a dancer. If you wish to raise a window, the window will raise, and if it doesn't raise, you better watch out: it's liable to get kicked out. If she was stressed and tightened up in the first place, that's what likely [pinched] the nerve."

Whatever had caused Betty's pain, Jerry recalled that the doctors "put her in a soft collar, gave her some Darvon, and told her to go home and relax."

Relaxing was not possible. The pain was relentless, and Betty ended up back in the hospital. This time the doctors put her in traction and prescribed stronger painkillers.

Knowing how much the kids had looked forward to the vacation, Betty urged Jerry to take them to the beach as planned. Meanwhile, at the hospital, Betty was strung up to various devices, and was given gold shots to treat the pain and inflammation. The doctors had determined that surgery was not an option because the damaged tissues were too close to the spinal cord, so the only choices to manage the pain were drugs and physical therapy.

"The first time the hospital attendants took me for therapy," Betty recalled, "I cried from the pain." She couldn't lie down as they wanted her to, so she sat on a chair, leaning forward across the treatment table as the attendant massaged and stretched her back.

After two weeks in the hospital, Betty was finally able to go home, but the doctors told her she needed to stay in bed for at least two more weeks with a traction setup.

Fortunately, Clara was there holding everything together. She nursed Betty, cooked and cleaned, and made sure the kids had rides and got to where they needed to be. "Clara was indispensable," Jerry recalled.

For Betty, the only way she could get through the day was to stay on top of the pain with the strong medication prescribed by the doctors. Before leaving the hospital, Betty had expressed her fear about being able to return to normal activities. She was so afraid she'd be out somewhere and the pain would start. The doctor's response: "Don't let the pain start. Keep your medication with you and take it every four hours."

It was doctor's orders, and Betty followed them. She was on pain meds around the clock, and every evening, at five, she'd have a cocktail, just as she'd always done. There was never a thought that mixing alcohol with the drugs she'd been prescribed would create a problem. She was not alone.

In the 1960s, there were no warning labels on medications, and few studies had been conducted regarding the possible problematic interaction between drugs and alcohol. It was a time when doctors were prescribing amphetamines and tranquilizers to women by the millions. The amphetamines provided a feeling of euphoria and energy, with the added benefit of suppressing appetite, while the tranquilizers such as Valium eased anxiety. The pills were so common, they were known as "Mother's Little Helpers."

That November, Americans voted overwhelmingly for Lyndon B. Johnson to remain in the White House, and while Jerry had worked tirelessly to help his fellow Republicans, the Democrats retained their majorities in both the House and the Senate. A group of congressmen approached Jerry and suggested he should run for minority leader. He had earned the respect of his peers during his sixteen years in Congress, and while this would be a great honor, he knew the additional travel it would entail would place even more of a burden on his wife.

That night, he discussed it around the dinner table with Betty and the four children. "If I became minority leader," Jerry said, "I'd have a real chance to become Speaker someday. On the other hand, the post would require a lot of traveling, and that would mean even less time with the family." They weighed the pros and cons, and as was always the case in the Ford household, the children were encouraged to speak openly and honestly.

After a lengthy discussion, finally, twelve-year-old Jack said, "Go for it, Dad." Betty and the three other children all agreed. It was truly a family decision.

That Christmas, the entire family went to the Boyne Mountain resort in Michigan, for what had become an annual family ski vacation. Even seven-year-old Susan was on skis, having learned the year before. Two days after Christmas, Jerry received a call informing him that the vote for minority leader was going to be very close, and he was urged to return to Washington. It wouldn't be the first vacation interrupted, and it certainly wouldn't be the last. Jerry won narrowly, by six votes, and on January 4, 1965, he was sworn in as House minority leader. Looking back, from Betty's perspective, it couldn't have happened at a worse time.

8

"Mom's Really Upset; You Need to Go Fix It"

With Jerry's new position as minority leader, his workdays stretched longer and longer. Most mornings, there were early breakfast dates on the Hill; most nights, there were late caucuses or parties involving constituents or lobbyists.

Socially, the Fords were plunged into a whirl of activity that sometimes had them making appearances at as many as three or four receptions in one evening. Betty would get dressed for a business dinner and drive into Washington carrying her long gown, Jerry's tuxedo, shirt, and shoes. After the dinner, she and Jerry would scramble up to his office on Capitol Hill and change into their formal attire for a black-tie charity gala or fund-raiser.

When Jerry was home, "he was wonderful," Betty said. "He helped with the dishes, played ball with the boys, watched Susan go through her dance routines, brought me coffee in bed in the morning. But we both knew his job came first."

As House minority leader, he had to show up in nearly every congressional district around the country where a Republican wanted his help. He was making easily two hundred out-of-town speeches a year. He became so focused on his work and his constituents that he couldn't see what was happening in his own household.

"Dad had tunnel vision," Steve Ford said. "He kept going. He expected her to get done whatever she was supposed to get done, and Mother sort of got left by the wayside." It wasn't that he didn't love her, "but because he didn't understand."

Betty knew how hard Jerry had worked to achieve this position and was immensely proud of him. She loved being "the wife of Minority Leader Gerald R. Ford," but at the same time, she was filled with self-doubt and feelings of inadequacy. "I couldn't accept that people liked me for myself," she said. And she was always self-conscious about the fact that she didn't have a college degree—especially at luncheons or dinner parties when conversations turned to where everyone had graduated from college.

As Jerry's prestige in Washington grew, Betty started becoming resentful. *Who do they think is making it possible for him to travel all over the United States giving all those speeches? He gets all the headlines and applause, but what about me?*

The more important Jerry became, the more her own self-worth and self-esteem declined. Betty began to resent his being gone so much, but, of course, she couldn't say anything. She'd been part of the conversation and had agreed to his aspirations. Still, at times she couldn't help herself. One night, Jerry got into bed and lay down beside her. She rolled over and said, "What are *you* doing here?"

When Jerry became minority leader, Mike and Jack were attending T. C. Williams High School, in Alexandria; Susan and Steve went to nearby Douglas MacArthur Elementary. The boys played football and baseball, while Susan had dance lessons, and had taken up horseback riding. There were orthodontist appointments, eye doctor visits, and, when you least expected it, always at the worst possible time, a broken bone or a tooth through a lip that required an urgent trip to the emergency room. Four kids, all going in different directions, with Betty in charge of juggling carpools, PTA meetings, and teaching Sunday school, as well as her ever-increasing responsibilities as wife of one of the most powerful men in Republican politics. The older boys "were going through adolescence and all that means," Betty wrote, "and I was having problems of my own with the change of life." On top of all that, the pain in her neck kept getting worse.

"I hated feeling crippled," she wrote. She was forty-seven years old, but she felt much older. The pills dulled the pain, and she realized that a drink or two in the evening helped her to relax at the end of a stress-ful day. The children saw that, at times, she was not always thinking straight.

"We kids took advantage of that," Steve said. "We learned how to get away with little things." The little things sometimes turned into big things, and Betty began to feel like she was "a doormat to the kids." It was all about to come to a head.

It was a Tuesday in August 1965. Jerry had been in meetings at the White House, and President Johnson had invited him to go for a cruise on the presidential yacht *Sequoia* that evening with a contingent of other congressmen. He'd called Betty to let her know he wouldn't be home until ten or eleven that night.

Clara had been at the house all day, and left at five, as she normally did. The school year hadn't started yet, all four kids were home, and Jack was pushing Betty's buttons.

"Jack's the son with whom I've crossed swords most often," Betty wrote. It wasn't uncommon for them to have bitter arguments, and this day was one of them. They were going at it back and forth upstairs. Downstairs, Susan, Steve, and Mike had come in from the pool. They heard the yelling, and then the sound of their mother sobbing behind the closed door of the master bedroom.

Jack came stomping down the stairs. "Mom's really upset," he announced. They'd had their scuffles before, but this time it seemed a line had been crossed. There was something different. He looked at Susan and said, "You need to go fix it."

Even though she was the youngest, somehow Susan was always the one that could calm down their mother.

"It's okay, Mom," she'd say. "We love you, Mom." That had become her role. The fixer.

Before anyone could do anything, Betty appeared at the foot of the stairs. Her hair was disheveled, like she'd been trying to pull it out, and her eyes—swollen and red from crying—were wild.

"That's it! I can't take it anymore!" she cried. "I'm taking Susan, and we're going to the beach!"

Susan, just eight years old, was terrified. She had never seen her mother like this before. *What does she mean? Where are we going? Are we going to stay in a hotel? What about Dad and the boys?*

And then the thought that always came next: *How can I fix it?*

But Betty was inconsolable. She was ranting and pacing, gathering things together, getting ready to leave. Later, she would admit that her intention was to let the "whole ungrateful family worry about where I was and whether I was ever coming home."

Mike realized they needed help. He snuck out the back door and raced across the street to their neighbors Harriet and Wendell Thorne's house.

"I need to get hold of my dad," Mike said. "And Clara. We need Clara." As the oldest child, Mike fell into the role of protector. He knew his mother would be mortified if anyone outside the family saw her like this.

Meanwhile, back at the house, Betty was packing her and her daughter's things. Susan was crying, scared to death. It wasn't long—although it seemed an eternity—before Clara showed up.

She took charge, in her calm, soothing way. "There, there," she said, as she wrapped Susan in her arms. "Let me go talk to Mother. Everything's gonna be all right."

Clara went upstairs and knocked on the door to the master bedroom.

"Mrs. Ford, it's Clara." Betty let her into the room, and while Clara would never reveal what was said or what she did, whatever it was, it was exactly what Betty needed to hear.

Clara had called Jerry, fortunately reaching him before the *Sequoia* left the pier.

More than fifty years later, Susan remembered the trauma of that evening as vividly as if it had happened the day before. "Dad went up with Mom, and then a doctor came. Clara came downstairs and took Steve and me and said, 'Come. Let us go for a walk.'"

Clara knew that Mike and Jack were old enough to realize what was going on, but Susan and Steve needed to be reassured. They walked up Crown View Drive as the late summer sun dropped below the horizon, and Clara tried to explain to them in terms an eight-year-old and a nine-year-old would understand.

"Your momma is sick," she said. She told them that Betty had been seeing a doctor—a psychiatrist—and he was going to help her get better. "It's not your fault," she said. "She loves you very much. But she just needs a bit of help right now."

After that, Susan remembered feeling scared of her mother, and embarrassed. She was afraid to bring friends home, and, more and more, she clung to Clara.

For Betty, going to therapy helped her realize that she couldn't be everything to everybody. "I'd been too busy trying to figure out everyone else's needs, that I'd had no time for Betty," she wrote. "I had to start thinking I was valuable, not just as a wife and mother, but as myself. And to myself."

Over time her self-esteem began to improve, and those feelings of uselessness and emptiness faded. She realized that her mental state had a lot to do with her exacerbating physical pain.

She wasn't alone. In 1963, Betty Friedan authored *The Feminine Mystique* about "the problem that has no name." The book, which would sell more than one million copies its first year in print, focused on the increasing unhappiness and empty feelings of women in America. Friedan wrote, "We can no longer ignore that voice within women that says: 'I want something more than my husband and my children and my home.'"

And while the visits to the psychiatrist helped, Betty didn't realize—and the doctor didn't ask—that she was using alcohol to cope. "I saw no reason to discuss my drinking," she would say years later. "I preferred to pretend everything would get better if I went back to dance class, or did some shopping, or took an afternoon off to write letters."

Meanwhile, each member of the family unconsciously slipped into roles to cope with something they didn't understand, but which only served to enable Betty's addiction.

Jerry would become a classic enabler, making excuses for his wife when she was late or had imbibed one drink too many at a social event, blaming it on an overzealous bartender.

Mike, the oldest, would quietly take over when his mother wasn't able to function. "I had to step in either indirectly or directly with my siblings to help with things like homework or driving Susan and Steve around once I got my license," Mike recalled. He'd run errands and do the grocery shopping—even fill in for Betty at church functions, in an effort to protect her.

"I didn't want her to look bad or feel like she hadn't done her job," he explained. "I didn't want her to feel that way."

Quite often in the families of an alcoholic, the second-oldest child becomes the scapegoat: one who develops angry and defiant behaviors. Jack would fall into that role.

"I think most of my family would say that she and I were, in a lot of respects, most alike," Jack acknowledged. "And so, that meant probably that we butted heads more often. I plead guilty to egging things on, at times."

Steve, a middle child, became the mediator. "No doubt that my role was to try to find a compromise to make peace," he reflected.

And Susan, the youngest, was the fixer.

From the outside, they were the perfect American family. And on the inside, they truly loved one another and were close. But the disease was there, lurking beneath the surface.

9

The Nixon White House

With the help of her weekly therapy sessions, Betty was feeling much better about herself and her situation in life. She realized there was nothing "terribly wrong" with her. "I just wasn't the Bionic Woman," she wrote. "And the minute I stopped thinking I had to be, a weight fell from my shoulders."

In March 1968, President Lyndon Johnson stunned the nation by announcing he would not seek reelection, and that year, after the tragic assassination of Democratic candidate Robert F. Kennedy, the presidential election was ultimately between the Republican candidate, former vice president Richard M. Nixon, and Democrat Hubert Humphrey, with anti-integrationist Alabama governor George Wallace siphoning votes as the choice of the newly formed American Independent Party.

When Nixon won the nomination at the Republican National Convention in Miami that August, he had asked Jerry Ford if he'd consider running as vice president on the ticket. But Jerry saw that there was a chance the Republicans might capture enough seats to win the majority, which would make him Speaker of the House—his ultimate goal, and what he'd been working toward the past twenty years. He thanked Nixon for the confidence in him but declined the offer. He just wasn't interested.

Nixon chose the relatively unknown governor of Maryland, Spiro T. Agnew, as his running mate, and as it turned out, the Republican ticket of Nixon and Agnew barely won the presidency—edging out Humphrey and Maine senator Edmund Muskie, but the Democrats retained control of the House and Senate. Ford would remain the minority leader.

Betty had always been very active, but after being diagnosed with the pinched nerve, she was reluctant to take part in many of her favorite activities, for fear of making things worse. She had always loved to ski, especially with Jerry and the children, but flying down a steep mountain on narrow wooden slats was far too risky. "That, and by the time she got four kids dressed and boots laced, she was exhausted!" Susan Ford recalled.

Still, the Christmas ski trips to Boyne Mountain in Michigan had become tradition, and now all four children, whom Jerry remembered picking out of countless snowbanks when they were seven or eight years old, were "zooming down the slopes and shouting gleefully, 'Hi, Dad! We'll see you later!'"

Unfortunately, one Christmas they went to Boyne, and there was barely any snow. It put a real damper on the trip and got them thinking about alternatives. Jerry had learned that Ted Kindel, one of his childhood friends from Grand Rapids—Ted's father had been Jerry's scoutmaster when Jerry became an Eagle Scout—had opened a hotel in Vail, Colorado. Kindel had gone out to Vail when it first opened in 1962 and, although there was just one gondola and two chairlifts, he saw potential. In 1963 Kindel built the town's first hotel, the Christiana, and in 1966 he became Vail's first mayor.

"Come on out to Vail," Ted urged his old friend. "You will love it."

So, for Christmas vacation 1968, the Fords flew to Denver, piled everybody into a rented station wagon, and drove west along the treacherous and windy Route 6, up and up and up. Around each new bend, there was an even more stunning view of craggy mountains so enormous that they made the mountains of Michigan seem like sand dunes. It was a much longer drive back then, before the completion of Interstate 70 and the Eisenhower Tunnel, but the Fords all agreed it was totally worth it.

Remembering that first year skiing in Vail, Susan Ford recalled, "It was amazing. The mountains were so much bigger, and there was so much snow."

Nestled at the base of the majestic snow-drenched mountains was the charming village of Vail. It was just a few blocks long at that time, and it looked like someone had taken a little town from Austria or Switzerland and plopped it right in the middle of Colorado. Ted Kindel and his wife, Nancy, introduced the Fords to everyone they knew, and within a couple of days, Vail already felt like home.

January 20, 1969, Betty and Jerry had prime seats for Richard M. Nixon's inauguration. Rows of tiered seats were set up on the inauguration platform on the east side of the US Capitol. The seats were assigned by a time-honored tradition, and as a member of the Joint Congressional Committee on Inaugural Ceremonies, Jerry Ford would be seated in the front row, stage left of the podium where Nixon would be sworn in, while Betty, as his wife, had an assigned seat across the aisle, in the third row. Under threatening skies, and the tightest security ever for a presidential inauguration, Betty watched her longtime friend Pat Nixon standing proudly next to her husband as he placed his left hand on, not one, but two family Bibles, and took the Oath of Office to become the nation's thirty-seventh president.

"I, Richard Milhous Nixon, do solemnly swear that I will faithfully execute the office of president of the United States, and will, to the best of my ability, preserve, protect, and defend the Constitution of the United States, so help me God."

One of President Nixon's goals was to open diplomatic ties between the United States and Communist China. At that time, there had been no direct relations with China for more than two decades, so it was truly historic when, in February 1972, Richard Nixon and the first lady—accompanied by three hundred staffers, press, and Secret Service personnel—traveled to mainland China and broadcast their journey for all Americans to see. The trip had such remarkable ramifications that Nixon called it "the week that changed the world." To continue the positive momentum in normalizing relations, Nixon suggested to the Chinese leaders that it was important to increase the number of visitors between the two countries. As it turned out, Majority Leader Hale Boggs and Minority Leader Jerry Ford, along with their wives, were among the first American visitors to be invited by the Chinese government.

At that time, "the chance to visit China was a rare opportunity indeed," Jerry said. And Betty, always ready for an adventure, was game to go.

Five days before they were scheduled to leave, in June, there was a report that five men had broken into the Democratic National Committee offices in the Watergate Office Building in Washington. Jerry recognized two of the names—G. Gordon Liddy and James McCord—and he wondered if anybody at the White House was involved. He told a colleague, "I don't give a damn who's involved or how high it goes. Nixon ought to get to the bottom of this and get rid of anybody who's involved in it."

Betty read about it in the newspaper, but amid preparing for her trip to China, didn't think much of it. The Watergate incident—what the White House called a "third-rate burglary" and what she saw as "an inept effort at God knows what"—would not only test the United States Constitution like never before, but also would send Betty and Jerry on a trajectory they never could have imagined.

On Friday, June 23, 1972, the Fords, the Boggs, and members of their staffs departed Washington and flew to Shanghai. Jerry Ford and Hale Boggs, despite their positions on opposite sides of the aisle, had a great deal of respect for each other and had bonded during their long months together as members of the Warren Commission. Betty and Lindy Boggs were also good friends, and this trip would cement the close relationship between the two families. (Sadly, just a few months after the trip to China, in October 1972, Hale Boggs was killed in a small-plane crash in a remote area of Alaska. Neither the plane nor his body was ever found.)

Betty found the trip fascinating and at times challenging. "The Chinese are likely to feed you anything," she recalled. One night, they were served sea slugs, a local delicacy. Sitting at formal dinners with their hosts, it would have been considered impolite to not eat what was served. For Betty, who didn't care for fish at all, "trying to choke down sea slugs" was a true testament to her diplomatic ability.

They traveled all over the country, including to Old Manchuria, where they were the first Caucasians to visit in twenty-four years. "The people were enthralled by us," she said. "Children would see our cars, and they'd come running from the rice paddies at full tilt."

It was an enormously educational experience from start to finish, but without a doubt, Betty was most impressed by how the Chinese used acupuncture in place of anesthesia. They were allowed to witness an operation in which the doctors removed a large ovarian tumor from a young girl. Betty was amazed that the girl was wide awake throughout the procedure, sipping tea and orange juice, clearly feeling no pain even as the doctors cut through her skin and sewed her back up. Thin acupuncture needles had been placed in her ankles, and a little machine between her legs made the needles vibrate. That image would remain seared into her mind.

Nineteen seventy-two was another presidential election year—another chance for the GOP to take control of the House. While Nixon was campaigning for a second term, Jerry was working as hard as he could to help Republicans get elected. From the time he and Betty returned from China in early July, he was gone almost constantly.

"Jerry and I thought President Nixon was doing a good job his first term in office," Betty recalled, and indeed, the American public agreed. On Tuesday, November 7, 1972, Nixon won reelection in a landslide against his Democratic opponent, Senator George McGovern of South Dakota. In the House of Representatives, however, the Republicans gained only thirteen seats—not enough for a majority. Realizing the opportunity the Republicans had that year wasn't likely to repeat itself in the foreseeable future, Jerry concluded that he was never going to become Speaker of the House. He had worked so hard toward that goal—in one year alone, he logged 138,000 miles and was gone more than 250 nights—but in doing so had sacrificed precious time with Betty and their four children.

By this point, the two older sons had reached adulthood and were each finding his own way. Mike, twenty-two, had graduated from Wake

Forest University the previous May (Jerry had given the commencement address) and was in graduate school at the Gordon-Conwell Theological Seminary in Massachusetts. Twenty-year-old Jack had attended college at Jacksonville University in Florida for two years but took time off to work on the Committee to Re-elect the President. Now he was transferring to Utah State University to study forestry.

Only Steve and Susan were still at home. Betty had dealt with Mike and Jack going through puberty, and now it was Steve and Susan. Jerry had been in charge of telling the boys about the birds and the bees, and one day, when Susan was about twelve or thirteen, Betty told her only daughter they needed to have a little talk.

Susan was about to go to camp for the summer, and Betty was concerned that she might get her period for the first time while she was away.

"Come sit up here," Betty said, tapping the kitchen counter. Susan hurled her body up onto the counter, so that even though her legs were dangling, she was nearly face-to-face with her mother.

Betty handed her a pamphlet that showed the differences in male and female anatomy, explained all about menstruation, and the mechanics of sex.

"It's really about the relationship between a man and a woman," Betty said. "One day you will kiss a boy . . . but whatever you do, don't ever let a boy stick his tongue in your mouth."

It was all Susan could do to keep from bursting out laughing.

"I can remember it to this day!" she recalled. "Because about ten days before, I had been French-kissed by some boy." *You are so late, Mother,* Susan was thinking. *You missed the boat.*

Susan kept quiet, trying to maintain a straight face, as her mother continued.

"You know," Betty said, "a boy did that to me once, and I bit his tongue and got on the trolley and went home."

"God, I'd have loved to have seen that!" Susan recalled. "And I don't doubt she did it."

It wasn't a long conversation, but at the end, Betty said, "Now, if you have any questions, please ask me."

In the late sixties and early seventies, the Alexandria public school system was going through a transition, as the city tried to achieve a racial balance among its three high schools. In grades nine and ten, Steve was bused to the predominantly black George Washington High School, where he was co-captain of the junior varsity football team, playing center and linebacker.

"Mother would come to all my games," Steve recalled with a smile.

During one game, Steve went down and was clearly in pain. The coach pulled him out and had him sit on the sidelines with an ice pack on his wrist. Betty, who was watching from the bleachers, had seen the hit and went into mother bear mode. She raced down to the field, and to Steve's horror, hoisted herself up and over the waist-high chain-link fence to get to the bench where he was sitting.

"Mom!" he hissed. "What are you doing?"

"What happened? What hurts?" Betty asked.

At sixteen, in the presence of his teammates and, more important, the cheerleaders, Steve was mortified. "Mom, get out of here. You can't be down here!" he said through clenched teeth. As soon as the game was over, Betty drove Steve straight to the emergency room, where it was determined he had broken his wrist.

Decades later, he looked back on the memory with a laugh and not a hint of embarrassment. "She was just a great mother that way," he said.

In 1972, his junior year, Steve was assigned to T. C. Williams High School, along with all the district's eleventh- and twelfth-grade students. There was a tremendous amount of racial tension, as depicted in the 2000 movie *Remember the Titans,* which was based on the 1971 T. C. Williams football season.

"We lived it," Steve Ford recalled. "Bricks were being thrown at windows, kids were getting into fistfights and smoking pot in the hallways." And while the Fords felt their six-foot-one son Steve could handle it, Betty and Jerry were concerned about sending their "baby girl" into such a volatile environment.

Susan had been best friends with "the Golubin twins"—Reagan and Elison—since elementary school, and the Golubin girls' parents were also concerned about the atmosphere at T. C. Williams. So, the Fords and the Golubins decided to have their daughters apply for admission to Holton-Arms, a private boarding school in Bethesda, Maryland.

"We all got in," Susan recalled. The girls stayed at school Monday through Friday and came home on weekends. One of the parents would pick up the girls Friday and one would take them back on Sunday.

By this point, Clara was no longer working for the Fords. A couple of years earlier, she had gone to Betty and told her that her father was suffering from Alzheimer's disease. She couldn't bear to put him in a home, and she needed to care for him full-time. Of course Betty and the family understood. Mike had gone to college, and the other kids were self-sufficient, able to help with household chores. Two or three times a week, the kids would visit Clara at her dad's house, which was only about ten minutes away. "Susan would come up, and we used to sew," Clara remembered. She was no longer at their home every day, but she was no less important to the Ford family.

This was their situation as the calendar turned from 1972 to 1973, and Richard Nixon was beginning his second term in office. Betty had been supportive of Jerry's political career ever since that first day he'd told her he wanted to run for Congress, before they were even married, and Jerry was well aware that she, too, had sacrificed a great deal. They'd always thought of each other as equal partners—more so than many other couples of that era. Perhaps it was because of the relatively older age at which they'd met and married, but any decision they made, they'd always made together. One of the many things Jerry had found attractive about Betty from the beginning, and still attracted him now, was her honesty and candor. She didn't tell him what he wanted to hear; she always told him how she really felt.

Recognizing that becoming Speaker of the House was most likely not going to happen, and that in less than three years their youngest children would both be off to college, they sat down to discuss plans for the future.

"We agreed that I would run one more time in 1974, then announce my retirement from public life in early 1975," Jerry recalled. At that point, he would be sixty-three years old—"still active enough to practice law or enter into a business partnership with friends"—and after so many years living on a congressman's salary, the opportunity to earn additional income as a private citizen was attractive to both of them.

"He promised me he would retire at the end of President Nixon's second term," Betty said. After twenty-four years as a congressman's wife, living in the Washington bubble, the thought of retiring, whether it be to Grand Rapids, or perhaps Florida or California, was something Betty found herself looking forward to with each passing month. She knew Gerald R. Ford's word was good as gold. There was no reason to think it wouldn't happen just like they'd planned.

10

A Five-Dollar Bet

If it wasn't for two *Washington Post* reporters following the story of the Watergate break-in, Jerry Ford might have been able to keep his promise. But no one could have imagined how, in the year 1973, America was about to be turned on her head, our Constitution tested beyond anything since the Civil War, and Gerald R. Ford, representative of the Fifth District from the great state of Michigan, would be smack dab in the middle of it all.

Around the dinner table at 514 Crown View Drive, everyone in the Ford family was expected to keep abreast of what was happening in the world, from politics to sports, and it made for lively debates. Betty and Jerry had always encouraged their children to ask questions and speak openly about how they felt. In 1973 there was much to discuss.

On January 30, 1973, former Nixon aides G. Gordon Liddy and James W. McCord Jr. were convicted of conspiracy, burglary, and wiretapping in the Watergate incident. Five other men pleaded guilty, but questions remained. Three months later, after *Post* reporters Carl Bernstein and Bob Woodward revealed a tangled web of secret funds and lies, Nixon's top White House staffers, H. R. Haldeman and John Ehrlichman, and Attorney General Richard Kleindienst, all resigned suddenly. At the same time, President Nixon fired White House counsel John Dean.

In May the Senate Watergate Committee began hearings that were broadcast live on television. It was a national soap opera with potentially dire consequences. Revelations from top officials appeared to be linking a Watergate cover-up to President Nixon.

When it came to Watergate, and Nixon's involvement, Jerry and Betty were convinced that their longtime friend had nothing to do with it.

Meanwhile, separate from Watergate, Vice President Spiro Agnew was being investigated for kickbacks and bribes he had allegedly received as governor of Maryland.

On October 10, 1973, Agnew, after months of denying any wrong-doing, admitted that he had failed to report $29,500 of income in 1967 while he was governor. He pleaded no contest to a single charge of tax evasion, was fined $10,000, and formally resigned the office of vice president of the United States, "effective immediately."

That night, Jerry and Betty were at home, when the phone rang around ten o'clock.

It was Mel Laird. Mel and Jerry had known each other a long time, having served in Congress together for many years. Mel had served as Nixon's secretary of defense, and, after Haldeman's and Ehrlichman's resignations, he had stepped in to become one of Nixon's advisors at the White House. A phone call from him at ten o'clock in the evening, however, was unusual.

Sitting in the family room, Betty could hear only Jerry's side of the conversation. "Let us think about it, and I'll call you back," he said.

Jerry hung up the phone and said, "That was Mel Laird. He wanted to know, if I was asked, would I accept the vice presidential nomination."

For the next hour, Jerry and Betty debated the pluses and minuses. First of all, Jerry wasn't sure he would be happy in the position. Traditionally, the vice president's job was chiefly ceremonial, with little impact on legislation, and Jerry couldn't imagine working at a slower pace. Then they talked about how it would impact the children, and the invasiveness of the press.

On the other hand, Jerry realized the vice presidency was an honor and would be a "splendid cap" to his career—a recognition of his long service in Washington.

"What about your promise?" Betty reminded him.

"That's the best part," Jerry said. He'd have to serve as vice president only until the end of Nixon's term: January 1977. Then he would leave public office, just as they'd planned.

"But it is highly unlikely Nixon would choose me," Jerry assured Betty. "I'm too valuable to him on Capitol Hill." Besides, there were other Republicans with national reputations and higher ambitions who seemed to be much likelier choices, such as John Connally, a former Democratic governor of Texas and US Treasury Secretary who'd recently switched parties; Governor Nelson Rockefeller of New York; and the governor of California, Ronald Reagan.

Betty agreed. It seemed there was only a very small chance Jerry would be chosen.

Jerry called back Laird. "We've talked about it and agreed that, if I were asked, I'd accept," he said. "I'll do whatever the president wants me to do, but we won't do anything to stimulate any campaign. I'm not promoting myself. We have made our plans, and we're happy with what we've decided to do."

The phone at 514 Crown View Drive had been ringing nonstop for the past two days, and Betty had put up with about as much as she could take. It was one reporter after another asking all kinds of ridiculous questions.

"Has your husband told you to get your hair done?"

"No," Betty replied with a smile. "I just had it done yesterday." Then she quipped, "And if you think my husband's worried about my hair, you have a wrong idea of my husband."

Another anxious reporter had called and asked, "Has your husband told you to go out and get a new dress?"

That one made her laugh. The small master bedroom closet in their split-level Alexandria home had become so overstuffed that they'd installed a rack that ran the entire length of one side of the bedroom to hold the collection of suits, gowns, and dresses Betty had accumulated over the years. She still loved fashion, and while Jerry rarely denied her anything, her ever-expanding wardrobe was sometimes a source of contention. The last thing he would ever suggest was for her to go out and buy a new dress.

Besides that, Betty thought, these reporters were barking up the wrong tree. There was no way President Richard M. Nixon was going to choose Jerry Ford as his vice president.

Ever since Agnew's departure two days earlier, rumors had been swirling about who Nixon would nominate to take his place. Only once before, in 1832, had a vice president resigned (and that was due not to personal scandal but to John C. Calhoun's clashing politically with President Andrew Jackson and deciding to vacate the office with just months left in the term to run for an open Senate seat in his native South Carolina), and Washington was abuzz as reporters tried to glean information from anyone possible. Ford's name had been mentioned among a dozen or so likely candidates, but in all honesty, Betty did not think her husband was a serious contender.

Jerry had promised her this was his last term in office, and he'd even told Nixon that was a "blood oath." No more campaigns, no more weeks on end with him traveling all over the country. Come January 1977, a little more than three years away, they were retiring, and Betty would finally have her husband back. Surely Nixon wouldn't choose a vice president who already had his sights set on leaving politics.

David Kennerly, a lanky, bearded, twenty-six-year-old photographer working for *Time* magazine, had been assigned to Vice President Agnew for the past year. When Agnew resigned in disgrace, *Time* sent out a bunch of reporters to cover the top candidates for his replacement, and as David recalled, "I drew the Gerald Ford straw."

Friday, October 12—the day the White House had said Nixon would reveal his pick—Kennerly called Ford's office to see if he could come in and take a few photos of him. Jerry's press secretary Paul Miltich said, "Sure. Come on in at eleven o'clock."

David had never met Jerry Ford before, but as he walked into the office, cameras slung across his body, he didn't bother to introduce himself by name. He said simply, "I'm here for *Time* magazine. You're on the list."

"Well, you're wasting your time," Ford replied good-naturedly. It was eleven o'clock in the morning, and at that time, the congressman was telling the truth. He hadn't received any indication that he would be chosen.

"Well," Kennerly said, "I'll just get a few shots, and at the very least, you'll have a nice picture for your wall."

Ford laughed. There was something about the photographer's nonchalant attitude that appealed to him. Kennerly spent about ten or fifteen minutes taking some photos with the natural light in the room—he called it "Rembrandt lighting."

At that moment, Kennerly was convinced that Ford truly did not think he would be the nominee. "He did not seem like a guy who was waiting by the phone for this call," Kennerly said.

That afternoon, at 514 Crown View Drive, Betty was just beginning to prepare dinner when Susan came striding into the kitchen. Home for the weekend from Holton-Arms, the sixteen-year-old was eager to find out if the rumors she'd been hearing were true. Even at school, she watched the news and read the papers; she knew her father was on the short list, but when she'd called and asked him, he'd been unusually quiet. Almost secretive.

"Mom, do you think President Nixon is going to choose Dad as vice president?"

"No, Susan, honestly I don't," Betty said. "Your father is much too valuable in the House getting legislation through. The president would never take him out. It wouldn't make any sense at all."

"Well, I think it's going to be him," Susan replied. "I'll bet you five dollars Daddy is the nominee."

Betty was so confident that Jerry was *not* going to be the nominee, she didn't hesitate one moment. "All right," she said with a confident smile. "You're on. Five dollars."

One of the perks of being minority leader was that Jerry had been assigned a government car, along with a wonderful driver named Richard Frazier. With Frazier behind the wheel, he could work in the car between meetings and on the way home.

Betty was in the kitchen when she heard the car pull into the driveway. She looked at the clock on the oven. It was just before six thirty.

That's unusual, she thought. With everything going on, she hadn't expected him to be home until at least eight.

As soon as Jerry walked into the house, Susan bounded up to him. "What's happening, Dad? Do you know who Nixon's gonna choose?"

Betty came walking out of the kitchen, eager to hear the answer too. "Do you know who it is, dear?"

Stone-faced, Jerry said, "The only thing I know is that the president is going to telephone his man soon." He checked his watch and said, "I'm going to go for a swim before dinner, and then I'll have to get back to the White House for the announcement."

While Jerry swam laps, Betty broiled a few steaks, and Susan set the table. Steve came downstairs and asked, "Does Dad know who it's going to be?"

"He says he doesn't know," Susan said. "I still think Nixon's going to choose him."

Betty shook her head. "I don't know who you've been talking to to get that idea, but it's not going to be your father."

After his fifteen-minute swim, Jerry went upstairs to dry off and get dressed.

"I'll be right down," he said. "I'll have to eat quickly and then get back to the White House."

Susan helped Betty serve the plates, and as soon as Jerry came down, they all sat down at the table. It was seven o'clock.

"Betty, why don't you say grace tonight," Jerry said. The four of them bowed their heads in prayer as Betty thanked the Lord for their many blessings.

"Amen," they said in unison. And then the phone rang.

Susan jumped up. Could this be *the call*? She grabbed the phone off the hook and answered, "Hello?"

As soon as she heard the voice on the other end of the line, a crestfallen look washed across her face. She held the phone out to her mother, the twenty-five-foot-long cord twisting in tight curls, and said, "It's only Mike. Here, Mom, he wants to talk to you."

Mike had seen the reports in the newspaper, and he, too, wanted to know what was going on. Susan had barely sat back down at the table when the upstairs phone rang.

The upstairs phone. The single line in her parents' bedroom that connected directly to the White House. It had been installed when Jerry became minority leader, eight years earlier, and the only other times she'd heard that phone ring was when they did the annual test. She leaped out of her chair and ran up the stairs.

Breathless, she answered, "Hello?"

A female voice said, "This is the White House calling for Mr. Ford."

Susan's eyes widened. Even for a kid who had grown up in the Washington political arena, to hear "the White House calling" was, like, *wow*.

In the most mature voice she could muster, she answered, "Yes, just one moment, please. I'll get him on the line for you."

Holding one hand over the mouthpiece, she shouted downstairs, "*Da-ad!* It's the White House!"

Jerry raced up the stairs and into the bedroom. Susan could hardly contain her excitement as she handed her father the phone.

"This is Jerry Ford," he answered.

General Alexander Haig, the White House chief of staff, came on the line and said, "The president wants to talk to you." Then, a second later, it was President Nixon's voice.

"Jerry, I've got good news, and I think Betty ought to hear it too."

"Well, I'm sorry, Mr. President," Jerry said, "but I'm on a line that has no extension. Can you hang up and call back on the other number?"

As he hung up the phone, Susan looked at him, incredulous. "Daddy, did you just tell the president of the United States to hang up and call back?"

"He wants to speak to your mother and me at the same time," Jerry replied. His voice was calm, but then, as he headed down the stairs, he heard Betty, still talking to Mike, and there was a sudden sense of urgency.

"Betty!" he hollered. "Get off the phone! The president wants to call!"

Betty hung up quickly, and seconds later, before she could fully comprehend what was happening, the phone rang again. She stood there, stunned, as Jerry dashed into the office, adjacent to the kitchen, and picked up the phone.

"Yes, Mr. President," he said. "Betty's getting on the line now." He nodded to Betty, pointing to the kitchen phone.

Betty could hardly believe what she was hearing. The rumors were true. The reporters had been right. Susan was right. President Nixon was nominating Jerry as his vice president. In less than two hours, the president was going to make the announcement from the East Room on live television, and he wanted both Jerry and Betty to be there.

The conversation was brief, and as soon as they disconnected, Jerry walked back into the kitchen. Betty was frozen in place.

"Don't worry, Betty," Jerry said as he put his arms around her. "We'll be okay. Vice presidents don't do anything. Everything's going to be fine."

Susan, realizing her mother was in a state of shock—and that they had no time to waste—took charge. "Mother, we've got to find you something to wear!"

Once again she raced up the stairs, and by the time Betty got up there, Susan was already flipping through her mother's wardrobe. "It can't be a print, and it can't be black. It should be a pretty color . . .

"What do you want to look like?"

They narrowed it down to an elegant, long-sleeved, chartreuse green dress that had a loose high-neck collar, a fitted waistline that fell into soft pleats, and a matching belt that accentuated Betty's slim figure.

Still in a daze, Betty slipped out of her blouse and slacks as Susan waded into the closet to find shoes and a purse to match. Betty put on the dress and then went into the bathroom to touch up her makeup. There wasn't time to fuss with her hair, so she simply ran a comb through it and spritzed a layer of hairspray.

Jerry walked into the room and said, "Come on, Betty, we need to go now. Frazier's got the car running."

"I'm almost ready," she said as she dabbed at her lipstick.

In the twenty-five years they'd been married, if there was one thing that frustrated Jerry about his wife, it was that she often kept him waiting. There was always "just one more thing" she had to do. A change of earrings, an extra swipe of blush on her cheeks. It was her way of taking control. And perhaps a little bit of revenge for all the times he wasn't there.

"Betty . . ." Jerry said. "We've got to go *now*."

"I think she was scared to death," Susan recalled years later.

With one last look in the mirror, Betty gathered up her courage, and then looked straight into her husband's eyes with love and pride, and said, "Let's go."

* * *

Because President Nixon wanted to keep his nominee a secret until the very last moment, Jerry was directed into the East Room, where he took his seat with the other members of Congress, while aides snuck Betty into Nixon's secretary's office through a side door. Betty sat nervously, watching the live news coverage on a small television set as the actual events were unfolding on the other side of the White House. After nearly ten minutes of anxiety-building suspense, you could tell Nixon was finally going to reveal the name of his choice for vice president.

"Time to go!" the aide said to Betty. They made "a mad dash" through the White House, and as they approached the East Room, Betty could hear people clapping and cheering. President Nixon was listing the criteria he had used in choosing his nominee, and when he announced that the man he had selected had served twenty-five years in Congress, everyone had bolted from their chairs, assuming it was Jerry Ford. The ovation went on for nearly a full minute.

Finally, President Nixon announced, "Distinguished guests and my fellow Americans, I proudly present to you the man whose name I will submit to the Congress of the United States for confirmation as the vice president of the United States, Congressman Gerald Ford of Michigan."

Before Nixon had even finished the sentence, the entire audience was on its feet, whooping and hollering, clearly pleased with the president's choice.

Jerry made his way to the podium, smiling with pride, and as the rousing applause continued, he scanned the room looking for Betty. Suddenly he saw the flash of her green dress out of the corner of his eye as she appeared in the doorway, being led in by a female staff member.

"Here's Betty," Ford whispered to Nixon. "Shall I call her up here?"

"Not yet," Nixon said under his breath. He was beaming, reveling in the enthusiastic ovation.

As Betty walked into the room, she had no idea where she was supposed to go or what she was expected to do. The aide whispered, "Go sit with Mrs. Nixon."

The first lady was at the end of the row of chairs, with daughters Tricia and Julie, and Julie's husband, David Eisenhower, seated next to them.

The standing ovation continued, with all eyes on the podium, as Betty crept gingerly toward her longtime friend, Pat. The only problem was, there wasn't an empty chair. All this pomp and circumstance, and no one had thought to reserve a chair for the wife of the nominee.

The applause died down, and everyone began to take their seats. "They told me to sit with you," Betty whispered.

"Oh yes, of course," Pat said as she scooted over to allow Betty to share the chair.

Jerry made a few remarks and then, finally, she was invited onto the stage to stand next to her husband and the president of the United States. Betty smiled as the crowd stood and clapped. Some even cheered. As the applause went on and on, cameras clicking, lights flashing, she looked over at Pat Nixon, and the soberness of the situation slowly began to sink in. A mix of excitement and sheer terror was building inside her.

Off to the side, Dick Keiser, the special agent in charge of President Nixon's Secret Service detail, was standing next to Jerry Bechtle—the newly assigned agent in charge of the new vice president's detail.

"Come on, Jerry," Keiser said, "let me have President Nixon introduce you to Jerry Ford."

Keiser approached Nixon and asked if he'd make the introduction.

"Sure," President Nixon said. People had surrounded Jerry and Betty, offering congratulations, when the president and the two Secret Service agents broke through the crowd.

"Jerry," Nixon said, "I'd like you to meet Jerry Bechtle. He's the agent in charge of your Secret Service detail."

Jerry Ford reached out to shake Bechtle's hand and said, "Nice to meet you, Agent Bechtle." Turning his head to Betty, he said, "And this is my wife, Betty."

They exchanged pleasantries, and Bechtle explained that he and a driver would be taking the Fords back to their residence.

"Okay," Jerry Ford said agreeably. "Just let us know when it's time to leave."

President Nixon turned to his vice presidential nominee and said flatly, "No, Jerry, you tell *him* when it's time to leave. The Secret Service works around your schedule. Not the other way around."

* * *

Back at 514 Crown View Drive, Susan had invited over some girl-friends to watch the coverage on television. But at the time, she didn't think it was that big a deal. "I wasn't convinced that the vice presidency meant much of anything," she said. "It wasn't going to affect my life. I was going back to boarding school, and everything was going to be the same as it always was."

But things had already begun to change. Steve Ford had gone to the T. C. Williams High School football game that evening—he'd decided to be a spectator rather than a player his senior year—but when he and his friend Kevin Kennedy drove back home, the streets in the neighborhood were all blocked off due to the press and security. So they parked the car a few streets away, and, rather than have to deal with the police, they thought it would be a good idea to climb over the back fence into the Fords' backyard.

As the two teenagers were scaling the fence, they were immediately confronted by Secret Service agents armed with loaded guns.

"What are you doing?!" the agents yelled.

Terrified, Steve explained that he was Gerald Ford's son, and he was just trying to get into the house. Looking back years later, Steve said, "It's funny now, but we were scared to death that night."

That week, David Kennerly's photograph of Gerald Ford staring out the window appeared on the cover of *Time*. It was the first cover for both. It wouldn't be the last.

11

Betty Ford, Second Lady

The morning after the announcement, Crown View Drive was invaded by the press. "You couldn't move without bumping into a reporter," Betty recalled. "You couldn't go out your front door."

And then there was the Secret Service. Even though Jerry still had to be confirmed by both houses of Congress before he would become vice president, because of the unusual circumstances, the Secret Service had decided he needed immediate protection. Everyone else in the family, Betty included, could come and go freely, but the vice president designate required around-the-clock protection. They set up a command post in the garage and used the driveway for the vice presidential limousine and the Secret Service follow-up car. Which meant the Fords had to park their own cars on the street.

On December 6, it became official. Both the Senate and the House of Representatives voted overwhelmingly in favor of confirming Gerald R. Ford as vice president. Knowing it was probable and imminent, Mike and Jack had come home—Jack had shaved his beard because he wanted to look respectable for his father, and Mike had brought a Jerusalem Bible—an English translation of the Scriptures from the original Hebrew and Greek texts—that he had purchased especially for the occasion.

Faith ran deep in the family, and for this auspicious event, it was important to Jerry and Betty to have the Bible open to a place that held meaning for them when Jerry took the oath.

They agreed on Psalm 20, which began, "May [God] answer you in time of trouble . . ."

It was a historic moment in the House chamber of the US Capitol, being broadcast on live television in America and around the world, and Betty was, literally, center stage. Wearing a long-sleeved turtleneck dress in bright orange wool crepe that popped amid the sea of men in dark suits, Betty stood behind the podium, holding the heavy Bible open to the designated page, with Chief Justice Warren Burger on her right, Jerry on her left, and the president off to her husband's side.

Betty held the Bible steady, beaming with pride, as Jerry placed his left hand on the open page and repeated the words prompted by Justice Burger. Up in the gallery, Mike, Jack, Steve, and Susan, sitting next to First Lady Pat Nixon, watched their father make history. When Jerry tripped up a bit on the last phrase, he corrected himself quickly and then laughed at his mistake. Betty looked into his eyes and laughed right along with him.

The crowd erupted into a standing ovation, and Jerry turned immediately to President Nixon and shook his hand. Then he walked over to Betty, put his right arm around her, and planted a kiss right on her lips. It was a tender moment—and unusual for such a public display of affection—but for everyone who witnessed it, there was no doubt about the love and admiration Jerry and Betty Ford had for each other.

Even though the new vice president had been minority leader for almost eight years, as the congressman from a small district in Michigan, he was still relatively unknown to most of America, and he realized his acceptance speech was his formal introduction.

He thanked President Nixon, his fellow members of Congress, and promised not to forget the people of Michigan.

"I'm a Ford—not a Lincoln," he quipped. The audience roared with laughter at the double entendre comparing two American automobiles—the Ford, identified with the common man, and the Lincoln, a car associated with the wealthy. Then he exuded humility, admitting his speeches could not match the eloquence of President Abraham Lincoln's. When the applause died down, he paused and turned to Betty, now seated on the platform off to his right.

Tears glistened in his eyes as the words formed in his mouth. "For standing by my side, as she always has," he said, his voice cracking with emotion, "there are no words to tell you, my dear wife and mother of our four wonderful children, how much their being here means to me."

As the audience erupted with applause, Betty smiled with appreciation. Up in the galley, the three sons looked at one another, wondering whether they should clap at the mention of themselves, while Susan wiped away a tear. But evident on the faces of all four was the sheer pride in the father they loved and adored. As Americans watched from their living rooms, they saw the Fords as the perfect all-American family: the handsome, athletic father who worked hard to support his family; the beautiful housewife and mother; the four attractive, wholesome children. The kind of family everyone wished they had. Perfect from the outside looking in.

The first big change was that the Secret Service moved into 514 Crown View Drive. Literally moved in, remodeled, changed the locks, and kept the keys. The agents needed a command post that would be manned twenty-four hours a day, and the only plausible solution was to convert the garage.

The Secret Service had given its requirements to the General Services Administration, which then had to request money from Congress. Special Agent Jerry Bechtle received confirmation of how much the garage conversion was going to cost, just as Vice President and Mrs. Ford were headed to a congressional reception. The director of the Secret Service had called Bechtle and told him, "You better tell the vice president the amount so he doesn't get blindsided at the reception by Congressman Mahon."

George H. Mahon, a Texas Democrat who'd been a representative since 1935, headed the Appropriations Committee that would have to approve the changes. In the limo ride to the reception, Bechtle, sitting in the front passenger seat, turned around and said, "Mr. Vice President, the cost estimate has come through for the conversion of your garage, and since you're liable to get asked about it by Congressman Mahon, I thought I'd better let you know what we're doing and how much it will be."

"All right," Vice President Ford said, "how much?"

"With all the communications we have to install and the construction on the house, it's going to be fifty thousand dollars."

Jerry and Betty looked at each other, their eyes wide in disbelief. Then they both burst out laughing.

"My God," Vice President Ford said, "the house cost only thirty-five thousand."

The driveway was already suffering from the weight of the armored vice presidential limousine, so the decision was made to dig out the driveway and replace the two garage doors with a solid brick wall and a bay window above. Inside, they would install a bathroom, a kitchenette, and a small sitting room, along with a complex electronic security and communication system. Holes were drilled for metal detectors and alarms; the windows would be fitted with bulletproof glass. Two structures that looked like telephone booths were set up in the corners of the backyard: sentry boxes for the Secret Service agents to stand post in inclement weather. Meanwhile, all the stuff that had previously filled the garage—bicycles, ladders, skis, rakes, a lawnmower—was crammed alongside the swimming pool until a shed could be built.

The Fords were so concerned about the disruption to the neighborhood, they wrote a letter apologizing for the inconvenience and placed it in each neighbor's mailbox.

As wife of the minority leader, Betty had been able to handle the social side of her life without any help, but being the wife of the vice president was a whole new level. While it had been common for Jerry and Betty to receive forty or fifty invitations each week, now they were inundated with as many as *five hundred* invites on a weekly basis. Jerry had his own staff, but Betty realized there were now more projects and obligations than she could handle herself, and she needed help.

The previous summer, Susan had worked at the White House selling White House guidebooks for the White House Historical Association with a couple of her friends from Holton-Arms—Barbara Manfuso and Lise Courtney Howe. ("We jokingly referred to it as the White House Hysterical Association," Susan recalled. "I was working there to make money to pay for my car insurance.") Betty had become acquaintances with Lise Courtney's mother, Nancy, who supervised the teenage sales-girls. As soon as Jerry's nomination was announced, Nancy had called and offered her assistance if Betty needed it. Betty immediately took her up on the offer.

It started out as a few hours here and there, but once Jerry was con-firmed as vice president, Betty hired Nancy to be her full-time personal assistant.

Meanwhile, in the time between Jerry's nomination and confirma-tion as vice president, the Watergate investigation was closing in on the White House. With increased calls for Nixon's impeachment, there was plenty of speculation swirling around the very real possibility that Ger-ald R. Ford could assume the presidency. The public wanted to know "Who are the Fords?"

The media became insatiable, and while Jerry had twenty-five years of experience dealing with the press, for Betty and the rest of the family, it was a brand-new experience.

"For all of us, it was fun for about ten and a half seconds," Susan said. "And then it wasn't."

Television talk-show host Dick Cavett brought in a crew with lights and cameras to film an entire hour with Vice President Ford, Betty, Steve, and Susan. It was presented that it would be nonpolitical, just a sort of "getting to know you" piece, complete with a tour inside their home. First, the television crew moved most of the furniture out of the living room onto the patio directly beneath a tree brimming with birds—prompting Betty to make a desperate plea to Nancy Howe: "Get down there as fast as you can and tell them to get that stuff covered so the birds don't deco-rate it!" But once on camera, Cavett went straight to politics, asking Jerry whether he would make a deal with Richard Nixon if the president were convicted of criminal charges.

"I have no doubt whatsoever that the president is not guilty of any criminal charges that might be forthcoming. I'm absolutely positive,"

Jerry said. But Cavett persisted. And while the vice president remained calm, his growing frustration was evident.

"Really, Dick, I don't think I ought to comment . . . as a matter of fact, I think the president is being unfairly accused, based on any evidence I've seen, for being involved in the execution or the cover-up of Watergate."

Cavett tried a different technique with Betty: "Is the thought of living conceivably in the White House appalling or overpowering?"

"I would say it is inconceivable," Betty answered. In an effort to cut off the questioning, Jerry added, somewhat tersely, "We're very happy here, and I think it's unwise to speculate on that, Dick. None of us have ever talked about it or thought about it."

From there, Cavett turned to Steve and Susan and asked a series of incredibly awkward questions.

"Do you know about the birds and the bees?" he asked. "Can you imagine anything more embarrassing than having your parents say, 'I'm going to have a serious talk with you'?"

Steve was clearly mortified, while Susan laughed nervously. *Yes, the only thing more embarrassing than that would be to be asked the question on a television program that's being broadcast into every living room in America!*

It was enough to make anyone cringe. Fortunately, Jerry jumped in and answered for them, stumbling over his words to explain that "somehow boys learn about it, and maybe girls are treated differently."

Without hesitation, Betty added, "If boys learn about it, girls learn about it too."

The conversation turned to skiing. Cavett asked Steve, "Would you guess that I'm a skier, to look at me?"

Steve looked at Cavett with incredulity. *Another dumb question.*

"Uh, well, anybody can ski," he answered.

"What about the drug scene around school?" Cavett asked Susan and Steve. "Do you see much pot or other hard drugs around school?"

The whole experience was incredibly uncomfortable, and, Betty recalled, "I was never so glad to see a bunch of people get out in my life."

* * *

Betty had little experience dealing with the press, and she would learn by trial and error. It was always a surprise to see how an interview would end up appearing in print or edited for television.

Dorothy Marks of Women's News Service described Betty as "a thoughtful, pretty woman with the erect carriage, slim figure, and really good legs of the model and professional dancer she once was." Marks asked her, "How do you see yourself as second lady?"

"I like to think of myself as a feminist," Betty said, "although I haven't joined any women's lib organizations. I guess you would say I have tried to put family first, knowing Jerry has had to put politics first. I have tried to support him by taking active roles in the Republican Women's Club, the Eighty-First Congress Club, the Congressional Club, and I'm ready to continue that support in this new job."

Betty agreed to an interview with Barbara Walters of the *Today* show. Her only stipulation was that she didn't want to talk about anything political; that was her husband's realm. After the normal pleasantries, Barbara looked down at her notepad and gave Betty a zinger.

"How do you feel about the Supreme Court's ruling on abortion?"

That January, in the landmark *Roe v. Wade* case, the Supreme Court had affirmed the legality of a woman's right to an abortion. It was extremely controversial, and now Betty was being asked to weigh in on it. So much for Walters's agreement not to ask anything political. Betty could have declined to answer, but she chose to answer honestly. That's just the way she was.

"I agree with the Supreme Court's ruling," Betty said. "I think it's time to bring abortion out of the backwoods and put it in the hospitals, where it belongs."

In another interview, she reiterated her approval of a woman's right to an abortion, adding that it was particularly appropriate for "some high school girls who are forced to marry, have their babies, and end up in marriages that are fiascos."

Betty's comments sparked an avalanche of mail, most of it negative. "Maybe I shouldn't have said it, but I couldn't lie. That's the way I feel," she said later. Her reputation for candor was established.

Time magazine assigned David Kennerly to cover Vice President

Ford full-time, and one of his first assignments was to photograph the family at a park near their house in Alexandria one Saturday morning. Being single and twenty-six, Kennerly went out with a friend the Friday night before and, in his words, "basically got hammered." He woke up with a massive hangover and couldn't remember what time he was supposed to meet the Fords.

"I had their phone number," David recalled, "so I just called the house."

Betty answered, and David said, "Hey, Mrs. Ford, this is David Kennerly. What time am I supposed to be over there?"

She could tell from his incoherent speech that he was hungover, but all she said was, "Ten o'clock. We'll see you then."

When David arrived at the house, Betty greeted him at the door.

"Well, good morning, David," she said with a smile. Before he could say anything, she handed him a cold beer and added, "Here, I think you're going to need this."

They both laughed, and in that moment, a very special relationship began.

After falling in love with Vail back in 1968, the Fords had purchased a third-floor, three-bedroom $50,000 condo at the Lodge at Vail the following year. Always budget conscious, Jerry and Betty saw it as a good investment in the growing mountain community. The entire family could stay there every Christmas, while it paid for itself as a rental property throughout the rest of the year.

The Secret Service sent out a call for any agents who knew how to ski and dispatched an advance team, renting a condo across the street from the Fords' place. There was no room inside for a command post, so they parked a truck on the street below and set up a table outside the front door where the agents would stand post around the clock. Along with the Secret Service, the Fords would be trailed by a small contingent of press.

"In fact, I learned how to ski courtesy of *Time* magazine," Kennerly recalled with a grin, "back when you could put that on an expense account." Betty had given up skiing at this point, but Kennerly recalled that the rest of the family were all good skiers. Though they didn't always ski together: the kids enjoyed the moguls and steeper terrain, while Jerry preferred the groomed intermediate runs.

"I'd go up on the chairlift or the gondola by myself, and no one knew who I was," Steve remembered. "There were a lot of people talking about how the vice president's up here . . . it was kind of amusing to hear what people have to say about your dad."

While Jerry and the kids were skiing, Betty shopped for Christmas decorations and last-minute gifts. This was her favorite time of the year. She loved Christmas, especially in Vail, and she did everything she could to make lasting family memories.

The condo had a two-story vaulted family room with a floor-to-ceiling stone fireplace and Betty insisted on a live Christmas tree that nearly touched the ceiling. She had saved every construction paper and egg carton ornament the kids had made since their kindergarten days, and those were mixed in with fragile glass balls and assorted ornaments they'd collected from foreign trips.

It was during this trip that David Kennerly began getting to know the family on a more personal basis. "They were so warm and friendly. Just a normal family," he recalled.

Kennerly was only three years older than Mike Ford, so he connected with the kids, but he and Betty hit it off too. "It wasn't like she was a motherly figure," the photographer said, "because she had a very young spirit. We really connected with humor."

Near the end of the trip, the Fords invited David to join them at a Chinese restaurant. They were all laughing and having a good time, when at the end of the meal, everyone got a fortune cookie. There were about fourteen people there, and they went around the table reading their fortunes aloud. When it came to Jerry's turn, he cracked open his cookie, read it silently to himself, and then slammed it down on the table.

Kennerly remembered that "he looked kind of shaken."

"So, what does it say?" Kennerly asked.

"Aw, nothing," Ford said.

Kennerly pried it out from under his hand and read it aloud. "You will undergo a change of residence in the near future."

Everybody had been laughing and carrying on, but suddenly the table went silent. Betty looked at Jerry, wide eyed.

"No, no, I hope not," Jerry said dismissively.

He certainly didn't believe a message in a fortune cookie had any bearing on his future, but there was no doubt both he and Betty were in sheer and utter denial. They seemed to think that if they didn't let their minds wander down that path, it just wasn't going to happen.

Susan Ford would remember that "It was our last private Christmas. The last one where we could just be ourselves."

Meanwhile, back in Washington, picketers were marching in front of the White House. One person held a placard that said "Pick Out Your Curtains, Betty."

In early March 1974, the Secret Service received some intelligence information that caused immediate concern. Newspaper heiress Patty Hearst had been kidnapped from her Berkeley, California, apartment by a left-wing revolutionary organization that called itself the Symbionese Liberation Army (SLA), and the FBI had obtained intelligence that Susan Ford was on the group's target list as well. Vice President Ford was notified, and he immediately called Betty to tell her there was a credible threat against Susan and that the Secret Service was assigning agents to her. It was a Friday afternoon, and Susan was being driven home from school. The agents would be there by the time Susan got home.

This was highly unusual because, at that time, the Secret Service was not required to protect the vice president's family.

Betty was understandably frightened. The thought that something could happen to one of her children because of Jerry being the vice president had never occurred to her.

"I was so excited for the weekend," Susan recalled. Her boyfriend Palmer Holt was coming up from Hampden-Sydney College in Virginia. "We had a hot weekend planned," she said.

When Susan arrived home from school, Betty calmly explained what the agents had told her.

"But Mom, I've got plans this weekend! Palmer's coming up. I don't want Secret Service agents following us around! No way!"

"Just go talk to the agents in the command post, Susan. It's for your own safety."

"Daddy is ruining my life!" Susan cried. She pulled a cigarette out of her purse and proceeded to light it, even though she knew her mother disapproved of her new habit. She took a long drag and then grabbed a can of Coke out of the fridge before stomping down the two steps that led to the garage turned command post.

Bob Innamorati, the agent assigned to Susan, recalled opening the door and seeing this tall, blonde, jeans-clad teenager with a Coke in one hand and a cigarette in the other.

"I honestly did not know what to expect," he said. "But I quickly realized that she was very smart and mature beyond her years."

After initial pleasantries, Agent Innamorati explained that yes, indeed, he and one other agent would be with Susan at all times, wherever she went.

"We've got tickets to see a concert in Georgetown tomorrow night," she said.

"Unfortunately, everything you do this weekend must be spontaneous," Innamorati said. "Nothing preplanned. You can't go to the concert."

For a sixteen-year-old, it was life shattering. "They were shutting down my social life," Susan recalled. "And I was pissed."

That spring, Mike came home with the wonderful news that he and his girlfriend, Gayle Brumbaugh, were engaged to be married. Betty wanted to give her daughter-in-law-to-be something that was precious to her and held meaning, so she presented her with a turquoise cross made by a Zuni Indian artist.

In a letter to Mary Lou Logan, a longtime friend from Grand Rapids, Betty wrote, "Mike is marrying a lovely girl from Maryland that he met in college. I could not have picked out a nicer young lady if I had done it myself."

Mike and Gayle were thinking about August 10, 1974, as a wedding date, but something inside Betty told her that August would not be a good time. Even though she still wouldn't allow herself to imagine any scenario that would put her and Jerry in the White House, she suggested to Mike and Gayle that they get married in July so they could enjoy the rest of the summer before they had to go back to school. They agreed and picked July 5.

It would be the same weekend as Susan's seventeenth birthday—and Susan wasn't happy about sharing it—but Betty followed her gut instinct.

It was one of those times she would look back on and say, "Somebody up there has been looking out for me for years."

On April 6, 1974, Betty Ford made her first solo trip outside Washington as second lady. The occasion was to launch a unique arts program that started in Michigan called the Artrain. Six railroad cars full of visual and performing arts exhibits were set to launch on a tour that would stop in twenty-four small towns in six southern states, beginning with Georgia.

Georgia's governor, Jimmy Carter, and his wife, Rosalynn, had invited Mrs. Ford to stay the night at the governor's mansion in Atlanta, where they would have a reception for her, and then a parade and dedication ceremony for the Artrain the following day.

Unbeknownst to Betty, her hostess was "really worried" about this visit. Rosalynn knew that her husband, a Democrat, was thinking of running for president in 1976, and his opponent might very well be Vice President Ford. "But, of course, I didn't tell her that," Rosalynn recalled years later. And her anxiety dissipated as soon as she met Betty.

"She was so warm and cordial," Rosalynn remembered. "She just put me at ease from the beginning."

The only staff Betty brought with her on this trip was her personal assistant, Nancy Howe. Having been around Betty for five months at this point, Nancy had seen how the pain medication Betty took caused some changes in her. For one thing, she moved very slowly, as if in a constant state of slow motion. Nancy knew the trip's schedule was timed to the minute, and no doubt she worried that if Betty was late, it would reflect poorly on her boss.

Shortly after arriving at the governor's mansion, once everyone was introduced and Mrs. Ford was settled in her room, Nancy pulled one of Mrs. Carter's staff aside and told her quietly, "Just so you know, Mrs. Ford takes medicine for a pinched nerve, and it often has an effect on her. It takes her a long time to get ready. So, for the parade tomorrow, we need to tell her that everything begins an hour earlier than it actually does."

That evening, at the appointed time for the reception, Governor and Mrs. Carter greeted guests as they arrived at the front door of the mansion. Everyone was eager to get a glimpse of, and hopefully the chance to speak to, the wife of the new vice president. This was, in a way, Betty Ford's debutante ball. And she was late.

The marble-floored Circular Hall was filled to capacity, and people were buzzing, wondering when the guest of honor would make an appearance. Thirty minutes after the reception had begun, Betty appeared, wearing a long, yellow knit dress she had borrowed from Nancy Howe, and as she glided down the long, winding staircase that looked like a set out of *Gone with the Wind*, the room fell to a hush. And then, suddenly, the crowd burst into applause.

Painter Jamie Wyeth, the twenty-seven-year-old son of famed artist Andrew Wyeth, remarked that Betty was "really quite beautiful" and that she had "a regal quality . . . a movie star feeling about her."

The Carters had invited some of their close political friends as well as some Georgia Republicans, and although Betty Ford was there to promote the arts, no one seemed interested in discussing Rembrandt or Renoir. Everyone was speculating about whether the well-coiffed woman in the yellow gown might soon be moving into the White House. Betty graciously greeted the guests as they proceeded through a reception line, and when some were bold enough to ask, she smiled coquettishly and said, "I'd rather not talk about that."

While that subject may have been off-limits, she was candid about most everything else. When someone inquired about her slim figure, she happily explained that she'd begun dieting a year earlier and had lost more than thirty pounds.

"Now I'm down to a size eight, less than a hundred ten pounds," she said proudly. Her secret? Lots of lettuce, cottage cheese, crackers, and tea.

"What do you think is the role of a political wife?" one reporter asked.

"I think we have to be supportive," Betty said. "I also think we have to be a sounding board for him. My husband has also said that I'm his toughest and best critic." And then, with a laugh, she added, "But sometimes I regret it."

She charmed the group with a story about how Jerry had come home one night recently after a long day and said, "I'm going right to bed."

" 'Oh no you're not,' I told him. There was a tango party coming up, and we needed to practice. So, I grabbed him and said, 'Okay, here we go! I'm going to teach you some great, dramatic tango steps.' "

Everyone was laughing as she demonstrated how she and Jerry were tangoing all over their small living room.

"She's got a right good personality," said one man—a Democrat friend of the Carters. "She's charming, her hair's arranged pretty, and she looks right at you when she talks to y'all."

A woman who had known Betty for some time but hadn't seen her in many years remarked to one of the reporters that what she liked about the second lady was that "none of this has changed her. She has great modesty. She's still as plain as an old shoe and sharp as a tack."

Later, when Betty and the Carters posed for photographs, Jimmy Carter bent down and whispered to her, "Do you ever become accustomed to this?"

She leaned into his arm and, with a big grin on her face, said, "Twenty-five years, twenty-five years." To the press and the public, this may have been Betty's coming-out party, but as far as she was concerned, she wasn't doing anything different from what she'd been doing for the past quarter century. It's just that now she was beginning to get some of the attention. And she kind of liked it.

The next day, despite Nancy Howe's surreptitious attempts to ensure Betty was on time, Rosalynn Carter recalled that "we were late everywhere we went that day," and that Betty seemed "a little drowsy."

Wall-to-wall people lined the parade route through Dalton—known as the "Carpet Capital of the United States"—and as the two women rode together in a convertible, Rosalynn was very much at ease, waving to the people and calling out, "Hello! Hello!" and "Hey, how are you?" She'd been in countless parades campaigning with Jimmy throughout the state.

Betty, however, wasn't quite sure what to do. Socializing at a reception was easy for her, but the last time she'd been in a campaign-type situation was back when Jerry was first running for Congress in 1948, before they were married. Her discomfort appeared to grow, and after a while, she said to Rosalynn, "You must know all these people."

Rosalynn was astonished. "No, I don't know them at all," she replied. She suddenly realized that even though they were both politicians' wives, Betty had basically been home raising children in Washington her whole married life.

Betty seemed just as surprised by Rosalynn's response, but from that point on, she joined in, waving to the strangers and calling out with a smile, "Hello, how are you?"

The parade ended at the Artrain, and it was time for the dedication. Sitting next to Rosalynn on the speakers' platform, Betty was nervous. She wasn't used to public speaking—even about nonpolitical issues such as the arts. She leaned toward Rosalynn and whispered, "Can't I just thank the mayor and sit down? I don't want to make a speech."

Rosalynn suggested it would be appropriate for her to say a few words. So, when it was time, Betty got up and stood at the podium.

Standing erect, looking out at the large gathering of people, Betty spoke off the cuff, without any prepared notes.

"Art is nonpolitical, and it is in the arts that we are all brought together," she began. She talked briefly about how her special interest in the arts was in dance and how dancing had been such an important part of her youth. It was a good little speech, and the people of Dalton, Georgia, loved it. As the crowd applauded, Betty seemed to become more at ease, having surmounted her initial fear.

As soon as the thank-yous and formalities were finished, Betty and Rosalynn were led to the Artrain for a tour of the exhibits. As they walked through, Betty commented on one of the trainmen's caps, and before you knew it, she had it on her head. It was purely spontaneous—perhaps after reminiscing about her dance experiences, it reminded her of the cap she'd worn at Bennington, back when she was just "Skipper"—and she kept it on as she walked through the train, clearly much more at ease than she'd been earlier. It was as if wearing a hat gave her a different persona and some much-needed courage. She became a woman who exuded composure, even if, in reality, she felt less than confident.

At the end of the traveling art exhibit, Rosalynn and Betty walked out of the Victorian-style caboose and stood on the rear platform. Below them, it was a festive scene with groups of preteen baton twirlers and uniformed Girl Scouts gathered next to choral groups and young girls in ballet costumes. Betty had a big smile on her face, with the conductor's cap still perched whimsically on her head. Someone handed her a pair of scissors, and as the crowd clapped and cheered, she clipped the ceremonial ribbon for the opening of the Artrain.

A few female reporters who covered the women's social pages and a couple of photographers were anxiously awaiting the opportunity to get some quotes for their stories. Cameras flashed, and reporters started firing questions:

"Mrs. Ford, how do you feel about the possibility of your husband becoming president?"

"I'll take it as it comes. After twenty-five years in politics, I've learned to roll with the punches."

And then, one of the reporters called out, "Mrs. Ford, are you on something?"

Evidently, the "drowsiness" Rosalynn Carter had observed earlier did not go unnoticed by the press.

Without hesitation, Betty answered, "Well, I do take Valium every day."

Her frankness surprised the reporters, and they wanted to know more. Why? How much? "Valium, three times a day, or sometimes Equagesic. That way I'm more comfortable," she explained unapologetically. "Otherwise I find I get nervous when I realize how much there is to do each day, and I get tense when I'm running late, so rather than wait till I get to the point where my neck goes into a spasm, I take a Valium."

Her openness surprised Rosalynn Carter, who knew that "any blemish on the public's image of a candidate's or an elected official's perfect wife, children, and idyllic family life can be a detriment." But Betty didn't realize that she had created a stir. She was just answering the question honestly. She had nothing to hide.

In 1974 Valium was by far the most prescribed drug in America. Its use as a minor tranquilizer for symptoms of anxiety accounted for a large share of the estimated fifty-seven million prescriptions written the previous year, and, to many, the little tablet had become as socially acceptable as a double martini before dinner. Betty's admission, however, didn't sit well with a lot of people who would read her comments in the newspaper the next day. Almost immediately, there was a backlash, as hundreds of people wrote letters accusing Betty Ford of being "a dope addict."

When the subject was brought up later, she shrugged it off. "I'm candid," she said. "I wouldn't deny it. I do take tranquilizers. People just don't understand they are for my neck."

Unlike Rosalynn Carter, who was more cautious about revealing personal matters because of her husband's likely upcoming bid for the presidency, Betty wasn't concerned about how her comments might affect her husband's political chances. It didn't matter. There weren't going to be any more campaigns. At the end of Nixon's term, Jerry was going to retire. He had promised. But besides that, Betty Ford was being Betty Ford. She didn't know any other way to be.

Secret Service agents on Jerry's detail were aware that she was drinking, but not to the point that they were concerned. What was more interesting to them was that Jerry made a tremendous effort to be home with Betty. He'd fly to the West Coast or the Midwest and very seldom spent the night. Even if there was an event in Los Angeles at eight o'clock in the evening, Jerry would insist on returning to Virginia that night, even if it meant arriving back in Washington at three or four in the morning.

Meanwhile, the Secret Service had its hands full protecting sixteen-year-old Susan. In many ways, by protecting the vice president's daughter, they protected the vice president and his wife from some potentially embarrassing situations. Even if Jerry and Betty never knew about it.

"My parents thought if you had the agents, you were safe," Susan recalled. "It was kind of a joke. Because their job was not to be your parent. Their job was to watch your behavior, not to correct your behavior; to make sure that I was safe."

The agents realized that to be a sixteen-year-old girl with two guys in suits hovering over you was not anybody's idea of normal, so they devised a way to give her some freedom while still being able to protect her.

"I used to carry a little remote that looked like a cigarette lighter that

I could put in my pocket," Susan recalled. "It was a panic button. And that way, they could back off me, like when I was at a fraternity party, with all these people, and if I felt uncomfortable or unsafe, I just hit the button, and it would come across the radios."

Susan had broken up with Palmer Holt and was now dating Gardner Britt, son of a Fairfax County car dealership owner, who was attending Virginia Polytech Institute and State University. One weekend, Susan and the Golubin twins went down to Virginia Tech to visit him. Betty and Jerry felt completely comfortable with the situation because the girls were being driven and protected by two agents. What could go wrong?

The girls attended a fraternity party Saturday night, and "we were underage drinking, I admit it," Susan said. The next day, "We were hungover, trying to sleep in the back seat on the way back home." Halfway between Charlottesville and Washington, they stopped at a McDonald's for some food and a much-needed restroom break.

They all ordered some food to go, and then the two male agents stood holding the bags of food while the girls went into the restroom. Suddenly there was the screech of a high-pitched alarm.

The agents raced to the door of the ladies' room, their hands on their guns.

"They thought I hit my panic button," Susan recalled. The other patrons in the restaurant were looking around, wondering, *What's going on? Who is in the restroom?*

"Turns out, it was actually the chime on the French fry cooker," Susan recalled with a laugh. "So, we just kind of took our bags, walked out the door, and quickly got into the car before anyone could recognize me."

In the eight weeks between when Gerald Ford was nominated for the position of vice president and the time he was confirmed, there was an intense investigation into his personal and professional life, the likes of which had not been seen before or since. The FBI's investigation of Ford was the largest, most intensive probe that the bureau had ever conducted into the background of a candidate for public office. Some 350 special agents had interviewed more than 1,000 witnesses, the IRS went over his tax returns line by line, and, overall, 1,700 pages of reports were compiled. "The process was like undergoing a physical exam in public view," Jerry Ford recalled.

The one thing that could have potentially caused problems was the one thing that had concerned Jerry the very first time he ran for Congress: the fact that his wife had been married, and divorced, before she became Mrs. Gerald R. Ford Jr.

"The *National Enquirer* was going to write a piece about the fact that she had been married previously," David Kennerly recalled. Betty was deeply concerned that it would be an embarrassment to Jerry. "Don't worry about it," Kennerly said. "Why don't you talk to Bonnie Angelo?"

Time had started a People section, which eventually spun off into *People* magazine, and Bonnie was the features reporter. "Maybe she'll ask you have you ever been married before? And you'll say yes. And she'll ask, 'Why haven't you ever told anyone before?' And you can just say, 'Well, no one has ever asked.' "

David Kennerly approached Angelo with the story tip. "You should talk to Mrs. Ford—she might have a story for you. You might ask her about her previous marriage."

"I didn't know she was married before!" Bonnie exclaimed.

"Well, yeah, nobody does," Kennerly said. In retrospect, he admitted, "I didn't mention anything about the *National Enquirer*."

That Sunday, there was a little item in the new People entertainment column of *Time* mentioning Betty's previous marriage.

"So, essentially it drove a stake through the story," Kennerly said. "It was literally a paragraph in the People section of *Time* instead of what could have been a front-page scandal in the *National Enquirer*."

"I think this is when my relationship with her got stronger," he reflected years later. "A reporter couldn't have done that," he said. There was a difference between reporters and photographers. "All I was doing was wanting to get in occasionally to take pictures."

Steve Ford, just about to turn eighteen, was in his senior year at T. C. Williams High School, and the school thought it would be wonderful to have the father of one of its students—who happened to be vice president of the United States—give the commencement address.

"I wasn't thrilled about it at the time," Steve recalled. "I was a pretty typical teenager, going, 'Come on, Dad, don't do that.' When you're eighteen years old and you're trying to lay low, to have your father come in and do the commencement isn't the way to stay below the radar."

Vice President Ford did indeed give the commencement address to the 1974 graduating class, and within a few months, there would be no way anyone in the Ford family could stay below the radar. History had them in the crosshairs.

12

The Unthinkable Happens

Mike and Gayle had moved their wedding date up a month, and Betty was pleased as could be when they got married on July 5 in Catonsville, Maryland. Among the bridal party were Jack and Steve as groomsmen, Susan as a bridesmaid, and the vice president of the United States as best man. So many family friends from Grand Rapids attended, the Fords practically rented a whole motel. It was a beautiful faith-based Episcopalian ceremony—a joyous day. The calm before the storm.

Eight years earlier, in 1966, Congress had passed an authorization to build a house for the vice president, but at the time Ford took office, funds still had not been appropriated. Meanwhile, the chief of naval operations resided in a beautiful old Victorian mansion on the grounds of the US Naval Observatory, just off Massachusetts Avenue NW, while vice presidents Hubert H. Humphrey, Spiro T. Agnew, and now Gerald R. Ford Jr. had all lived in their private residences, each of which had to be converted, at considerable cost, to bring them up to the security standards of the Secret Service. In May 1974, a decision was made to use the US Naval Observatory mansion as a temporary residence for the vice president and his family, much to the indignation of its current occupant, Admiral Elmo R. Zumwalt. This home, too, needed to be updated and upgraded, and as second lady, Betty was expected to make all kinds of decisions for the remodeling.

When Betty toured the house for the first time, accompanied by the White House curator, Clem Conger, and his assistant, Betty Monkman, she quickly realized that a lot needed to be done to turn this vacant house into a place that was not only a livable home for their family but also suitable for all the entertaining that was expected of the vice president and his wife. The admiral had moved out, and while he had left a few things, there were no paintings on the wall—not even a table in the dining room.

"It was far more expensive and time-consuming than anyone had expected," Jerry Ford recalled, "but Betty kept at it with her characteristic enthusiasm and drive."

For the past several months, Betty had been meeting with officials of the navy and the Secret Service to determine what changes would have to be made. She was planning to go to New York City the week of August 7 to look at furnishings. Before she went to New York, however, she wanted Jerry to approve the areas she'd selected for the family living quarters and for entertaining guests. She had made arrangements to go back to the house with her husband and all the appropriate participants on Thursday, August 1. At five thirty that evening, Betty was waiting in the limousine outside the Old Executive Office Building, waiting for Jerry to finish up his day and drive with her to the Naval Observatory house.

What she didn't know was that the vice president's day had been quite eventful. Tormenting, actually. At three thirty, Chief of Staff Alexander Haig had gone to Jerry's office and revealed some disturbing news: the US Supreme Court had just ruled that sixty-four conversations taped secretly by Nixon in the Oval Office had to be turned over to US District Court Judge John Sirica, the judge presiding over the Watergate incident. Haig had just heard or read transcripts of the tapes.

"I want to alert you that things are deteriorating," he told Jerry. The new tapes contained evidence that would contradict Nixon's version of events in the scandal and would prove that the president knew about the cover-up six days after the June 1972 break-in at Democratic National Committee headquarters. Haig proposed six options that had been discussed among Nixon's staff as to how things might unfold. The sixth option, recalled Jerry, "was that Nixon could agree to leave in return for an agreement that the new president—Gerald Ford—would pardon him."

Haig didn't come right out and ask, but it certainly appeared that he was trying to gauge the vice president's willingness to make such a deal. Jerry told Haig he didn't think it was appropriate for him to make any recommendations at all.

The fact that Nixon had lied to him was crushing news, though. Nixon had repeatedly assured Ford that he was not involved in Watergate, and Jerry had chosen to believe him and give him the benefit of every doubt. They had been friends for more than twenty-five years. He was angry and hurt.

"Throughout my political life," Jerry wrote, "I was truthful to others; I expected others to be truthful with me."

"I want some time to think, Al," Jerry said. He wanted to talk to the president's attorney, James St. Clair. And he added, "I want to talk to Betty. She deserves to be brought up to date."

"It was really important to him; he didn't want to think of this as dragging her into this task," the Fords' oldest son, Mike, said. "He always considered he and my mom as a team: as a parent team in raising the children, and as a team in the White House and in public life too."

Nixon was going to leave one way or the other, and Jerry was going to become president. At this point, it was just a matter of how and when. He could hardly wait to talk to Betty—not only to confide in her what was going on, but also to get her take on the situation. It was her opinion he valued above all. But first, there was this meeting at the new vice presidential residence.

"The exercise at this moment, I felt, was ridiculous," Jerry recalled. "The possibility that we'd ever live in that house was slim, and getting slimmer all the time." But to change plans at the last minute would invite reporters to ask questions. That was the last thing he needed.

As they walked through the house discussing draperies, furniture, and china, Jerry grew more and more impatient. He couldn't say anything to Betty in front of anyone else. He wanted badly to get home to talk with her about it alone. By the time they got back to the house, however, they were running late for a dinner engagement at the home of

Washington Star society columnist Betty Beale and her husband, George Graeber. He certainly couldn't bring it up in front of them.

It wasn't until around eleven o'clock that he finally got the chance to talk to Betty alone. Sitting together in their family room, Jerry described the disturbing meeting with Alexander Haig. As he recalled, "Her eyes widened in disbelief."

She was "dumbfounded" that Nixon had lied to them, and yet, instead of being angry, Jerry would remember that her immediate reaction was compassion. She was terribly sad for President Nixon, Pat, and their family. They had been friends for so many years, and Betty's first thoughts were how this was going to affect them, not her.

But then, the totality of it finally hit her, and in her soft voice, she said, "My God, this is going to change our whole life."

"Neither she nor her husband were emotionally prepared to ascend to the White House," David Kennerly confirmed.

Despite the mounting pressure against Nixon, the Fords had believed him; they couldn't fathom that he would lie to them. Some might say they were naive, but, really, it was just one more example of their characters: lying wasn't something they could do any more than cheat, steal, or kill. A person's word was his or her honor. Knowing that Nixon had betrayed not only them but also the entire country was devastating.

Jerry told Betty about the various scenarios Haig had presented for Nixon's departure and asked what she thought.

"You should not get involved in making any recommendations at all, Jerry," Betty said firmly. "Not to Haig, not to Nixon, not to anybody." Jerry agreed. With the weight of the world hovering over his shoulders, Betty was his pillar.

"I really think he got a lot of strength from her," Mike Ford said. "And I think he gave strength to her as well."

It was one thirty by the time Jerry and Betty went to bed and turned out the lights. Lying there in the darkness, each of them silent in thought, their hands reached out and touched. And then, together, they began to pray.

"God give us strength, give us wisdom, give us guidance as the possibility of a new life confronts us.

"We promise to do our very best, whatever may take place.

"You have sustained us in the past.

"We have faith in Your guiding hand in the difficult and challenging days ahead.

"In Jesus's name, we pray."

And then Jerry recited from the book of Proverbs the prayer that throughout his life had always been a source of strength during times of crisis: "Trust in the Lord with all thine heart; and lean not unto thine own understanding. In all thy ways acknowledge Him, and He shall direct thy paths."

The next day, Betty wrote a letter to her friend Mary Lou Logan in Connecticut, thanking her and her husband for coming to the party they'd had in honor of Mike and Gayle in Washington, and also politely declining Mary Lou's invitation for Betty to chair a bicentennial ball.

In closing, Betty wrote, "right now I am quite involved in trying to furnish the Admiral's house with as little money as possible, since it is only being considered as a temporary residence for the vice president. I must admit it is a great challenge for me."

Even with what had transpired the day before, it seemed that Betty still did not fully comprehend how quickly and dramatically her life was about to change.

"I didn't see it because I didn't want to see it," she wrote in her memoir. "I think the possibility so terrified me that I was blocking it out."

The phone rang and rang and rang. Cameras and reporters swarmed onto Crown View Drive. "Every time you went in and out of the house, they were shouting questions at you," Steve recalled. "Mom was really getting the most of it, but we kids would go through the same thing."

Yes, Betty was right. This was going to change their whole lives. And there was nothing they could do about it.

On Thursday, August 8, Jerry called Betty from his office. He'd just had a seventy-minute meeting with the president.

"Nixon is going to announce his resignation to the nation on live television tonight," he said. "I'll be sworn in at noon tomorrow."

"Up until then," Betty wrote, "I'd kept hoping that something would happen which would save the president, save the office, save all of us, hoping it wouldn't end the way it ended."

But it was happening, and fast. "From Thursday night through Friday, I was like an actor on a set, being told where to go and what to do," she recalled.

Mike and Gayle were in the process of moving to Boston, trailering a U-Haul full of wedding presents, and when they got there, the Secret Service met them and gave them tickets to fly back to Washington.

Jack Ford was on horseback working as a ranger in Yellowstone National Park. The Secret Service had to send in a helicopter so they could break the news that his father was about to become president of the United States, and then lift him out so he could get back to Washington in time to witness the swearing-in.

Steve Ford was at work mowing lawns for the US National Park Service. The Fords had always required their children to have summer jobs in a variety of occupations. That afternoon, he and his crew were picking up trash along the George Washington Memorial Parkway going out to Mount Vernon. "Here I was working with all these guys, long-term government employees working for the Park Service, and they're wondering if my dad's going to become president of the United States and become their boss."

Betty was going through the motions. What would she wear? What about Gayle and Susan and the boys? It was picking out clothes, figuring out logistics, and the telephone just kept ringing and ringing. "I was numb," she recalled.

When Jerry got home at around eight thirty that evening, Mike, Gayle, and Jack still hadn't arrived. At nine, Jerry, Betty, Susan, and Steve gathered in front of the television in the small family room and watched, in stunned silence, as President Nixon announced, "I will resign the presidency, effective at noon tomorrow. Vice President Ford will be sworn in as president at that hour."

It was surreal.

Mike, Gayle, and Jack finally arrived a bit later. Upon seeing his mother, Mike recalled, "She was not particularly well at that time. Her pinched nerve, and all the wear on her from him being away. She was not very strong."

Jerry, too, was concerned about how Betty was handling all of this, but it was out of their hands. There was no choice but to move forward. Tomorrow he'd be giving the most important speech of his life. It was up to him, and him alone, to reassure the nation that everything was going to be okay. And yet, he was honestly concerned that his emotions would get the best of him. He couldn't afford to break down.

So, before he and Betty went to bed that night, Jerry practiced his speech in the privacy of their bedroom at 514 Crown View Drive in front of the one person whose opinion, to him, mattered most.

The morning of August 9, 1974, Jerry went to his office early, accompanied by Phil Buchen and former congressman John Byrnes—two close friends turned advisors—while the rest of the family scurried to get ready. Two limousines took them to Jerry's office in the Old Executive Office Building next door to the White House complex, where they had been directed to wait while Nixon gave a private farewell to his Cabinet members and staff in the East Room. Jerry was going over his speech while Betty and the children watched Nixon's remarks on the television set in Jerry's office.

Just before nine thirty, Secret Service agents and a military aide escorted Jerry and Betty to the Diplomatic Reception Room on the ground floor of the White House. President Nixon had finished his remarks, and now he and his wife, Pat, were waiting there to walk outside with the Fords.

All the people had filed out of the East Room, joining military personnel and staff—two hundred or more—on the South Lawn. Dozens of White House employees, many of whom had worked for three, four, or five presidents, came out onto the first-floor balcony and the second-floor Truman Balcony to witness this unprecedented scene. From maids and butlers, to secretaries, sergeants, and men in dark suits, there was barely a dry eye to be found. Just beyond the crowd, an army helicopter, olive green with a white top, which denoted it as one of the presidential fleet, was waiting to take the disgraced chief executive away from the White House for the last time.

"People were crying," Betty recalled, "and it still seemed impossible to me that this was happening." Somehow, Betty managed to put on a brave smile as she walked out the door to face the crowd and the cameras. The powder-blue skirt and jacket with white piping she had cho-sen to wear was subdued—she hadn't wanted to stand out or appear to be overshadowing Pat Nixon—and while the clothes hung a bit loose over her thin frame due to the weight she'd lost in the stress of the past few weeks, what everyone watching would notice was the way she held herself with such grace. She pulled Pat Nixon close on her left side, and Jerry on her right, wrapping her arms around each of them, as President Nixon walked alongside his wife, hands by his sides. Nixon smiled at the crowd in a broad, awkward grin, while the man who was about to replace him looked straight ahead, a pained look on his face.

The two couples walked from the White House toward the helicop-ter, through a cordon of uniformed military personnel holding rifles at attention in salute. "My heavens, they've even rolled out the red carpet for us," Pat said. "Isn't that something?" It was a peculiar thing to say. But everything about this juncture was extraordinary. There was no script for a moment like this.

And then Pat added, "Well, Betty, you'll see many of these red car-pets, and you'll get so you hate 'em."

"The moment was terribly painful for all of us," Jerry recalled. "We were trying to put up the bravest, strongest front."

When they reached the helicopter, its rotors just beginning to spin, Jerry leaned over and kissed Pat on the cheek.

"We wish you the best. Health and happiness," he said.

Pat turned toward Betty, and the two ladies, friends for a quarter century, both realizing this might be the last time they would see each other, put their cheeks together, and kissed in sad farewell.

President Nixon turned to Jerry, stuck out his hand, that awkward smile still plastered across his face, and said, "Goodbye, Mr. President."

"Goodbye, Mr. President," Jerry replied. He shook Nixon's hand, but still there was no smile.

Richard Nixon walked up the few steps to the door of the helicopter and then turned around to face the crowd, as he flung his hands high up into the air, his fingers formed into his trademark *V* for victory sign.

There was no cheering, no applause. Clint Hill, the assistant director of the Secret Service, responsible for all protection, remembered stand-ing on the lawn watching and thinking to himself, *What does he think he has won?*

"We couldn't help but feel sorry for a very dear friend and his wife," Jerry would say years later. "But at the same time, to be honest, I was anxious to turn around, walk in, and get started on my new responsibilities."

Jerry grabbed Betty's hand and whispered, "We can do it. We're ready."

They turned around and walked back toward the White House, along the red carpet, their hands clutched together tightly, with fingers intertwined. No more words needed to be said. The only thing they knew for sure in that moment was that, whatever lay ahead, they would get through it. They had their faith and each other.

Just before noon, Betty and Jerry were escorted to the East Room, where the swearing-in would take place. It was the same room where, under three glittering crystal chandeliers, less than three hours earlier, President Nixon had made his farewell speech; the same room where Betty and Jerry had knelt and prayed alongside the casket of President John F. Kennedy, nearly eleven years earlier. Those walls held a lot of history. And now the people that filled the room—the Fords' children; other family and friends from Michigan; congressional friends, both Democrats and Republicans; members of the Cabinet; and the press—were there to witness yet another unforeseeable, unthinkable, historic moment.

"Most presidents get nominated, win an election, get sworn in, and then there are galas and balls, parties, celebrations. This time there was no celebration. It was a dark moment hanging over the White House," Steve Ford recalled.

As soon as Jerry and Betty entered the room, everyone rose, clapping with somber appreciation. The clapping continued as they walked to the front of the room and stepped up onto the low stage, joining Chief Justice Warren Burger, who approached from the opposite side.

Jerry recalled feeling a sense of awe. "At that historic moment, I was aware of kinship with my predecessors. It was almost as if all of America's past presidents were praying for me to succeed." He looked across the room and saw two hundred people who believed in him—none prouder than his four children, who were seated in the front row.

A military aide handed Betty the Bible, the same one on which Jerry had taken the oath of office ten months earlier as vice president. This time, however, they had decided to open it to the Book of Proverbs: *Trust in the Lord with all thine heart; and lean not unto thine own understanding.* There was no doubt in their minds; their lives were in God's hands.

As soon as the clapping had ceased, Chief Justice Burger looked at Jerry and said, "Mr. Vice President, are you prepared to take the oath of office as president of the United States?"

"I am, sir," Jerry said. He raised his right hand and placed his left hand on the Bible.

Betty's face revealed all the emotions swirling inside: disbelief, shock, terror, profound love, and immense pride, as her husband stood next to her and repeated the words spoken by the chief justice.

"I, Gerald R. Ford, do solemnly swear that I will faithfully execute the office of president of the United States, and will, to the best of my ability, preserve, protect, and defend the Constitution of the United States, so help me God."

"The words cut through me, pinned me to the floor," she recalled of that moment. The audience stood and clapped. For the first time that day, Jerry smiled, and then turned to Betty and kissed her. They stood together for a few moments as cameras clicked and flashed, and then Chief Justice Burger went to the podium and announced, "Ladies and gentlemen, the president of the United States."

Betty looked as though she might faint. Thank God there was a chair, and it was time for her to sit. Jerry went to the podium, looked out at the audience, fully aware that the entire world was watching. He gave the speech as he had practiced, in a measured voice, each word chosen carefully.

"Mr. Chief Justice, my dear friends, my fellow Americans. The oath that I have taken is the same oath that was taken by George Washington and by every president under the Constitution. But I assume the presidency under extraordinary circumstances never before experienced by Americans. This is an hour of history that troubles our minds and hurts our hearts . . ."

He held his emotions, his voice cracking just twice: first, when he said, "I am indebted to no man and to only one woman, my dear wife, as I begin this difficult job," and when he asked for prayers for Richard Nixon and his family.

It was not a long address, but for years to come, the passage that all would remember was when he declared, "My fellow Americans, our long national nightmare is over."

For Betty, it felt as if the nightmare had just begun. She would recall August 9, 1974, as the saddest day of her life.

During normal transitions, one presidential family moves out of the White House, and the new family moves in the same day. In this case, it was impossible. The Nixons' daughter Julie and her husband, David Eisenhower, had stayed behind to pack their family's things; Jerry had told them to take their time. So, after photos were taken with the family in the Oval Office, Jerry went straight to work assembling his Cabinet and prioritizing the needs of the country while the rest of the family returned to their home in Alexandria.

When Jerry came home around eight o'clock that evening, tailed by the press, the neighbors were standing in the street cheering. "Way to go, Jerry!" "Great new government job!"

Betty had invited a dozen or so close friends to join them for a casual celebratory dinner of ham, salad, and lasagna, and by the time Jerry walked in, people were laughing and having a great time.

"The morning had begun with tears, lives being broken, people being broken, and now there was laughter," Betty wrote. Everybody wished them well, and "Jerry was in his shirtsleeves pouring champagne."

Betty had on an apron, and as she pulled a tray of lasagna out of the oven, she quipped, "Jerry, something's wrong here. You're president of the United States, and I'm still cooking!"

It was crazy but true.

One of the kids had invited photographer David Kennerly to join them that evening too. He had been around so much the past ten months that he'd almost become part of the family. He could always make Jerry laugh, and he and Betty had become especially close.

"She had a fantastic sense of humor," he recalled. "I could tell her all the off-color jokes that I would never tell President Ford because he wouldn't get them or he'd be offended. She wanted to hear it all; she wanted to hear the gossip."

When the party started to break up, Jerry said, "David, I want you to stay after everyone else leaves."

The kids were still there, talking in the kitchen, but once all the other guests had left, Jerry and David sat down in the living room. "We sat on the couch, and he was smoking his pipe," David remembered.

"How would you like to be my chief photographer at the White House?" Ford asked.

David had thought about this. He had wondered if perhaps President Ford might offer him the job, but he wasn't sure about it. Kennerly had seen how Nixon's chief photographer, Ollie Atkins, had limited access. He had to make appointments with Nixon's secretary, and there were many times when Nixon just shut him out. David didn't want any part of that.

"I'd like to do it," the photographer said, "but on two conditions: one, I report directly to you, and, two, I have total access to everything that's going on all the time."

President Ford took the pipe out of his mouth and looked at him. David suddenly regretted opening his mouth. "Here I was twenty-seven years old," he recalled, "and I thought, *Okay, I'm going to call my parents up and tell them how the president offered me a job, and I told him to shove it.*"

But that didn't happen. The new president started laughing. "You don't want Air Force One on the weekends?" David breathed a sigh of relief and laughed along with him.

Ford said he was fine with the arrangement David had proposed, but he wanted to inform Al Haig, his chief of staff, and make sure they handled the new appointment appropriately with Ollie Atkins.

The president looked at his watch and said, "Hey, let's go watch the eleven o'clock news."

They went into the den, but when Jerry flipped the power switch on the television, it wasn't working.

"Oh, for crying out loud," he said. "Come on upstairs. We've got a TV in the bedroom."

Susan and Betty had changed into their nightgowns and robes and already had the television on.

"He's been president for ten hours, and there I am in the master bedroom," David recalled, "sitting on the edge of the bed with the first lady and Susan, watching the swearing-in and the long-national-nightmare-is-over speech on TV."

At the end of it, David stood up and said, "Well, I've got to go . . . and"—he added as an afterthought—"um, you've got a big day of being president tomorrow."

Everybody burst into laughter. Betty stood up and gave him a hug, and then Jerry grabbed him by the hands. "Will working for me be a problem for your colleagues?" he asked. "Because of everything that's happened with Nixon?"

"No, no, Mr. President," David said. "Not at all. They all like you and will be glad to have me as an advocate for them in the White House." It almost brought tears to his eyes—that at the end of this long, emotion-filled day, the president would be concerned about him.

Finally, everyone was gone, and it was just Jerry and Betty, alone in their bed. Holding hands, they drifted off to sleep, knowing that, indeed, they had a big day of being president and first lady ahead.

The next morning, David Kennerly was at the *Time* office across from Lafayette Square, when an announcement came over the intercom.

"David Kennerly, call the operator."

David got on the phone, and it was President Ford. Not a secretary; the president himself.

"Do you still want to come and work for me?" President Ford asked.

"Yeah, I'm ready to go."

"Well, you better get over here right now," Ford said. "You've already wasted half a day of the taxpayers' money."

"To this day, I think one of the deciding factors in me getting that job," David said, "was the fact that I got along so well with Mrs. Ford. She had a great deal of influence on him.

"Being a photographer is an extremely intimate job," he continued. "There is a trust factor because you are there for a lot of very personal moments."

Indeed, within weeks, David Kennerly would find himself taking pictures of the president and first lady during some of the most emotional times of their lives.

PART THREE

◆

BETTY FORD, FIRST LADY

T here is no job description for first lady, no guidebook, and for
Betty Ford, who had never imagined herself in the role, the only
way she knew how to handle the situation was to be herself.

"Okay, I'll move to the White House," she said, "do the best I can,
and if they don't like it, they can kick me out, but they can't make me
somebody I'm not."

Outspoken and surprisingly candid, Betty Ford was refreshingly
relatable, and as it turned out, she was exactly what America needed.
At a time when the women's rights movement was gaining momentum, there hardly could have been a better spokesperson. Betty's openness about everything from her personal health issues, to her views on
premarital sex and smoking marijuana, sparked important and timely
national conversations. After so many years living in Jerry's shadow,
Betty Ford was in the spotlight, and as she began to realize the power of
her platform, she became determined to make the most of it.

13

The Ford White House

Saturday, August 10, Betty woke up to the sound of people calling out, "Good morning, Mr. President!"

Her husband had gone downstairs in his baby-blue short pajamas, opened the front door, and picked up the newspaper on the front stoop, only to find a bevy of reporters and photographers waiting to snap his photo. After making himself breakfast—orange juice and a toasted English muffin with peanut butter—the president of the United States got dressed and headed to his new office at the White House.

Betty took her time getting up. She had never been a morning person, and she wasn't going to change suddenly just because Jerry had a new job. At ten o'clock, she got a call from a White House aide.

"Mrs. Ford, we are just wondering what you are going to do about the state dinner."

"What state dinner?" Betty asked.

"King Hussein is coming on the sixteenth."

A state dinner in six days. For the king of Jordan. Fortuitously, Betty and Jerry had entertained King Hussein at the US State Department during the vice presidency, and Betty knew that the White House was filled with people who knew how to give state dinners, but still, it was up to her as the first lady to make a guest list, and choose the menu, flowers, and music.

Other than Nancy Howe, she didn't have a staff, and Nancy's previous experience was supervising teenagers selling guidebooks in the lobby of the White House. Fortunately, several of Pat Nixon's staff had agreed to stay on, and Betty was going to have to rely heavily on them.

The phone was ringing constantly with requests from the media. She needed a press secretary. She needed a social secretary. She didn't even know what else she needed, but she knew she needed help.

Betty turned to Nancy and said, "Why don't you go ask a few members of the press who they might recommend for a press secretary? And let's get some gals in for interviews."

There were dozens of reporters camped outside and across the street at the Abbruzzeses' house. Police had roped off Crown View Drive at the junction with Cloverway, and the Secret Service wouldn't allow anyone on the Fords' property, so Peter and Louise Abbruzzese had opened their garage to the press, letting them use it as a makeshift pressroom and for shelter from the rain. They let the reporters and photographers use the electrical outlets in the garage and even welcomed them inside the house to use the bathroom and telephone. Louise kept a pot of coffee brewing all day, and at six o'clock, Peter would come out with a pitcher of martinis.

Sunday, the Fords went to church at Immanuel Church-on-the-Hill in Alexandria, just as they'd done for over twenty years. That afternoon, Steve pulled out the hose and filled a bucket with dish soap to wash his Jeep. In one sense, nothing had changed. They were still living in their average middle-class neighborhood, doing everyday things. "Literally ten months earlier, my dad was a congressman from Grand Rapids, Michigan, getting ready to retire," Steve reflected.

But now the public was fascinated, and everything any member of the family did or said was newsworthy.

A team of movers arrived at 514 Crown View Drive, and Betty supervised the packing of their household items as they prepared to move into the White House—which things they'd bring, which things would go into storage. She had just carefully folded Jerry's World War II US Navy uniforms into a box, which had yet to be closed and taped, when her husband walked in. He happened to see the open box and wondered if they were worth keeping.

"I guess we should send them to Goodwill," he said.

Betty looked at him in disbelief. "Jerry," she said, suppressing a laugh, "I think some of this stuff may be a little important now. We'd better keep them."

The Nixons were still moving their possessions out of the White House, but to expedite the Fords' moving in, Chief Usher Rex Scouten suggested Betty come over for a tour to decide how they might want things changed to suit their family's needs and lifestyle.

Betty and Susan arrived at the White House at the appointed time on August 13 and were met by Scouten, Curator Clem Conger, and Mrs. Nixon's social secretary, Lucy Winchester, whom Betty had asked to stay on for the time being.

The residential quarters of the White House occupied the top two floors—twenty-five rooms in all, with twelve and a half bathrooms. There was a family kitchen, which had been added by Jacqueline Kennedy, adjacent to the "informal" dining room, the walls of which were covered in antique wallpaper depicting Revolutionary battle scenes. Betty found the wallpaper "depressing" and could hardly wait to tear it down and paint the room a bright, sunny yellow, but she'd already realized that Clem Conger felt strongly about the historical continuity of the house. Mindful of his feelings, she decided to wait to have that conversation once they'd moved in. She had no intention of changing the public rooms on the ground and first floors, but she was determined to make their living quarters as comfortable for the family as possible.

Scouten showed them to the room that had been Tricia Nixon's, and suggested Susan might like to take that one.

"It was Pepto-Bismol pink," Susan remembered. "And I am not a pink girl." Of course, any of the rooms could be painted or decorated any way the family desired, but that all came out of their own pocket. Besides, the pink room didn't have an attached bathroom. Up until the recent Secret Service renovations in which a portion of her closet was turned into a half bath, she had shared a bathroom with her three older brothers her entire life, and the one thing she was looking forward to most was having a bathroom entirely to herself. Susan wound up choosing the bedroom that Julie and David Eisenhower had used, which did have its own bath as well as a sitting room.

But Betty knew there was one other thing that would make her daughter happy.

"Susan has always wanted a brass bed," she said to Rex Scouten.

Conger looked aghast. "Oh, a brass bed really doesn't fit the era of the house."

Betty smiled at the curator and said, "If you have a brass bed in storage, that would be lovely."

Conger didn't reply, but apparently he got the message from his new boss. It didn't take him long to find an exquisite brass bed that a family in Missouri was more than happy to donate on a temporary basis to the daughter of the president.

Ever since the Eisenhowers, the previous presidents and first ladies had separate bedrooms, and Conger assumed that President and Mrs. Ford would do the same. It was the wrong assumption.

After walking through what had been known as the president's bedroom and the first lady's bedroom, Betty decided that the "president's bedroom" would make a wonderful den. They'd have Jerry's favorite blue leather chair and footstool in there, his exercise bike, his pipes and pipe rack, and their old television set. She'd hang on the walls their family photos that showed the children growing up. And the first lady's bedroom? That's where she and the president would sleep—together.

"Jerry and I have shared the same bed for nearly twenty-six years, and we're not going to change now," she said. She planned to bring their own bed—two twin-size mattresses attached to a king headboard—along with their own sheets, bedding, and pillows. From the reaction in the room, she thought her wishes were viewed as the equivalent of deciding to sleep in a tent on the South Lawn.

"Clem Conger's taste was impeccable," Betty wrote, "but he was more in tune with Pat Nixon than with me." Ever the professional, Conger took detailed notes and set the wheels in motion to make the necessary arrangements.

Dick Hartwig, the special agent in charge of Mrs. Ford's Secret Service detail, recalled it was during that meeting that he realized how grounded she was. "She didn't want to have the presidency make her something she wasn't. She wasn't a rock star; she didn't want to be a rock star. She just wanted to be Betty Ford."

After viewing all the rooms, Betty and Susan were offered iced tea, and they stayed a while longer, chatting idly with the staff. Soon Betty was informed that there were some press people waiting outside to ask her a few questions. In fact, they'd been waiting outside in the heat for quite some time, and Betty felt awful that she hadn't been told earlier.

She walked quickly outside to answer all their questions about the tour and plans to redecorate. "I really don't consider it my house," she responded to one query. "I consider it the house of the people." And, "No, we won't be selling our home in Alexandria."

It wasn't long before word got out that the new first lady intended to share a bedroom with the president.

"People started saying I was disgraceful and immoral," Betty recalled. "I didn't care. I wanted to be a good first lady, I was perfectly willing to be educated about the duties of a first lady, but I didn't believe I had to do every single thing some previous president's wife had done."

One thing Betty Ford was good at was throwing parties. With the help of Nancy Howe, and the talents of the White House employees who had been there through several administrations and had thrown dozens of state dinners, exactly one week after her husband took office, Betty managed to orchestrate a memorable evening honoring the king and queen of Jordan that would set the tone for this new administration.

It was a black-tie affair for 120 guests, and Betty looked exquisite in a long-sleeved, flowing white gown designed by an Alexandria, Virginia, boutique owner named Frankie Welch. It was tied at the waist and had light strands of feathers from elbow to wrist that added a modern, elegant flair. Betty had chosen a four-course menu that began with cold poached salmon, followed by roast sirloin of beef bordelaise with mushrooms and artichokes, a Bibb lettuce salad with Brie cheese, and chocolate mousse for dessert. She and the president had gone over the seating chart together to match people with others they thought would spark good conversation.

After dinner, President Ford and Mrs. Ford led the guests into the

East Room for dancing to the tunes of Howard Devron's Orchestra. There was no stuffiness to this event. Newspaper headlines the next day said it all: "Fords Bring Dancing Back to White House."

Reporters who had covered White House parties for years said they hadn't seen anything as open and relaxed in recent times. Betty was in her element as both she and the president danced with one guest after another until midnight. At one point, everyone was laughing and clapping as President Ford took center stage on the dance floor to the Jim Croce hit "Bad, Bad Leroy Brown."

"It was one of the liveliest parties in the executive mansion since the Johnson administration," one guest said.

Three days later, Betty joined Jerry on his first trip outside Washington—to Chicago—where he spoke to the Veterans of Foreign Wars about working out an amnesty program for Vietnam conscientious objectors. It was their first trip on Air Force One, and it was also the day they'd be moving into their new home. After the president's speech, they returned to Andrews Air Force Base and then transferred to a helicopter, which flew over the congested Washington traffic and landed directly on the South Lawn of the White House.

"It's a very strange feeling," Betty said. That morning, she had left the family's beloved home in Alexandria—the place "in utter chaos, crates and cartons everywhere, chunks of our lives uprooted and labeled for storage"—and when she walked into the residential quarters of the White House, all the things they'd designated to move with them— clothes, knickknacks, assorted furniture—were all there, unpacked and placed exactly where she'd told Rex Scouten she wanted things to go.

She'd had ten days to get used to being first lady, but physically moving into the White House gave it a sense of reality that hadn't been there before. Now, any time she left the privacy of the living quarters, her every move would be monitored by the Secret Service.

Everyone in the family had been assigned a code name, all beginning with the letter P. President Ford was "Passkey"; Mrs. Ford was "Pinafore"; Mike, "Professor"; Jack, "Packman"; Steve, "Peso"; and Susan, "Panda." The agents used the code names when communicating by radio to announce when a member of the family was moving, and where he or she was going. New names were assigned to the individual family members of each new administration, but the code names for places—such as Andrews Air Force Base and Camp David—had remained the same since the Eisenhower administration. After living on a street called Crown View Drive for the past nineteen years, Betty Ford would learn that her new residence at 1600 Pennsylvania Avenue was known to the Secret Service as "Crown."

The political twist of fate that put Betty Bloomer Ford into the White House—from Grand Rapids, to Crown View Drive, to "Crown"—and had her meeting kings and queens, was unprecedented and, seemingly, entirely unpredictable.

The sudden and dramatic change was "a very traumatic experience," Betty would recall. But she had never backed away from a challenge, no matter how difficult, and she wasn't about to start now. And while being first lady was certainly not a position Betty Ford had ever aspired to, let alone imagined she might become, as it turned out, she was exactly what America needed.

"The day the Fords came into the White House, it was like spring had come overnight after a long, cold winter," Secret Service Agent Bob Alberi recalled. "The previous six months of the Nixon administration had been painful for everyone. Nobody talked to anybody." It had been so tense that the agents charged with protecting President Nixon were concerned that he might harm himself.

Just twenty-seven years old at the time, Alberi vividly remembered the first time he met Betty Ford.

"What's your name, young man?" she asked.

He was shocked. *The first lady wanted to know his name?* President and Mrs. Nixon had never spoken to him—they'd barely even looked at him.

"My name's Bob Alberi," he said.

"Nice to meet you, Bob," she said. "Where are you from?"

"Arlington, Virginia, ma'am."

"Where'd you go to high school?"

"Gonzaga. My father worked at the Pentagon."

Agent Alberi was assigned to President Ford, "but from that moment on," he said, "anytime I saw Mrs. Ford, she would always stop and say, 'Hi, Bob, how is everything going?' Both President and Mrs. Ford were delightful," he said. "It was a terrific change."

From the start, Alberi noticed that the new president and his wife had a very special relationship. "President and Mrs. Ford would hold hands in the car, like they were newlyweds," he said. "It was so refreshing."

Ordinary Americans, too, seemed to feel like the Fords were just the "family next door." Betty received hundreds of pieces of mail each week. Many were letters of encouragement and praise, while others asked questions about what she ate, what her husband ate, or commented on something they'd read about her. Still others offered advice. One woman from Cincinnati wrote:

> *Dear Mrs. Ford,*
>
> *Someone close to the President should convince him to change his hairstyle. His hair should be parted on one side, arranged over the top, properly shaped, and then lightly sprayed. I believe my husband has less hair than the President, but the results of my efforts have been pleasing and revitalizing to him.*

Nancy would read some of the letters aloud, and they'd have a good laugh together, but Betty was adamant that every letter needed a response. She and Nancy came up with a standard response that would acknowledge the well-meaning advice graciously:

> *Dear _____*
>
> *Mrs. Ford asked me to acknowledge your recent letter in which you shared your views and feelings with her. Please know that the President and Mrs. Ford are always pleased to have the benefit of comments from fellow citizens, and they appreciate the effort you made to convey your opinions.*

Betty took her role seriously, and while she couldn't respond personally to every letter, she wanted to make sure that people who'd taken the time to write to her were at least acknowledged—no matter how silly their comments or requests.

* * *

When the Fords moved into the White House, Steve Ford was a couple of weeks away from starting his freshman year at Duke University. The check for admissions had been sent, but at eighteen years old, the idea of moving into the freshman dorm with Secret Service men carrying guns and radios—"that is not the group you want to hang out with," Steve recalled. "It seemed overwhelming."

Shortly after they'd moved into the White House, Steve walked into the Oval Office and said, "Dad, I'm not ready to go to college. I want to take a year off. I'll go back to school next year. But I want to get used to this whole thing of you being president." Steve told him he wanted to go out West and become a cowboy.

"It's not what my dad wanted to hear, and, obviously, he had more important things on his plate than me not going to college. But Mom and Dad were great parents, and they allowed us kids to find our own way."

So instead of going to Duke, Steve headed out to a Montana ranch with his Secret Service detail of ten guys, who exchanged their coats and ties for cowboy hats and boots.

The press was focused on the aftermath of Nixon's resignation, but President Ford had a country to run and little time for the media. Thus, Betty, who was largely unknown to the public, was the next natural place to look for stories. The number of requests to speak with her was so extraordinary that the White House Press Office decided the only way to respond to the volume was for the first lady to hold a press conference of her own.

September 4, 1974, was the first time a president's wife held a full-scale White House news conference, and the State Dining Room was filled to capacity with nearly 150 reporters and photographers from around the world. Wearing a tailored shirtdress in a warm butter yellow, with a scarf as an accent around her neck, Betty sat with her back to the fireplace in a high-backed chair, a secretary desk adorned with a vase of flowers the only thing between her and the roomful of press.

Covering the first lady was relegated mostly to female reporters, and as they fired away questions, Betty appeared relaxed, unafraid to touch any subject.

There were questions about liberalizing abortion laws—she was for it. Advising her husband on inflation? She noted that the government needed to tighten its belt just as housewives had to balance a budget and keep a checkbook. Breaking into a smile, she added, "At least *my* checkbook has to balance." She was poised, beautiful, candid, honest, and surprisingly funny.

"Mrs. Ford, what sort of footprint would you like to leave at the White House? How would you like to be remembered?"

"Well, I would like to be remembered in a very *kind* way," she said, with another smile that brought laughter from the audience. And then, turning more serious, she added, "Also as a constructive wife of a president. I do not expect to come anywhere near living up to those first ladies who have gone before me. They have all done a great job, and I admire them a great deal. It is only my ambition to come close to them."

Time magazine's Bonnie Angelo asked, "Are you keeping a diary or some sort of record that might—"

"Bonnie," Betty interrupted, laughing, "I hoped you were keeping it for me!"

The room erupted in laughter. With no preparation, no notes in front of her, Betty Ford made no pretense and presented a woman far more sure of herself than any of them had expected.

Three days later, she took her first trip alone as first lady, to Birmingham, Alabama. It was a trip that had been scheduled six months earlier, and she wanted to honor her commitment. She was one of eleven women being honored as "Legendary Women of America," as part of a fund-raiser for St. Vincent's Hospital in Birmingham. After getting a tour of the maternity ward and holding a newborn baby for the photographers, Betty agreed to answer questions from the press. First, she wanted to clarify her previous statements on abortion.

"I'm all for babies," she said. "I have four children of my own and am looking forward to having a grandchild. As far as the matter of abortion, that is a matter of the Supreme Court. The Supreme Court made the ruling, and the Supreme Court is the law of our land. And as long as that is the law of our land, I abide by the law of the land."

Clearly, the West Wing staff had coached her after her previous remarks sparked controversy. The Equal Rights Amendment? She was all for it. The ERA was a proposed amendment to the Constitution that would provide for the legal equality of the sexes and prohibit discrimination on the basis of sex. Betty felt so strongly about it, she was even willing to go on the road and campaign for it. And when she was asked how she felt about legalization of marijuana, she refused to answer but added that of her own children, "I'm sure they've tried it. Children try everything, don't they?" She quickly caught herself and added, "But they definitely did not like it, and it is not used."

The Associated Press headline the next day: "Mrs. Ford Says She Thinks Some of Her Children Have Used 'Pot.'"

The mostly female press corps that covered first ladies could hardly believe what they were hearing. She was the most accessible first lady in recent times, and to a public used to canned and predictable first lady comments, one reporter wrote, "she is like champagne after *vin ordinaire*. Following the mannequin mask of Pat Nixon, the polished political astuteness of Lady Bird Johnson, the glacial elegance of Jackie Kennedy, the resistance of Mamie Eisenhower and Bess Truman to public exposure, Betty Ford remains, astonishingly, a real person."

Sally Quinn of the *Washington Post* wrote, "Betty Ford, in the first month of her stay in the White House as first lady, has managed to speak out on several controversial issues that most politicians' wives would never dream of getting involved in.

"Abortion, marijuana, amnesty, equal rights amendment, social mores, her relationship with her husband, her views on psychiatry, her own mental condition, tranquilizers, the Nixon pardon . . . Just ask, and you'll get an answer—a straight answer. She'll tell you plainly what she thinks about anything, without a moment's hesitation, without any sense of fear."

In an interview with *McCall's* magazine, Betty noted that she was surprised by the delving nature of some of the questions. "They've asked me everything but how often I sleep with my husband," she said. And then, knowing full well it would be printed, she added, "and if they'd asked me that, I would have told them: as often as possible!"

Inside the White House, the staff was equally as surprised with the openness of this new first lady. One day Betty called for Curator Clem

Conger's assistant, Betty Monkman, to come up to the residence. She wanted to discuss the possibility of having the wallpaper with the Revolutionary War scenes removed from the dining room.

"And so, I went up there, and there was Mrs. Ford in her bathrobe in the West Sitting Hall," Monkman recalled. It was late morning, around ten thirty or eleven. "I mean, I have talked to many first ladies, but never in their bathrobe. So that, to me, said something . . . that she felt so comfortable about herself and who she was."

Later, Betty would look back on those first few weeks and reflect that "in the beginning, it was like going to a party you're terrified of, and finding out to your amazement that you're having a good time. You never know what you can do until you have to do it."

Privately, Betty was very spiritual. Her faith was far more important to her than most knew. Hanging in her bathroom, where she'd see it first thing in the morning, and as the last thing at night when she was brushing her teeth, was a plaque with the Prayer of Saint Francis:

> *Lord, make me an instrument of Your peace.*
> *Where there is hatred, let me sow love.*
> *Where there is injury, pardon;*
> *Where there is doubt, faith;*
> *Where there is darkness, light; and*
> *Where there is sadness, joy.*
> *O divine Master,*
> *Grant that I may not so much*
> *Seek to be consoled as to console;*
> *To be understood as to understand;*
> *To be loved as to love;*
> *For it is in giving that we receive;*
> *It is in pardoning that we are pardoned; and*
> *It is in dying that we are born to eternal life.*

The plaque was one of the personal items she'd brought with her to the White House. It was a tenet of who she was and how she chose to live her life on a daily basis. She could never have imagined how prophetic the references to pardoning at the beginnng and end of the prayer would be.

From the moment Gerald Ford took office, he struggled with the decision of what to do about former President Nixon. As with many difficult decisions he'd had to make over the course of his career, he discussed it with Betty.

They were sitting in what had been President Nixon's bedroom, the room they had turned into a den with all their familiar belongings surrounding them. As he smoked his pipe, Jerry told Betty he was thinking about pardoning Nixon. He'd been wrestling with the decision, weighing the pros and cons. Ultimately, he'd concluded that too much of his time was being consumed by the mess Nixon had created, and it was detracting from his ability to run the country effectively.

Despite how Nixon's reckless actions and outright lies to her husband had dramatically altered the course of her own life, Betty was not bitter or vengeful. It wasn't in her.

"I think Nixon has suffered enough," she said. Compassion was always at her core. She realized the ramifications a pardon would have and knew that many Americans wanted to see Nixon tried in court, and yet President Ford would recall that "she felt enormous sympathy for his family."

In the end, Betty said what she always did whenever there was a tough decision her husband had to make.

"I'll support whatever you decide," she told him.

On September 9, 1974, one month after Gerald Ford took the oath of office, he pardoned former President Nixon for any crimes he had committed or may have committed. It was not a popular decision. The outcry was swift and fierce, with Ford's favorable rating in a Gallup poll plummeting overnight from 71 percent to 49 percent.

In a letter to her friend Mary Lou Logan, dated September 12, 1974, on White House stationery, Betty wrote:

We were all a little reluctant to leave our home of twenty years which has brought us much joy. However, everyone here has been so gracious and helpful that we soon felt at home.

The children have adjusted quite well to living here. Susan adores all of her room on the third floor and is quite settled in with her friends coming and going as usual. For a while, Steve continued to slip back to our old home on Crown View, but I feel he had adjusted to the change before he left to go out west. I was worried that Jack would not like having the Secret Service around and all of the formality of the White House, but he adjusted the fastest of anyone.

They were all getting adjusted to this new normal, feeling like they'd finally passed the tests God had laid out before them.

14

Going Public with Breast Cancer

With so many new obligations, Betty had become increasingly reliant on Nancy Howe to help manage the endless requests, phone calls, and invitations. The two were comfortable with each other and found ways to laugh and have fun. At one point, Betty commented that petunias were the only things that could stand the heat in Washington in the summer—meaning not only the heat of the sun but also the heat of Congress when all the members want to go home, and they start racing through legislation and getting all disagreeable. Nancy thought it was so amusing, and so typical of Betty, that she began calling her "Petunia."

There was an office in the East Wing of the White House designated for use by the first lady and her staff, but Betty preferred to conduct her business from the residence. She set up a small desk in the West Sitting Hall of the residential quarters, so she could write letters and answer phone calls without having to go through the time-consuming process of hairdressing and makeup. If she didn't have to go out, she'd often remain in one of her elegant bathrobes until lunchtime. Nancy would come upstairs each morning, and she was usually the last person to leave before Jerry returned at the end of his workday. With appearances at charity luncheons and the constant social planning, there was little time for friends or personal interests.

Nancy Howe had scheduled a routine gynecology checkup for herself at Bethesda Naval Hospital on September 26. Given the tumult of the past thirteen months, Nancy knew that Betty hadn't had any time to look after herself.

"Come along with me," Nancy urged her. "You're due for a checkup." Betty agreed, and off they went.

As the doctor checked Betty's breasts, her mind was busy with all the things she still needed to do that day. He asked her to wait for a minute and then, without any explanation, returned with Dr. William Fouty, the chief of surgery. She lay there as Dr. Fouty reexamined her breasts; then he told her she could get dressed. Neither physician indicated anything was unusual, and the two ladies returned to the White House.

Unbeknownst to Betty, the doctors at Bethesda had contacted Dr. William Lukash, the chief White House physician. Upon returning to the residence, Betty received a message that Dr. Lukash wanted to see her in his office on the ground floor at seven o'clock that evening.

Meanwhile, that afternoon, Susan felt like she was coming down with a cold and stopped by Dr. Lukash's office to get some medication. He told her to shut the door and sit down.

"There's something I need to tell you," he said. "Your mother has a lump in her breast, there's a good chance it's cancer, and she doesn't know, so hush-hush, don't say anything to anybody."

Susan was in complete shock. "It was devastating. Totally devastating," she said. "I had never been so scared in my life." She ran upstairs to her room, sobbing. "We have just been through this unimaginable roller coaster, and now I'm going to lose my mom? This is not fair."

Her fears were not unfounded. At that time, in 1974, a breast cancer diagnosis was akin to a death sentence. A radical mastectomy was the best option to prolong life, but with reconstructive surgery in its infancy, it typically also meant permanent disfigurement. When Susan was about ten years old, her Grandma Ford had had both her breasts removed, and Susan remembered seeing the grotesque scars under her corset. The word breast was considered almost vulgar or pornographic, unspoken to the point that in the 1950s and 1960s, women who died from breast cancer were often listed as dying from "a woman's disease."

That evening, Dr. Lukash met with President and Mrs. Ford in his office and explained that the doctors at Bethesda had found a suspicious lump in Betty's right breast.

"They want to operate immediately," he said.

"Well, they can't operate immediately," Betty interjected. "I have a full day tomorrow."

As it turned out, the hospital couldn't schedule her surgery until Saturday morning, but she would be admitted Friday night. Dr. Lukash explained that early Saturday morning, Betty would be put under general anesthesia, and the surgeon would perform a biopsy: removing a sample of the suspicious tissue, which would then be examined under a microscope by a pathologist. If the lump was benign, Betty would be discharged. However, if it proved malignant, they would go ahead and remove her breast while she was still under anesthesia.

There were no other options. This was what the doctors recommended and what was standard practice at the time. Betty would go into surgery not knowing whether she had cancer; not knowing whether she'd wake up with one of her breasts cut from her body.

As soon as they were alone, Jerry put his arms around Betty and kissed her. "I'm sure everything's going to turn out all right," he said. "We're lucky you had the examination, and we're luckier still that you will receive the best care."

He was deeply concerned. And so was she. But neither of them was the type to get panicky in a crisis. "We didn't allow ourselves to break down," Jerry said. "We had to deal with reality."

When they sat down for dinner with Susan, it was obvious she'd been crying and that she already knew.

Betty and Jerry had always been open with their children, and they immediately called Mike, Jack, and Steve—all in different places—to let them know what was going on. Everyone was scared. They were a close family, but they also realized they were no longer just any family. The eyes of the world were on them, and they had to decide when and if they would disclose the situation to the public. *Cancer* and *breast* were two words that were whispered, not broadcast to the world, and rarely had a first lady shared something so deeply personal. But at the same time, after the secretiveness surrounding the Nixon administration, President Ford had vowed that he would be transparent with the American people.

Both Betty and Jerry were scheduled to attend groundbreaking ceremonies for the Lyndon Baines Johnson Memorial Grove on the Potomac, in Virginia, Friday morning; then Betty was to give a luncheon speech for the Salvation Army. Since this was the first time the Johnson family had been together in Washington since LBJ's death in January 1973, she had invited Lady Bird Johnson, her two daughters, Luci and Lynda, and their husbands for tea at the White House.

"I want to go through my activities without making any kind of announcement," Betty insisted. The plan was for her to check into the hospital around six o'clock the following evening. Then the White House would send out a press release.

"She was adamant about going public with it," photographer David Kennerly recalled. "And women didn't do that—not in 1974. And not only that, but President Ford agreed, and he stood by her. It had nothing to do with politics, and it had everything to do with the love and support for his wife."

That night, Betty and Jerry lay in bed, and after kissing good night, they held hands and prayed.

They were the president and first lady of the United States. But on this night, they were simply a man and a woman facing the terrifying unknown of cancer.

The next morning, Betty and Jerry went through the motions, and no one would have guessed anything was wrong. Betty was happy to see her friend Lady Bird, and was eager to show her and the Johnson daughters how she had added her own touches to make the White House living quarters their home. She brought them into the bedroom that she and Jerry shared, and as the Johnson family members looked at the Ford family photos on the wall, none of them noticed the packed suitcase sitting on the bench at the foot of the bed.

Just before six o'clock, Betty entered the hospital, accompanied by Nancy Howe and Ric Sardo, a Marine military aide who had been assigned to her and whom she adored. Once she was securely in the presidential suite, the White House sent out a press release announcing that Mrs. Ford had checked into Bethesda Naval Hospital. The wording about her upcoming procedure was blunt.

"The purpose of the surgery is to determine through a biopsy whether the nodule is benign or malignant. Should it prove to be malignant, surgery would be performed to remove the right breast." It was announced on the evening news, and, before long, there were reporters and cameramen staked outside the hospital, their searchlights shining up at the windows of Betty's hospital suite.

Mike and Gayle had flown down from Boston, and they accompanied President Ford and Susan to have dinner with Betty. Everyone was trying to be lighthearted, avoiding the subject of the surgery and the unknown, but it was difficult to hide the fear they all felt inside.

"We were all scared to death," Mike remembered. The one person who was holding it together best was Betty herself.

"She and Dad had talked about whether to share this very personal issue," Mike recalled, "and Mom said, 'I just feel like there are other women out there going through the same thing, and they're scared, and here I am getting the best medical care in the world. I have an obligation. I need to talk about this.'"

"She showed no apprehension," President Ford confirmed. Finally, it was time for all of them to leave. "I held her for a long moment and then squeezed her hand," he said. "She gave me a loving smile and squeezed my hand right back."

It was a somber ride back to the White House. And even though he had Mike, Gayle, and Susan with him, President Ford would recall it as the loneliest night of his life.

"The thought that the woman I loved might be taken away from me was almost too much to endure," he wrote. He called down to the florist and asked that they send three dozen red roses to Betty's suite. They were her favorite, and he wanted her to see them as soon as she woke up.

Before he went to bed, he wrote her a short note on White House stationery. He would give it to her the next morning.

Dearest Mom
  No written words can eloquently express our deep, deep love. We know how great you are, and we, the children and Dad, will try to be as strong as you.

Our Faith in you and God will sustain us. Our total love for
you is everlasting.
We will be at your side with our love for a wonderful Mom.
xxxx Jerry

At six thirty the next morning, the family went up to the presidential suite at the hospital, and there was Betty, sitting in her favorite robe, smiling to greet them like she was the hostess of a party. Pointing to the toeless socks they'd put on her, she said with a grin, "Here's one for *Women's Wear Daily*."

"She was the strong one, holding us all up," Susan recalled.

Photographer David Kennerly was there taking photos. "No fear," he said. "I didn't see any fear outwardly or inwardly. She was like 'Come on, we're just going to deal with this.'"

Even Dr. Lukash remarked on it. "Throughout this ordeal," he said, "Mrs. Ford exhibited an atmosphere of confidence, and, more interestingly, I thought that she demonstrated a kind of inner strength that sustained the first family, her close staff, and even the doctors."

President Ford returned to the White House while Susan, Mike, and Gayle waited in the suite. "We all sat around and prayed," Susan remembered.

Jerry was sitting in the Oval Office, trying to focus on the speech he was to give later in the day at a summit conference on the economy, when Dr. Lukash called. It was not good news. The nodule had been removed, and the pathology report determined it was malignant. They wouldn't know for several days whether the cancer had spread, but with Betty still under anesthesia, Dr. Fouty was going to perform a radical mastectomy.

President Ford's aide, Bob Hartmann, was with him in the Oval Office, and could tell that his boss was struggling to hold it together.

"Go ahead and cry," Hartmann said. "Only strong men are not ashamed to cry."

Tears streamed down the president's face, his emotions pouring out. "Bob, I just don't know what I'd do without her. I just don't know what I'd do."

When Dr. Lukash informed Susan, she crumpled. She thought for sure this meant her mother was going to die, and she couldn't control her sobs. "How am I going to live the rest of my life without my mom?" she wondered.

Her worries were not unreasonable. In 1974 Betty Ford was one of more than ninety thousand women diagnosed with breast cancer; thirty-three thousand women died.

Along with the breast and some supporting muscle, the doctors removed lymph nodes from Betty's armpit. Traces of cancer had been found in three. At the time, women who had no cancer cells in their lymph nodes had a 75 percent chance of surviving five years after breast cancer surgery and a 65 percent chance of surviving ten years. However, women with cancer cells in one or more lymph nodes had only a 50 percent chance of surviving five years, and three out of four women were dead within ten years.

The family discussed it, and the consensus was to be completely open about Betty's surgery and the prognosis. Within hours of the operation, the three physicians involved—Dr. Lukash, Dr. Fouty, and Dr. Richard Thistlethwaite—appeared at a press conference at the White House. They revealed the details of how the lump had been detected in a routine exam, just seven months since her previous checkup, and that primarily because the cancer had been detected early, the first lady's prognosis was excellent.

What happened next was remarkable. Across the country, the phone lines at doctors' offices and organizations such as the American Cancer Society were inundated with calls from women—thousands upon thousands of women—looking to make appointments for breast exams.

"Even before I was able to get up," Betty recalled, "I lay in bed and watched television and saw on the news shows lines of women queued up to go in for breast examinations because of what had happened to me."

A spokesperson from the American Cancer Crusade said that its phones were "ringing off the hook. It's a tragedy for Mrs. Ford, but she may have saved an awful lot of women's lives."

The White House, too, was overwhelmed with phone calls and correspondence. Twenty-six-year-old Nancy Chirdon was a secretary in the Military Office of the vice president, and since a new vice president had not been confirmed yet, she was brought in to assist Mrs. Ford's staff to respond to the flood of mail.

"One Sunday, I was sitting at home," she remembered, "and I got a call from a man whose wife had just been diagnosed with breast cancer. He was so distraught and didn't know what to do, so he had called the White House asking to speak to Mrs. Ford." The White House operator, not knowing what else to do, had forwarded the call to Nancy, at home.

"People saw in Mrs. Ford a woman who was so relatable that they felt like they could just pick up the phone and talk to her," Nancy said.

Literally overnight, Betty Ford removed the stigma from breast cancer. No longer was it a source of shame, but a disease like any other that needed to be addressed and treated. Newspaper articles described how women could perform their own self-exams, complete with drawings of women's breasts, and explained how mammograms—a relatively new imaging technology available only in a small number of places—could detect potential tumors.

In the first week after Betty's surgery alone, more than thirty-five thousand men, women, and children sent cards and letters to the first lady.

"This was a revelation," said breast cancer survivor and advocate Nancy Brinker, who founded the Susan G. Komen Breast Cancer Foundation in 1982. "It really had never happened before. And with it, she began a movement of patient empowerment, advocacy, information, and a real desire to create a prevention and a cure of the disease."

A fourteen-year-old wrote that her mother had the same kind of operation three years ago, and that she could truly sympathize with her. "I will even go so far as to say I don't think there's anyone in this country, except of course those who know you personally, who feels as bad about this as I do," the teen wrote. "This has nothing at all to do with my political beliefs, since I would never in my entire life dream of voting for a Republican, but I will pray for you every night and please get better!"

Women offered advice and encouragement from their own experiences: "This operation makes us stronger women than we were before." Others wrote of their admiration: "One thing you have demonstrated to the American people is that you are not superhuman. You're just a super lady."

On her last full day in the White House, Betty told photographer David Kennerly, "I've always wanted to dance on the Cabinet Room table." January 19, 1977. *Courtesy Gerald R. Ford Library*

Baby Elizabeth Ann "Betty" Bloomer in her mother, Hortense's, arms. Denver, 1918.
Courtesy Gerald R. Ford Library

Betty, age 3, with her teddy bear.
Courtesy Gerald R. Ford Library

Betty (left) with two friends at Whitefish Lake. Circa 1925. *Courtesy Gerald R. Ford Library*

Betty (left) honed her dance skills under the tutelage of Martha Hill (seated, center) and Martha Graham (not pictured) at Bennington College School of Dance. Summer 1937. *Courtesy Gerald R. Ford Library*

Mary Snapp (left) and Betty Bloomer (right) in "Scenes from Scaramouche" at a Calla Travis School of Dance performance in Grand Rapids, Michigan. May 1936. *Courtesy Gerald R. Ford Library*

As the "Martha Graham of Grand Rapids," Betty takes a sensuous pose in a benefit performance of "Fantasy." 1942. *Courtesy Gerald R. Ford Library*

Betty, age twenty-four, modeling for Herpolsheimer's Department Store. Grand Rapids, Michigan, 1942. *Courtesy Gerald R. Ford Library*

Joyful newlyweds, Betty and Gerald Ford, on their wedding day, October 15, 1948. Grand Rapids, Michigan.
Courtesy Gerald R. Ford Library

Congressman Gerald Ford and Betty attend a Grand Rapids campaign event with presidential candidate Dwight D. Eisenhower and his wife, Mamie. October 1, 1952.
Courtesy Gerald R. Ford Library

Betty, age thirty-four, with newborn Jack and two-year-old Michael in their apartment in Parkfairfax, Virginia, 1952.
Courtesy Gerald R. Ford Library

Mike, Jerry, Jack, baby Susan, Betty, and Steve (in highchair) in the kitchen of their home at 514 Crown View Drive, Alexandria, Virginia, 1958. *Courtesy Gerald R. Ford Library*

Clara Powell was like a second mother to the Ford children. Here with Mike and Jack on Jack's first birthday, 1953. *Courtesy Gerald R. Ford Library*

Clara Powell snuggles with Steve and Susan at 514 Crown View Drive, Alexandria, Virginia. Circa 1960. *Courtesy Gerald R. Ford Library*

Ford family Christmas photo, 1960.
Courtesy Gerald R. Ford Library

Betty playing with
Steve and Susan on
the swing set in the
backyard of their home
on Crown View Drive,
as Mike plays ball in
the background, 1962.
*Courtesy Gerald R. Ford
Library*

The Ford family on skis at Boyne Mountain, Michigan, 1965.
Courtesy Gerald R. Ford Library

As a congressman's wife, Betty Ford was profiled in an article entitled: "How does she dress so well and not spend a fortune?" for *Ladies Home Journal,* April 1961. *Courtesy Gerald R. Ford Library*

After being sworn in as vice president, Jerry Ford unabashedly kissed Betty, much to the surprise of House Speaker Carl Albert. *AP Photo*

"You'll get so you hate these red carpets," Pat Nixon whispered to Betty as the Nixons departed the White House, after President Nixon resigned in disgrace. August 9, 1974. *Courtesy Richard M. Nixon Library*

Betty was stoic as her husband was sworn in as the 38th President of the United States by Chief Justice Warren Burger in the East Room of the White House on August 9, 1974. *AP Photo*

For the first ten days of Gerald Ford's presidency, the family continued to live in their Alexandria home. President Ford and First Lady Betty Ford having breakfast in their kitchen, August 18, 1974. *Courtesy Gerald R. Ford Library*

Betty Ford wishes President Ford a good day at the (Oval) office as he exits their Alexandria residence, August 18, 1974. *Courtesy Gerald R. Ford Library*

Betty Ford with her personal assistant, Nancy Howe, in the White House, August 25, 1974.
Courtesy Gerald R. Ford Library

Betty Ford conducts her first press conference as first lady in the East Room at the White House, surprising members of the press with her openness and candor. September 4, 1974.
Courtesy Gerald R. Ford Library

As Betty Ford gave a tour of the Fords' White House bedroom to Lady Bird Johnson, daughters Lynda and Luci, and Lynda's husband, Chuck Robb, she did not disclose that she was going to Bethesda Naval Hospital to undergo breast cancer surgery that evening, and no one noticed the packed suitcase at the end of the bed. *Courtesy Gerald R. Ford Library*

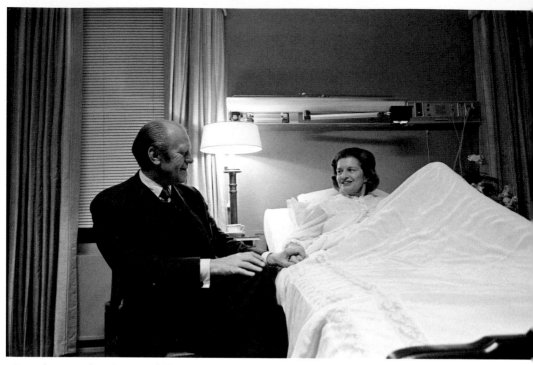

President Ford with Betty following her urgent breast cancer surgery at Bethesda Naval Hospital. October 2, 1974. *Courtesy Gerald R. Ford Library*

Eager to show everyone how well she was recovering, Betty tossed a football—a gift from Washington Redskins coach George Allen—to President Ford in the hospital hallway, barely a week after her breast cancer surgery. October 4, 1974. *Courtesy Gerald R. Ford Library*

Betty gives President Ford a warm embrace in the Oval Office, as the president playfully admonishes the photographer. December 6, 1974. *Courtesy Gerald R. Ford Library*

Betty and daughter Susan share a playful moment in the president's chair in the Oval Office. December 8, 1974. *Courtesy Gerald R. Ford Library*

Onlookers stop and stare as First Lady Betty Ford walks through Vail, Colorado, laughing with friends Sheika Gramshammer and Gloria Brown. December 24, 1974. *AP Photo*

The Fords open presents on Christmas morning 1974 in Vail, Colorado. *Courtesy Gerald R. Ford Library*

Thousands wrote that her bravery in going through surgery prompted them to get checked; people sent $1 and $5 bills with handwritten notes designating the money go to research organizations such as the American Cancer Society; and men wrote to President Ford thanking him for helping them understand better how to be supportive of their own wives going through not only the physical trauma but also the emotional impact of breast cancer.

Betty realized that the loss of a breast was not going to diminish, in any way, her husband's love and affection for her. Still, she knew the first time he saw the wound, it would be a shock.

"She had Dad walk into her hospital room when they were changing her dressings so that he saw it with the nurse there for the first time," Susan remembered. "With all the drains and the ugliness of surgery, it was not pretty."

The one thing Betty worried about was whether she'd be able to wear the kinds of evening gowns she adored, many of which were cut to accentuate a woman's breasts.

"Don't be silly," Jerry said. "If you can't wear 'em cut low in front, wear 'em cut low in back."

There were some difficult moments, like the evening Dr. Lukash brought Betty a little brown bottle of pills and told her it was chemotherapy, to ensure the disease wouldn't spread. She would have to take the pills for five days in a row, every five weeks, for two years. At first, it was upsetting.

Every time I look at these pills, she thought, *it's going to remind me of the fact that I've had cancer.* But then, in typical fashion, she put the negative thoughts in the back of her mind and focused on what she needed to do to move forward. Betty kept a positive attitude, working hard at the exercises prescribed to get back her strength and celebrating every step of progress. The first day she could pick up a cup of tea with her right hand was a triumph. Just one week after the surgery, she had made tremendous strides, and on that day, she decided to surprise her husband when he arrived for his daily visit. She always knew when his motorcade rolled up to the hospital because through the window, she could hear the noisy army of press that always preceded him.

Betty got up out of bed, and, under the supervision of a nurse, she walked out of her room to stand by the elevator.

"Shh!" she whispered to the Secret Service agents lining the hall, breaking into an impish grin as she held one finger to her lips.

The elevator doors opened, and as soon as Jerry saw her, he froze. "What are you doing out here?"

"I came out to surprise you," she said, grinning.

He embraced her, kissed her on the lips, and then said, "I have a surprise for you too . . .

"It's a present from George Allen," he said as he handed her a football. Two days after her surgery, the Washington Redskins had beaten the Denver Broncos 30–3 in a home game, and all the players, along with Coach George Allen, had signed the ball.

"What a wonderful gift!" Betty exclaimed.

She held the ball and looked at the signatures as they walked together back toward her room. Jerry got a few paces ahead of her, and suddenly she had an idea.

"Here, catch!" she called out to him.

Jerry whipped around, just in time to see her raise her right arm, football in hand, and draw it back. The ball came at him and he caught it, effortlessly, at his chest. David Kennerly was in prime position to capture the spontaneous pass, and the next day, the photo appeared on nearly every front page of every newspaper in America. It was indeed a photo that was worth more than words could say: the playful smile on the first lady's face as she demonstrated the strength she'd regained one week after losing a breast to cancer was a priceless inspiration to anyone struggling with adversity.

Many people were still angry at President Ford for pardoning Richard Nixon—it was an anger that would persist until his last days in office— but there was an empathy for him at this time, and nothing but love and admiration for the courageous woman at his side.

Meanwhile, there were several high-profile social functions at the White House on the schedule, and there were questions whether they should be canceled. From her bed at Bethesda Naval Hospital, Betty insisted that nothing should be stopped because of her.

Barely a week after learning her mother had breast cancer, and still unsure what the prognosis was for her long-term recovery, seventeen-year-old Susan Ford made her debut as White House hostess. She had gone to visit her mother in the hospital that afternoon, eager to get approval for the sleeveless red chiffon dress she had bought for the occasion.

"Oh, Susan, it's beautiful," Betty said. "You'll look lovely. But I do think because it's a formal affair, you should wear my long white gloves. That will pull it all together. Ask Nancy Howe—she knows where I keep them."

That night, in the Blue Room, Susan got a taste of her mother's obligatory duties as first lady. At 9:40, after having dinner upstairs in the family residence, Susan walked down the grand staircase on the arm of her father, the president of the United States, to make an appearance at the reception for the diplomatic corps. For forty minutes, she stood, poised and smiling, shaking hands with all 315 guests as they passed through the receiving line. Some may have noticed her shifting from one foot to the other, unused to standing still for so long in high-heeled shoes meant more for show than comfort, and at one point, as she looked down the line and couldn't see an end to the people, she whispered to her father, "When is it going to stop?"

When it finally did stop, President Ford gave her a hug and kiss. He was proud of her.

And then they took to the dance floor, with the orchestra playing Maurice Chevalier's "Thank Heaven for Little Girls." It was a bittersweet moment for both of them: a special moment between father and daughter, and yet both thinking about the woman in the hospital and the reason they were having this dance together.

"I knew that if she died," Susan said, "I would have to do more events like that."

The long white gloves were hot, the shoes uncomfortable for a girl more accustomed to blue jeans and sneakers, but for the next hour and a half, Susan danced with one ambassador after another. "At seventeen, dancing with all those much older men was not high on my list," she recalled, "but I did it for my mother."

Throughout the two weeks Betty was in the hospital, President Ford was under a tremendous amount of stress. Susan could see how his overwhelming concern for Betty combined with the pressures of the country were taking a toll on him. In an effort to cheer him up, she and David Kennerly decided to surprise him with a golden retriever puppy. The Fords had always had dogs, but their last golden retriever, Sugar, had died shortly before Jerry became vice president. (Keeping it a surprise proved to be somewhat difficult when the kennel owner from whom they were purchasing the dog asked relentless questions to ensure it would be placed in a suitable home. When asked if the new owner owned his own home and had a steady job, Kennerly had replied, "The people are a friendly middle-aged couple who live in a big white house with a fence around it. It's public housing." And the job? "He's sure to be in town for a couple of years," Kennerly assured the kennel owner, "but beyond that, I can't tell you.")

The president was thrilled with the eight-month-old golden retriever, and they decided to name her Liberty.

When Betty was finally released from the hospital, her return to the White House was like a national homecoming party. Looking out the window of the presidential helicopter as it landed on the South Lawn, Betty got a bird's-eye view of the crowd that had gathered to welcome her home.

Hundreds of people stood outside the White House gates with signs that said "We Love You, Betty" and "Welcome Home." The press was there, of course—cameras and reporters from all over the world—and everyone who worked in the White House was lined up outside the Diplomatic Reception Room. Members of the staff had strung hundreds of the colorful "Get Well" cards on a cord and draped it like a garland across the Truman Balcony.

Janet Ford, the sister-in-law Betty considered to be her best friend, had come from Michigan to help Betty during her recovery. She and Susan were standing on the lawn, with Liberty, waiting for Betty's arrival. As soon as Betty stepped out of the helicopter, Susan ran to her mother and wrapped her arms around her like she never wanted to let her go.

"I had no words for the joy I was feeling," Betty recalled. "I could only look, and touch, and smile, and hold on."

15

A Reluctant Role Model

Four days after Betty returned home to the White House, she and Jerry celebrated their twenty-sixth wedding anniversary. They had a quiet lunch upstairs in the family dining room, topped off with a special dessert the White House pastry chef had made: two hearts sculpted out of ice cream. Then Jerry told her he had a surprise for her.

"Come on out on the balcony," he said.

Television host and country-and-western star Tennessee Ernie Ford and his touring group were gathered on the South Lawn. When President and Mrs. Ford appeared on the balcony, the singer began serenading them with "Anniversary Waltz."

Betty stood there leaning on the rail of the Truman Balcony, dressed in a peacock-blue dressing gown, holding hands with her husband, swaying to the music, a tender smile across her face.

"It was a fantastic anniversary," she wrote. "Just to be alive and well and home was wonderful."

While Betty had been in the hospital, it became clear that hiring a press secretary and social secretary were of immediate importance. Nancy Howe thought Betty should get rid of everyone on the staff who had served in the East Wing under Mrs. Nixon, but Betty balked at that. Yes, she wanted to make her own imprint, but she had compassion for the people who were on the staff, had been doing a good job, and, through no fault of their own, suddenly had a new administration. The calligraphers in the Correspondence Office, the women who worked in the Social Office—they were craftswomen, nothing political about them. Betty decided they should stay. "From that moment on," Nancy Chirdon said, "those staff people had a tremendous amount of loyalty to her."

Prior to going into the hospital, Betty had interviewed several women for the important position of press secretary and ultimately chose Sheila Weidenfeld. Sheila had been a talk-show producer for NBC in New York City, working with Joan Rivers, David Brenner, and Maury Povich, and had recently moved to Washington because of her husband's job. Several members of the press corps had recommended her for the position.

Petite and brash, thirty years old at the time, Sheila recalled of her first meeting with Mrs. Ford, "Neither of us had any idea what the role of the first lady's press secretary entailed." They'd both be learning on the job.

Sheila fielded the phone calls from the female reporters covering the first lady, and was surprised by the intimate questions they asked. They wanted background on her life and what her plans were, as well as details about what she ate and what she was wearing for every occasion. Pat Nixon had wanted nothing to do with the press, and now "you had this woman who had revealed that she had breast cancer, and she was new, and it was exciting times again," Sheila said. "People were really eager to know more about her."

Sheila's mission was "to get the first lady off the social page and onto the front page," but Betty Ford herself, with her bold decision to go public with her breast cancer, had already accomplished just that.

Before they knew it, the Fords were preparing for their first Christmas as the first family. Planning for White House Christmas decorations typically begins nine or ten months in advance and is one of those duties that is relegated to the East Wing. It was a huge undertaking under normal circumstances, but even with everything else going on, Betty Ford put her personal stamp on it. The White House was closed to the public for three days as hundreds of volunteers came in and transformed the various public rooms into a magical Christmas wonderland with a theme centered around handmade ornaments—encouraging Americans to save money during these difficult economic times and spend more time with family. The chefs made gingerbread houses; trees were decorated in almost every room; and crèches were set on mantels and tabletops.

Forty thousand Christmas cards were sent out—paid for personally by President and Mrs. Ford—and then there were the parties. Parties for children of the diplomatic corps, parties for children of the White House staff and employees, nightly parties for various political groups. Betty recalled, "The Christmas parties started, and I didn't think they'd ever stop." And while most of the Christmas parties were subsidized, the Fords decided to host a party for a thousand members of the press, for which the liquor tab also came out of their own pocket.

Amid all the revelry, President Ford was scheduled to meet the president of France, Giscard d'Estaing, on the West Indies island of Martinique in mid-December, and Betty had decided to join him. Two days before the trip, however, the first lady experienced severe pain. She still took medication for her pinched nerve, but on top of that, she had also developed osteoarthritis. Her brothers, too, suffered from the chronic joint condition, so it wasn't surprising that she would be diagnosed with it as well, especially after so many years of dance, but she noticed it tended to flare up when she was stressed, and when it did, it was debilitating.

A press release explained that Mrs. Ford would not be accompanying her husband as scheduled, but no one believed the reason was because of osteoarthritis.

What's really wrong with her? Is it a recurrence of her cancer?

There was a mistrust of what was coming out of the White House Press Office, but the incapacitating discomfort Betty felt was real. One day Sheila went upstairs to see Mrs. Ford and found her lying in bed, the room completely dark.

"She was obviously in great pain," Sheila recalled. "She looked so pale, so weak." It gave the press secretary a new appreciation for everything the first lady was dealing with. Seeing her like that, Sheila realized "what a tremendous obstacle her health was, and how courageous she was to be able to go through bouts like this, never knowing when they would come and for how long."

During these times, a nurse was with her almost around the clock, applying hot compresses and administering extra pain medication as prescribed by Dr. Lukash. Anything to help relieve the torturous pain. Within a few days, that episode was over, and she was back to the frenetic pace of being the president's wife.

Christmas would be spent at Vail, as usual, but things were completely different now that Jerry was president. The previous year, he'd traveled with a small Secret Service detail, but now he had a much larger group of men protecting him, and Betty and each of the four kids had agents too. Dick Keiser, the special agent in charge of the Presidential Protective Division, asked the guys on the detail, "Who skis?"

Larry Buendorf was the first to respond, "I'm a good skier," he said. He'd grown up in Minnesota and had been skiing almost since he could walk. He also realized they'd need to do an advance before the president got out to Vail, which would require two weeks of "mountain familiarization"—or, basically, two weeks of free skiing.

With the Secret Service and the additional equipment they needed with them, there was no way the Fords could stay in their condo. Dick Bass, an oilman from Texas, who was one of the founders of Vail and had become a friend of the Fords, offered them use of his home at 312 Mill Creek Circle. It was a large wood-and-stone residence near the base of the gondola, with plenty of bedrooms and large, open living spaces. The agents would stay in condominiums close by, and, of course, the press would descend upon Vail over the holidays too. In fact, Sheila Weidenfeld had learned that NBC had rented the house next door to the Bass house. She could foresee all kinds of potentially embarrassing situations, but when she informed Mrs. Ford, the reaction surprised her.

Betty just laughed and said, "I guess I'll have to keep the drapes pulled."

Because they now had a much larger house, President and Mrs. Ford told Jack and Steve they could bring their girlfriends, and Susan could bring her boyfriend out to Vail. Several days before they were to leave, Susan's boyfriend called and said he had hurt his back, and the doctor told him skiing was out of the question. Not wanting to be the only one without a companion for the week, Susan invited Barbara Manfuso, one of her best friends at Holton-Arms.

Barbara and Susan had been close since freshman year. "I knew them before her dad became vice president or president," Barbara recalled. "To me, they were just Susan's parents."

The morning of December 22, President and Mrs. Ford, Mike and Gayle, Susan, carrying two cats in a box, and Barbara, holding Liberty on a leash, set off on Air Force One for Colorado. Thirty-six other passengers joined them, including Chief of Staff Donald Rumsfeld, Press Secretary Ron Nessen, and Dr. Lukash and their families; seven members of the press; and ten Secret Service agents.

They'd been airborne for about an hour when a Secret Service agent came into the compartment where Susan and Barbara were sitting and said, "Miss Manfuso, President and Mrs. Ford want to see you up front."

Barbara froze and looked at Susan with wide eyes. *Oh, my gosh*, she thought, *I'm already in trouble, and we've only been gone an hour.*

"You better get up there," Susan said. "I'll come with you."

The two girls walked up the aisle into the presidential cabin, and as Barbara opened the door, everyone inside yelled, "Surprise!"

It happened to be Barbara's eighteenth birthday. "I remember Susan's mom and dad sitting there," she said. "There was a cake with candles lit, and Mrs. Ford had a huge smile on her face." Betty knew that Barbara felt anxious about being away from her family at Christmas for the first time, so she had arranged for the White House pastry chef to make a special cake, and had wrapped all kinds of presents for her.

"It was really sweet," Barbara remembered. "I was so touched. With everything she had going on, to make sure my birthday was celebrated on Air Force One. That was something she did not have to do."

In the past several years, Jerry and Betty had become friends with one of Vail's most colorful couples, Sheika and Pepi Gramshammer. Both originally from Austria, they spoke with distinctive German accents and ran a small hotel and restaurant called Hotel-Gasthof Gramshammer. The ruggedly handsome Pepi was a former professional ski racer, and he had become one of Jerry's favorite ski partners. Sheika, a stunning beauty with an infectious smile, had been a model and Las Vegas dancer before moving to Vail, and she and Betty hit it off from the moment they first met. "She was a mother I never had. When I had an issue, she was a sister I never had, and she was a friend," Sheika remembered with fondness. "I could talk to her, and when she was in trouble or had an issue, we talked about it. We were like old souls reunited."

Their *gasthof*, or "guesthouse," had a ski and sport shop called Pepi Sports attached on the ground floor, for which Sheika did all the purchasing. She recalled the first time she went to New York on a buying trip, no one had ever heard of Vail. She had to explain that it was a new resort between Denver and Aspen. But after the Christmas of 1974, everyone in the world knew of Vail. Still, the Fords remained the same.

"We were always included in all the activities when he was a congressman," Sheika said. "And then he became vice president, and he still came, but they hadn't changed at all. It was still the same. Just they had another title."

The Fords were determined to have as normal a Christmas as they always had, but the army of press that had accompanied them wanted to peer into every aspect of their family holiday. They had photographers following President Ford down the mountain as he skied with Pepi and a few members of his Secret Service detail, eager to catch a photo of any of them falling. Still others tried—usually without much success—to keep up with the Ford children, who were all expert skiers and could easily ditch the novice press corps.

Pepi had offered all the Secret Service agents a generous discount on skiwear, and when Larry Buendorf had first gone out, he'd bought himself a bright yellow jacket. Sheika loved to ski behind him, calling out "Hey, yellow bird!"

President Ford had one ski outfit, and he always wore the same thing. "We were concerned because you could spot him a mile away," Buendorf recalled. "So, we asked him to mix it up. Pepi set him up with some new jackets, pants, and hats, and he was good about changing his outfit every day after that."

Meanwhile, Betty was still trying to regain her energy after surgery, so she didn't venture out too much. She would meet friends for lunch or spend her days shopping—nothing newsworthy, except for the fact that it was the first lady meeting friends for lunch or going shopping.

But the press was so starved for information about her, the next day in the newspaper there'd be a photo of Betty thumbing through the racks at the Gondola Sport Shop with the scintillating caption: "Mrs. Ford Goes Shopping."

A couple of days into the trip, Susan's boyfriend called to tell her he had been cleared to ski and was flying out to spend the rest of the week with her. The night of Gardner's arrival, Susan went with her agents to Denver to pick him up at the airport. Her friend Barbara stayed back at the house rather than make the three-hour round-trip drive. Everybody had gone to bed, and Barbara was sitting in front of the fireplace feeling kind of mopey, knowing she'd be the third wheel as soon as Gardner arrived.

"Susan's mom came out and made a cup of tea, and sat with me until Susan and Gardner came back," Barbara recalled fondly. "We talked about all kinds of things for the three or four hours they were gone, and she stayed up with me so I didn't have to be alone. That was so typical of her."

It had become a family tradition for everyone in the family to draw names and then fill a stocking for that person. According to Barbara, Mike and Gayle had drawn her name, and when she came downstairs on Christmas morning, her stocking was overflowing onto the mantel.

"They went so overboard," she said. "Everyone made me feel like I belonged; like I was part of their family."

With the snow outside, and a roaring fire in the fireplace, Betty and Jerry sat together on the couch as everyone else sprawled around wherever they could find a seat: on chairs, on the floor, on the hearth, taking turns playing Santa to hand out the gifts. There was nothing Betty loved more than having her whole family together, laughing, teasing one another, making memories. It had been one heck of a year, and they'd made it through, their family bond stronger than ever before.

During the flight back to Washington, Special Agent in Charge Dick Keiser got word that President Ford wanted to speak with him in the presidential cabin. He walked in, and Jerry and Betty were sitting there together, looking very relaxed, having had a nice week with friends and family.

"Hey, Dick," the president said. "You guys did an excellent job this week. I felt very comfortable, and we all had a wonderful time."

"Thank you, Mr. President," Keiser said. "I appreciate that."

"There's just one question I have. You know, you asked me to wear different outfits every day?"

"Yes, sir. We appreciated you doing that for us."

"Well, you know, Dick," the president said with a smile, "Larry Buendorf had that bright yellow jacket and he wore it every day. Anybody who was looking for me, all they had to do was find the guy in the yellow jacket and know that I'd be right next to him."

Betty couldn't help but snicker as she watched the six-foot-two, fearless special agent blush bright red. "Yes, sir, Mr. President," Keiser said. "You have a point. A very good point. We will reevaluate our procedures."

Ever since Betty had seen the women lining up for breast cancer screenings and mammograms, she had come to recognize the power of her position—a power that could be used to help others. The calendar had turned to 1975, and with her mastectomy behind her, Betty was eager to start the New Year working for the causes she cared about most.

First on the agenda was the Equal Rights Amendment—something Betty could relate to from her own experiences. It sought to level the playing field for women in all aspects of life—including divorce, property ownership, and employment. Betty felt strongly about this and was determined to use her platform, and her ability to speak directly to the president, to turn the ERA into a reality.

16

The First Lady Speaks Out

Nineteen seventy-five had been declared International Women's Year, after nearly a decade of work by the Presidential Commission on the Status of Women (PCSW). The PCSW was established in 1961 under President John F. Kennedy to investigate questions about women's equality in education, the workplace, and under the law. After much urging from Betty, on January 9, 1975, President Ford signed an executive order establishing a National Commission on the Observance of International Women's Year. Although this order didn't have any legal or legislative force, "it had moral force," Betty said. It meant the president of the United States was standing up for women and the Equal Rights Amendment, and against "legal inequities between sexes."

Betty stood next to her husband in the Cabinet Room, packed with press and supporters. With pen in hand, President Ford looked up at his wife and, with a teasing smile, said, "Before I sign this, Betty, if you have any words of wisdom or encouragement, you are welcome to speak."

Amid the laughter, Betty didn't hesitate to respond. "I just want to congratulate you, Mr. President," she said, grinning broadly. "I am glad to see that you have come a long, long way."

More laughter, as the president shook his head with amusement. "I don't quite know how to respond to that."

To get the Equal Rights Amendment ratified as part of the US Constitution required thirty-eight states voting to approve it. Thus far, they were five states short. Equal rights for women was something Betty felt strongly about, and she was determined to use her influence, both privately with her husband—"pillow talk at the end of the day, when I figured he was most tired and vulnerable"—and publicly.

Her first overt action was to write a letter to a member of the North Dakota State Assembly just a few days before it came up for vote there. The assemblyman read her letter aloud during the session, and it made an impact. North Dakota became the thirty-fourth state to ratify the amendment. Now only four states were needed. Over the course of the next few weeks, as various states were about to vote, Betty picked up the phone and called prominent state legislators urging them to support the ERA. For a state lawmaker to receive a personal phone call from the first lady was impressive, and even those who disagreed with her often bragged about getting the phone call, which gave her side of the issue an elevated position.

When a group protested that the first lady was using a White House telephone line—suggesting she was using taxpayer dollars to lobby for the ERA—Betty had an outside line installed so she could continue making calls as a private citizen from her "home office."

Indeed, the ERA had some formidable opposition, the loudest voice of which was Phyllis Schlafly, a Republican Party activist who had created an antiamendment campaign called Stop ERA. Schlafly believed that family and traditional values were under attack. She opposed the ERA because she believed it would open the door to same-sex marriage, abortion, the military draft for women, coed bathrooms, and the end of labor laws that barred women from dangerous workplaces. She claimed that equality would be a step down for most women, who, she said, "are extremely well treated" by society and laws. Schlafly painted women who were for ERA as bra-burning women's libbers. She rallied throngs of housewives against ERA and went around the country talking about motherhood.

Meanwhile, Betty made call after call to lawmakers across the country, explaining her feeling that women should have the option to be homemakers, and there was nothing wrong with that—she herself had raised four children and not had a career—but even housewives should have equal opportunities for education, an equal chance to establish credit, and equal Social Security. If a woman entered the workplace, she should be given the same rights as any man and earn equal pay for the same work. She spoke in her naturally soft voice, employing flattery, gentle persuasion, and charm, using the power of her position to get her point of view heard.

For legislators with daughters, there was conversation on the cost of raising a girl: "It just isn't right that we pay so much to educate them, only to find that they don't have the same chance to use their education." For those more liberal leaning, she talked about her career before marriage, and for those who thought the ERA would destroy families, she reminisced about the joys of being a mother to four children. It wasn't about forcing women to give up being mothers or housewives, but about giving them equal rights no matter what path they chose.

"Frankly, I enjoy being a mother, and I am not about to burn my bra—I need it!" she told one reporter. But she took to proudly wearing a "Ratify ERA in 1975" pin on her lapel, so there was no doubt about which side she was on.

Not since Eleanor Roosevelt had a first lady been so willing to take an unequivocal position on a controversial, and highly emotional, political issue. Thousands of letters poured into the White House—three-quarters of them against Mrs. Ford's position on the ERA. When asked about the criticism, Betty told the press, "I'm going to stick to my guns on this. I expected criticism, and I'm not bothered by it."

One day Betty looked out the window from the third floor and saw a group of protesters gathered outside the White House holding signs that said "Betty Ford Is Trying to Press a Second-Rate Manhood on American Women" and "Women Want Equal Pay, Not ERA." This gave her the distinction of being the first president's wife to be picketed for her own political stance.

When asked about the voluminous amount of negative feedback, Betty commented that she thought those who were for the amendment were sitting back and not writing. That did the trick. Thousands more letters arrived at the White House, and within two weeks, the tide had completely reversed, with nearly 6,000 letters favoring the ERA versus 2,500 against.

It was around this time that Betty realized there was some inequality at 1600 Pennsylvania Avenue too. She was returning to the White House from an event one day, just as the president was preparing to leave. The presidential limousine sat parked outside the South Portico, its flags with the presidential seal on either side of the front hood flapping in the breeze, as the first lady's driver brought her car to a stop just behind it. As she got out of the car, she turned to Agent Dick Hartwig and joked, "Why don't *I* have any flags? I'm the first lady. Don't I deserve a flag?"

Everyone laughed, and they went inside.

That night, Agent Hartwig told his fiancée, Sally, the story. He adored Mrs. Ford, and would often share anecdotes about her sense of humor.

"We should make Mrs. Ford a flag," Sally suggested. So, she and a friend got to work designing a special flag for the first lady, and about two weeks later, Agent Hartwig brought it to the White House.

He arranged for David Kennerly to be there, along with several members of the first lady's staff, to surprise Mrs. Ford with a tongue-in-cheek ceremonial presentation of the handmade first lady flag.

It was blue satin, trimmed with white lace and braid decorated with red and blue stars. In the middle of it, carefully stuffed, shaped, and formed was a pair of red and white lace-trimmed bloomers, in honor of Betty's maiden name. In bold white letters on top of the bloomers it said: "Don't Tread on Me," and at the bottom "ERA." It even had an opening along the left side so that it could be attached to a fender pole on the car.

"She really got a kick out of it," Agent Hartwig recalled. "Of course, we couldn't actually fly it from the car," he said, but she hung it from the front of her desk in the East Wing, keeping it proudly on display from that day on.

In the end, the ERA would not get the required number of states necessary to add it to the Constitution—even though Congress ultimately extended the deadline, it officially failed in 1982—but Betty vowed to keep on fighting, and at least she had her own first lady flag.

Another major issue plaguing the country at this time was high inflation. People were struggling to make ends meet in the stagnant economy, and while President Ford was working on financial policies to get the country growing, Betty announced that she would make her own small contribution by no longer spending money on expensive designer clothing. But with public functions to attend almost daily, she needed far more dresses, both day and evening, than she ever had before. Shortly after they returned to Washington from Vail, Betty read an article in the newspaper about an up-and-coming New York City designer named Albert Capraro who used only American-made fabrics and designed dresses that sold for as little as $70.

One of the perks of being first lady, she had discovered, was that whenever she wanted to call anyone, all she had to do was pick up the phone and ask the White House operator to connect her.

Capraro, who had just gone into business for himself after eight years as an assistant to Oscar de la Renta, was sitting in his Manhattan office and sketching some ideas for his summer collection when the phone rang.

"Mr. Capraro? This is Betty Ford. I noticed your designs in the *Washington Star-News*, and I was wondering if you'd be willing to come to Washington to discuss making some clothes for me."

Two days later, Capraro arrived at the White House with a book of sketches. The thirty-one-year-old designer, who sported what he called a "Renaissance beard," had an animated personality, and Betty liked him immediately.

She brought him into her closet, so he could see what she already had in her wardrobe, to show him the styles she preferred. Suits, dresses, and evening gowns were organized by color, and every piece had a card attached to the hanger, on which she or Nancy Howe would write where, when, and to what event the outfit was worn, including the shoes and accessories she'd worn with it.

"These are two of my favorites," she said, pulling out two Oscar de la Renta dresses.

Capraro laughed. "Those are my designs!" he said. "I designed those when I worked as an assistant for Oscar."

As they sat down to look over sketches, they bonded with their shared passion for fashion, talking chiffons and jersey, silk and suede. He took her measurements and recorded them carefully in a notebook, and after a few hours, she'd ordered twelve outfits. The best part was that she'd managed not to stray too far over the $1,000 budget her husband had authorized. Additionally, Capraro agreed to design some evening gowns for her out of some magnificent silk fabrics the president had brought back from a recent trip to the Far East.

As soon as word got out that the first lady had ordered her spring wardrobe from him, Albert Capraro became a household name. Betty was delighted. "She loved helping someone new," Susan Ford said. And Capraro was equally charmed by his newest client. He noted how her eyes changed from blue to green depending on the clothes she wore and described her as a "perfect model: size six, five feet five and a half inches tall, a hundred and six pounds."

Capraro would go on to design many fashions for both Betty and Susan. "We always had fun with Albert," Susan recalled.

As in most work environments, there is inevitably discord among coworkers, and the first lady's office was not immune. Betty had come to rely on Nancy Howe as an all-round assistant—a pseudo chief of staff—but over time Nancy became the center of controversy.

"I called her the palace guard," Press Secretary Sheila Weidenfeld said. "She was always upstairs with Mrs. Ford and kept tight rein on who was allowed to see the first lady, and when."

Nancy was paid as White House staff, and while her role was undefined, there is no denying she was devoted to Betty Ford. She'd typically arrive at the White House around seven in the morning to handle the personal letters that arrived daily for the first lady. At nine she'd head upstairs to the residence, and with Betty still in her dressing gown, the two would go over everything from the 170 invitations a week to appear somewhere, to Betty's clothing needs, planned remarks, and guest lists for state dinners or other functions. Unless Betty had a luncheon event, the two would eat together—usually a sandwich or a salad—in the light-filled North Lobby.

Newspaper columnist Betty Beale had written several articles about Howe and her unequivocal access to the first lady, articles for which Nancy had happily provided comment. Nancy had stated that she was "the only White House staffer regularly in the mansion for a nightly aperitif with Mrs. Ford and the president when he joins the two of them around 7 pm in the North Lobby sitting room," Beale wrote. The article described Nancy as "vivacious" and "bubbly," noting that the Southern-talking aide had adopted a private name for Mrs. Ford. She called her "Petunia," and according to Nancy, the name "tickled" the first lady.

But Nancy's control over Betty's schedule—and the annoying "Petunia" this and "Petunia" that—increasingly became a flashpoint with others. Even Susan started complaining that she'd often get blocked when she wanted to have a private conversation with her mother.

"It's not a good time," Nancy would say.

"She interfered with our relationship," Susan recalled. And even though Susan had mentioned the problem to her mother, Betty couldn't imagine getting along without Nancy and didn't realize the extent to which Nancy was controlling everything.

On Sunday, March 2, 1975, the Fords were at Camp David when Betty opened the paper to the *Family Weekly* magazine supplement and saw the headline "Betty Ford's Best Friend."

It was all about Nancy Howe. "There's a new job description at the White House these days—best friend to the first lady," the article began. "Since government service has no such title, however, Nancy Lee Howe, who is the virtual shadow of the first lady, is listed as 'Special Assistant to Mrs. Ford.'"

Betty was furious. She did not think of Nancy as her best friend. Yes, they spent a great deal of time together, and theirs was a friendship that went beyond simply an employer-employee relationship, but clearly Nancy had done an interview, without Betty's knowledge, and had proclaimed herself "best friend."

Betty called Sheila Weidenfeld. "She was hysterical," Sheila recalled.

Sheila explained to the first lady that she had discouraged Nancy from talking to the reporter—it was inappropriate, and she'd never endorsed the idea. But Nancy proceeded anyway.

"She is not my best friend!" Betty sobbed. "I am so mad. I am so mad that right now, as I talk to you, I am rolling this article up into a ball and throwing it into the fire, where it belongs! I'm going to fire Nancy!"

The worst part, really, was that Susan had been trying to tell her mother for months how controlling Nancy was, how others on the staff had been complaining about her "palace guard" attitude, and how she had isolated Betty from her other friends and even family members. Betty had seen only loyalty and devotion, until now.

Between Susan, David Kennerly, and a call from her military aide Ric Sardo, whom Betty had come to trust and whose opinion she valued, by the end of the day, Betty had calmed down. She wouldn't fire Nancy, but she would certainly be more cognizant of how things were being run.

It had become tradition for the Fords to spend Easter in Palm Springs, where a number of their friends spent the winter. The president liked the golf, and Betty enjoyed the dry, warm weather getaway during what was typically a dreary time in Washington. Normally the Fords stayed at Thunderbird Country Club, but this year Jerry's close friend Fred Wilson, a wealthy insurance executive, and his wife had offered their home, which would accommodate the needs of the Secret Service for security purposes.

As it happened, the Easter getaway, the last weekend in March, coincided with tragic news coming out of Vietnam. One of the few bright spots for Nixon in 1973 was the signing of a peace agreement in January, followed by the withdrawal of US troops, which was completed on March 29 of that year. But the North Vietnamese Communists violated the cease-fire, and by 1974, the peace between the two sides had crumbled. The North Vietnamese were sweeping into the south, capturing major South Vietnamese cities, and a human tragedy was rapidly unfolding. A week earlier, President Ford had sent General Fred Weyand, the army chief of staff, and Graham Martin, the US ambassador to Vietnam, back there for an assessment. David Kennerly—who had spent time in Vietnam and had won the Pulitzer Prize for the haunting photographs he'd taken there prior to becoming the chief White House photographer—had asked if he could go along to provide President Ford with a personal, nonpolitical account of what was happening. The visit was cut short as he became part of an emergency evacuation of Americans. Upon returning to the United States, Kennerly flew directly to Palm Springs.

It was eleven o'clock at night when he arrived at the Wilson house, where President and Mrs. Ford were both waiting to greet him. Betty was in her robe, and as soon as she saw David, she ran to him and threw her arms around him.

"Oh, David!" she exclaimed. "We heard your helicopter was shot at! We were so worried!"

It was true. For the next five hours, David recounted harrowing stories of what was happening on the other side of the world. He had broken away from the officials who were involved in meetings to get into the countryside and had even traveled into Cambodia with the help of two CIA agents. He shot dozens of rolls of film of people suffering—such as a woman who'd been hit by shrapnel, dying in her husband's arms—but it was one photo of a little girl wearing a dog tag, with a look of utter hopelessness in her eyes, that tore him to pieces. He'd barely gotten out of Phnom Penh before it fell to the Khmer Rouge, the Cambodian Communist guerrilla force. Then, while flying over the South Vietnamese port of Cam Ranh Bay, his helicopter had been shot at by frustrated South Vietnamese soldiers—friendlies.

"Cambodia is gone," Kennerly said bluntly. "And I don't care what the generals tell you; they're bullshitting you if they say that Vietnam has got more than three or four weeks left. There's no question about it. It's just not gonna last."

Both Betty and Jerry hung on his every word. They trusted him implicitly.

"Mr. President," Kennerly said, "those people are scared to death. We've got to get those people out of there. Not just the Americans."

The Fords listened to his stories all night. And the next day, after he'd developed the photos, they saw the horrifying reality in black and white.

President Ford announced that because of the rapidly deteriorating situation in Vietnam, there were going to be a series of thirty "babylift" operations:

"I have directed that money from a two-million-dollar special foreign aid children's fund be made available to fly two thousand South Vietnamese orphans to the United States as soon as possible."

Tragically, the first plane, carrying around three hundred passengers, mainly orphans, crashed just minutes after takeoff, killing more than half of those on board.

Betty was crushed by the news of so many innocent children dying. The whole situation in Vietnam just seemed to go from bad to worse.

The babylift operation continued, and the next day the Fords flew up to San Francisco to receive the first planeload of orphans to arrive in the United States. The plane was filled to the brim with children, many unsettled and sick after such a tiring and emotional journey.

Because of her chemotherapy, Betty's resistance to disease had been suppressed, and her doctors had said she couldn't mingle with the children. She was restless, standing in a separate viewing area, watching as her husband held and comforted some of them. She wanted to hold the children, make them feel better. She had even considered adopting one of them for her own. But just to hug them would have been enough, and she couldn't even do that. It broke her heart.

While the Fords were in Palm Springs, Nancy Howe and her husband, James, had traveled to the Dominican Republic with their daughter Lise Courtney as guests of a flamboyant South Korean businessman and lobbyist named Tongsun Park. It is illegal for anyone working in the government to accept personal gifts worth more than $50 from a representative of another government, and because of Nancy's connection to the White House, the press had been nosing around. Indeed, there was an ongoing White House inquiry into the relationship between the Howes and Tongsun Park.

They came home, and three days later, James W. "Jimmy" Howe shot himself to death.

Betty was shocked and deeply saddened when she learned of Howe's death and the allegations. But mostly she was concerned about Nancy. She called Nancy immediately and tried to console her.

Betty attended the funeral privately, with no press. To her, this was a purely personal matter. But the following day, it was announced that Nancy would no longer be employed at the White House. The press had a field day and insinuated that Betty Ford had fired her longtime personal assistant and "best friend" in the midst of Howe's grief.

"Well, I didn't fire Nancy Howe," Betty later said adamantly. "When I was told she had to leave, I cried. Her own psychologist and another psychologist met with Dr. Lukash and decided that she wasn't in shape to stay on. There was a feeling that the circumstances of Jimmy's death would make it difficult for her to handle a sensitive and burdensome job."

That, and the ongoing investigation into the Howes' relationship with Tongsun Park. It was a terrible situation all the way around. Because of the investigation, Betty would not be permitted to speak to her friend for months. "It broke my heart," she said. "I wanted in the worst way to be with Nancy through that period."

Nancy Howe was never charged with any wrongdoing, but Tongsun Park would eventually be indicted on charges of illegally influencing US politicians and officials in connection with the Korean Central Intelligence Agency.

That same week, North Carolina voted down the Equal Rights Amendment, which meant it would not be passed in 1975. It had been a rough week. And while Betty had her burdens, she knew they didn't compare to the weight her husband shouldered. Two weeks after Jimmy Howe's funeral came the fall of Saigon, on April 30.

As President Ford would recall in retrospect: "The South Vietnamese forces were inadequate to protect us, and our only choice was to get out all American personnel, military and civilian, and as many of our South Vietnamese friends as possible. Our forces were literally surrounded at the embassy. It was some hectic, tragic twenty-four hours. To see that transpiring was probably as low a point in my administration as any."

Upstairs at the White House, Betty sat with Susan, David Kennerly, Dr. Lukash, Ric Sardo, and Sheila Weidenfeld as news of the evacuation came in. They learned that two US Marine guards had been killed.

"They were only nineteen and twenty-two," President Ford said. He looked so weary. With children near those same ages, Betty sensed her husband's feelings of helplessness.

Reaching over to touch him, she said softly, "You should write notes to their parents."

He nodded. "Yes. Yes, I will."

Jerry hadn't wanted this job; hadn't asked for it. Betty's heart ached for him, knowing the responsibility he carried alone.

At the end of May 1975, Betty went on her first overseas trip as first lady. She'd been scheduled to go to Japan and Martinique the previous fall, but breast cancer had intervened. Now she was feeling great, and she was excited to accompany President Ford on a whirlwind trip to Belgium, Spain, Austria, and Italy.

Every day of the six-day trip was planned to the minute, detailed in a loose-leaf notebook with a plastic cover marked simply "Schedule." Betty had gotten much better about her notorious lateness, but to help ensure that she would be on time to events, while still looking her best—"there wasn't any time to come into a city and ask which way to the beauty salon"—the president paid to have her hairdresser, Jim Merson, come along.

Additionally, Betty was given personal background papers on everyone she would meet. There was a photo of the person in the upper-right-hand corner, and on the left side was written the person's name, how he or she should be addressed, individual interests, history, any imprudent or taboo subjects, and where each one ranked in the political pecking order.

The trip was filled with pomp and circumstance. Colorful parades, lavish dinners in palaces with kings and queens, princes and princesses. The schedule was arduous, but Betty kept up and told the accompanying press, "My health is good, and I'm having a ball!"

Meanwhile, back in Washington, history was being made, as the first-ever senior prom was being held in the White House.

"Be good," Betty had said as she kissed Susan goodbye the morning they left. But she wasn't worried. She was leaving her daughter with the best chaperones in the world: Aunt Janet and the Secret Service.

Susan nearly didn't have a date; she had recently broken up with her boyfriend Gardner Britt. But the seventeen-year-old ended up asking twenty-one-year-old Billy Pifer, a premed student at Washington and Lee University she had met a few weeks earlier. To begin the evening, Susan and Billy, along with three other couples, enjoyed a preprom dinner of beef Stroganoff and a glass or two of white wine, while cruising down the Potomac on the presidential yacht *Sequoia*. Then Secret Service agents drove the party back to the White House just in time to welcome the other seventy Holton-Arms High School seniors and their dates for one unforgettable senior prom.

The senior class had raised $1,300 to pay for refreshments—Swedish meatballs and quiche, along with a nonalcoholic punch—and two bands. Most of the young men had hair that touched their shoulders, as was the style at the time, and the girls wore long dresses pinned with corsages presented to them by their dates. Susan looked beautiful in a long, peach-colored Albert Capraro dress she and her mother had picked out together in New York, and she was every bit the poised hostess. The press was on hand to capture the unique White House event, and Betty would read that her daughter was dancing (butt) cheek to (butt) cheek, otherwise known as the bump, with her tuxedo-clad date until one thirty in the morning.

One of the things President Ford had missed ever since moving to the White House was his daily swim. An indoor swimming pool had been installed in the West Wing during Franklin D. Roosevelt's administration and had been enjoyed by presidents and their families until Nixon had it removed to make space for a Press Room. President Ford, being an avid swimmer, recognized that a swimming pool would make a good addition to the White House, not only for him and his family but also for future residents. A White House Swimming Pool Committee had been formed the previous fall, and private donors, many of whom were friends of the Fords from Grand Rapids, funded the design and construction, which was overseen and approved by the Secret Service as well as the Fine Arts Commission. When the twenty-two-by-fifty-four-foot pool was completed in July, President Ford invited the press to take photos of him swimming laps, and from then on, he used it almost daily when he was in residence.

One of the biggest questions that still loomed over President Ford was whether he would run for president in 1976. A group of conservative Republican senators had concluded that because neither the president nor Vice President Nelson Rockefeller had been elected to office (Ford had appointed Rockefeller under the terms of the 25th Amendment), it would be in the best interest of the Republican Party, and of the country, for the 1976 presidential nomination to be sought and won in an open convention.

Jerry had promised Betty he would retire in 1977—but that was before their world had turned upside down. As with every major decision, the Fords discussed it as a family. A presidential campaign was a completely different ball game than a congressional campaign in the

Fifth District of Michigan, and it would involve everyone in the family. They were coming up on one year of being in the White House, and no one was more surprised than the first lady when she finally came to realize she had enjoyed it.

"I was willing to take on four more years in the White House," Betty said. "And when the time came, I felt Jerry would be the best man for the job." The children agreed, and on July 8, 1975, Jerry Ford announced that he would seek the Republican Party's nomination to run for president in 1976.

With Nancy Howe gone, Betty needed to find a replacement as soon as possible. Nancy Chirdon, who had been brought in to help with the mail after Betty's mastectomy, had stayed on as an assistant to Sheila Weidenfeld, and she had impressed the first lady. Betty had learned a great deal from the Nancy Howe situation, however, and she decided to have two assistants share the duties equally. Nancy Chirdon would be one, and Carolyn Porembka, who had been Nancy Howe's secretary, would be the other.

While there were always far more invitations than Betty could accept, there was one event she wouldn't miss for all the world: a gala fund-raiser for the fiftieth anniversary celebration of Martha Graham's dance company. She flew to New York City for a sneak preview of the upcoming one-night presentation of *Lucifer*, a ballet that Graham had choreographed especially for Rudolf Nureyev and Dame Margot Fonteyn. It was the first time she had seen Martha Graham since she'd left New York City nearly forty years earlier, promising to return after six months.

At eighty years old, Martha was still as toned and perfect as Betty remembered. In response to reporters covering the event, Betty said Martha had always been a source of strength.

"She was my teacher, and she shaped my whole life," Betty said, choking back emotion. "She gave me the ability to stand up to all the things that I have had to go through with, I believe, much more courage than I would have had, had it not been for her." She turned to her mentor and beamed. "Thank you, Martha!"

Comedian and film director Woody Allen had paid $5,000 to be

Mrs. Ford's escort to the star-studded gala. He too had studied under Martha Graham, but quit because, he said, "he didn't like wearing leotards." He showed up in a tuxedo and black-and-white Converse sneakers, while Betty looked ravishing—as glamorous as any of the movie stars in attendance—in a flowing lavender Halston gown. Glowing with elation, she was back in the world of dance that was so much a part of her soul. During intermission, Betty appeared with Martha, Woody, and Woody's girlfriend, actress Diane Keaton, to speak to the press.

"This means a very great deal to me," Betty said. "One of the most exciting things in my life."

"And how do you feel being the first lady's escort?" a reporter called out to Woody Allen.

"We're just good friends," he quipped.

At the end of the performance, Betty was invited onstage. The crowd stood and cheered as the first lady of the nation and the first lady of modern dance exchanged curtseys and bouquets of roses, a reunion forty years in the making.

As Betty soaked in the applause and adoration that evening, little did she know that the steely courage Martha Graham had instilled in her was about to be tested yet again.

For several months, Don Hewitt, the executive producer of TV's *60 Minutes,* had been trying to snare an interview with Mrs. Ford. Sheila Weidenfeld knew the show would be a great way for the American public to really get to know her, but at the same time, if she wasn't confident enough or well prepared, it could destroy not only her reputation but also be politically disastrous for the president. Sheila had been putting off Hewitt with the excuse that Mrs. Ford's health was still fragile, and she just wasn't ready. Finally, by the summer of 1975, with Jerry's announcement to run, the time seemed right, and Betty agreed to do it. It would be her first in-depth television interview since she'd become first lady.

The CBS crew arrived at dawn to begin setting up in the third-floor solarium. Meanwhile, Betty had her makeup and hair done before getting dressed for her television debut. She'd chosen a beige-peach jersey dress with soft, flowing long sleeves, accented with white linen trim on the collar and waist, designed by Cuban American designer Luis Estévez. A long scarf in the same color as the dress, which she had draped loosely around her neck and fastened with a decorative pin at her collarbone, gave the outfit an added pop of sophistication without being over-the-top.

Don Hewitt and forty-three-year-old correspondent Morley Safer came up to the second-floor West Lobby sitting room to meet Betty before they began the interview.

"I had never met her before," Safer recalled. "And I didn't expect to find a woman so strong and straight and frank."

Hewitt and Safer were pros at making their subject feel comfortable and relaxed, conversing in idle chitchat, while saving the zingers for when the cameras rolled.

As soon as everything was ready, they proceeded upstairs to the solarium.

"When we sat down to talk, there was no period of awkwardness or discomfort; we chatted with great ease," Morley Safer said.

"Look," Betty said, "you can ask me anything you want, and I'll tell the truth. I'm such a lousy liar, if I tried to lie to you, it would be transparent anyway."

Sheila Weidenfeld stood off to the side, watching and listening intently as the interview progressed. From what she observed in the monitors, she thought Betty appeared relaxed and had an "enthusiastic, excellent camera presence."

As Safer pried and probed into her personal life and that of her family, Sheila felt she was "open but not outspoken. Honest. She sounded just plain intelligent. The words seemed as legitimate as the smile."

"I was delighted," Sheila said. "So were they. So was she." The show would air three weeks later, a day after the one-year anniversary of the day Gerald Ford had been sworn into office.

That Sunday, August 10, 1975, the Fords had flown to Vail. Everyone was excited to see Betty's television debut, and that evening, she and Jerry, along with Don Rumsfeld, Press Secretary Ron Nessen, and some friends from Vail, all gathered around the television in the living room of Dick Bass's house.

The ticktock-ticktock signature sound of the *60 Minutes* broadcast began, and then Morley Safer appeared. "Elizabeth Ann Bloomer was her name when she was born in Chicago fifty-seven years ago and grew up in Grand Rapids," he began.

Safer gave a brief synopsis of her life up to marrying a congressman—without mentioning him by name—and moving to Washington. "Then followed more than twenty years of housewifery and the obscurity that comes of living in the shadow of a politician. Well, a year ago this weekend, Jerry and Betty Ford found themselves in the unsought position of president and first lady. When we went to the White House to chat with Betty Ford, we expected to find, quite honestly, a rather bland and predictable political wife. We found instead an open woman with a mind of her own, prepared to talk about anything. No taboos."

Then, there she was, from head to shoulders filling up the entire screen, her reddish-brown hair perfectly coiffed, her eyes sparkling, looking equal parts glamorous model and woman next door.

"I told my husband if we have to go to the White House, 'Okay, I will go,'" Betty said. "'But I'm going as myself. And it's too late to change my pattern. And if they don't like it, then they'll just have to throw me out.'"

It was a wonderful beginning. Safer asked her about the difficulties of being a political wife.

"I had twenty-six years of experience as the wife of a congressman," she said, noting that she had learned a bit in all that time. "You know, I wasn't sitting around being a dummy."

In an effort to probe deeper, Safer asked, "But would you advise your daughter to marry a politician?"

"That's a hard question," Betty answered as she broke into a smile.

"Would you advise against it?" Safer queried.

"No, I would not advise her against marrying a politician," Betty said, her lips pressed together, with a slight uptick at the edges, just short of a smile. "I wouldn't pick one out for her though," she quickly added with a laugh.

It was terrific. Betty was sitting with perfect posture, as she always did, but she'd draped her arm casually on the back of the overstuffed yellow sofa, which made her come across like she was having a spontaneous chat with a neighbor. And even when Safer began asking more personal questions, Betty wasn't ruffled at all.

He asked about the political pressures on a marriage and even went so far as to ask if she worried about her husband philandering with "some of the attractions in this city."

"I have perfect faith in my husband," she said. "And he really doesn't have time for outside entertainment." She paused, and then, with a glint in her eyes and a coy smile, she quipped, "Because I keep him busy."

Jerry grabbed a small pillow from the sofa and, suppressing an embarrassed smile, tossed it at her. He hadn't expected his wife to discuss their sex life on national television.

Safer addressed her admission that she'd seen a psychiatrist. "I found it very helpful," she said without shame.

They talked about her outspokenness on the ERA and how she would continue to work toward getting it passed, and on her formula for a successful marriage.

"It shouldn't be fifty-fifty. It should instead be seventy-thirty, with each side giving seventy and expecting thirty in return . . . and when you're going overboard like that, trying to please each other, you can't help but be happy."

He tried to get her to expose problems in the marriage. What did they fight over?

Only "very minor details," she admitted. Most disagreements were "probably because I was late."

Money? "No, we never had any money to fight over," she retorted with yet another engaging smile.

And what kind of influence did she have on her husband? Betty acknowledged that, yes, she had urged him to put a woman in a Cabinet position, and he had named Carla Hills to be US Secretary of Housing and Urban Development, but she was also working on another.

"If I can get a woman on the Supreme Court bench, then I'll feel I would have accomplished a great deal."

Safer noted that Betty had spoken out about subjects that were considered taboo for the wife of a president, such as abortion. Before he could finish his thought, she interjected, "Well, if you're asked a question, you have to be honest, exactly how you feel. And I feel very strongly that it was the best thing in the world when the Supreme Court voted to legalize abortion, and, in my words, bring it out of the backwoods and into the hospitals where it belonged. It was a great, great decision."

And what about people living together before they're married? "Well, they are, aren't they?" Betty replied with a laugh. Her candor was so refreshing and yet startling at the same time. No first lady had ever appeared on television like this before.

Then came a zinger. "What if Susan Ford came to you and said, 'Mother, I'm having an affair'?"

There was ever so slight a pause before she replied, "Well, I wouldn't be surprised. She's a perfectly normal human being, like all young girls."

Uh-oh. Everyone in the living room in Vail took a deep breath.

Betty went on, "If she wanted to continue it, I would certainly counsel or advise her on the subject. And I'd want to know pretty much about the young man she was having the affair with."

Oh dear.

"In some cases," Betty added, "perhaps there would be less divorce."

Next, Morley Safer turned to the issue of drugs, and whether she worried about her own children "going wrong" with drugs.

"We've brought them up with a certain moral value," she said, but added, "I'm not saying that they haven't tried it, because I'm sure they've all probably tried marijuana."

The wife of the president of the United States had just admitted her children had probably dabbled in an illegal substance. *Oh my.*

"Would Betty Bloomer have been the kind of girl who would have experimented with marijuana?" Safer asked.

"Oh, I'm sure I probably, when I was growing up, at their age, I probably would have been interested to see what the effect . . . I never would have gone into it as a habit or anything like that. It's the type of thing young people have to experience, like your first beer or your first cigarette, something like that."

Safer seemed like he could hardly believe this was the first lady of the United States, and he attempted to make that point: Wasn't it unusual for her to be speaking out on all these previously "forbidden" issues?

Betty, full of confidence, almost defiant, interjected, "But also, didn't the fact that I had the cancer operation and the publicity of that save a lot of people's lives?"

Safer had to admit that was true. "Was that a conscious decision?" he asked.

"Definitely," Betty said. "I felt that if I had it, many other women had it. Because I had no idea about it whatsoever, and it came about as a complete surprise. One day"—she snapped her fingers—"like that. And the next day, I was in the hospital. And I thought there are women all over the country like me, and if I don't make this public, then their lives will be gone. They're in jeopardy."

Betty professed that it was her faith in God that carried her through the difficult times in her life, and acknowledged proudly that both she and the president prayed every night before going to sleep. Finally, Safer asked about the current state of her health.

Without hesitation, she said she'd never felt better. "Absolutely marvelous." But that didn't mean she was going to live forever. "Some people go three years, some people go four years, but . . . I'm convinced in my own mind that I'm completely cured."

And what about that pinched nerve? That, she admitted, still gave her trouble, but "You know, everybody can't be perfect," Betty said. "You have to suffer a little to appreciate life."

And with that, the segment ended. Betty looked over at Jerry and said, "Well?"

"I think you just cost me ten million votes," President Ford deadpanned. And then, breaking into a smile, "No, I think you cost me twenty million votes."

"Nonsense!" Don Rumsfeld chimed. "She won you thirty million votes!"

The morning after the interview, "All hell broke loose," recalled Patti Matson, the first lady's assistant press secretary. "Her exact words, as quoted in the newspapers, were startling to many and outrageous to others. If a person hadn't seen the interview in person, there was no context, no understanding that her statements were in direct response to specific questions. Without seeing it, many wouldn't have heard the tone of her answers or seen her soft demeanor."

Indeed, the *New York Times* declared, "Betty Ford said today that she wouldn't be surprised if her daughter Susan, eighteen years old, decided to have an affair . . . Mrs. Ford suggested that in general, premarital relations with the right partner might lower the divorce rate."

And with that, the outcry began. "My stock with the public did not go up," Betty recalled. "It went down, rapidly." The White House was inundated with letters, wires, and phone calls, two-thirds of them against her. "The furor after *60 Minutes* terrified me. I was afraid I might have become a real political liability to Jerry."

Indeed, Morley Safer acknowledged that "Even though Mrs. Ford had said more or less the same things in print, the reaction to her saying them on television caused a national stir, and it brought the biggest mail response we've ever had."

More than half the letters were in this vein: "I don't know which was more tasteless, your questions or her answers." Another viewer wrote, "Your appalling interview with Betty Ford was the last straw. It sickens me to know that a person with such . . . values is our first lady."

But there was quite a bit of mail like this: "What a woman! Jerry sure is a lucky guy to have her by his side."

A woman in Dallas wrote: "Because of her, I just might vote Republican for the first time in my life." And still another: "Regardless of who is elected president in '76, I move Betty Ford be retained as first lady."

Feelings at the White House were mixed too. "I had a little trouble with Donald and Dick," Betty said, referring to Don Rumsfeld and Dick Cheney. "They were unhappy about my *60 Minutes* interview."

Indeed, despite Rumsfeld's initial quip that Betty had won her husband "thirty million votes," the segment had caused so much controversy that Rumsfeld and Cheney had brought up the subject with President Ford.

"We think Betty needs to lay low for a while," Cheney advised. "Do you think you could get her to tone it down?"

President Ford looked at his two aides and said, "If you want Betty to tone it down, then you tell her."

When White House press secretary Ron Nessen issued a statement saying the president "had long ceased to be perturbed by his wife's remarks," that caused yet another round of critiques.

It was decided that an acknowledgment letter be sent by Betty to everyone who responded negatively to her appearance. Sheila Weidenfeld and Betty worked on it together to make sure it had just the right tone. The letter would not be revealed directly to the press, but Weidenfeld's plan was that some ordinary citizen would pass it along. Eventually, one recipient handed it over to the *New York Times,* which printed it in its entirety.

Thank you for writing about my appearance on the "60 Minutes" interview. The concern which inspired you to share your views is appreciated.

I wish it were possible for us to sit down together and talk, one to another. I consider myself a responsible parent. I know I am a loving one. We have raised our four children in a home that believes in and practices the enduring values of morality and personal integrity.

As every mother and father knows, these are not easy times to be a parent. Our convictions are continually being questioned and tested by the fads and fancies of the moment. I believe our values to be eternal, and I hope I have instilled them in our children.

We have come to this sharing outlook through communication, not coercion. I want my children to know that their concerns—their doubts and their difficulties—whatever they may be, can be discussed with the two people in this world who care the most— their mother and father.

On "60 Minutes," the emotion of my words spoke to the need of this communication, rather than the specific issues we discussed.

My husband and I have lived twenty-six years of faithfulness in marriage. I do not believe in premarital relations, but I realize many in today's generation do not share my views. However, this must never cause us to withdraw the love, the counseling, and the understanding that they may need now, more than ever before.

This is the essence of responsible parenthood. It is difficult to adequately express one's personal convictions in a fifteen-minute interview. I hope our lives will say more than words about our dedication to honor, to integrity, to humanity, and to God.

You and I, they and I, have no quarrels.

Sincerely, Betty Ford

Sheila Weidenfeld would refer to it later as "the perfect letter." Indeed, as soon as it became public, the tide turned. After conducting yet another poll, the *New York Daily News* declared "Keep Speaking Out, Betty!"

When asked "Should Betty Ford have aired her views on premarital sex, pot, and abortion?"—60 percent responded "yes"; 32 percent, "no"; and 8 percent, "don't know."

The reaction to Mrs. Ford's remarks appeared to depend very much on the age, education, and income of the respondent. Among people under age thirty-five, 80 percent approved of her, as did those who had college degrees and earned more than $20,000 in annual income.

Amid the furor, to show she had no regrets or blame, Betty sent Morley Safer a photo of the two of them taken during the interview. She inscribed it:

> Dear Morley,
>   If there are any questions you forgot to ask—I'm grateful.
>   Sincerely, Betty Ford

17

Two Assassination Attempts

One year after moving into the White House, in an interview with *McCall's* magazine, Betty said, "I think I have learned over the past months the positiveness of the position—which I hadn't realized before. I have grown. I have come to realize the power of being able to help."

Ironically, the White House, a place she'd once dreaded, is what gave her a new sense of herself. The article stated, "And while she acknowledged a loss of privacy and anonymity as first lady, the role gave her an exalted status and a chance to influence public thinking that is unparalleled for any other woman in this country."

On Friday, September 5, Betty was upstairs in the White House, sitting at the small desk in her study and talking on the telephone, when the White House operator cut in.

"Mrs. Ford, I have an emergency call from Mr. Keiser."

Before she could even wonder why Dick Keiser, the special agent in charge of President Ford's Secret Service detail, would be cutting in, Keiser said, "Hello, Mrs. Ford. Not to worry. The president is all right. There was an incident in Sacramento. A woman with a gun."

Betty was too stunned to say anything. Keiser reiterated, "The president is all right. He is in a meeting with Governor Jerry Brown now. I'll give you more details as soon as I have them."

As soon as his meeting with the governor was finished, Jerry called Betty. He knew the agents had already informed her, but he just wanted to reassure her he was fine.

Every president receives threats, and, at that time, President Ford was getting about a hundred per month. "But I had never worried about them because of my confidence in the professionalism of the agents guarding me," Ford wrote. Betty was concerned, but he assured her that his confidence had not been misplaced; Larry Buendorf and the other agents had done a superb job.

Later, she would learn how quickly it happened; how close her husband came to being shot.

It was shortly before ten in the morning, and the sun was shining brightly when the president came out of the historic Senator Hotel in downtown Sacramento, California. The Secret Service had his limousine waiting, ready to transport him to the Statehouse building two blocks away.

President Ford turned to the acting agent in charge, Ernie Luzania, and said, "Ernie, it's such a beautiful day, I'd rather walk than drive."

"Of course, Mr. President," Luzania said. Across the street, the police had set up rope lines, and a crowd had gathered, hoping to catch a glimpse of the president.

"Hello, Mr. President!" people shouted, waving.

"Suddenly he darts across the street," Agent Larry Buendorf recalled, "and, of course, we just fell into position. My position was at his left side, right next to him."

President Ford was smiling, reaching out to the crowd with both hands, as the people clamored to have the chance to shake his hand. A petite young woman wearing a long red dress stepped forward. Just as the president stuck out his hand toward her, she reached down and pulled out a Colt .45 from an ankle holster hidden beneath the hem of her dress.

Larry Buendorf saw the unusual movement, the flicker of metal.

"Gun!" he shouted as he leaped forward to grab the pistol.

Buendorf twisted the woman's hand behind her back, disabling her, as the other agents formed a protective cocoon around the president and whisked him away. The woman would be identified as Lynette "Squeaky" Fromme, a twenty-six-year-old follower of Charles Manson.

"The pistol was loaded with four rounds, and she was pulling the slide back when I hit it," Buendorf recalled. "So she never chambered her round."

President Ford went into the scheduled meeting with Governor Brown, and at first, he didn't even mention what had happened. When someone else told the governor, Brown asked, in disbelief, "Why didn't you tell me, Mr. President?"

"Well, I didn't think it would be very polite to tell you that one of your constituents tried to kill me on the way to your office," Ford said with a smile.

The entire family was shaken to its core. "I remember Mom telling us we need to be good soldiers," Steve recalled.

"Don't let Dad know you're worried. He's got the weight of the world on his shoulders, and we can't let him know how scared we are. We'll put on smiling faces."

When the president arrived back at the White House, Betty was waiting, eager to see him, and give him a long embrace.

Looking back many years later, Steve said, "You know, that was a great thing about Mom and Dad. They both knew how to handle situations."

Agent Larry Buendorf had remained in Sacramento for debriefing by the FBI, but as soon as he returned to the White House, Betty grabbed him and gave him a hug.

"I'm so thankful you were there, Larry," she said.

"Everyone did the right thing at the right time," Larry replied, not wanting to accept special recognition. "It's our job. It's what we train for."

From that point on, every time the president left the White House, Betty would go on the balcony and wave goodbye as the helicopter took off from the South Grounds. "It was very scary. I would pray that he came back safely," she said.

From that day on, Betty was understandably anxious about her husband traveling, and when he had another trip to California two weeks later, she decided to accompany him. It was her first time joining Jerry on a political trip—what Sheila Weidenfeld referred to as a "handshaking" trip in which Betty came as "wife" in the most traditional sense: "a sweet smiler, who beams with pride at the magnificence of the oratorical power of her man."

"I was appalled," Sheila recalled. "Don't take the woman Americans have come to respect as an honest, forthright, intelligent lady who speaks her mind and make her into a podium princess!"

President and Mrs. Ford left Washington Friday afternoon, September 19, and after stopping in Oklahoma City for appearances at several events—including a thousand-person Republican fund-raiser—they flew on to Los Angeles, arriving late that night, where they stayed at the Century Plaza Hotel. The next two days, they were guests of Leonard Firestone, the US ambassador to Belgium, and his wife, Nicky, at their home, Ryomi, in Pebble Beach. The president played golf at Cypress Point Golf Course, and Betty joined him later for a private lunch with the Firestones, as well as a number of prominent guests: former Republican congressman Jack Westland; longtime friend Leon Parma, an executive with Teledyne Ryan Aeronautical Company; and local celebrities such as actor Clint Eastwood, entertainer and television mogul Merv Griffin, and famed photographer Ansel Adams, along with his wife. Betty enjoyed meeting so many interesting people, and despite her press secretary's view that she was along as a "podium princess," President Ford always enjoyed having her by his side, and she loved being there.

It had been a jam-packed few days, so when the president had a speech in San Francisco that Monday, Betty decided to spend a relaxing morning in Pebble Beach. She'd meet him later at the airport in San Francisco for the return flight to Washington.

Betty's plane was scheduled to arrive at the San Francisco International Airport in time for her to transfer to Air Force One and be aboard when the president's motorcade arrived. During the short flight from Monterey, Secret Service agent Dick Hartwig was trying to make radio contact with San Francisco, but he couldn't raise anyone. The channels had been closed.

Just before landing, a call came through. "Move Pinafore to Angel with all possible speed."

In code, that meant, "Get Mrs. Ford to Air Force One as quickly as possible." But with no other information, Hartwig wasn't concerned.

When they arrived at the airport, Betty noticed that the Secret Service cars were not lined up as they usually were, and there were agents standing all around the presidential plane. Dick Hartwig and Pete Sorum, her staff advance man, each grabbed one of Betty's arms and whisked her up the steps and inside Air Force One. She walked into the presidential cabin and was surprised to see Jerry already there, sitting with his staff.

"Well, how did they treat you in San Francisco?" she asked breezily.

President Ford turned to Rumsfeld, "You tell her, Rummy."

There had been another assassination attempt. And this time, the gun *had* gone off. Another woman, Sara Jane Moore, a political leftist, fired one shot, but narrowly missed the president.

As soon as Air Force One took off, the stewards were summoned. "Quite a few martinis were consumed on the flight back," press secretary Ron Nessen recalled.

Susan was upstairs in the White House solarium with a friend who was visiting from Vail. They were lying on the floor watching television. "We had two televisions in there so you could watch two different things at the same time, which we thought was very cool," Susan recalled. "The phone rang, and it was one of my agents. I got the news just before both stations broke into a news report of the assassination attempt."

Steve Ford was at his girlfriend's parents' house, also watching television. There was an urgent knock on the door. One of his agents, who had been sitting outside in the car, came in and said, "Shots were fired at your father, but he's okay." At the same moment, a special news bulletin interrupted the regular programming they'd been watching.

"The country hears, 'Someone has shot at the president,'" Steve reflected. "But we hear, 'Someone tried to kill your father.' It's a dramatic difference."

On October 25, Betty flew to Cleveland, Ohio, to give the keynote speech at a three-day conference for International Women's Year. Three thousand people filled the auditorium as Betty stepped up to the podium. She knew that, in the wake of the controversy her remarks on *60 Minutes* had sparked, this was an important speech—not just for her personally but also for women all over the world.

For those who knew her, it was evident that speaking before such a crowd was still outside her comfort zone. For those in the audience, she appeared humble, relatable. After thanking the people for the privilege of addressing them, she began to deliver the speech, which she and her staff had crafted meticulously word by word.

"While many new opportunities are open to women, too many are available only to the lucky few," Betty said. "Many barriers continue to block the paths of most women, even on the most basic issue of equal pay for equal work."

Within a few sentences, the crowd erupted in applause. Betty smiled appreciatively.

"And the contributions of women as wives and mothers continue to be underrated." More cheering and applause.

In the twelve-minute speech, Betty said that the limits on women originated from emotional ideas on what women should or shouldn't do, and that they have been "formalized into law and structured into social custom."

Despite the backlash from her previous statements on *60 Minutes*, she did not hesitate to reference her views on the Equal Rights Amendment.

"But my own support of the Equal Rights Amendment has shown what happens when a definition of proper behavior collides with the right of an individual to personal opinions. I do not believe that being first lady should prevent me from expressing my views."

The crowd went wild. This was exactly what they wanted to hear from their first lady.

"I spoke out on this important issue because of my deep personal convictions," Betty continued. "Why should my husband's job, or yours, prevent us from being ourselves?" She paused, and then delivered a zinger: "Being ladylike does not require silence."

Betty went on to say that part of their job—and hers—was to remove the "cloud of fear and confusion" from people who found it difficult to accept the national social changes taking place: namely, the idea of the Equal Rights Amendment.

"I have had the best of two worlds: that of a career woman earning my own living, and that of a homemaker and mother raising four individual and delightful youngsters. I am equally proud of both periods in my life. We have to take that 'just' out of 'just a housewife' and show our pride in having made the home and family our life's work."

The speech was not long, but it was intended to clarify the issues that were causing the emotional hysteria around the ERA, and to point out why she felt it was so critically important.

"Freedom for women to be what they want to be will help complete the circle of freedom America has been striving for, for two hundred years," Betty said. "As the barriers against freedom for Americans because of race or religion have fallen, the freedom of all has expanded. The search for human freedom can never be complete without freedom of women."

The audience roared with approval, bursting into a standing ovation.

"They loved her," Sheila Weidenfeld remembered. "And she was delighted."

That December, President and Mrs. Ford made a momentous trip to the People's Republic of China to tour the sights, learn more about the culture, and foster better relations between the PRC and the United States. Eighteen-year-old Susan got a pass from Mount Vernon College to accompany her parents on what would undoubtedly be a supreme educational experience. It was a four-day trip halfway around the globe during which each member of the Ford family became highly visible ambassadors. Susan set off to photograph the Great Wall, President Ford attended politically important meetings, and Betty wanted to meet Chinese dancers.

It was arranged for Betty to visit the Dance School of the Central May 7 Art College in the capital of Beijing, and she was truly enthralled as she went classroom to classroom watching various dance performances by students of all ages. The dancing was different from anything she had studied, but when the students asked her to join them, she didn't hesitate.

Betty admitted to being somewhat rusty in her steps, but jumped in to join the fun, much to the surprise of the students. "The wife of a president could *never* do that," they whispered, giggling.

Oh, but they hadn't met this wife of this president. Betty smiled, kicked off her shoes, and gracefully followed along to the instruction of student Yu Chan-ha, who guided her in the northern Chinese folk dance. With her arms raised, toes pointed, a smile too natural to fake, Betty was in her element. As soon as she joined in the rhythm, the press cameras flashed, and in newspapers the next day, some reporters suggested that this moment opened more bridges between the two countries than the talk of the diplomats.

One of the most popular television shows in the 1970s was *The Mary Tyler Moore Show*. Actress Mary Tyler Moore played a single woman working in the male-dominated world of TV network news, and although it was a comedy, the show addressed many of the same issues Betty had been speaking out about: premarital sex, women's health, equal pay for equal work. When the show's producers asked Betty if she'd be willing to do a cameo, she agreed happily.

Betty's short appearance—she had just six lines—was filmed in the Hay-Adams Hotel across the street from the White House, shortly before Thanksgiving. The premise of the episode is that Mary and her boss, gruff Lou Grant, played by Ed Asner, are attending a broadcast news seminar in Washington, DC. Grant has bragged about introducing Mary to the movers and shakers he knew in the Capitol, but when a social gathering appears to fall apart, Mary is convinced he'd made everything up. In the end, Grant gets a phone call from Betty Ford, inquiring about whether the president had left his pipe in Grant's hotel room. Grant hands the phone to Mary to speak with the first lady, but Mary, thinking it's all part of a ruse, hangs up on her. Betty had a wonderful time doing it, and when the show aired the following January, her stock went up even further.

What few people knew was that that scene almost didn't make it. The morning of the filming, Betty had a last-minute case of stage fright. She was late to the shooting, and, Mary Tyler Moore would recall, "She had trouble remembering her dialogue, even as I helped her out by giving her cues while standing just to the side of the camera. I felt so sad that this lovely, warm lady couldn't master it on her own."

Even those closest to Betty Ford were confused by the first lady's behavior. Something was going on, but no one could quite figure out what it was. Meanwhile, the calendar had turned to 1976—the nation's bicentennial anniversary, and the year Betty Ford's husband was campaigning to remain president of the United States.

18

"Betty's Husband for President!"

"Nineteen seventy-six is a jumble in my head," Betty wrote in her memoir, "full of days when I just went quickly from one thing to another, changing my clothes. There were state dinners one right after another, and the bicentennial, and campaigning. Campaigning for a solid year."

Indeed, 1976 would test Betty like she'd never been tested before. Former California governor Ronald Reagan had announced his candidacy to challenge President Ford for the Republican nomination, forcing the Ford campaign to pull out all the stops. Because President Ford was, as David Kennerly had once put it, "busy being president," much more pressure fell on Betty, as well as all four Ford children, to actively campaign. The spotlight was on all of them.

In late March, the weather was dreary in the Capitol, and Susan got an invitation to stay at a friend's house in sunny Jamaica for a long weekend. To convince her parents to let her go, she asked her friend Bay Anderson, who had worked at Holton-Arms and was a few years older, to be a "chaperone." A couple of days before they were to leave, Bay came to the White House to help Susan pack.

Clothes were strewn across the bed, and the girls were giddy as they planned their adventure. Betty heard the laughter and came walking into Susan's bedroom.

"Oh, are you two girls getting excited for your trip to Jamaica?" Betty asked as she examined the clothes Susan had laid out.

"Oh yeah," Susan said nonchalantly. Among the T-shirts and shorts, Betty pulled out a skimpy turquoise bikini that was already tucked in the open suitcase.

"Susan, you are not taking this bikini."

"But, Mom . . ." Susan complained.

"No, Susan. Your father is president of the United States. You can't be seen in nothing but strings."

Grudgingly, Susan set aside the bathing suit. But as soon as her mother walked out of the room, it went right back in.

As it turned out, that same weekend, Jacqueline Kennedy Onassis was in Montego Bay, Jamaica, too, with her son, John. At fifteen, John F. Kennedy Jr. still had Secret Service protection—after the assassination of President John F. Kennedy, a law was passed providing Secret Service protection to children of presidents until the age of sixteen—and Susan's agents were in touch with John's. Shortly after they arrived, Agent Tommy Pabst told Susan that John Kennedy wanted to meet her.

"I really wanted to meet him too," Susan recalled. "But I especially wanted to meet his mother because I'd heard so much about her."

Word had gotten out that Jackie Onassis was on the island, and paparazzi were everywhere. But the agents worked everything out so that Susan, Bay, John, and the former first lady had tea together at the Round Hill Hotel without any photographers getting wind of it.

On another day, Susan wasn't so lucky. She and Bay were lying on towels at the beach, working on their suntans, with the agents in swim attire next to them. Susan sat up and grabbed the bottle of suntan oil next to her. Bay was a bit too far away, so Susan said casually, "Tommy, can you put some suntan oil on my back?"

It was purely innocent, but the next day, a photo of the Secret Service agent slathering oil on the back of the president's daughter wearing the forbidden turquoise bikini appeared in the *National Enquirer*.

"Of course I got in trouble," Susan remembered. "And I have a feeling Tommy got in trouble too."

* * *

In 1976, CB radios were one of the hottest new trends. Citizens-band radios, with a range of fifteen to twenty miles, had been used by truckers to communicate on the road, and now they were catching on with average consumers who liked the idea of having a "handle"—a code name of sorts—and talking in a cleverly disguised language. There was even a novelty song about the CB radio craze, "Convoy," by C. W. McCall, which, in January of that year, was the number one single in the country.

Peter Secchia, a friend from Michigan, who was organizing the campaign in Michigan and Wisconsin, had the idea to use CBs for what he called a "scatter blitz." They had a caravan of Ford supporters, each vehicle equipped with a CB radio, and when Peter yelled out "Scatter blitz!" over the radio waves, everyone would jump out of the cars, "scatter," and then "blitz" the area with Ford 1976 flyers and other campaign paraphernalia.

When Betty came to Wisconsin, Peter suggested that she rally the supporters with a send-off over the CB radio. It was new technology, and at first Betty had trouble getting the hang of it. But soon she figured out how to hold down the button while she spoke into the radio. "Keep on talking for President Ford," she said. "We appreciate your help in keeping the Fords' '10-20' at 1600 Pennsylvania Avenue." In CB lingo, 10-20 meant "location."

Truckers loved it, and the press ate it up. Soon the entire country was talking about Betty joining the CB community, and there were contests to come up with her CB handle. She settled on "First Mama," and her popularity soared with a group that she probably would not have reached otherwise.

The long-anticipated bicentennial on July 4, 1976, brought many celebrations and events around the country, and President and Mrs. Ford were the grand masters of the nation's two hundredth birthday celebration.

The president made appearances in Valley Forge and Philadelphia, Pennsylvania, before meeting Betty in New York City, where they each landed in separate helicopters aboard the aircraft carrier USS *Forrestal*. From the flight deck, President Ford rang the bicentennial bell thirteen times—one for each of the original thirteen colonies—sparking off a magnificent parade of tall sailing ships in New York Harbor.

"No tribute could be more spectacular," the commander in chief said. The sailing vessels, which had come from twenty-two nations, were "an escort of grace and beauty into the third century."

It was an incredible sight. Even more spectacular was the sight looking down from the helicopter. Millions of New Yorkers were everywhere: hanging out of windows, standing on rooftops, throngs of people gathered along the Hudson River, and surrounding the Statue of Liberty on Ellis Island. After the traumas of Vietnam and Watergate that had so divided the nation, the bicentennial celebration was something around which all Americans could unite. The day ended back at the White House, and as night fell, Betty and Jerry gathered with a small group of friends and family to watch the dazzling fireworks show over the Washington Monument. Standing on the Truman Balcony, as the colorful bursts lit the night sky, Betty and Jerry stood with their arms around each other, exhausted and overwhelmed by the magnificent sight.

Three days later, President and Mrs. Ford hosted Queen Elizabeth II and Prince Philip for what Betty would recall as the "most glamorous" state dinner during her time in the White House. Plans for the white-tie dinner had been in the works for months, and anyone who had any connection whatsoever was vying for an invitation to what some were calling "the social event of the century." It didn't disappoint.

As with all the state dinners, Betty was very involved with every detail. She and the president had gone over the guest list together, which included Lady Bird Johnson, Ella Fitzgerald, Cary Grant, Willie Mays, Billy Graham, Barbara Walters, David Brinkley, and two celebrities specifically requested by the queen herself: comedian Bob Hope and actor Telly Savalas, who was then starring in the popular crime drama *Kojak*. Betty had spent hours with social secretary Maria Downs drawing up the seating chart, and for the musical entertainment, they'd invited one of the most popular duos at the time, the Captain and Tennille. Dinner would be elegant American cuisine: New England lobster, followed by "Saddle of Veal" with rice and broccoli, and ending with dessert of "Peach Ice Cream Bombe" and fresh raspberries.

The day began with a grand arrival ceremony, after which President and Mrs. Ford brought the queen and the prince upstairs to the Yellow

Oval Room for a private lunch that included Susan and Jack, both of whom were living at the White House at that time. Afterward, Queen Elizabeth and Prince Philip returned to Blair House to prepare for the evening's festivities.

For the dinner, Betty had chosen an elegant mint-green chiffon gown with a lace neckline and flowing sheer sleeves designed by Luis Estévez. Just as she was dressed and ready to go downstairs and greet the royal couple, Jack, who was on hiatus from college, came rushing into the bedroom, searching for studs to put into the shirtfront of his rented tuxedo.

"You're *never* going to be ready," an exasperated Betty huffed, as Jack rummaged through his father's drawer. There was no time to help him search. Betty and the president had to get downstairs to greet their royal guests.

After the initial pleasantries in the main hall, President and Mrs. Ford brought the queen and the prince upstairs for some quiet time before the festivities began.

"Mrs. Ford wanted guests to have a good time, and she worked to put people at ease from the moment the head of state arrived at the White House," assistant secretary Matson recalled. "They would be escorted upstairs to the personal living room in the family quarters. Mrs. Ford understood that a formal dinner at the White House might be nervous-making for guests, and her natural warmth and empathy for others cut across diplomatic lines."

As the elevator doors opened at the second floor, "Jack came flying in, still fiddling with his shirtfront," Betty recalled. "He stood there, mouth open, gaping at the four of us."

Without missing a beat, Queen Elizabeth, dressed in a citron-colored organza gown bedecked with medals, a diamond tiara perched on her head, turned to Betty and, smiling sweetly, quipped, "I have one just like [him] at home."

An elaborate dinner was served in a big tent outside the Rose Garden. "We had violinists stationed along the paths, and to be out in the gorgeous night air, with the moon shining down, and the violins playing as you walked by, was unforgettable," Betty remembered.

Unfortunately, the queen's first dance was also unforgettable. The US Marine Band had a set list of songs to play for the evening, and the tunes were organized in groupings of three. There were no titles on the music, they were listed only by number. The band had just finished one song, when President Ford escorted Queen Elizabeth out to the dance floor. The crowd parted, and the band began to play the next song on its list: which just so happened to be "The Lady Is a Tramp." It was purely coincidental, but it would go down in the annals of White House history as one of the most embarrassing gaffes ever.

Rain poured outside the tent, but nothing could dampen the evening. Captain and Tennille sang their hit "Muskrat Love," Bob Hope had everyone in stitches with his one-liner comedy routine, and the dancing went on and on and on. It was after midnight when the royal guests finally departed, but Betty and the president weren't ready for the night to end. When the band started playing "Chattanooga Choo Choo," Betty grabbed Bob Hope's hand, and the two performed an impromptu floor show for the guests. Everyone loved it, and no one more than Betty herself. She had played hostess to a queen, but on this night, Betty was America's princess. Finally, just before two in the morning, she wanted one last dance with her husband. Swaying cheek to cheek under the crystal chandeliers, Betty was thrilled with the way the evening had turned out.

"If I hadn't kept mixing up Your Highness and Your Majesty—he's His Highness, she's Her Majesty—I'd give myself four stars for the way that visit went off," she wrote.

The next day, the first lady's staff came in, and there on the wall outside their offices was a poster-sized photo of Betty Ford dancing with the incredibly handsome legendary film star Cary Grant.

Betty had written an inscription on the photo: "Eat your hearts out, girls!"

"That gives you a sense of a certain playfulness of her humor," Patti Matson recalled. "She liked us to enjoy ourselves . . . she had a sense of perspective. Work didn't have to be a grind; you could accomplish things and have a good time too."

But amid the good times, something was happening to Betty, and as the campaign wore on, members of the first lady's staff began to become more and more worried about her.

"Mrs. Ford used to be visited periodically by her arthritis specialist," recalled her personal assistant, Nancy Chirdon. Betty had been seeing him since they'd lived in Alexandria. "He loved coming to the White House, but there was no member of the staff or family that appreciated his visits," Nancy said. "He would come up and talk to her, visit with her, but after each visit, the next day—and the next week—she couldn't function well."

One of Nancy's responsibilities was packing the first lady's pillbox: a black case that held all of Mrs. Ford's prescription medications.

"There had to be at least ten bottles lined up side by side in the case," she recalled. "She took it with her all the time." One of the prescriptions was her chemo treatment, which she had to take monthly, but Nancy didn't know exactly what everything else was. "When she had an episode of pain, she'd take a pill. She didn't feel comfortable speaking in public unless it was just off the cuff," Nancy explained. "She just felt as if everything hung on her words. She was conscious during the campaign of her popularity and also of her controversy. The West Wing powers that be and the campaign officials weren't always happy with her, which caused even more pressure, which caused even more pain."

There appeared to be a clear correlation between her stress level and her pain, and the relentless campaign travel schedule made it worse. "We had different mattresses, different pillows, everything was different," Nancy said. Because Betty never knew when the pain would strike, a navy nurse was assigned to travel with her. The nurse would provide hot compresses and massage, but Betty was in complete control of her own medication and took it as needed.

Nancy began to notice dramatic changes in her boss: the first lady's energy was low, she experienced mood swings, and more and more frequently, she was slurring her words. "She didn't seem to be there."

Press Secretary Sheila Weidenfeld also started noticing the changes, and it worried her—not only for Betty's health but also for the image she was projecting as the wife of the presidential candidate. At a reception at the Claremont Hotel in Oakland, California, Sheila recalled that Mrs. Ford "looked exhausted and sounded as though she were having trouble concentrating." She had actually referred to herself as "president," but quickly realized it and added, "Actually, you know, I was president of the Senate wives when my husband was only vice president. I used to kid him about that all the time!"

But then she rambled on about fate and God, without seeming to have a clear point. Later that evening, Sheila mentioned it to one of the Secret Service agents.

"I think she's being overscheduled," he said. "You can only push a human being so far, especially a delicate lady like Mrs. Ford. They're overpushing."

The problem grew worse. Everywhere Betty went, she was greeted with tremendous enthusiasm, but as she went from fish frys for fifteen thousand people to hospital dedications, one speech site after another, in and out of limousines and planes, there was more slurred speech.

Betty noticed the mistakes too, and she was embarrassed. After one speech in which she had "rambled incoherently," she sobbed to Sheila, "How could I do that? I just can't get over it. All those stupid mistakes!"

She vowed never to open her mouth again without a complete text of prepared remarks. Still, Sheila noticed the first lady would be in hysterics one minute, but then she'd pull herself together for a press conference and handle it flawlessly. It was a constant state of highs and lows, completely unpredictable, and while Betty seemed to realize something was wrong, she didn't know what it was.

Sheila didn't understand either. Was it a physical problem or an emotional problem? Or something else altogether? "Where do you draw the line between concerned friend and press secretary?" she wondered.

Nancy Chirdon became so concerned that she decided to talk to the navy nurse about the situation. They concluded that maybe nobody was looking at the medications the doctors were prescribing.

"We figured it was the medication because it was a causal effect," she explained. "You could see the effect it would have on her speech and her demeanor after she would take the medication. But she was like a lot of people, particularly women: when the doctor told you to take something, you take it. And we didn't question it. So, she would take the medication, and we would notice the effects."

After one trip during which Betty's speech was especially slurred, Nancy told the nurse, "I just think there's something wrong here. I want to talk to Dr. Lukash."

The nurse agreed and offered to come with her. A rear admiral, William Lukash was the nurse's superior, so they knew this could be an uncomfortable conversation. But they felt they had no choice. They were deeply concerned about the first lady's health and well-being.

The two women, both just twenty-six years old, walked into Dr. Lukash's office, where he was sitting at his desk.

"Doctor," Nancy said, "I think that the medication Mrs. Ford is on may be too strong."

Doctor Lukash looked at her and stood up, so that he towered over the two petite women.

"What makes you think so?"

Nancy described the effects she saw: the slurred speech, the erratic moods, the way she seemed to zone out after taking some of the pills.

"Those are properly prescribed," he said with a hint of defensiveness. And then, his eyes piercing into hers, he asked, "Where did *you* go to medical school?"

Nancy had not expected this kind of reaction. "I just thought you should be aware," she added. The nurse backed her up. "Yes, we just thought you should be aware."

"Listen," Dr. Lukash said. "I understand the medications Mrs. Ford is on."

"He didn't say 'It's none of your business,'" Nancy recalled, but they were dismissed. Nancy never told Mrs. Ford that she and the nurse had gone to Dr. Lukash. "She would have been mortified. And, as far as I know, the medication was never adjusted."

Separately, Sheila Weidenfeld also confronted Dr. Lukash, after one particularly bad trip to California.

"Is Mrs. Ford all right?" Weidenfeld asked the White House physician.

"What do you mean?" Lukash responded, perplexed. Sheila went on to recount some of the things she'd witnessed. "She was in very bad shape. I've never seen her so depressed. I think it's the pressure. She just can't take it."

"Well, she's all right now," Dr. Lukash said. He didn't think there was anything to worry about. But Sheila persisted. She tried to convince the doctor that the first lady's schedule was causing unnecessary pressure, and it had to be eased up. Additionally, she added, "The pills she is taking are having a very bad effect on her."

"The pills are for her pinched nerve and arthritis," he explained. Another dismissal.

The public, and the press, thus far, hadn't seemed to notice anything unusual. Indeed, Betty's popularity kept growing. The *National Enquirer* asked its readers, "Who would make a better president, Gerald Ford or his wife, Betty?" The result: "a clear victory for his wife, 54 percent to 46 percent."

Social secretary Maria Downs recalled being with Betty in the elevator one day "when her polls were just skyrocketing, and his were down." The first lady turned to Maria and said, "Oh, Maria, what I would give to change polls with Jerry."

Across the country, buttons and bumper stickers sprang up with slogans such as "Betty's Husband for President," "Keep Betty in the White House," "I Love Betty," and even "Betty for President." They weren't the result of any campaign consultation brainstorm. It happened spontaneously nationwide. And to keep the momentum going, more events were added to the first lady's schedule.

The Democrats held their convention at Madison Square Garden in New York City, and on July 15, they selected Georgia governor James "Jimmy" Carter as their presidential nominee. Meanwhile, Ronald Reagan and President Ford were running neck and neck. The Republican nominee would be decided at the Republican National Convention in Kansas City, Missouri, a month later.

Coming into the convention, it was very close. The magic number of delegates needed to get the nomination was 1,130 and James A. Baker III, who would soon be named President Ford's campaign manager, was privately projecting that President Ford was going to get 1,135. Not much margin for error.

The convention opened on Monday, August 16. That night, when Nancy Reagan and Betty Ford entered the convention hall, each received a rousing ovation. The next morning, the press turned it into a popularity contest, won by applause, noting that "the president's wife was applauded long and noisily, but not so long and noisily as was Ronald Reagan's wife."

The following night, once again the wives came to the hall. Mrs. Ford arrived first, wearing a bright yellow dress. As she stepped into the guest section in Kemper Arena, she pumped her right arm, waving to the crowd with a winner's gesture. Standing next to her, Susan was dressed in a white T-shirt with a red button pinned to it that said "I Want Betty's Husband for President," and on Betty's other side stood popular singer Tony Orlando. The crowd went crazy, clapping and hollering for a full five minutes.

An hour later, Mrs. Reagan arrived in a red flowered dress, waving to the crowd as she took her place on the opposite side of the hall. But just as the applause started for her, the convention band started playing "Tie a Yellow Ribbon 'Round the Ole Oak Tree"—the song Orlando and his group Dawn had turned into a number one hit three years earlier. Tony spontaneously grabbed Betty, and the two started dancing in the aisle. All heads turned away from Mrs. Reagan and up to the first lady in the yellow dress and her famous dancing partner. The next morning, the headline in the *New York Times* read: "Betty Ford Bests Nancy Reagan on Applause Scale."

It was a nail-biter of a convention, but President Ford ultimately won the delegates needed and became the Republican nominee.

That final night, President Gerald R. Ford knew his acceptance speech was critical. "Nothing was more important," he recalled. "It just had to get the campaign off and running."

One of his aides brought in a videotape machine so he could watch himself. "At first, it wasn't too good," he acknowledged. He worked on his delivery and then gave the speech in front of his most ardent critic.

"It's much too long," Betty said. "And, you know, Jerry, you have a tendency not to smile. You look like you're ready to shoot someone."

"As usual, she was right," Jerry recalled. They made some cuts, and he worked on smiling.

When he delivered the thirty-eight-minute speech, the delegates applauded an incredible sixty-five times. At the close, the sounds of bells, whistles, and horns erupted as the crowd chanted its support. President Ford had announced Kansas senator Robert Dole as his running mate, and when the speech concluded, Dole and his wife, Elizabeth, joined Jerry and Betty on the stage, along with Ronald and Nancy Reagan, in a show of party unity.

With Betty beaming at his side, "Suddenly," President Ford recalled, "I felt her hand in mine, and all of us—as if by some unspoken signal—clasped our hands and raised them high above our heads."

There was a deafening roar from the crowd, and for everyone watching, the love and pride Betty Ford felt for her husband in that moment was unmistakable.

Coming out of the campaign, a Gallup poll had President Ford trailing Jimmy Carter by 10 points. It was going to be an uphill battle. Jack and Susan had been campaigning all year, but now even Steve, Mike, and Mike's wife, Gayle, joined in. How things had changed in the two years since their father had been thrust into the White House.

"It was something we as a family all came to embrace and commit to," Mike Ford said. He and Gayle were both graduate students, and instead of taking a full course load, he took only one class that fall semester—on a Wednesday—so that he could spend four or five days traveling around the Northeast. "We gave it our all to share the good message of Jerry Ford and his strong leadership, integrity, and the way he brought the country back together, healing the scars of Vietnam and Watergate."

Steve Ford, who'd been attending California State Polytechnic University, Pomona, decided to quit school to campaign for his dad. Betty was skeptical about whether his prime motive was to campaign or to avoid school—especially when, at a family strategy meeting, Steve presented his unique idea to take two friends and a Winnebago camper decorated with banners and stickers and drive through the western United States.

"We took that motor home from California to Oregon, Washington, Idaho, Montana, Wyoming, Utah, New Mexico, and finally ended up in Arizona," Steve recalled, years later. "Lots of small towns and many miles. These were the folks I related to, since I had been working on cattle ranches in the West."

Wearing jeans, Western shirts, and cowboy boots, Steve didn't put on any airs. And when people asked him why he was doing it, he'd say "My father's done a lot for me in the last twenty years, and this gives me a chance to pay him back in a small way."

Steve's sentiments summarized the feelings of the whole family.

Betty joined him in Downey, California, where she proudly introduced herself as "Steve's mother" to a group of voters assembled in a parking lot, and then spent a few hours working the phones at the Republican headquarters.

"Hello, this is Betty Ford," she'd say.

Frequently, the response she'd get was, "You're kidding."

"Yes, really, I'm Betty Ford, calling from Downey," she'd repeat, trying to convince the disbeliever. There'd be a pause, and then a request.

"Well, all right," Betty would say, "go and get your tape recorder."

The previous six months had been taxing, but the next three months were grueling. Betty crisscrossed the country: lunch in a university cafeteria in Oregon; a stop in Sioux Falls, South Dakota, to say hello to a thousand Shriners; a stop in Independence, Missouri; five minutes to meet in an airplane hangar; and on and on. There were plenty of eighteen-hour days. The family split up to cover as much territory as possible, and by Election Day, the race was razor close. In Buffalo, Betty had been invited to be the grand marshal of the Pulaski Day Parade, and the Carter forces countered by sending to town his running mate, Senator Walter Mondale of Minnesota. Betty knew they'd wind up in the reviewing stand together at some point during the festivities, and the press would want pictures of the meeting.

When Senator Mondale came up on the platform, Betty smiled and graciously shook his hand. Then she said, "I have something for you." She reached into her pocket and pulled out a green-and-white campaign button. Green and white were the Carter campaign colors, but the button said "Keep Betty in the White House."

"I believe these are your colors," she said, pinning it right on his lapel. It took Mondale a minute to realize what it said, but as soon as he did, he laughed, and then promptly took it off.

Tuesday, November 2, 1976, the campaign ended where Jerry Ford's career and his marriage to Betty Bloomer had begun twenty-eight years earlier, in Grand Rapids. They flew in separately—he from Canton, Ohio, and she from Harrisburg, Pennsylvania.

As soon as they saw each other, they hugged and kissed. Then together they rode, standing in an open car, hand in hand, through the streets of their hometown, waving to the cheering crowds. It was an amazing spectacle. Fifty thousand people—one-quarter of the city's population—had turned out to express their love and enthusiasm for Jerry and Betty Ford. In a speech at the grand, historic Pantlind Hotel, Ford reflected that the two and a half years he'd been president had been "troubled, and they have been tough. But," he said, "we're going to make America great again."

The president had traveled sixteen thousand miles in ten days and had given so many speeches that his voice was hoarse. He'd thrown out his notes and, with tear-filled eyes, said, "I say to you calmly that I want your prayers for confirmation, but tomorrow I ask for your votes, and I won't let you down."

He turned to Betty and handed her the microphone.

Betty looked out at the crowd. Seeing so many familiar faces and old friends brought back a flood of memories from what seemed to have been a different lifetime.

"I just want to say how absolutely, completely, ecstatically thrilled I am to be here tonight and how proud I am of Jerry and the job he's done. I hope you go out tomorrow and give that old ballot box a good pull for Jerry Ford!"

America had fallen in love with this outspoken, fearless first lady, but nowhere in America did they love her more than in Grand Rapids.

The next morning, Jerry and Betty voted, and then boarded Air Force One to head back to the White House. Whether they'd stay there another four years was now in the hands of the voters.

19

Last Days in the White House

Election Night, 1976

That evening, Betty and Jerry invited a group of close friends and family to watch the election returns in the White House residential quarters. Susan, Steve, Jack, Mike, and Gayle were there, along with Clara and President Ford's brother Tom; Grand Rapids friends Peter and Joan Secchia; former major league baseball player and popular television sportscaster Joe Garagiola, who had played a big role in the campaign; Senator and Mrs. Robert Dole; Senator Jacob Javits of New York; singer Pearl Bailey; as well as assorted staff and others who came and went as the evening progressed.

It was an informal atmosphere, with people gathered around several television sets, sitting in chairs, on sofas, or wandering from room to room. Betty and Pearl Bailey sat together cross-legged on the floor in front of one of the televisions for a while, like two young schoolgirls.

The early evening brought a sense of excitement. There was a feeling that President Ford had narrowed the gap so much on Governor Carter that he might win—that he *could* win. In those days, the Democratic states were red and the Republican states were blue on the television electoral map, and when a state would go blue, Garagiola would call out, "Here we go, Prez! Here we go!" He was the head cheerleader. "Go blue!"

Then around eleven thirty, the mood started to change. President Ford took two calls within that next hour, and the news was not good. At one twenty in the morning, NBC declared that Carter had won New York, and shortly thereafter, Texas went red too. It wasn't looking good, but there was still a narrow path to enough electoral college votes for victory. At roughly three o'clock, Dick Cheney and Bob Teeter, a pollster, came up and talked privately with Ford. The president had all but lost his voice, so he asked Greg Willard to gather everyone together.

Cheney and Teeter explained that the way it was going, the way the numbers were shaping up, the tally of electoral college votes was simply too close to call; the final totals in the key states of Ohio, Wisconsin, and Hawaii likely wouldn't be known for several more hours. At three twenty, Ford realized that "there wasn't a darn thing that I could do," so he went to bed.

Betty couldn't go to sleep until she knew for sure that they'd lost. She stayed up with Susan, Mike and Gayle, Steve, and a few others. Susan was sprawled out on the floor, and the rest of them sat in chairs gathered around the television when, at 3:38 a.m., NBC news anchor John Chancellor announced, "We project that James Earl Carter will be the thirty-ninth president of the United States."

No one said a word. Even though they knew it was probably coming, to hear it announced was like a stake in the heart.

After a few moments, Betty turned to Mike and Greg Willard, who were both sitting to her right, and asked, "Do you think we should wake him up?"

"No," they answered in unison. "Let him sleep."

At that point, NBC cut to a live video feed of Jimmy Carter in Plains, Georgia. Betty looked at the television and said, "Governor, I hope you know what you're getting in for."

Everyone chuckled. Leave it to Betty to lighten the mood. And then she said, "You know, I had the craziest thing happen to me when I was in Pittsburgh . . ." She began to tell a funny story from the campaign trail, and suddenly everyone was laughing hysterically. As soon as she finished, Susan piped up, "Oh, Mother, you won't believe what happened to me in this one parade . . ." Soon it was this cacophony of everyone telling stories of funny things that had happened during the campaign.

Finally, about four thirty, Betty went into the bedroom to change into her nightgown and robe. When she came back out, she said, "Okay, everyone, it's going to be a busy day. Let's all get some sleep."

She was standing in the archway between the West Sitting Hall and the Center Hall, and Mike, Gayle, Steve, and Susan got up and walked over to hug her good night.

They'd invited Greg Willard to spend the night on the third floor, and as he walked toward the elevator, he made eye contact with Betty. With a despondent look on his face, he mouthed, "Good night."

Mrs. Ford walked over to him, and he said, "Oh, Mrs. Ford, I'm so sorry. I really thought he was going to pull it out."

Betty looked at him sternly, in a motherly way, grabbed him by the hands, and said, "Now, you listen to me, young man. When we walk out of here on January twentieth, we're walking out with no regrets and many wonderful memories. We'll walk out with our heads high, filled with pride, and you're going to walk out with your head high along with us."

She kissed him on the cheek and said, "Now, go get some sleep."

That moment, Greg remembered, was "quintessential Betty Ford." Of course she was disappointed at the loss, but she wasn't going to dwell on it. "She could have been despondent, angry, or bitter; instead, she summoned that remarkable Betty Ford inner strength and focused squarely on the future."

The day after the election, David Kennerly recalled, "was a day when more than a few tears were shed, among the family and those of us who were close to them. It was a tough loss." To make things worse, President Ford could barely talk. And the press was waiting for him to give his concession speech.

Around eleven in the morning, President Ford was in the Oval Office with Dick Cheney and a couple of other staff members. He called the White House switchboard and asked them to get Governor Carter on the phone. When Carter answered, Ford whispered, "I can't talk. I'm going to have Dick Cheney read my statement."

Sitting in a chair across the room, on an extension, Dick Cheney read the president's brief concession. It was official, but a press conference was scheduled for twelve fifteen.

At noon, Betty, Mike, Gayle, Jack, Steve, and Susan joined the president in the Oval Office.

"David," Betty said to Kennerly, "I want a photo of all of us behind the desk, just like we did the day the president took the oath of office."

Everyone was crying, and no one wanted a photo, but they weren't going to turn down Mother. They gathered behind the desk, and no one could even force a smile. Betty turned to Jack, who was at her right, and grabbed him under the chin.

"Chin up, kid," she said with a grin. "Look, there are worse things that could have happened."

"That moment," David Kennerly recalled, "was so indicative of her strength. She was holding everyone up. That photo is one of my all-time favorites." In the sequence of photos that follow, everyone is smiling—they are forced smiles—trying to be as brave as Mother.

It was time to go to the press room. Jerry reached out to Betty and whispered, "I can't read the concession speech. Will you do it for me?"

She looked into his eyes, so filled with disappointment and sadness. It was the first election he'd ever lost. "Of course I will," she said.

The family walked out the door of the Oval Office and paraded somberly down the colonnade past the Cabinet Room, turned right, and entered the door to the press room.

President Ford went first, and the rest followed. As they stepped onto the small stage, gathering around the podium, the members of the media applauded.

President Ford stepped forward to the microphone. "It's perfectly obvious," he said, his voice crackling and hoarse, "my voice isn't up to par, and I shouldn't be making very many comments, and I won't. But I did want Betty, Mike, Jack, Susan, Steve, and Gayle to come down with me and to listen while Betty read a statement that I have sent to Governor Carter."

His eyes were sad, but he gathered strength from having his family around him.

"I do want to express on a personal basis," he continued, "my appreciation and that of my family for the friendship all of us have had, and after Betty reads the statement that was sent to Governor Carter by me, I think that all of us, Betty and the children and myself, would like to just come down and shake hands and express our appreciation personally."

He paused and then said, "Now let me call on the real spokesman of the family." Behind him, Susan, Mike, Jack, and Steve broke into laughter as he turned to his wife and said, "Betty."

Laughing at that unexpected introduction, Betty stepped up to the podium and kissed her husband on the lips.

It had been just three years since they'd first shocked the public by kissing each other on the lips in front of the entire world when Jerry had been nominated to be President Nixon's vice presidential appointee. There'd been countless public displays of affection since then—for they had bared their personal struggles and triumphs with the country. They didn't know how to hide their emotions. With the Fords, what you saw was who they were.

Dressed in a gray suit with a white high-collared, feminine blouse, her hair and makeup perfect, Betty stepped up to the microphone as Jerry moved aside. *Don't show any emotion*, she thought to herself. *Not for the country's sake, but for the family's.*

She looked out to the audience of press, and in her soft, soothing voice, she said, "The president asked me to tell you that he telephoned President-elect Carter a short time ago and congratulated him on his victory. The president also wants to thank all those thousands of people who worked so hard on his behalf, and the millions who supported him with their votes. It's been the greatest honor of my husband's life to serve his fellow Americans during two of the most difficult years in our history. The president urges all Americans to join him in giving your united support to President-elect Carter as he prepares to assume his new responsibilities."

As Betty spoke, the news cameras zoomed in on President Ford's face. Watching Betty read the statement, his eyes conveyed the heartwrenching grief he felt for not having been able to sway the country. But in his demeanor, you couldn't help but notice how proud he was of his beloved Betty for her courage in that moment.

And then Betty read the telegram. Her voice was clear, strong, and deliberate, and on her face was a smile filled with pride.

Dear Jimmy, it is apparent now that you have won our long and intense struggle for the presidency. I congratulate you on your victory. As one who has been honored to serve the people of this great land both in Congress and as president, I believe that we must now put divisions of the campaign behind us and unite the country once again in the common pursuit of peace and prosperity. Although there will continue to be disagreements over the best means to use in pursuing our goals, I want to assure you that you have my complete and wholehearted support as you take the oath of office this January. I also pledge to you that I and all members of my administration will do all that we can to insure that you begin your term as smoothly and effectively as possible. May God bless you and your family as you undertake your new responsibilities. Signed, Jerry Ford. Thank you very much.

The audience of press clapped, and then the president, Betty, and their family walked out among them, shaking hands, chatting with the reporters. It was an odd relationship between the political family in the fishbowl and the press, whose job it was to expose everything about them. And while each member of the Ford family had his or her quibbles with members of the media, the patriarch of the family had set an example by respecting them for the job they'd done. As Betty smiled graciously and shook hands, she wasn't focusing on what had gone wrong, or how they might have done things differently—she was already looking ahead to the future and the pleasures of private life, thinking to herself: *All I have to do is get us all through the next three months, until the day we leave the White House.*

Betty had put up a good front when she'd given her husband's concession speech, but as the days went on, she became somewhat melancholy at Jerry's having lost the election after twenty-eight years of faithful service to the country. She thought the American people had made a big mistake. In a sense, she was out of office too. "People with low self-esteem crave reassurance from the outside world," she wrote later. She realized she was one of those people, and in her two and a half short years as first lady of the United States, she'd received about as much reassurance as any human being could get. Sure, Betty had her critics, but she'd been voted one of the most admired women in America. And the best part of it all was that she was just being herself. She hadn't changed to fit what she thought people wanted her to be. She'd just been Betty, and that's who people loved.

In an article for the *Evansville Press*, writer Judy Clabes summed up the nation's adoration of Betty Ford with an article entitled "We'll Miss You, Betty Ford." It began, "You didn't ask to be first lady. But when it was thrust on you, you were there, doing it up right when we needed you most.

"You were frank, honest, open, natural—all the things we had begun to think first ladies couldn't be. But most of all, you were human. You made us more comfortable with ourselves."

The article went on to describe the controversy she'd stirred up, and that while people didn't always agree with her, "we couldn't help but love you for the way you were making us feel again." Clabes wrote about how Betty was obviously a devoted mother and loving wife—"you kissed and hugged your husband for all the world to see"—and yet she was her own person, always expressing her own mind.

"You made us proud, Betty Ford . . . it was we who prayed for you when we learned of your pending mastectomy. But it was you who gave us strength. You were open, forthright, unashamed, courageous—giving hope to thousands of women who had been through that hell, saving countless others from a similar fate."

The article reminded readers of Betty dancing the bump with Tony Orlando and the "Betty Ford for President" buttons. "We'll miss your unrehearsed laugh, your warmth, your steadying influence . . . at the time when we needed you most, you were almost too good to be true. But that's the best part of all. We did believe again, and you didn't let us down."

The day before the inauguration, Betty realized this would be her last opportunity to say goodbye to the White House employees and staff who had, for the past two and a half years, day in and day out, made her life so tolerable, so easy, and, if she really thought about it, some of the best years she'd ever had.

Photographers David Kennerly and Eddie Adams from *Time*, who was doing a piece on President Ford's last day in office, were walking around with Betty and a few of her staff members as she poked her head into offices, saying goodbye. It was all very informal.

"We walked by the Cabinet Room, which has always been—or had been certainly up until that point—a very male domain," Kennerly recalled.

Suddenly Betty stopped and, with a look of mischief, said, "I've always wanted to dance on the Cabinet Room table."

Kennerly was the only one in that little group who didn't think she was kidding.

"Well, Mrs. Ford," he said, "this is your last chance."

She took her shoes off, and hopped up onto the table. "She was very fragile looking, but as a former dancer, she was extremely agile," Kennerly remembered.

Taking her place in the center of the table, in one fluid movement, she crossed her right leg over the left, foot flexed standing on the toe, just as her left hand went to her hip, and her right arm stretched to the ceiling. It was a pose rehearsed over a lifetime, prepared for this spontaneous finale.

David Kennerly captured it in three or four short clicks, and then Betty Ford brushed her hands together and said, "I think that'll about wrap it up for this place."

Inauguration Day, 1977

The schedule for Inauguration Day was planned nearly to the second, and on this day, Betty knew she couldn't be late. They'd set an alarm, but Betty and Jerry both awoke at dawn. They began the morning with what had become their normal routines: Jerry eating his breakfast in the dining room as he read the newspaper, while Betty took hers in the sitting room. Jerry knew that Betty didn't like to talk before ten o'clock if she "had any choice in the matter," and today, of all days, was one in which they both respected the other's need to be alone in thought.

The first order of the day was to greet the Carters at the White House for coffee before the ride to the Capitol, and Betty was anxious to get it over with. The tradition for the outgoing president and first lady to host the couple that will be moving into the White House later the same day has got to be one of the most awkward, and emotional, social situations there is—especially when your successors have beaten you in a hard-fought campaign. But both Betty and her husband were the gracious hosts they'd always been. "We were all human beings, civilized, and the thing you want to do is be as pleasant as possible," she wrote, and although she smiled for the obligatory photos, it was strained, and later, she would not be able to recall a word that was said.

When it was time to go, Betty put on her fur coat and walked arm in arm with her husband, still the president of the United States for one more hour, out the door to the North Portico. Pasting on yet another smile as they walked through the sea of photographers, she tried not to think about the fact that this was the last time they'd walk out these doors. Their life in the White House was over.

President Ford and President-elect Carter rode together to the Capitol in the presidential limousine, with the Secret Service in the follow-up car directly behind them. Third in line came Betty and Rosalynn Carter in their own car.

"I'm sure her thoughts are as deep and varied as mine, but, like most people, we don't express them," Mrs. Carter wrote in her memoir. Instead, they chatted about Camp David, where the Fords had just spent their last weekend.

"The food is so delicious there," Betty said. "I'm going to have to go on a diet."

She was gracious, but counting the minutes until the torturous obligation was over.

As they came out the west side of the Capitol, Betty looked out at the mass of people gathered at the bottom of the steps, cheering and clapping, and that's when it hit hardest. She waved, forcing a smile. And then, as she and Jerry walked down the steps, their hands intertwined, it was all she could do to keep the tears from pouring out. It was so difficult. It just hurt.

"All our married life was being left there," she wrote. "We were married, we went to Washington, looked for a place to live and found it, our children were born there, Jerry's twenty-eight years of work had been there," and now she felt like "the whole thing had just gone down the drain."

PART FOUR

◆

BETTY FORD, AFTER THE WHITE HOUSE

Just as suddenly as Betty had become first lady, in an instant, that title, that role, was gone. Now what? What do you do after you've reached such a pinnacle? She was fifty-nine years old, moving to the next phase of her life, looking forward to retirement with the husband she loved and adored. Even though they'd lost the election, Betty and Jerry were proud of the way they'd conducted themselves in their short time in the White House, and at this point in their lives, with book deals and television deals, they could enjoy a lifestyle that had never been possible before.

But something was wrong. Something was terribly wrong. Everyone agreed: "Something has to be done about Mother."

Few outside the Ford family were privy to what happened; how it all unfolded. But ultimately, Betty's "problem" would become public.

It is a testament to Betty Ford's resilience, her deep-seated strength and determination, combined with the sincere love and commitment of her devoted husband, that the outcome would become one of her greatest achievements.

20

"Kiss Today Goodbye"

Along with a full Secret Service detail, four staff members personally chosen by President and Mrs. Ford moved with them to Rancho Mirage, California: President Ford's military aide, Bob Barrett; Greg Willard from the White House Advance Office; and Annie Grier and Joy Chiles from the Press Office. The four of them had been working tirelessly in the eighty days between the election and Inauguration Day to facilitate the Fords' transition from the White House to their postpresidency life in the desert. There were myriad administrative complexities: organizing presidential papers; coordinating staff and facilities authorized by the General Services Administration; and sorting through millions of pages of documents and mementos to be preserved for the presidential library. Add to all this the personal aspects: boxing up clothes, furniture, and personal belongings not only from the White House but also things that had been put in storage when they moved out of 514 Crown View Drive two and a half years earlier.

After a few days in Pebble Beach, where President Ford played in the Bing Crosby Pro-Am golf tournament, the Fords flew to Houston for a benefit dinner in memory of famed NFL football coach Vince Lombardi, and finally arrived in Palm Springs on Friday, January 28. Plans were under way to build a home in Rancho Mirage, but in the interim, Jerry and Betty moved into a partially furnished $375,000 house they leased from Emily DeWare, a Texas heiress, in the exclusive gated hill-side community of Thunderbird Heights. Some of the Fords' furniture and a few personal effects went into the house, while the Secret Service set up a command post in a portion of the garage, surrounded by boxes of the Fords' belongings piled from floor to ceiling.

The four staff members rented a bungalow on the Thunderbird Country Club grounds, just down the hill from the DeWare house. It had two tiny rooms with a kitchenette in the middle. For the next several weeks, the kitchenette served as the "Office of the Thirty-Eighth President of the United States." It was so incongruous that, at times, the staff members would pause, look at one another, and burst out laughing: Wow, what a change from 1600 Pennsylvania Avenue! But if the change was sudden and drastic for them, it was even more so for Betty and the president. Within just a few days, the starkness of it all became palpable.

The Fords were living in the DeWare house on a narrow, isolated street. They couldn't just walk down to the clubhouse and have lunch. They had to be driven to go anywhere—and that meant being driven by the Secret Service. They had a few friends in the desert and would attend sporadic black-tie galas. Occasionally, people would invite them over for dinner, but having the former president and first lady to dinner was an event—it wasn't like the informal backyard barbecues they'd enjoyed with neighbors on Crown View Drive.

They hadn't been in Rancho Mirage much more than a week before President Ford started traveling, while Betty was left to set up house and somehow fill her days. All through February and into March, the president was gone a great deal. There were speeches at universities, corporate boards trying to entice him to join, and more invitations to charity events and golf tournaments than he could possibly accept. It was not the retirement Betty Ford had envisioned.

"Those of us on the staff immediately recognized how lonely it was for them—especially for Mrs. Ford," Greg Willard recalled. "It was inescapable how blasted lonely it was out there. And, as their staff, we felt this odd sense of responsibility to somehow fix it. Unfortunately, there simply wasn't a good fix."

Everyone around the Fords, even the Secret Service agents, was feeling it. They all wanted to get Betty out and about. On one occasion, with the president away on an overnight trip, Greg stayed back in Rancho Mirage and stopped by the DeWare house to see Betty.

"Mrs. Ford, a bunch of us have been talking about this new movie *A Star Is Born* with Barbra Streisand and Kris Kristofferson. Come on and go with us to see it tonight."

"Yeah! That sounds fun! I'll go!" she said.

Greg bought bags of popcorn for everyone, and as the group sat there in the darkness, he kept reflecting on how remarkable the situation was. Just a few months ago, when she was first lady, living in the White House, there were so many invitations; so many people who wanted every moment of her time. Now here she was, sitting in a dark movie theater, surrounded by only her husband's personal aide and her Secret Service agents. Yesterday's news.

The Fords had been in Rancho Mirage about six weeks when an opportunity for a trip to New York City popped up. The Eisenhower Exchange Fellowship had asked Jerry to give a speech to a group of trustees and major contributors. Both Jerry and Betty were in contract negotiations with NBC for some television appearances, and several top publishing houses were bidding for their memoirs. It was an ideal time to meet with the various parties to iron out the details.

A year earlier, during a campaign stop in New York City, Betty had attended a performance of Broadway's latest hit *A Chorus Line*. Directed and choreographed by Michael Bennett, the show was an emotional glimpse into the struggles and triumphs of a group of dancers auditioning for a Broadway musical, and with its powerful music by Marvin Hamlisch, it had gone on to win nine Tony Awards, including Best Musical of 1976. When Betty first saw the show, she was flooded with memories of those heady days in New York City when she, too, had visions of becoming a professional dancer. She had been wanting to see it again, and for Jerry to see it, and now was the perfect chance.

Betty called the staff office to see if tickets to the show could be arranged for her and Jerry. She then asked, "Who's going on the trip with us?"

"Annie Grier and I are scheduled to work the trip," Greg Willard replied.

"Well, then, let's get four tickets. You and Annie are going with us. You two need to see it."

In New York, Harper & Row Publishing offered Betty and Jerry a joint contract for an estimated $1 million to write their memoirs, separately but equally. No previous president and first lady had ever made a similar two-book deal that placed their experiences as public figures on an equal basis. Trevor Armbrister, an author and former *Saturday Evening Post* reporter, would help President Ford with his book, while Betty selected Chris Chase, a female freelance writer suggested by the publisher to assist with writing her autobiography. Betty's book was scheduled to be published before Jerry's, in the fall of 1978.

The evening of Monday, March 21, the sold-out crowd at the Shubert Theatre was getting restless. It was eight minutes past showtime, the house lights were still on, and there was a group of prime middle orchestra seats unoccupied in the otherwise full theater. Suddenly there was a commotion in the back. The entire audience turned to see what was going on. As soon as they saw President and Mrs. Ford walking down the aisle, pandemonium erupted throughout the theater.

Everyone stood up and started cheering. "Bravo! Bravo!"

President Ford smiled and nodded, clearly appreciating the raucous ovation. But it was Betty who was taking it all in—her face was filled with pure, unmitigated joy. You could see it in her eyes; it was sheer happiness. After weeks of quiet loneliness, to have this kind of reception was like a shot of adrenaline to her soul.

People were reaching out their hands, and while the agents tried to gently push them back, Betty and Jerry graciously offered their hands in return as they made their way down the aisle. As soon as they were seated, with their two guests on either side of them, the agents took their seats in the row behind.

Finally, the lights went down, and the show began.

Onstage, a group of dancers, some dressed in leotards, others in street clothes, were following instructions during an audition: "Five, six, seven, eight . . ."

From the moment the dancers came onstage, it was as if Betty was reliving those months in New York City in her twenties when she was one of those idealistic girls on the stage; when her only dream was to be chosen by Martha Graham as one of her principal dancers.

Betty could no more hold still in her seat than she could not breathe. As the dancers glided across the stage, stood on their toes, and kicked their legs up to their foreheads, her own feet, in designer heels, pointed and flexed as if she were silently dancing the numbers right along with them.

Greg and Annie glanced at Betty from time to time and couldn't help but smile at the glee on her face. For six long weeks, those around the Fords had wondered, *How do we fix this? How can we cure her loneliness?* For this night, at least, the answer was right here at the Shubert Theatre on West Forty-Fourth Street. It was as if this play had been written for her, about her.

She sat there mesmerized. The story line was about a group of dancers in their twenties and thirties, sharing the heartbreaks of their childhoods and how dance had saved them, baring their souls to the director whose decision would change the course of their lives.

One girl sang how dance was her escape; how going to the ballet made her forget her worries. Betty listened intently to every lyric, and every so often she'd turn to look at her husband to make sure he was enjoying it as much as she'd hoped he would. He was. About halfway through the show, a female dancer named Val began singing a song called "Dance Ten, Looks Three," in which she described with shocking frankness how she had undergone plastic surgery to enhance her "tits and ass" in order to get more jobs.

There were quiet gasps in the theater. Everyone knew President and Mrs. Ford were in the audience, and they weren't sure how this was going to go over, given the former first lady's mastectomy. The president sat there, watching, listening. Suddenly Betty started slapping her leg in time to the rhythm, laughing, and moving her shoulders up and down. It put Jerry immediately at ease, and when he broke into a beaming smile, the rest of the audience relaxed.

When a line in the song referenced how the new breasts had enhanced the girl's sex life, Betty turned to Jerry, laughing, with a naughty glint in her eye. She loved it! And she loved that it made her husband blush.

Nearly two hours in, at the very end of the musical, the choreographer asked the dancers, "If today were the day you had to stop dancing, how would you feel?"

There was a pause, and actress Priscilla Lopez, as Diana Morales, her voice pure and poignant, began singing, "What I Did for Love." Betty reached over and clasped her husband's hand, tears welling in her eyes as the opening lyrics began.

"Kiss today goodbye . . ."

It felt as if she were singing to Betty and Jerry; as if the song had been written just for them, just for this moment. The past three years had been an emotional roller coaster. They'd landed in the White House— not what they'd wanted at all, but they'd thrived, and Betty had loved it. And then they'd worked so hard to be reelected, only to lose in a heartbreaking defeat. She was almost afraid to look at her husband, for fear they'd both break down.

The song was all about remembering what the dancers had been through, how they'd danced their hearts out, purely out of love, and looking back, they had no regrets.

Betty and Jerry turned and looked into each other's eyes, fighting the tears, as their hands squeezed so tightly, it was as if they were embracing.

As soon as the curtain fell, the entire audience rose to its feet with applause.

"Bravo! Bravo!" Betty was clapping with all her might. "Wasn't it wonderful, Jerry?" Her entire being was sparkling.

"It was, Betty. It was perfect!" the president replied with a huge smile.

Suddenly Betty had an idea. She turned to Greg Willard. "Do you think we could go backstage?"

"Yes, ma'am," Greg said. He'd been on their staff long enough to know exactly what she wanted and how to make it happen. "I'll take care of it."

They made their way backstage, and Betty was in heaven. She was beaming with joy as she grasped the hands of the dancers and told them how wonderful they were, how much she and the president had enjoyed the performance.

"The choreography was marvelous!" she exclaimed. "Now show me, how did you do that one move?"

And then the dancers were moving their arms and counting "five, six, seven, eight," and Betty was moving right along with them. This was her language, and she was just so happy. It was the happiest she'd been in months, and she didn't want the evening to end.

Meanwhile, several of their Secret Service agents were waiting outside with the motorcade, wondering what was going on to delay the scheduled departure. Agent Marty Venker got on the radio.

"Follow-up—Venker. Passkey's ready to go, but Pinafore is definitely not."

Everyone knew what that meant. No one was leaving until Betty was ready to go.

Several days later, back in Rancho Mirage, a bulky package was delivered to the DeWare house gate. The Secret Service agents carefully examined the package and its contents. Inside was a VCR tape, along with a handwritten note from a seventh-grade boy in Pennsylvania.

The agents brought the package to the staff to decide whether the Fords should see it—you never knew what kind of crazy stuff people might send. Greg Willard examined the package and was intrigued by the young boy's heartfelt note. He went into the living room, inserted the video into the VCR player, and pressed Play.

The boy had created a tribute to President and Mrs. Ford, splicing together video clips of them from a network television broadcast during President Carter's inauguration. Included were Marine One, the presidential helicopter, lifting off from the Capitol with the Fords aboard, followed by a series of clips of the two of them at Andrews Air Force Base, and finally, Air Force One taking off to deliver them to California. In place of the network audio commentary, the boy had dubbed a different soundtrack: it was "What I Did for Love," the song from the musical they'd just seen in New York.

Greg was gobsmacked. *That song! What are the odds?!* It was a short video, just long enough for the entire song to play, just long enough to tug at your heartstrings.

Betty was outside on the patio reading, and when she came in, Greg said quietly, "Mrs. Ford, if you have a minute, I think you want to look at this."

"What is it?"

He handed her the note and said, "You won't believe this, but the video's background music is that wonderful song from *A Chorus Line*—the one you and the president loved so much."

Mrs. Ford looked at him in disbelief. "'What I Did for Love'?"

"Yes," Greg said. "It's really quite moving."

"Well, yes, I'd like to see it."

They sat down together on the sofa and watched the video. Neither of them spoke, as the cascade of emotions welled up inside.

When the president returned later that afternoon, Betty said, "Jerry, you've got to see this . . ."

From that point on, "What I Did for Love" was *their* song.

The first week in April 1977, President Ford had a five-day stint as a visiting professor of political science at his alma mater, the University of Michigan in Ann Arbor, so he and Betty used it as an opportunity to spend the following Easter weekend with friends and family in Grand Rapids. They were both looking forward to a relaxing weekend surrounded by people who knew them from way back—and hosting a dinner party for those who had helped raise money for the White House swimming pool—but out of the blue, as happened so frequently, Betty's pinched nerve flared up, leaving her in severe pain the entire weekend. Sunday morning, she managed to attend the Easter service at Grace Episcopal Church—where she and Jerry had been married—but by the end of the service, she was in such excruciating pain, she could barely move.

Jerry was scheduled to give a speech in Louisville, Kentucky, a couple of days later, but they decided to return first to Rancho Mirage. The Fords were traveling on a military jet, which stopped in Oklahoma City to refuel. During the stop, everyone got off the plane to stretch, but Betty didn't move from her seat. One of the agents stayed with her, and no one asked why she remained on the aircraft. Finally, they took off for the last leg back to the West Coast.

As the aircraft prepared to land, two staff members took seats near

Betty in the front cabin, where she had been sitting the entire flight. They couldn't help but notice that she had her right hand clasped tightly over her left hand. As the plane came to a stop, Betty pulled away her right hand, and they could see a huge welt next to her wedding ring, where she had been squeezing her left hand. They didn't say anything—it wasn't their place—but their antennae were up. *What is going on?*

It had been a long day of travel, and it was late, so the staff members returned to their apartment, while the agents took President and Mrs. Ford back to the DeWare house. Greg Willard had just unpacked and was ready to plow into a backlog of paperwork, when the phone rang. It was the president.

"Greg, can you come down here to the house. Mother and I need to talk to you."

He could tell by his boss's tone of voice that it involved something very urgent.

"Of course," he said. "I'll be right there, Mr. President." When Greg walked in, Jerry and Betty were sitting in the living room, Betty in a nightgown and robe. She was wincing in pain, her eyes weary, and it was obvious she was in agony.

"As you can see, Mother is in terrible pain," Jerry said. "We want to talk about surgery."

Betty looked up, her voice a whisper. "I can't live like this. I can't do it. I know the risks of surgery; I've considered them before. I want to proceed down the surgery path."

"Can you look into it, Greg?" the president asked. "Find out what we need to do?"

"I'll call Dr. Lukash, sir," Greg replied. "He'll be the best one to guide us and get the process started quickly. I'll call him at the White House now."

Dr. Lukash had stayed on with President Carter as the White House physician, and within thirty minutes, he was aware of Betty's situation and her desire to consider surgery. Lukash immediately contacted the medical staff at the Eisenhower Medical Center in Rancho Mirage.

The next day, Greg Willard and the Secret Service agents met privately with administrators at the hospital to make the necessary arrangements. The medical team decided that Betty first needed to have a myelogram: a diagnostic procedure in which contrast dye would be injected into her spinal column, followed by multiple CT scans of her spinal region to try to determine what was causing her severe pain. The procedure was scheduled for the following morning.

Betty arrived at the hospital bright and early and was prepped for what was expected to be a routine, hour-long procedure. President Ford remained at their residence, expecting that his wife would be back home for lunch. The procedure itself was uneventful, and when it was over, the doctors told Betty everything went fine.

"We'll examine the results and keep you under observation for a few hours," they told her. "You should be able to go home by early afternoon."

By early afternoon, however, it was clear that Betty Ford wasn't going anywhere. She'd become very ill. Greg Willard recalled somberly, "By late afternoon, she was clearly not well; she was struggling."

President Ford was summoned to the hospital and was rushed immediately to Eisenhower by his Secret Service agents. Something was very wrong. Betty had become noncommunicative, extremely nauseous, and was experiencing tremors throughout her body.

The doctors huddled together, studying her charts, and concluded finally, "We have to admit her. She's having a very bad reaction to the myelogram dye. It happens in about five percent of people, and the dye just needs to work its way through the system." According to the lead physician, "She probably won't be able to go home this evening. Out of an abundance of caution, we'll admit her and keep her here overnight."

President Ford had never seen his wife in such bad shape, and everyone was very concerned. This was supposed to have been a routine diagnostic procedure meant to determine whether she could have the surgery that she hoped would ease her constant pain.

She was taken to a hospital room that had a small connected anteroom with a sofa. That evening, a very worried Greg Willard slept there, in what would turn out to be his first of several overnight stays. The president returned home but called repeatedly during the night to get the latest reports.

Betty slept some that night and seemed to be a little more comfortable; nevertheless, she remained noncommunicative, and the tremors continued.

The medical team continued to administer IV fluids, still convinced that once the dye was flushed from her system, it was just a matter of time before the adverse reaction would pass. President Ford's visits to Eisenhower continued with increasing urgency. His appearance was grim; he felt helpless. As he would leave the house for Eisenhower, the agents would call ahead to the anteroom to report that he was on his way. As soon as he reached the hospital, he would receive the latest medical update before proceeding into Betty's room. The doctors kept assuring him it was just a bad reaction, but that still didn't address the obvious question: When was it going to stop?

So far, the president's staff had managed to keep the hospitalization quiet; no press had gotten wind of it. But they knew it was just a matter of time before something leaked. By the second night, a new fear surfaced that Betty's breast cancer may have metastasized to her brain. The medical team decided she should undergo a brain scan to see if that horrific possibility might explain her symptoms. To make certain the scan and her movements within the hospital remained totally private, the procedure was performed in the middle of the night, with just medical personnel, Secret Service agents, and staff huddled in the cramped radiology control room.

As the scans got under way, one of the group quietly asked the radiologists, "Tell us what you're *not* looking for? What is it we all hope *not* to see?" The response was stark: "It just doesn't make sense that she's having this prolonged reaction to a myelogram. What we do *not* want to see are differentiated shades within areas of the brain scans. The concern is that there might be lesions—metastatic tumors or a benign mass—that have developed on her brain that could be causing this."

The results of the scans turned out to be a relief—no lesions, no metastatic breast cancer, no brain tumors. *Thank God.* But what, then, was causing her to suffer so? The doctors still couldn't explain it. However, by the third day, Betty began to rebound. She was more alert, and her tremors had receded. But she remained extremely weak. Finally, on the fourth day, Betty was allowed to go home.

Ironically, everyone had become so consumed about her horrible reaction to the myelogram, they'd forgotten the reason she'd come to Eisenhower in the first place: When could she have surgery?

The answer she received was not what she had hoped to hear. The source of her pain could not be remedied by surgery. The situation was inoperable. Betty was devastated. Despite all she had been through the past several days, to know that she had no choice but to live with her debilitating pain for the rest of her life was crushing.

What no one recognized at the time—including some of the top medical professionals in the country who'd been consulted—was that the wretched reactions Betty had suffered in the hospital had absolutely nothing to do with the myelogram dye: they were classic symptoms of drug withdrawal.

Once she came home, everyone around the Fords, including Jerry, sensed that "something was not right." They just didn't know what. Over the course of the next several weeks, Betty's strength was slow to return. She persevered just to have an occasional lunch at the house with a friend or with Annie Grier and Joy Chiles. Afterward, she inevitably needed to rest. In the meantime, Jerry maintained his frenetic travel schedule, jetting around the country from one speaking event to another. Lady Bird Johnson had invited the Fords to the LBJ Ranch, in central Texas, in early May, and Betty had been looking forward to the visit. But when the time came for the trip, she just didn't have the strength to go, so Jerry went alone.

Looking back, it's clear what was happening. Mired in pain, all alone there in the desert, seemingly a million miles away from the pinnacle of the White House and her friends, it's not at all surprising that Betty Ford began spiraling down. Armed with a cabinet full of pills— all prescribed by her doctors—she'd mix and match depending on the aches or stresses of the day. No one around her knew exactly what she was taking or in what combinations, but they blindly assumed that the doctors knew best. She saw her internist every week for vitamin B shots and refills for any of the vials that were getting low. Around five or six o'clock each evening, she'd ask Benjy, the former White House navy steward who had stayed on to work for the Fords, to make her a drink—usually a vodka tonic. And while she might have a second drink, none of the staff perceived her alcohol consumption as anything outside of the parameters one would have considered, in the '70s, as moderate social drinking.

To those around Betty, there was no indication she had a problem with alcohol or prescription drugs. But in retrospect, it's clear that by this point, the mix of pills, depression, pain, and booze had already begun its stealthy and relentless takeover.

21

A Downward Spiral

With Betty's health issues, one of the first orders of business was to find new doctors. No longer could she simply call downstairs to Dr. Lukash for a sleeping pill or a pain pill; no longer did the doctors come to her.

Dr. Joseph Cruse came highly recommended as an ob-gyn—he had worked at the Walter Reed Army Medical Center in Washington, DC, and was now affiliated with the nearby Eisenhower Medical Center—so Betty and Susan both began going to see him.

Dr. Cruse, himself a recovering alcoholic, realized Betty had a problem the first time he met her. "I had a long hallway from my reception desk to the consultation room. She had to hold on to the wall all the way down. And then she came in and sat down and kind of blinked at me."

Susan would accompany her mother to the appointments, and when Dr. Cruse asked Mrs. Ford questions, Susan usually answered. Cruse found himself in a difficult position—just like Betty's internist and cardiologist. Because Mrs. Ford had come to him as a gynecology patient, he felt it was out of line for him to suggest that the former first lady had an addiction problem.

The summer of 1977, the Fords flew to Vail, as had become their typical routine. Betty loved the clear, crisp mountain air and the small-town feel. Friends there such as Sheika Gramshammer knew her before she was first lady, and she could just be herself.

Still, there were so many obligations, even as the wife of a former president. The mail had declined somewhat, but invitations and requests for appearances still came in daily. There was no way Betty could go back to handling it herself, as she had when Jerry was a congressman, but unlike the funds that were provided to the outgoing president for an office and staff, there was nothing for the outgoing first lady. Betty needed an assistant, and one who was willing to move back and forth between Rancho Mirage and Vail.

Twenty-six-year-old Caroline Coventry was working at Pepi Sports when she heard that Betty Ford was looking for a new personal aide. She followed up with President Ford's assistant, Bob Barrett, who promptly set up an interview at Dick Bass's house.

"I introduced myself, and Bob Barrett talked for thirty minutes straight," Caroline recalled. "He never asked me a question. And I thought, *Will this guy ever stop?*"

Barrett knew that Caroline had worked at Pepi Sports, and, apparently, she had all the skills he thought Mrs. Ford would need in an assistant. Finally, Barrett said, "Would you like to meet Mrs. Ford?"

Caroline was caught off guard. She hadn't expected to meet the former first lady at this initial meeting. But what could she say? "Of course," she said. "I'd love to meet Mrs. Ford."

"Great," Barrett said. "I'll call and let her know we're coming."

Caroline was even more surprised when Bob Barrett brought her into President and Mrs. Ford's bedroom, and there was Mrs. Ford, sitting up in bed.

"She was wearing a beautiful bright-pink quilted silk bathrobe," Caroline recalled. It stuck out in her mind because she'd never imagined meeting the former first lady in her bedroom, let alone in a bathrobe.

"Mrs. Ford," Barrett said, "I'd like to introduce you to Caroline Coventry. We've been talking about the job as your assistant."

Betty smiled. "It was a genuine smile," Caroline recalled, "and then she said, 'Hello, Caroline. Would you like to come here and work?'"

Mrs. Ford's speech was slurred, but other than that, Caroline remembered, she was as happy and as nice as could be. *What do you say when you are facing the former president's wife, and she asks if you want to work for her?*

"Oh, of course," Caroline answered with a smile. And that was it. "It happened very fast," she remembered. "It was done before you realized it."

Her duties were loosely defined, but, basically, Caroline would assist with anything and everything, from sorting mail and handling correspondence, to running errands and helping with packing for trips. She was eager to please, and with her warm, bubbly personality, she fit in from the start. Susan was there all summer, and she and Caroline became friends.

In a letter to a friend, Caroline wrote, "They treat me just like family. I eat dinner with them, with their whole family. Never have I known such a nice family. They treat you as one of the tribe, and it is a real pleasure. Susan is like a sister, and Mrs. Ford takes a joke just like my mother. Normal dinner conversation is about what's the latest in the White House."

In those first couple of months in Vail, however, Caroline could see that her new boss had a problem: she was relying on too many pills. Caroline's father was a doctor, but she'd grown up in a household in which nothing stronger than aspirin was ever prescribed. Still, she could easily recognize the signs.

"There were good days and bad days, and it all depended on how much medication she took," Caroline recalled. Others noticed it too. While writing an article about the Fords' post–White House life for *New West* magazine, reporter Mary Murphy interviewed friends and acquaintances in Vail, including a waitress at Pepi's Restaurant who told her that Mrs. Ford had been through "a bad summer. She walks slowly, she eats slowly, she smiles slowly, as if it hurts her to move."

Indeed, when Murphy first met Betty in Vail, she noted that "Betty Ford looked five years older than she did last November. Her cheeks were puffy, her skin pale, her green eyes dulled and distant, and her words, although quite coherent, were spoken with the uncertainty of someone learning English."

Sheika Gramshammer chalked it up to her pain. "*Poor darling*, we thought, *she can't get through an evening without pain pills. And every* once in a while, she might have one bourbon too many, but everybody does that sometimes."

The signs were there, but no one spoke about it. Caroline Coventry thought, *This is the former first lady. She has the best medical treatment available. Surely someone has spoken to her about this. Surely.*

At the end of the summer, it was time to return to Rancho Mirage. Susan Ford had been attending college in Kansas but decided to leave school, move out to Palm Springs, and try to get a job as a photographer. She'd broken the news to her parents, and they'd said, "Fine, but we're not going to support you financially." They'd help her buy a condo, but then she was on her own.

President and Mrs. Ford had purchased a plot of land on the Thunderbird Country Club golf course in Rancho Mirage, next door to their good friends Leonard and Nicky Firestone, and were in the process of designing and building a house. Betty hired a well-known and much sought-after Beverly Hills interior decorator named Laura Mako to help furnish their new residence.

"They went from a modest life in a very modest suburban house to the White House, and this was the first time she had ever worked with an interior designer or even had the option of buying new furniture," Caroline recalled. "It gave Mrs. Ford something to do. Something to concentrate on. She thought it was fun and exciting to be in this position. This was a whole new adventure, and she was enjoying it, especially since there was an additional expendable income they had not experienced before."

Indeed, for the first time in their lives, Jerry and Betty had some extra money to spare. There were the presidential and congressional pensions he'd earned, but the bigger money came from the NBC contract and $1 million joint book deal. On top of that, President Ford was in high demand for speaking engagements, and he was as surprised as anyone to realize he could make $10,000 for one speech. He was traveling all over the country, and in May 1977 alone, he was gone twenty-eight out of thirty-one days. Meanwhile, Betty was in Rancho Mirage, still at the rented house. Laura Mako noticed that as they were choosing furniture and fabrics, there were times Betty would take a pill and then drift off. Some days, Laura would have to go over the same things they'd covered the day before. Of course, she couldn't say anything. This was the former first lady.

In addition to the decorating, Betty was working with writer Chris Chase on her autobiography. They had a routine in which Chase would come over to the house in the morning, and they'd sit together talking, "Betty going on and on and on," as Chase recorded it. "She was not a hard person to work with," Chase said, and everything would be fine until about lunchtime. Chris never saw her take any pills, but Betty might have a drink at lunch, and after that, "we really couldn't work," Chase said. "Right after lunch, we'd just give it up."

Caroline Coventry didn't observe Betty's drinking during the day, but she did notice that her employer was always very thirsty. "She always had iced tea. And she'd carry a glass of water around with her in a highball glass." Caroline assumed that the mix of medications dehydrated her.

There were luncheons and meetings Betty would attend, and when she went out, she knew only too well how to put herself together enough to be presentable in public. Caroline loved watching Mrs. Ford put on her makeup. She'd sit down at the vanity in front of the mirror, and was very serious about how she applied her eye shadow, lipstick, rouge. "It was an art that she had perfected," Caroline recalled. "She had a lot of pride in her looks."

Betty didn't exercise, but Caroline recalled that she was so flexible, "she was like a rubber band. She was amazing. I think she was just built that way." And she maintained her slim figure simply by not eating much at all. "When you're on that many drugs, food is not important, you're so out of it," Caroline explained.

There was an immense amount of mail, and it was Caroline's responsibility to answer every letter within twenty-four hours, along with maintaining Mrs. Ford's schedule and basically assisting with all levels of her life.

But every day, Caroline felt like she was wearing a "black hat."

"I was the bad news in the morning, because I'd be trying to get her dressed, and it felt like I was constantly hounding her. It wasn't fun. It was hard."

Caroline tried to figure out new ways to get Betty up and moving, and to appointments on time.

"I would set the clocks ahead by fifteen minutes or make the times on her schedule fifteen minutes earlier," Caroline said. "But she was too smart for that."

"Oh, Caroline, you're not fooling me," Betty would say.

"Sometimes she would surprise you, but basically, she was pretty predictable when she was in that state. In the state of taking all those meds," Caroline recalled. "Everything moved very slowly. Things couldn't get addressed because you'd ask her something, and by the time she thought about it for twenty minutes . . . it's like, okay, do you have a decision? So it was hard to get any business done."

As the weeks went by, Mrs. Ford declined more and more invitations, and then the invitations stopped coming. "Her friends all sort of knew what the problem was," Caroline said. And her friends were very active: playing tennis, golf, attending luncheons. It got to the point they just couldn't tolerate being around her.

"Wherever I went that fall, I was in a fog," Betty acknowledged later. "Sometimes a euphoric fog, sometimes a depressed fog."

Bob Hope's wife, Dolores, invited her to serve on the board of Eisenhower Medical Center, but while she faithfully attended meetings, Betty would sit there without saying a word. Friends began whispering that she was "kind of a zombie."

"She was painfully lonely," Caroline remembered. "Susan couldn't be there all the time and was totally burnt out with the situation, so I became her friend, her daughter, her confidant—whatever it took. It was difficult to satisfy that position because I wasn't a very good codependent, and it took a lot of that."

Like anyone who lives with someone addicted to drugs and/or alcohol, Caroline felt like she was constantly treading water, trying to keep both herself and Betty from drowning. It was so mentally and physically draining, it couldn't go on indefinitely without a casualty.

In September 1977, Betty was scheduled to travel to Moscow as part of her deal with NBC, to narrate the Bolshoi Ballet's performance of *The Nutcracker*. The show would be taped and then aired in the United States in December, at Christmastime. The president's assistant, Bob Barrett, offered to accompany her. It was decided that instead of Caroline Coventry, it would be better for Carolyn Porembka, Betty's former White House secretary, to go on the trip. She was used to traveling with Mrs. Ford on overseas trips, and as Caroline Coventry put it, she "knew how to take care of her. It was clear it was going to be a juggling act."

Even though it was just September, it was already very cold in Moscow. So cold that Betty slept with her fur coat draped over her in bed.

In addition to Bob Barrett, Carolyn Porembka, and her Secret Service detail, Betty had a translator, and the NBC cameras that accompanied her wherever she went. It wasn't so bad when she was touring the local sites, or the ballet school, where she interacted with the children, but when it came time to tape *The Nutcracker* performance, she was filled with anxiety. Sitting in the theater box with cameras on her, she was nervous about how she was coming off.

"I was not a professional," she wrote later, "and our three directors—a Russian, a Frenchman, and the NBC guy—spent hours yelling at each other."

She was so scared, she could hardly read the cue cards. "I'd sit for ages in that box, and when they excused me," Betty said, "I'd head for the ladies' room and take another pill."

22

The Turning Point

While Betty was in Moscow, Caroline Coventry stayed in Rancho Mirage, handling the never-ending correspondence, trying to keep everything organized for Betty so that things would run as smoothly as possible.

One day President Ford was away, and Caroline was alone in the house. She walked into the master bath—she was always in and out of there, assisting Betty with a zipper she couldn't reach on a dress, helping style her hair, trying to rush her along when she was late for an appointment, organizing things in the closet—but on this day, she went to the vanity where Betty would sit and do her makeup, and opened one of the drawers.

Oh, my God. There were dozens of prescription pill bottles, all different kinds of medication—some with dates that had expired, and others that were more recent—and as she started picking them up and reading the labels, Caroline instantly realized what was going on.

"That was her juggling act, right there," Caroline said. "She would take different things to compensate for different feelings during the day. She knew her meds well enough to know what she had to take to make herself feel good. She was very much in control of all of them."

Her mind spinning, Caroline went into the office, grabbed a notepad, and carefully listed everything in the drawer.

"I had this legal pad, and I wrote and wrote and wrote," Caroline said. "The amount of medicine was staggering. It filled three pages." But then it dawned on her that this wasn't everything. "I didn't know half of what was in that drawer because she'd taken the other half to Moscow."

Caroline had no idea what the drugs were for or what they did, but she thought if she could figure it all out, she might have some idea which medications were having such a detrimental effect on Mrs. Ford's personality. She headed straight to the pharmacy.

"I want all the information on all these drugs and what they do," Caroline said as she handed the pharmacist the list. The pharmacist gave her a stack of material; Caroline took it back to the house and started reading. Without a medical degree, much of the descriptions and jargon didn't make sense to her, but she could see that Mrs. Ford had pills for pain, pills for sleep, pills for digestive problems, constipation—you name it, she had it.

The more she learned, the more terrified she became. If Mrs. Ford was taking these meds, mixing and matching them by her own volition, it was like she was playing Russian roulette. Caroline was so distraught, she made the bold decision to go straight to Mrs. Ford's doctor in Palm Springs.

Dr. Williamson, a general physician in his late sixties or early seventies, was "old school," Caroline recalled. "I felt the need to talk to him. I wanted him to know that his prescribing these meds was having an adverse reaction on Betty Ford that, in turn, was affecting her family, friends, and social environment. It was a matter of ethics."

The receptionist led Caroline into Dr. Williamson's office. He was sitting behind a big wood desk next to a window with a view of the mountains. It was a gray day, and Caroline was struck by the fact that the only light in the room came from the cabinet behind the desk. Framed certificates of the doctor's medical degrees hung on the walls.

Caroline's father was a doctor, and she had a tremendous amount of respect for the medical profession. But after discovering the massive amounts of medication this doctor had prescribed to Mrs. Ford, she could hardly contain the fury that was building inside her.

She sat down on the edge of the chair as if she wouldn't be there too long. And she wasn't.

"Why are you giving all these drugs to Mrs. Ford?" Caroline

implored as she waved the filled legal pages in front of him. And then, looking straight into his eyes, she blurted out, "You're going to kill her!"

Dr. Williamson looked away and sighed. "I thought she'd never come back if I didn't give her what she asked for."

Caroline's stomach was churning. She couldn't believe what she was hearing. *Give me any kind of answer, but don't tell me that*, she remembered thinking to herself. She was beyond distraught. *Now what?* she thought as she stormed out of the office. She couldn't tell President or Mrs. Ford what she'd done. It was a complete betrayal of confidence, and she'd most certainly be fired. But she had to do something.

Caroline wondered how long this had been going on. Since the White House? Before? A few members of the household staff had come to Rancho Mirage from the White House, and she broached the subject cautiously with one of them.

"When he told me the routine in the White House, I had this vision of two hands, outstretched with palms up, and someone giving her a handful of pills in one hand and a vodka in the other," Caroline remembered. She was seething.

"To this day, that image of the two hands, pills in one and a drink in the other, and knowing how it affected Betty Ford, is a constant reminder to never mix the two."

The problem was, however, that in the White House, the staff served at the pleasure of the first lady, and even though they saw what was going on, it would have been extremely difficult not to fulfill her requests. It wasn't the staff's position to tell the president's wife what she should or shouldn't do. "It was the hardest thing for me to accept," Caroline said. "That somebody would give her alcohol and medication at the same time."

She decided she had to speak to President Ford.

Up to this point, Caroline had had little interaction with the former president, and when she did, it was very formal. Typically, she would discuss something with Bob Barrett, and then Bob would take it to the president. But Bob was in Moscow with Mrs. Ford, and because this was such a personal issue, she decided to go directly to President Ford.

She caught him alone in his office one day and said, "President Ford, we have to do something. Mrs. Ford is taking all these drugs, and it's not working."

President Ford looked at her and, with a weariness in his voice, said, "Caroline, we have done everything we can. We've sent her to psychiatrists, we've sent her to doctors, massage therapists, acupuncture. There's nothing left to do."

He was filled with despair. Within the past eight months, he'd seen his wife deteriorate into someone who barely resembled the vivacious, active woman he had married. He still loved her, deeply, but Caroline got the feeling that he had made peace with the fact that this was the way life was going to be from now on. When he traveled, he didn't have to deal with it. And golf was his escape.

"They rarely quarreled," Caroline said. "He just appeased her. It was the easiest way to deal with it."

That fall, Susan bought a condominium in Palm Springs, and Caroline moved in with her to share expenses.

"Caroline would come home and tell me all the god-awful things about my mother that day," Susan recalled. "So the two of us would talk about it. But neither of us knew what to do."

"Susan was really there for me as a sounding board," Caroline said. "She was the only one that really understood what I was seeing, hearing, and thinking."

Because Caroline was often alone with Betty day in and day out, she was the target of Betty's mood swings and unreasonable demands. "She didn't realize she was hurting me," Caroline said, her eyes welling with tears as the painful memories returned. "She didn't know because she was too drugged out. She didn't know how she affected her children or her husband. It's not any one moment. It's the overall hurt that you get. You put up with it. You tried as hard as you could to get beyond it any way you possibly could. It was a daily challenge."

Susan, too, found it incredibly difficult to be around her mother at that time. Sometimes she'd visit her father in his office and avoid her mother completely. And there were times when her mother had committed to an event, but then it would come time, and both Susan and her father would realize Betty was in no condition to be in a social situation.

"She would say her neck hurt, and then she'd take a pill and wouldn't feel like doing her hair and makeup," Susan recalled. "I was more the parent in the relationship, and I protected her."

So Jerry would tell everyone Betty had the flu, and often Susan would go in her place. "Dad and I covered for her."

Betty would often call Susan and say, "Come over, and let's have lunch and go shopping."

"I'd get over to the house at eleven thirty or eleven forty-five, and she was still in her robe," Susan recalled. "And it was like watching someone in slow motion getting dressed. It was just forever. And we'd maybe barely get out the door by two thirty to go shopping."

During the day, it wasn't alcohol, it was medication. "She was not a daytime drinker," Susan said. "Occasionally, I saw her have a glass of wine at lunch, but that was not a regular occurrence."

"We wanted to carry on as if everything was fine," Mike Ford said, "but no one really wanted to admit that we were seeing our mother really change and become withdrawn and emotional and really sick. We were in denial."

When Betty returned from Moscow, Caroline didn't dare mention what she'd done, and things carried on as they had before. When they'd first arrived in Rancho Mirage, Betty had frequent invitations to lunch with friends such as Dolores Hope and Nicky Firestone, but those invitations began dropping off. And it was easy to see why.

"Eating with her was torturous," Caroline recalled. She'd pick up the fork, take a bite, and then chew the mouthful so slowly. Everything was in slow motion. Minutes would go by before she'd pick up the fork again. She didn't eat in front of the television. The radio wasn't on. No animation in her discussions. Just slow, deliberate, and quiet. After a few bites, she might comment to the chef, "Oh, Odie . . . this is so good!"

When there were no invitations or outings on the schedule, Betty would stay in her robe all day. The pink robe. "She wore the same robe every day," Caroline said. "Quilted silk. Every morning. If we weren't in it at four in the afternoon, we were doing pretty well. She was struggling every single day to find some sense of order in her life."

From October to December, Caroline accompanied Betty on numerous trips throughout the country, including the National Women's Conference in Houston with First Lady Rosalynn Carter, and a trip to Grand Rapids, where Betty was an honorary patron of a new art exhibit. Caroline remembered it as a blur. "There was lots of traveling and trying so hard to be on time, to be alert. Just trying to make it."

* * *

In mid-December Betty flew to New York City for an interview with Tom Brokaw on NBC's *Today* show to promote the airing of the Bolshoi Ballet's *Nutcracker* that she had attended and narrated in September. Of the countless interviews Brokaw conducted during his decades-long broadcasting career, this one with the former first lady would remain vivid in his mind.

"She was not in good shape when she arrived," Brokaw remembered. "She was sleepy, her eyes were drooping, and she could barely articulate why she was there." Under the glare of the lights, the cameras rolling, Betty stumbled over her words, with a forced smile pasted across her face. Brokaw did his best to carry her through the interview, trying to prevent her from completely humiliating herself. Meanwhile, standing nearby, Betty's staff watched, frozen in place.

"I remember having this wide-eyed exchange with her staff," Brokaw said. "It was a full realization of what she was going through at that point. We were all astonished."

This was not the same woman he had seen just two years earlier when he attended a white-tie state dinner at the White House. "President Ford had this down-home, Main Street charm, and Betty elevated him with her style and grace. At that dinner, I really thought she had found her place." Brokaw had never seen any indication of a problem during Ford's presidency, but now it was unmistakable.

After the interview, Betty flew back to California. President Ford was gone, so Caroline offered to stay and watch *The Nutcracker* on TV with her. After all the buildup, they were both excited to see how it turned out.

"We sat in the bedroom," Caroline recalled. "Two chairs in front of the TV."

An announcer came on and said, "*The Wonderful World of Disney* will not be presented this evening but will return next week at its regularly scheduled time."

Then there was Betty Ford, a close-up shot of her filling the whole screen. Dressed in a dark-brown fur coat with a collar, an apricot turtleneck, and dangling earrings encrusted with green and pink jewels, Betty looked elegant and warm.

From the family quarters of the White House, Betty Ford looks out over the West Wing to get a glimpse of her husband as he walks to the Oval Office, January 20, 1975. At times, she said she felt like "a bird in a gilded cage." *Courtesy Gerald R. Ford Library*

Betty's outspoken support for the Equal Rights Amendment sparked controversy, but she refused to be silenced. Hollywood, Florida. February 26, 1975. *Courtesy Gerald R. Ford Library*

President Ford, Susan, and Betty share a light moment at Camp David, March 2, 1975.
Courtesy Gerald R. Ford Library

Mike, Gayle, President Ford, Betty, Jack, Susan, and Steve on the South Lawn of the White House. September 6, 1976. *Courtesy Gerald R. Ford Library*

Betty shows off the ERA "Bloomer" flag presented to her by one of her Secret Service agents. L to R: Nancy Chirdon, Agent Dick Hartwig, Betty, Carolyn Porembka, military aide Ric Sardo, photographer David Kennerly. June 24, 1975.
Courtesy Gerald R. Ford Library

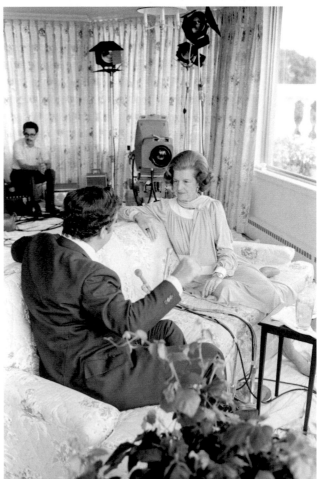

Betty's candid answers in her interview with Morley Safer for *60 Minutes* sparked unprecedented controversy. July 21, 1975.
Courtesy Gerald R. Ford Library

Betty greets President Ford on Air Force One, unaware of an assassination attempt, moments earlier, outside a San Francisco hotel. September 22, 1975. *Courtesy Gerald R. Ford Library*

First Lady Betty Ford answers questions from the press about early detection of breast cancer. New York City. Nov. 7, 1975. *Courtesy Gerald R. Ford Library*

After the assassination attempts, Betty routinely waved goodbye to President Ford from the White House balcony, and said a prayer, every time he departed on a trip. *Courtesy Gerald R. Ford Library*

When First Lady Betty Ford enthusiastically joined a group of Chinese dancers during a presidential visit to Beijing in December 1975, some said she opened more bridges between the two nations than the talks of the diplomats. *Courtesy Gerald R. Ford Library*

Comedian Woody Allen paid $5,000 to be First Lady Betty Ford's escort at the 50th anniversary celebration of Martha Graham's dance company. L to R: Diane Keaton, Martha Graham, Betty Ford, Woody Allen. New York City, June 19, 1975. *AP Photo*

First Lady Betty Ford, aka "First Momma," drew large crowds during the 1976 presidential campaign because she was so popular. San Jacinto, Texas. April 21, 1976. *Courtesy Gerald R. Ford Library*

Betty joined son Steve on a campaign stop in California during his sweep through the west in a Winnebago motor home during the 1976 presidential campaign. *Courtesy Gerald R. Ford Library*

Betty takes Queen Elizabeth II on a tour of the White House. July 7, 1976. *Courtesy Gerald R. Ford Library*

First Lady Betty Ford dancing with Britain's Prince Philip following the state dinner in honor of Queen Elizabeth II and Prince Philip. July 7, 1976. *Courtesy Gerald R. Ford Library*

Betty got a lot of attention when she danced "the bump" with entertainer Tony Orlando onstage during the 1976 Republican National Convention in Kansas City. August 17, 1976. *AP Photo*

First Lady Betty Ford and comedian Marty Allen dancing in the Grand Hall of the White House following a state dinner honoring the president of Liberia. September 21, 1976. *Courtesy Gerald R. Ford Library*

President and Mrs. Ford brought dancing back to the White House during state dinners and they were often the last ones on the dance floor at the end of the evening. August 3, 1976. *Courtesy Gerald R. Ford Library*

Betty and White House chief photographer David Kennerly had a close relationship and shared a bawdy sense of humor. *Courtesy Gerald R. Ford Library*

Betty tries to cheer up son Jack for a family photo in the Oval Office after the election loss, November 3, 1976. L to R: Steve, Jack, Betty, President Ford, Susan, Gayle, and Mike. *Courtesy Gerald R. Ford Library*

Because President Ford lost his voice in the waning hours of the 1976 presidential campaign, Betty stepped up to read his concession speech to the press. L to R: Steve, President Ford, Susan, Mike, Gayle, and Betty (at podium). *Courtesy Gerald R. Ford Library*

The living room of the Fords' home in Rancho Mirage, California, where the family held an intervention to address Betty's drug and alcohol addiction on April 1, 1978. *Courtesy George Gutenberg Architecture & Interior Design Photography*

Betty and Caroline Coventry share a light moment as they unpack boxes during the Ford's move to their newly constructed home in Rancho Mirage, CA. The intervention took place days later. March 1978. *Courtesy Caroline Coventry.*

Liza Minnelli, Elizabeth Taylor, and Betty Ford at Studio 54 in New York City, May 1979.
Getty Images

Dr. Joe Cruse, Betty Ford, and Leonard Firestone break ground for the Betty Ford Center,
October 1981. *Courtesy Hazelden Betty Ford Foundation*

Jerry and Betty stroll hand in hand in Vail.
Courtesy Russ Ohlson

Betty Ford and daughter Susan Ford Bales.
Courtesy Susan Ford Bales

Betty Ford in front of Firestone Hall at the Betty Ford Center, 1990. *Courtesy Hazelden Betty Ford Foundation*

To Betty Ford,
Congratulations on the Medal of Freedom
So Well Deserved — Warm Regards.
Geo Bush

11-18-91

First Lady Barbara Bush, Betty Ford, and President George H.W. Bush as Betty is presented the Medal of Freedom. November 18, 1991. *Courtesy Gerald R. Ford Library*

Betty and Jerry Ford with their children, grandchildren, and great-grandchildren in Vail, Colorado. This was the last family photo before President Ford's death. Summer 2002. *Courtesy Susan Ford Bales*

Greg Willard briefs Mrs. Ford as Air Force One arrives in Washington, DC, for the state funeral of President Ford. December 29, 2006. *Courtesy Gerald R. Ford Library, David Kennerly*

Betty Ford prays at her husband's flag draped casket in the US Capitol Rotunda, December 29, 2006. She slept with that flag next to her until her death in 2011. *Courtesy Gerald R. Ford Library, David Kennerly*

Jerry and Betty at their Alexandria home, August 1974.
Courtesy Gerald R. Ford Library,
David Kennerly

"Good evening," she began. "I'm speaking to you from the Bolshoi Theatre in Moscow."

Oh dear, Caroline thought. *This is not good.* She was smiling, and she looked beautiful, her hair perfectly styled, her makeup expertly applied, but the words came out of her mouth like she was, well, drugged.

The shot zoomed out, and another woman appeared on the right of the screen.

"During my visit to the Soviet Union, my interpreter and guide has been Katya . . . uh . . ." She hesitated, clearly struggling with the last name, and turned toward the woman.

"Chakovskaya," interjected the woman.

"Ah, thank you, Katya," Betty said with a smile.

Okay, Caroline thought, *that wasn't too bad. That's a hard name to pronounce.*

"Tonight we're going to attend a gala performance of a favorite Christmas fantasy: *The Nutcracker* by the world-famous Bolshoi Ballet. Now, won't you join us, please? We'll have a lovely time. It will be delightful."

The next scene showed Betty and Katya walking up the stairs of the Bolshoi Theatre. They had removed their coats, and you could see Betty's floor-length gown. High necked, with draping sleeves, in a beautiful shade of apricot.

Titles appeared on the screen:

NBC presents The Nutcracker *by Peter Tchaikovsky*
Story Teller Mrs. Betty Ford
With Katya Chakovskaya

The orchestra began playing, and there was Betty again. She had on a permanent smile as she spoke, but her eyelids were heavy. It looked like she was reading from a teleprompter, but the words were slurred. "Tonight we are seeing a slightly different version of *The Nutcracker*, but in many ways, it is the same. The story about a little girl who has a dream. I've always known her as Clara, but here in Moscow, she is known as Mascha."

The camera cut to the conductor and the orchestra, with the music playing as Betty continued her narrative.

"There's a Christmas party, a beautiful tree, marvelous toys, a mysterious magician . . . to entertain the children, and dolls that come to life and a special gift for Mascha: a toy nutcracker that turns into a prince."

The curtain is drawn, and the ballet begins with Tchaikovsky's exciting theme in the background. *Bum bada-da-da dum dum dum dum*. Betty disappears, and the dancers take over.

Thank God, Caroline thought.

The ballet itself was magnificent. The costumes, stunning; the dancers, absolute perfection. But every ten minutes or so, the camera would return to Betty, reading from the teleprompter explaining what was happening in the ballet, her words slurred and devoid of feeling or emotion.

Betty explained that, during intermission, the audience had been informed that the dancer performing as the prince had injured his leg and could not continue. After an hour delay, two other Bolshoi stars took over the principal role.

She struggled to pronounce things properly—and not just the Russian names, but simple words like "enduring popularity."

She came on again before the last scene, and by this time, her eyes were nearly closed. You could see her false eyelashes moving, and it looked like it was all she could do to keep her eyes open as she stumbled through the words. It was painful to watch.

When it was all over, Betty turned to Caroline and said, "That was pretty bad, wasn't it?"

Caroline didn't know what to say other than to be perfectly honest. She simply looked at Betty and said, "Yeah, it was."

"There wasn't much discussion after that," Caroline recalled, "because she was destroyed. She knew that she had really blown it."

The next day, the press reviewed the program as "something of a disaster," and called her "sloe-eyed and sleepy tongued."

"And they were right," Betty would acknowledge, years later. "I was so overmedicated."

But nobody said anything. The pills were prescribed by doctors, and everyone thought she needed them.

"So I went on having pain and taking pills. And feeling guiltless," Betty said.

* * *

"Christmas vacation in Vail that year was utter hell," Caroline recalled. Betty was in a constant daze, and she rarely got out of her bathrobe the entire vacation. "For the first time, the kids came to me."

Mike, who hadn't been around his mother in several months, noticed that she was manifesting a lot of unhealthy signs. "She was incoherent, kind of shuffling around, not eating right. And the slurred speech, the not getting dressed until late in the day, had become a lifestyle."

The kids were so frustrated, and at one point, Steve turned to Caroline and said, "Caroline, can't you just get Mom dressed in the morning?"

"Yeah, I'll try," Caroline said. *As if that would solve everything*, Caroline thought. She wished it were that easy. It seemed such a small thing to ask, but it was such a huge task. Although Steve was sincere in his request, he didn't realize what a constant daily struggle it had been for Caroline since the day she started the job. Everyone realized something had to be done about "Mother's problem," but no one knew what to do.

The children would remember it as the worst Christmas ever, while Betty was completely oblivious. "We were up in Vail, there was a lot of good snow, we were together, and I had my pills."

After Christmas, back in California, Caroline tried her hardest to get Mrs. Ford dressed in the morning. No luck. Every day was such a chore to get the smallest things done. President Ford would recall that it seemed like Betty was "in second gear," and it became "increasingly difficult to lead a normal life." It was easier for him to travel. He couldn't stand to watch his wife get up in the morning and take a handful of pills, and then another handful at night, on top of a couple of drinks.

The master bath in the rented house was floor-to-ceiling pink marble, and one night, while the president was away, Betty took a bad fall in the bathroom. No one was there, so it was never clear exactly what happened, but she managed to get herself up and back into bed. The next morning, she realized she'd chipped a tooth.

"She was scared to death for fear anyone would find out," Caroline Coventry recalled. An appointment was made with the dentist, and the agents whisked her away to have the tooth fixed. Caroline realized it could have been worse. What if she'd hit her head?

The new house in Rancho Mirage next door to the Firestones was nearly complete, and everyone seemed to think that perhaps once the Fords moved into their permanent home, Betty would be better.

Caroline always opened the mail and sorted through it, and one day a long letter came from someone in Germany. It was written completely in German, so Caroline asked one of the Secret Service agents if he could find someone to translate it. A few days later, the agent came back with the translation. The letter was from a woman who had seen Betty on the Bolshoi *Nutcracker* TV special and recognized that she had a problem. "I understand what's wrong with you. I've been there." She wanted Betty to know that there was someone out there who had been through the same thing and to let her know where she could go to find help.

"The agents warned me not to get involved," Caroline remembered. They reminded her that she was not a friend, not a family member—she worked for Mrs. Ford, just as they did. It was not their place to judge or advise the family or Mrs. Ford on how she was living her own life.

"Stay out of it," they said.

But Caroline decided that if she showed the letter to Mrs. Ford, perhaps she'd see herself in it and indeed seek help.

"On February 20, I tried my lonely intervention," Caroline recalled. She took the letter into the living room, where Betty was sitting, her hands trembling. In her soft voice, Caroline tried to be as delicate and tactful as possible.

"You know, Mrs. Ford, I got a letter from someone that understands that you're taking these pills. She understands how bad you feel, and she's very considerate in how she wrote this letter."

Betty appeared to be in a dazed state. But suddenly she came undone.

"I am so mad!" she yelled.

"She just came unglued," Caroline recalled. "Yelling and screaming at me."

"I've already tried to take myself off some of these medications!" Betty cried. "I've already tried to do that." It was true, she had tried. But when she stopped taking one medication or another, she would begin to go through withdrawal, so then she'd compensate for the withdrawal with something else.

Betty flew into a rage, and, as tears streamed down her face, she stormed into the bedroom. Caroline felt terrible. After a few minutes, Caroline walked quietly into the bedroom, where Betty was lying on the bed, convulsing with sobs.

"I'm sorry, Mrs. Ford. I'm sorry. I was just trying to help."

"Get out of here!" Betty screamed. "You don't need to try to make me feel good. You don't need to soothe me."

Caroline left the room, shaking. She'd never seen Mrs. Ford like this before, and she was deeply concerned.

Caroline went to the Secret Service command post and told them what had happened.

"You've got to have somebody posted at various points throughout the house," she said. "Just be there in case she falls. I'm worried because she's all alone in the house, and she's just so upset." Normally, the agents wouldn't be inside the house, but Caroline knew that oftentimes an alcoholic will die of something unrelated to the disease, such as a fall. The image of Betty lying on the floor of the pink-marble bathroom when she'd chipped her tooth haunted Caroline.

The agents chastised her for going against their advice. "We told you not to get involved," they said. They'd been right. Now look what had happened.

She went home to the condo and poured out everything to Susan. She was just trying to help. Trying to *do something*.

"Susan understood," Caroline said. "She knew what it was like. She had lived through all of that as a child."

Indeed, for most of Susan's childhood, Betty had been self-medicating in varying degrees, and Susan's coping mechanism was to try to fix whatever problems arose. There would be times when things seemed normal, but then there'd be another episode, another incident. Looking back, Susan came to realize that she was often the parent in the relationship, trying to protect her mother. There was no question that Betty's condition was far worse than ever, but even Susan was out of answers. What could you do?

Caroline didn't blame Mrs. Ford. "That was a rude awakening. And that's why they don't do interventions like that. But I didn't know that. Nobody knew that."

The next morning, hesitant to greet Mrs. Ford after the previous night's incident, Caroline stayed in the office and answered mail. Her nerves were on edge, and one day that week—the days were all a blur— Dr. Cruse's office called, wondering why Caroline had missed her personal appointment that had been scheduled.

Caroline, too, was seeing Dr. Cruse as her gynecologist, and with her "mind in the clouds," she'd completely forgotten. She made another appointment. When Dr. Cruse came into the examination room, he could tell by the look on her face that she wasn't well.

"What's wrong, Caroline?" he asked.

She started sobbing and just let everything out. "I was so strung out," Caroline recalled. "I basically had a nervous breakdown right there in his office. It wasn't pretty."

Dr. Cruse, a recovering alcoholic who had seen how loved ones of alcoholics were affected, knew exactly what was going on. "Don't worry about it," he said soothingly. "I'll talk to Susan."

A few weeks later, Susan, who was working as a freelance photographer, got an assignment that would finally open the door to a solution. Dr. Cruse was an outspoken advocate for sobriety in the community. He was working with a treatment center for chemically dependent kids called Turnoff, in the high desert, and asked Susan if she'd take some photos for them.

"I didn't know anything about Alcoholics Anonymous or Al-Anon at that time," Susan recalled. She was just twenty years old, and it wasn't commonly talked about. Dr. Cruse drove her up to the facility, and as she took the photos, she learned about the program and was struck by the wonderful things the center was doing to help the kids turn around their lives. On the drive back to Palm Springs, Susan told Dr. Cruse about a friend she had, who had a problem. She was taking too many pills, and she'd changed so much, Susan didn't know what to do.

"You're talking about your mother, aren't you?" Dr. Cruse asked.

Tears filled Susan's eyes as she nodded. "Yes. I just don't know what to do. It's tearing our family apart."

Dr. Cruse told her there was a fairly new technique called an "intervention," in which the person was confronted in a loving way and convinced he or she needed treatment. It worked best if the whole family was involved.

The intervention technique had been developed in the 1970s by an Episcopal priest named Vernon Johnson, who had made it his life's goal to help addicts achieve sobriety. In a study of two hundred recovering alcoholics, his main question was: "What made you want to stop drinking?"

Johnson saw the value in having family and loved ones confront the addict—not ganging up and blaming her or him—but showing they cared. The family members would write letters to the addict providing detailed evidence of past events in which the addict had hurt them and how it had made them feel, focusing on caring rather than condemnation.

As a team, the end result of the intervention must be the agreed-upon goal that the addict seek treatment—not as punishment, but to improve the addict's life.

Susan knew this was what had to be done. She called her father and told him what Dr. Cruse had said. But Jerry wasn't sure this was the right thing to do. It sounded so hurtful. Besides, it was going to be difficult to get Jack, Steve, Mike, and Gayle there all at the same time. And Clara Powell. Susan knew they needed Clara there. But everyone was spread across the country, living his or her own life.

Dr. Cruse convinced President Ford to meet with him at his office after hours one evening. "I knew she had a problem," Cruse said. "It was clear she was under the influence of prescription drugs." When the president arrived with two Secret Service agents, Cruse explained how the intervention needed to work. It had to consist of the family, and each would give a personal experience. Then they had to present her with consequences if she didn't agree.

President Ford could not imagine doing this to his beloved wife. He knew it would tear her apart. "Joe," he said, "can't you go do it by yourself?"

"He didn't want to do it," Cruse recalled. "What do you say to the president?"

* * *

Meanwhile, the new house on Sand Dune Road was complete, and Betty was excited to finally be moving in. The single-story, five-bedroom, six-and-a-half-bath, 6,300-square-foot house sat at the end of a cul-de-sac on nearly one and a half acres of land overlooking the thirteenth fairway of the prestigious Thunderbird Country Club, with stunning views of the mountains in the distance. The Firestones' home was next door on one side, and President Ford's office was in the home previously owned by movie legend Ginger Rogers on the other side.

A thirty-foot-tall olive tree at the front of the property had been saved, so that as you entered the front door, the tree's branches reached out like welcoming arms. Inside, high ceilings and large, open spaces filled with natural light. The guest bedrooms, kitchen, and dining room wrapped around the backyard where a swimming pool was under construction. Eventually the yard would be landscaped with palm and citrus trees, and a row of rose bushes along one wall, but when they first moved in, there was just a big hole in the ground.

Next to the master bedroom was a cozy den for watching television, lined with bookcases to be filled with family photos, books, and memorabilia, and the president's favorite blue leather chair and ottoman. The center of the house was the expansive sunken living room decorated in soothing blue, green, and white.

All the new furnishings were in place, but then three moving vans arrived with their additional furniture and belongings from Grand Rapids, Crown View Drive, and the personal items from the White House, all of which had been in storage. The truckloads of boxes were unloaded into the garage. Every morning, Caroline would meet Betty at the new house, and they'd tear through boxes, trying to find places for everything. It was a monumental chore, Jerry was traveling, and with no end in sight, Susan suggested they fly Clara out to Palm Springs to help set up the house. Clara agreed and was there within a week.

Finally, Betty had everything she'd wanted for so many years: her husband was retired, and they'd moved into their dream home. She'd picked out everything: the bathroom faucets, the light fixtures, the fabrics for drapes and furnishings. The huge John Ulbricht painting of Betty was hung in the living room, and it looked exquisite. Why then, if all her dreams had come true, did she feel so empty inside?

To cure the emptiness, she turned to her gourmet collection of drugs. "I did a little self-prescribing," she would admit later. "If one pill is good, two must be better—and when I added vodka to the mix, I moved into a wonderful, fuzzy place where everything was fine, I could cope."

23

The Intervention
and Treatment

Betty seemed to be getting worse day by day. In a moment of frustration, Susan called Dr. Cruse and said, "We have to do something now. We can't wait to get everyone together."

So the next morning, Susan, Dr. Cruse, and Caroline attempted the "mini-intervention."

It didn't work. They hadn't caught her early enough before she'd taken her pills, and the three of them weren't strong enough to handle her resistance.

"You are all a bunch of monsters!" Betty yelled. "Now, get out of here! Get out of my house and never come back!"

"I was devastated," Susan said. "Here Dr. Cruse had promised me that we were going to help my mother, and all we'd done was fall flat on our faces, and my mother had kicked me out of her house."

"It was a big mistake," Cruse admitted. "The Secret Service escorted me out and told me I wasn't welcome back on the property." Later that evening, President Ford called Dr. Cruse and said that Betty had called him. "She's clearheaded," President Ford said, "and she told me she wants half of our house, and she's going to New York."

"It gave me goose pimples," Cruse said. But then Ford added, "Don't worry, she's said that before."

Susan went home, and later that night, just like she'd done so many times as a little girl, she turned to Clara to help figure out what to do. "Boy, was I glad she was there," Susan said. "Because at that point, Clara was the only person Mother would talk to."

"Don't worry," Clara said. "Mother's fine. I've got her settled down."

In the meantime, Dr. Cruse had called psychiatrist Joseph Pursch. A captain in the US Navy, Dr. Pursch headed the Alcohol Rehabilitation Service at the navy's Regional Medical Center in Long Beach. Together he and Cruse decided they had to do a proper intervention, and it had to be done as soon as possible; Betty Ford's life was at stake.

"Captain Pursch was quite a personality," Caroline Coventry recalled. A Chicago native, Pursch had been raised in Yugoslavia but returned to the United States as a World War II refugee during his teens. Now in his midforties, he spoke with a noticeable Eastern European accent, and "he commanded your attention," Caroline said. "And you listened."

Dr. Pursch brought in Pat Benedict, a navy nurse who worked with him, and met with Susan, Clara, and Dr. Cruse. Susan was terrified about how it would work, but Benedict reassured her everything would be okay.

"When I met Pat Benedict, it was like somebody had taken a hundred-pound weight off my head," Susan recalled. "Because she understood what I was going through. I'd tell her stories, and she'd heard them all before." The nurse explained to Susan that her mother had a disease, and it could be cured—if they could convince her to go through treatment.

For the intervention to work, they had to have the entire family there. Everyone had agreed, except Jack. He had given up hope that the problem would ever be corrected, and he worried they'd only be hurting her.

Clara was the one who finally convinced him. "We've got to do this for Mother," she said. "If we lose, we lose; but we will have given it our best shot." Finally, Jack came around.

Plans were made for everyone to meet in Rancho Mirage. The intervention would take place April 1, one week before Betty's sixtieth birthday.

"You felt very, very guilty," Caroline Coventry recalled. "Because we were all working behind her back, making arrangements for everyone to fly in and make sure they had a place to stay in Palm Springs for this intervention. And Mrs. Ford didn't have a clue."

Everyone met in President Ford's office for some coaching and to understand how their mother had gotten to this point.

"The doctors literally gave us a set of instructions," President Ford recalled. They told the family how Betty was going to resent it, and that she was going to cry, but everyone had to be firm and united. In the process, Jerry, and all of them, realized how they had actually been enablers.

"I would make all kinds of alibis about why we were late getting someplace, or why Betty didn't show up at all," Jerry said. "And it was getting worse, not better. My pleading with her was exacerbating the situation, because she would resent it, as though I was being a nitpicker."

"We began to understand the nature of chemical dependence and how it had taken over her life," Mike Ford recalled. "And at that point, I was really prepared to march in there and lay it on her."

"It was so tense," Caroline recalled. "But as we all walked from the office to the house that morning, I knew God was with us."

The intervention was brutal. For nearly two hours, the family spoke about things they'd been holding inside for years. It was like walking through fire, feeling the scorching pain throughout your entire body; and when you got to the other side, you had searing, open wounds— wounds that would eventually heal and turn into scars—but, by the grace of God, you were still alive, and no one had died.

At first, Betty was strong, her iron will front and center. But eventually she succumbed to reality, and the tears came out in sobs. "No one had ever seen her cry like that before. It took every ounce of energy in her body," Caroline recalled.

Betty had been blindsided, and she couldn't come to terms with what she was hearing.

"I had given my whole life to my family," she remembered thinking. "My whole idea was being a super mom and perfect wife. I had played a role that I thought was a very good one, and dedicated many hours and all my time to it, and to think I had failed? That was a terrible thing."

Then Dr. Pursch took over. "Mrs. Ford, are you willing to go into treatment?" he asked. Betty nodded and tried to smile like she meant it. "Yes," she said through tears, "I want to get well."

Dr. Pursch explained the first thing that needed to happen was for her to be detoxed from all the drugs she was taking. He was confident she could stay at home during the detoxification process, as long as she allowed the navy nurse Pat Benedict to move in and supervise everything. It would probably take a week, and while it was going to be the most difficult thing she'd ever done, it was essential.

After that, Betty had a choice. She could choose to go to Alcoholics Anonymous meetings and learn how to live a sober and drug-free life, but that would take months, if not years, to have the effect she could get in a four-to-six-week intensive in-patient treatment program. There was one at the pioneering Hazelden center, outside of Minneapolis, or special arrangements could be made for her to be committed to Dr. Pursch's program at the naval facility in Long Beach.

The nurse knelt beside her and said, "Betty, I have had a problem too. I took a lot of amphetamines in Vietnam, and then Valium to level the nerves. I will help you."

She could tell she wasn't really getting through. Betty didn't want to hear about Pat's problems. And then, Pat added, "I've also had a breast removed."

That resonated. Betty reached out and patted her on the cheek.

By this point, everyone was emotionally drained. Dr. Pursch suggested they take a break for lunch. He and the others would leave so that Betty could have some time alone with her family. After that, everyone would reconvene in the living room. The doctor suggested that Mrs. Ford get dressed, and, he told her, they'd be collecting all her medications and disposing of them.

Betty nodded. She understood. As everyone got up, Betty went into her bedroom.

"I got dressed and put myself together to prove how really well I was," she said. And then she went to the drawer in her bathroom, pulled out the four or five pills she normally took at noon, and swallowed them with a glass of water.

After lunch, Dr. Pursch returned with a whiteboard and an easel. He began writing the names of each drug Betty was taking and how many milligrams a day of each. When he added them up, the amount was so staggering, it shocked Betty herself.

Even though she was "sedated to the teeth," the message got through loud and clear. "When they confront you with that kind of evidence, you have to be a real dummy not to realize you're in trouble," she would say later.

President Ford was stunned. He saw the pharmacy bills each month, and while his apprehension about the amount of medication had been growing, he'd never actually counted the pills.

"I was more concerned with the pills than the alcohol, because the amounts she was drinking didn't seem abnormally high," he said. "It was a couple of vodkas before dinner, and maybe she'd want a couple of bourbons after dinner." But neither he nor anyone else had understood how the combination of alcohol and pills magnified the effect—until Dr. Pursch laid it all out for them in black and white.

Pursch brought in a movie projector, and they watched educational films about alcohol and drug dependency. It was a crash course that made the family realize how they'd all been in denial. Everyone was lost in his or her own thoughts, remembering incidents over the years that now were so clearly warning signs of Betty's growing dependence on alcohol and prescription drugs. The first step, before anything else, was to get all the drugs and alcohol out of the house.

Dr. Cruse, Caroline, and Susan took anything and everything they could find—even the over-the-counter stuff.

"There were bottles and bottles and bottles," Susan recalled.

"I took out an entire grocery bag filled with bottles," Dr. Cruse said. "We found more later. She had hidden them."

That night, Clara cooked pot roast, and the family had dinner together. "It was like the family was a family once again," Susan recalled. "It was like everything had been torn down, and there was nothing to hide anymore."

They'd walked through the fire and come out alive. Now, it was time for the truly hard work to begin.

It was decided that Betty would go through the detoxification process at home, with Pat Benedict administering the detoxification medication and supervising her around the clock.

"It was horrible what that body went through. Just horrible." Caroline shuddered at the memory. "She was worse off than they thought. She spent the whole first day throwing up, just trying to get it out of her system. She had the shakes, her body ached, she got the twitches. She had a lot of massage. They did everything they could to try and keep her comfortable, but it was holy hell."

"It was miserable. Horrible," Susan remembered. "I would stop by, but she really wanted to be in her bedroom where it was dark and desensitized. I'd give her a hug and a kiss and leave."

Betty would later write: "I shook so much I didn't need an electric toothbrush. And in bed at night, my legs kept moving, I couldn't lie still." She knew the only way she was going to get through this was to turn to God.

Over and over, as she lay in bed, she repeated the Serenity Prayer: "God, grant me the serenity to accept the things I cannot change; courage to change the things I can; and wisdom to know the difference."

"President Ford was very strong," Caroline remembered. "But can you imagine him watching all of this? He was just finding himself, too, because this was new territory. He took care of her. He cherished her; it was obvious. It wasn't like he ever slept in the other bedroom. He was always there for her all night."

Privately, President Ford was deeply worried. He went to the nurse and asked, "Why does she keep throwing up? When will it stop?"

"Mr. President, this is the worst day she'll ever have," Pat told him. She promised to have her up and bathed and walking the next day.

True to her word, Pat got Betty dressed in a blue skirt and a bandana around her head, and out they went for a walk on the golf course. Pat carried Valium and a syringe in her pocket in case of an emergency. They went past the president's office, and Betty waved. Then, as they continued along the path, all of a sudden Betty reached over and put her arm around Pat.

In that moment, Pat realized Betty was going to be okay. "She wanted to get well, and that's half the battle."

Betty was weaned off her pills slowly, while Pat administered measured doses of the powerful sedative Librium to help ease the withdrawal symptoms. Day by day, the symptoms diminished, and at midnight on April 7 she took her last Librium.

"Steve was there," Betty recalled. "And he and Pat and I celebrated in the kitchen with glasses of Cranapple juice."

The next day, Saturday, April 8, was Betty's sixtieth birthday. The Firestones had planned a small dinner party with just Leonard, Nicky, Dolores Hope, the president, and Mrs. Ford, but Betty didn't want to go. Her pinched nerve was bothering her, and without medication, she said she was miserable. What she didn't say out loud was that she knew there'd be a cocktail hour, and she wasn't ready to face it.

Pat Benedict had been in constant contact with Dr. Pursch about Betty's progress. When she called to tell him of Betty's unwillingness to go to the dinner party, Pursch said, "I want her up and dressed and at that party."

Not only did Betty make it through the cocktail hour, but she also stayed through dinner. "I marveled that I was able to eat some soup without shaking and slopping it all over the table," Betty recalled.

"It had been a brutal week," Caroline recalled. "And then we got in the car and drove to Long Beach."

The Secret Service had arranged for Betty to enter the hospital through the back entrance to avoid the possibility of any press, but beyond that, Dr. Pursch had made it clear to everyone that Betty Ford was not to be given any special treatment. "I believe you have to treat VIPs like any other patients, so there were no officers wearing their medals to greet her when she arrived, as there had been at Bethesda, when her husband was president. And I think this frosted her," he said.

Pat and Caroline accompanied the former first lady, while two agents stayed close but inconspicuous. There was silence as they rode in the cavernous elevator designed for hospital gurneys, up to the third floor. The doors opened, and the first thing Betty saw was a big plaque that said ALCOHOL REHABILITATION CENTER.

"I almost turned right around and got back into the elevator," Betty reflected. "I was not ready for that." She'd admitted she had a pill problem. But alcohol? No way. She was not an alcoholic. Her image of an alcoholic was a homeless man on the street drinking out of a paper bag.

According to Caroline, "She was a wreck. I don't think she ever anticipated what it was going to be like. First of all, the hospital was not luxurious. It's run by the navy. It's not the Ritz-Carlton. And then they took her to her room and there were four beds."

Four hospital beds—more like cots, really—military grade. The US Navy's drug and alcohol rehabilitation program had started quietly in 1965, using the principles of Alcoholics Anonymous to help active-duty navy personnel and their dependents. But it wasn't until 1974 that the navy admitted alcohol addiction was a serious problem, and the program was given its own space in the Naval Regional Medical Center, Long Beach.

Betty's apprehension had been building, and when she walked into that room, saw the stark facilities, and realized she was going to be sharing a room and one bathroom with three other women, her emotions reached a crescendo. Gritting her teeth, she turned to Dr. Pursch and said, "I am accustomed to having a private room."

Her reaction was not unexpected. Pursch had dealt with navy admirals who felt they deserved special treatment too.

"Well, then," he said, "I'll have the other women come and get their things. I'll tell them they have to move out."

He knew Betty well enough to know that she wouldn't allow others to be removed just so she could have special treatment. And he was right.

"Oh no, you're not going to make anyone move for me," she said as she set down her purse on the one free bed in the room.

Caroline remembered how extremely difficult it was for Betty. "She had lost all her privacy. That was the biggest thing. Her privacy, and her dignity."

The next rude awakening was what to do with Mrs. Ford's clothes. She'd worried endlessly about what to pack for an anticipated four-week stay, and had brought several pieces of luggage. The closet space allotted for her was fourteen inches wide.

Knowing the press would inevitably find out, Betty had agreed to a statement that was released once she was safely admitted to the hospital: "Former First Lady Betty Ford was hospitalized Monday at the Long Beach Naval Hospital for an overmedication problem. Mrs. Ford states, 'Over a period of time, I got to the point where I was overmedicating myself. It's an insidious thing, and I mean to rid myself of its damaging effects. There have been too many other things I've overcome to be forever burdened with this detail.' "

There was no mention of an alcohol problem.

Every minute of every day for the next four weeks would be planned out for Betty. She was handed the "Policies and Routine for Patients," and because this was a naval installation, everything was in military time. It was boot camp for alcoholics. A critical part of the treatment was for patients to work the twelve steps of Alcoholics Anonymous.

0630	*Reveille*
0630 – 0730	*Breakfast*
0745 – 0830	*Muster/Cleanup*
0845 – 1015	*Group Therapy*
1030 – 1145	*Education Sessions*
1145 – 1230	*Lunch*
1255	*Muster*
1300 – 1430	*AA Meeting/Al-Anon*
1430 – 1515	*Films*
1530 – 1600	*Jogging*
1800	*Dinner*
1915	*AA Meeting*

For group therapy, Betty was placed in Group Six—they called themselves the "Six-Pack." There were five men, including a twenty-year-old jet mechanic who'd been drinking from the time he was eight; a young officer whose drinking had resulted in two failed marriages; and a naval clergyman "addicted to drugs and drink." Betty was the oldest in the group, the only female—and the only member with Secret Service agents standing outside the door.

Everyone was required to wear name tags with just first names on them, so wherever Betty went, the sailors would yell out, "Hi, Betty!"

There were far more men than women, and while the rooms were segregated by sex, the sessions were not. At first, it was disconcerting to her. "I was not a model patient," she admitted. "I had a bit of the celebrity hang-up. I considered myself a very special person who had been married to a president of the United States, and I didn't think I should have to discuss my personal problems with just anybody."

But she was expected to do everything everyone else did. "They had to clean the toilets and wastebaskets, and were in meetings almost every minute of every day," Caroline recalled. It was negotiated that Betty would not, in fact, have to clean toilets—that seemed to cross a line for a former first lady—but other than that, there were few exceptions allowed. "They were kept very busy. That was part of the whole protocol. She would say she was so tired, and they'd say, 'You never die from being too tired.' They were tough."

Betty listened to the others' stories, but she simply couldn't relate to them. "I could not say I was alcoholic," Betty would say later. "I didn't relate to any of the drunk stories I heard. I had never had an urge to hang out at bars, I wasn't about to get kicked out of the navy if I didn't shape up, nobody was suing me for running over their cat while under the influence."

She knew she had a problem, or her family wouldn't have even considered the intervention. But she was still in denial. "There's an enormous difference between other people's thinking you're alcoholic and your thinking you're alcoholic. I was perfectly happy not to drink," she said. "I was longing for pills, not pilsener."

There were lots of tears those first few days. Just going through the motions. Betty trying to appease everyone, without admitting her problems were as bad as everyone else's. One of those first evenings, Dr. Pursch arranged for Betty to attend a women's AA group in Laguna Beach.

The Secret Service agents drove Betty and Caroline, and then waited outside. At the beginning of every AA meeting, the attendees are required to introduce themselves with first names only, and to admit their addiction to alcohol.

As they sat down, Caroline grabbed hold of Betty's hand. She knew this was going to be hard for her boss. When it came to Betty's turn, she stood up and with strength pouring forth and "not a quiver in her voice," she said, "My name is Betty, and I'm an alcoholic."

"The hand I held gave me strength and faith," Caroline wrote in her diary that night. "Only one regret. The president wasn't there to share a most memorable day."

"I was very proud of her," Caroline said. "She was taking these huge steps, and I wished the president could have been there to witness it."

Within the first week of Betty's treatment, President Ford, Steve, and Susan arrived to attend a five-day family session. The family members were put in different groups—not with Betty or one another, but in groups with other patients who knew Betty.

"I wasn't convinced that what I was saying wasn't going to get back to my mother—my deepest, darkest secrets," Susan recalled.

In one of the first sessions, President Ford had been in a group, and when he left, Susan took his place. "You kind of go in and tell your story," she recalled. When somebody made the comment that her father had taken credit for getting the intervention together, "It set me on fire," she said.

"No he didn't!" Susan blurted out. "*I'm* the one that did all the work. I'm the one that put the pieces together. Where does he get off taking all the credit?!"

"The whole family is so raw with emotions as you're going through it," she remembered. "It's just exhausting. It's wonderful, but exhausting. You get rid of stuff."

In one group session, the counselor read a short story called "Warm Fuzzies."

"It was like taking my heart and pulling it out," Susan remembered. "It was like the way I felt about my mother, and how she had taken everything away from me. I never had a chance to be a kid. I was always covering for her." Tears poured down Susan's face as the emotions came pouring out. "When is it going to be my turn?" she wondered aloud.

President Ford attended group sessions with five or six recovering alcoholics, went to some meetings with Betty, and sat in lectures with dozens of other patients and their families. "For the first time, I learned about alcoholism . . . being a disease," he said. "I learned that I was making all these excuses an enabler does."

At first, Steve Ford felt a great deal of angst about going to the treatment center. But Pat Benedict reassured him and explained how important it was. The first day, he went to the cafeteria, where his mother was eating lunch with several of the sailors. There were admirals and seamen, and they were telling jokes, and she was laughing and having a good time. As he walked up to the table, he heard one of the sailors telling a dirty joke.

"I was so offended," Steve recalled. "This is my mother! You can't tell dirty jokes around my mother!" Later, he complained to Dr. Pursch.

"Steve, this is exactly what your mother needs," Pursch said. "She is no longer the first lady, she is Betty. She takes that hat off, and she gets to be equal with everybody else." Pursch made him realize that having been first lady was part of the problem. "Her doctors would prescribe whatever she wanted," Steve said, "because they didn't want to make a first lady mad."

In one group session, they were talking about the fact that if your parents were alcoholics, then it was very likely the children would become alcoholics too.

"I made the dumb statement 'Oh, no, I'll never be an alcoholic,'" Steve said. "They jumped all over me. 'Do you think your mother decided to be an alcoholic?' And I had to accept it that, yes, I have a good chance of becoming an alcoholic because of my family background."

On April 15 Steve was visiting his mother, when a local television crew approached him. "Steve, is your mother an alcoholic?" the photographer blurted out.

Steve Ford had been raised to be honest. When someone asks a question, you answer it.

"I know that the problem exists," he said. "My mother does drink, just as many other people do in this country. To what extent, I couldn't tell you. There always seems to be a problem mixing alcohol with drugs. The Good Lord seems to be challenging her with tasks, and she hasn't failed yet."

Betty still had not admitted to a problem with alcohol, and she was less than pleased with her son's remarks.

"She had begun to pull back and get into her denial again," Dr. Cruse recalled. "She thought she wasn't as bad off as a lot of the sailors and wives and so forth. That's what the disease does. She was scared and angry and frightened and puzzled. She was hoping to continue to reserve for herself the right not only to drink but also not to be labeled a drunk."

Pursch summoned President Ford, Caroline, Bob Barrett, and Pat Benedict, and another mini-intervention took place.

Dr. Pursch looked Betty straight in the eyes and said, "We are here because something needs to be faced, and that is that you are also dependent on alcohol."

Betty turned to her husband, hoping for some support—some kind of affirmation that she wasn't. When he didn't speak up, she said, "If you're going to call me an alcoholic, I won't stand for it."

Dr. Pursch had spoken with not only President Ford but also with Susan, Dr. Cruse, and other members of the family, and he knew the truth. "So far, you have talked only about drugs, but you are going to have to make a public statement saying you are also dependent on alcohol."

"I can't do that," Betty said, her voice beginning to quiver. "I don't want to embarrass my husband."

Pursch stood up, his eyes steeling through Betty. "You're hiding behind your husband," he said. "If you don't believe it, ask him."

Betty was beginning to hyperventilate. "Well?" she asked, looking at Jerry.

Jerry winced. He didn't want to cause her any more pain, but after attending the sessions, he'd come to realize that he'd been enabling her for far too long. "No," he said. "It won't embarrass me."

Still, Betty couldn't agree to making a public statement that she was an alcoholic. But Dr. Pursch was not going to let her get away with it. He kept pushing.

Dr. Pursch was "ruthless," Pat remembered. "I was sitting next to her . . . her little eyes were filling, her little nose was running, and I put my arm around her and just held her."

"Betty," Dr. Pursch glared, "you're just as alcoholic as anyone can be, and you're using your husband to hide behind."

"Pursch was very tough," Jerry recalled. "I think he felt Betty wasn't responding, she was in denial . . . and he thought he had to shock her."

"He knew that if she put it out there, that if she committed to it to the American public, then she'd damn well better live up to it," Caroline said. "You have to have something to live up to. Some pressure on your back to stay sober."

Betty was heaving with sobs. Crying inside and out.

"I had cried so hard my nose and ears were closed up, my head felt like a balloon, all swollen," Betty remembered. She was mad and hurt that Jerry hadn't spoken up to defend her. "He hadn't allowed me the out I was looking for."

Ultimately, Betty agreed to release a statement—a carefully worded statement written with the input of Dr. Pursch, President Ford, and Bob Barrett—and on Friday, April 21, Barrett read it at a press conference held outside the hospital.

Barrett stood at the microphone and said, "Here is the statement from Mrs. Ford: 'I have found I am not only addicted to the medication I have been taking for my arthritis but also to alcohol. This program is well known throughout the country, and I am pleased to have the opportunity to attend it. I expect this treatment and fellowship to be a solution for my problems, and I embrace it not only for me but all the many others who are here to participate.'"

The impact was enormous. America loved and respected Betty Ford, and her announcement brought home, in a powerful way, that this disease could touch virtually any family in the country. On top of that, Pat noted, "she opened the door for *women* to seek treatment."

"To the laymen, it was just a statement," Caroline said. "To us, it was Betty Ford getting well."

After reading the statement, Barrett and Dr. Pursch answered questions. When asked whether Mrs. Ford would be speaking publicly, Barrett replied flippantly, "We've never had too much success in keeping Mrs. Ford's mouth shut. Somewhere along the line, she'll be saying what she wants to when she wants to."

Dr. Pursch added, "Mrs. Ford is a gutsy lady, and I expect her to do very well. We're taking it one day at a time."

When asked about details of the drugs she was taking, Pursch declined to give specifics but said they were "medications any of us would get from a family practitioner if we went to him with the pain she had."

Barrett emphatically denied the problem involved any negligence by doctors treating Mrs. Ford.

Sometime in the second week of treatment, Betty had a revelation. During one group session, a young woman got up and said she didn't know why her family was making such a big deal about her drinking.

"My drinking hasn't caused my folks any trouble," the girl insisted. Betty had been in sessions with some of the woman's family members, and they had talked about how her drinking had indeed caused trouble for each of them. Betty remembered all the things her own family had told her during the intervention, and in that moment, she realized that by not admitting she had a problem with alcohol, she was in denial every bit as much as that young woman.

It was Betty's turn to stand up next.

"I'm Betty, and I am an alcoholic," she said. "And I *know* my drinking has hurt my family." As she said it out loud, a wave of relief spread through her.

She realized suddenly that while she couldn't identify with the habits or backgrounds of the other patients, she could identify with the disease. "We were all suffering from the same thing, and it didn't matter where we came from or how we got here. If we could have done something about our sickness on our own, we'd have done it."

Day in and day out, Betty was immersed in therapy and education about alcoholism and drug addiction. There were speakers who shared their own stories of recovery; role-playing sessions that showed how the disease affected loved ones; and films and lectures about the disease and its detrimental effects on the body. Betty learned that although she had detoxed and hadn't taken drugs or so much as a sip of alcohol since that last handful of pills immediately after the intervention, it would take more than *two years* before she was completely cleansed of the chemicals that had built up inside her body due to the long half-life of the medications she'd been taking.

"We learned that alcoholism kind of comes in two ways," Caroline said. "It either is a chemical dependency that is genetic or you build that up. You start drinking in college, and it builds up, and over forty years it catches up with you. You don't always have the chemical dependency gene."

The more Betty learned, the more it became clear that her genetics predisposed her to the disease. Both her father and one of her brothers were alcoholics. And she learned that the spouse and children of an alcoholic typically assume various codependent roles in order to cope: enabler, hero, scapegoat, lost child, mascot.

The enabler steps in to protect the alcoholic/addict from the consequences of her behavior, making excuses to prevent embarrassment and thus minimizing the consequences of addiction. The hero attempts to be the model child, excelling in everything he does, and taking over family responsibilities. The scapegoat acts out, is very independent, and is often seen as the "problem child," as he diverts attention from the alcoholic's behavior. The lost child demands little and receives little attention, which often results in his inability to develop close relationships. The mascot is the attention seeker, often clowning around to defuse the stressful situations caused by the alcoholic.

As Betty listened and learned, it was as if the counselors were describing her husband and each of her children. Their personalities had formed around her addiction.

Meanwhile, outside the walls of the hospital, people all over the world were reacting to Betty's admission that she was an alcoholic and was embracing treatment.

"I was astonished at the amount of newspaper coverage, the editorials commending my heroism, my candor, my courage," she said. "I hadn't rescued anybody from a burning building, I'd simply put my bottles down. It was my family, not I, who had been 'candid' and 'courageous,'" Betty wrote, years later.

Indeed, she wasn't feeling courageous at all. Three weeks into the treatment, her nerves were raw. "People don't understand the mood swings of a recovering alcoholic," Betty explained. She went to the hospital beauty parlor, and when the stylist had cut one side of her hair very short, she looked in the mirror in horror and asked, "What are you doing?"

"Caroline told me you wanted it short so you could swim in the pool," the hairdresser said.

Betty was furious. As soon as she saw Caroline, she screamed, "I could kill you for doing this to me!"

"She was so angry," Caroline recalled. "She was frustrated and angry, and she couldn't take it out on the doctors or Pat, because they'd say, 'Uh-uh-uh.'" There were times it got very ugly, and Caroline received the brunt of her anger.

"Her words hurt," Caroline acknowledged. "I was under so much pressure to make sure everything was going well, but while President Ford, Susan, and Steve came and went, I was there the whole time." At night, Caroline would return to her motel room across the street from the hospital and fall into bed, exhausted, and, many times, crying her eyes out. "I was a mess," she said.

Mike and Gayle Ford came out for a weekend to attend the family sessions. "Part of it was this is a family disease," Mike said. "And we all had to take responsibility and learn about what are the trigger points and how do you address that as a family. So, we were learning all that. New language, new responsibilities, and how to help Mom."

Then came another crisis. Betty's autobiography was in galleys, ready to go to print, and the publisher called and said it wanted her to write another chapter—a chapter about her drug and alcohol addiction, and the treatment at Long Beach.

"No, I won't do it," Betty said. "It has nothing to do with the book."

"It was a crisis," Jerry said. "The publishers were uptight, and we had to very delicately convince Betty that it was a proper conclusion to *The Times of My Life*. There was no other responsible way to end the book. I felt the request of the publishers was legitimate, and the problem was to prevail on Betty, make her believe that she could, in her early recovery, be forthright and go public."

Chris Chase, the writer, flew out from New York. She attended sessions with Betty to understand how the treatment worked, and Betty had to relive the intervention all over again.

After twenty-eight days in treatment, Betty was released from the hospital. More than three dozen reporters and photographers were waiting outside the front door behind a rope line along with a group of spectators.

"Mrs. Ford, how do you feel?" a reporter called out.

Betty smiled and said, "Just fine." When the crowd began clapping in a show of support, she turned and gave a wave and then got into the back seat of the car.

"I know that she felt so vulnerable," Caroline recalled. "I wasn't even the person in rehab, and *I* felt like this virgin going out into the world.

You know, you live in this protective bubble for four weeks, and you don't talk to anyone for four weeks. And I remember driving out of there, and experiencing this feeling of being so scared because now you have to do it all yourself. And that was me. Just imagine what *she* felt like."

President Ford greeted his wife with a long hug and a tender kiss when she arrived back at their home in Rancho Mirage. He was so proud of her. But then he broke the news that a group of Republicans were having a reception at the house, and she was expected to greet them. Not only that, but NBC was coming to do an interview.

Betty broke down and cried. She begged not to have to do it, but the television crew had already arrived from New York.

"Nobody had consulted me, nobody had consulted my doctors," Betty said. It had been on the schedule, and no one had realized how fragile she would be, still going through drug withdrawal, which would take at least a full year. It was as if everyone thought that after four weeks in rehab she'd be completely well and able to uphold whatever duties were expected of her—just like she'd done at the White House. Feeling like she had no choice in the matter, Betty finally agreed to do it.

She sat next to President Ford in the television room and, gritting her teeth behind the forced smile, said she was "just fine."

"It was a cruel intrusion," she said later. "There was no way I should have been put under such pressure. I was upset with my husband, with politics, with everything and everybody."

What she was feeling inside was not apparent to the public. Across the country, people were lauding her courage.

"What she has done is the most significant advance in the history of alcohol treatment," said Dr. Luther Cloud, president of the National Council on Alcoholism, in New York. "This might well mark the end of the stigma."

At Alcoholics Anonymous, there was hope that Betty Ford's courage would increase the recognition that "alcohol addiction is a physical disease, not a moral sin."

President Carter had invited President and Mrs. Ford to the White House for the unveiling of their official White House portraits, and on May 24, 1978, barely two weeks after her release from Long Beach, Betty was back at the White House—the first time she'd been there since Inauguration Day the year before.

During the ceremony, President Carter said, "Betty Ford has earned the admiration of our nation for her courage and complete candor. She is the most popular person in our country today."

24

Recovery

Letters started arriving by the thousands. "When we got back from Long Beach, there were two huge garbage bags full of letters," Caroline Coventry remembered. The letters came from people whom she had helped, people who understood her situation, people who were looking at friends and family who had problems. "They were the most unbelievable letters you can even imagine," Caroline said.

Caroline would open and read the letters, and while she knew Betty couldn't possibly read each and every one, Caroline would take the most poignant letters to her.

"I always made sure she had the letters that were really interesting and really hit the point, whether it was about alcoholism and drugs or whether it was a really nice letter written to her about people she had helped in general."

Betty wanted Caroline to type personal responses to every letter, but it was an impossible task. Finally, they agreed to order cards with standard responses to send as acknowledgments.

"I ordered Crane stationery with the initials EBF on it like it was water," Caroline recalled.

* * *

"I was on a high because my life was all coming together," Betty recalled. "Everybody was happy with me, I'd gone and done something about my alcoholism and drug dependency, I was the apple of everyone's eye."

Betty was beginning to eat healthy, and she'd learned that exercise needed to be a key component of each day. At first, she had the feeling that after her twenty-eight-day crash course and treatment, she didn't need to attend AA meetings every day. But the first months of recovery were not easy. Staying sober was hard work. Those who had been in recovery far longer knew how easily one could relapse. Dr. Cruse had introduced Betty to another female recovering alcoholic named Meri Bell Sharbutt, who took Betty under her wing. A former big band singer, Meri Bell made sure to call Betty daily and accompanied her to AA meetings every single evening. At the meetings, people inevitably came up to Betty and introduced themselves, and it was Betty's habit to be gracious to anyone who approached her. That always got a reprimand from Meri Bell.

"You're not here to play former first lady," Meri Bell would scold. "You're here for the same reason the rest of us are here. To stay sober and work the program to the best of your ability."

"Once in a while, during the first year of my sobriety, I felt like a Martian," Betty wrote. As she sat in those AA meetings and listened to stories of young women prostituting themselves to get drugs or alcohol, using four-letter words Betty had never uttered in her life, she could not see any reflection of herself. But over time she began to understand that she did indeed share the same disease as those women, and also their hopes for a drug- and alcohol-free future.

Betty still had arthritis and debilitating pain in her neck, but now she had to rely on massage, hot packs, and hot showers for relief. Her emotions were fragile too.

When they first got to Vail that summer, she was in her bedroom one day, lying on hot packs, and she saw a mouse running along the floorboards. It wasn't unusual—the house was in a wooded area—but when she saw two mice one day, she mentioned it to Jerry and Jon, the house caretaker.

"Do you realize we've got mice?" she asked. "They come out of the closet, run across the room, behind the television, over the draperies, and then go back into the closet."

Jerry turned to Jon and said with a smile, "She must be drinking again."

He was kidding, and had no idea how what he thought was a flippant joke would make her feel. She held her tongue in front of Jon, but later, when they were alone, she said, "I know you were kidding, but you have no idea how raw my wounds are. So please don't ever say anything like that to me again, particularly in front of someone else. Because it hurts."

And although she had openly admitted being alcoholic—and had been praised for it—there was still a measure of denial that was easily fed by seemingly innocent comments. Friends would say, "Oh, Betty, you just can't be alcoholic. I never saw you when you were out of it."

And Jerry would pipe in, "Well, you know she never had any trouble with alcohol until she got tangled up with those pills."

"This was dangerous stuff for me to hear," Betty admitted. "I had to turn it off and go back to my support groups. Because the voice of the siren, murmuring, 'You were never an alcoholic,' fed my own denial."

It was truly one day at a time. There were plenty of times when she was tempted. During a trip to New York City a few months into her recovery, she and Jerry were hosting a dinner party in their hotel suite at the exclusive Pierre for some of the NBC executives. The hotel staff knew that during past stays, President and Mrs. Ford typically liked to have a martini in their suite at a certain time each night. No one had directed otherwise—and Jerry still enjoyed his martini—so a pitcher of martinis was delivered to their room prior to the party.

Betty looked at the pitcher and thought how nice it would be to have a small drink—it would help her be calm and cool when the guests arrived. If she took a small amount and poured it in a bathroom glass, no one would ever know. She wrestled with the decision, like the cartoon of an angel on one shoulder and the devil on the other, each trying to persuade her what to do.

She didn't drink the martini. "The evening went beautifully," she recalled, "and I realized I could do it without my old crutch." She was learning that sobriety was progressive, just like alcoholism was progressive. Betty Ford would reflect often on that one decision—so small to some, but enormous to the recovering alcoholic—which would give her the strength she needed to face many other challenges and events.

Throughout that summer of 1978, Betty had been thinking about something she'd long wanted to do that would give her even more confidence and make her feel good about herself: she wanted to have a face-lift.

"The president was very supportive," Caroline Coventry remembered. "Whatever she wanted." Doctors were interviewed, and Betty finally decided on an Iranian doctor in Palm Springs. There was some concern because she needed to go under general anesthesia, but Dr. Cruse and Dr. Pursch closely supervised the procedure at Eisenhower Medical Center to ensure that only minimal medication was used.

As with everything she did, Betty was open about her face-lift. And while there was plenty of criticism, Betty lifted the veil of secrecy on the procedure, giving many women the feeling that it was not only all right, but perfectly acceptable. Once again it was "the Betty Ford effect."

Surgeons' offices across the nation were suddenly besieged by callers who had seen the results of Mrs. Ford's cosmetic surgery and wanted to do the same for themselves.

"There's been such a precipitous increase in face-lifts that I have a four-month delay," one plastic surgeon in Chicago said.

Betty's memoir, *The Times of My Life*, had been delayed to allow for the addition of the chapter about her stay in Long Beach, and in early November, it was finally published. On November 9, *Reader's Digest* magazine threw a star-studded party at the Waldorf Astoria Hotel for two hundred Ford family friends and former members of President Ford's administration to celebrate the launch of the book and the remarkable woman herself.

Betty looked stunning in a flowing chiffon gown in varying shades of peach and coral, her hair styled and makeup applied professionally to enhance her "new" face, which was being revealed in public for the first time. Barely six months into her recovery, it was a huge event, putting Betty into the spotlight—not something the professionals at Long Beach would have advised—but Betty loved it.

Henry Kissinger was master of ceremonies, and his monologue, delivered in his thick German accent, had the crowd roaring with laughter. In response to rumors circulating that Jerry Ford was considering running for president again in 1980, Kissinger said, "Betty is supposed to be opposed to another campaign in 1980, so I asked her if she had changed her mind, and she said, 'No,' she still doesn't want to be president." After all the jokes, he got serious and said, "Betty has done more for women than anyone. She is irrepressible, joyful, and she gave class to the White House."

Entertainer Pearl Bailey moved around the room, singing cabaret style, and, at one point, she pulled Betty out of her seat for an impromptu soft-shoe dance. "My sister," Pearl said, "you wrote a book of courage."

When Tony Orlando began singing a moving rendition of "You Are So Beautiful," President Ford took Betty's hand, and together they danced in front of the crowd, holding each other close.

There were so many special moments, but the most poignant one came at the end of the evening, when President Ford made his remarks at the podium. After everything he'd seen his wife go through the past six months, he had a difficult time keeping his emotions in check. Tears glistened in his eyes as he told Betty how much she meant to him and the rest of the family.

"Thank you for putting up with us, for understanding us, for trying to help us. We cannot express adequately our gratitude, our pride, and our love for thirty years of a wonderful relationship, and we thank you so much, Betty," he said.

It was so moving, so evident the love between the two of them. As people in the audience wiped away tears, Betty stepped up to the microphone, grabbed her husband's hand, and said, "This is where my strength is." Looking around the room filled with friends representing each phase of her life—Grand Rapids, Alexandria, the White House, Palm Springs—all gathered there in her honor, she spoke from the heart, confiding in the group the surprising reflections she'd had while writing the book. "It was marvelous when we were all there in the White House," she said. "It was one of the happiest times of my life.

"I feel as though I have to pinch myself to realize it is all true," she said of the evening. "I am thrilled to be here, and I thank you, everyone, for coming."

The *Washington Post* noted: "Her manner and voice bore no resemblance to the halting, stilted tone that sometimes surfaced in the days when she was overly sedated."

* * *

Betty was indeed riding high, and everything seemed to be going her way. Then Susan dropped a bombshell.

For the past year or so, the Fords' daughter had been in an on-again, off-again relationship with Chuck Vance, one of the Secret Service agents on her father's protective detail. "It was a very rocky relationship from the beginning," Susan said, "because he was afraid he was going to lose his job." She argued that she wasn't the protectee—she no longer had Secret Service protection—just the daughter of a protectee, and that shouldn't matter. They tried to keep their relationship quiet, but eventually things became so serious, Susan decided she had to tell her parents.

"My mother was beside herself," she recalled. Susan had just turned twenty-one, and Chuck was sixteen years older, divorced, and had two adopted children. The Secret Service immediately transferred Chuck to the field office in Riverside, California.

"It was a surprise for everybody," Agent Bob Alberi said. No one in the Secret Service had seen it coming. "It was a shocker; completely out of left field."

A few months later, Chuck was transferred to Los Angeles, and when that happened, Susan told her parents she was moving with him, and they were going to live together.

Neither Betty nor Jerry supported the decision, and they didn't hide their feelings.

"I hope you've thought about this," Betty said to Susan. "And I really wish you were engaged before you go and live with him."

That infuriated Susan. "I was throwing things back at her that she'd said," Susan recalled. "Remember what you said on *60 Minutes*?" she argued. Ironically, those words about what she would do if her daughter had "an affair" came to the forefront, but Betty and Jerry were mostly concerned about the age difference.

"Susan was our youngest child, our only girl, and we didn't think anybody was good enough for her," Betty wrote.

"There was no fondness there between my mother and Chuck," Susan said. When the two got engaged and made plans for a February 1979 wedding, it was one of many challenges that tested Betty's sobriety that first year.

She admitted she had temptations. "I liked alcohol," she said frankly. "It made me feel warm. And I loved pills; they took away my tension and pain." Through her daily support groups, she realized that she hadn't "got this problem licked. To the day I die," she said, "I'll be recovering."

In January 1979, President Ford was invited to the Middle East to meet with the leaders of Oman, the United Arab Emirates, Saudi Arabia, Jordan, Egypt, and Israel, and Crown Prince Fahd of Saudi Arabia had personally extended an invitation to Betty as well. She was just beginning to get into a routine, feeling comfortable in her home, and to go on such a long trip at this stage of her recovery, she felt, was just too soon. "I didn't want to go out and test the waters," she said. "This would be a semiofficial visit to the Middle East, and I wasn't ready for a lot of responsibility."

But Jerry urged her to join him. "I wasn't comfortable leaving her alone for two weeks," he admitted. Plus, after all he'd learned during the therapy sessions at Long Beach, he'd realized how important it was for their marriage for them to do things together.

Betty felt like she was abandoning Susan at a critical time, just before the wedding, but reluctantly agreed to go.

It turned out to be a fascinating trip at a historic time. The Shah of Iran and his wife, the Empress Farah Diba Pahlavi, whom the Fords had entertained at the White House, had just fled their home country in the midst of an uprising against the Shah's regime, arriving in Egypt at the same time as President and Mrs. Ford. The six of them visited the city of Aswan together. In Israel, they walked the streets that Jesus had walked, and were hosted by Prime Minister Menachem Begin. In Saudi Arabia, Betty sat between Crown Prince Fahd and the Saudi oil minister, Sheikh Zaki Yamani—a very unusual occurrence in a country where men and women were always segregated at public events. In Jordan, King Hussein piloted a plane and flew Betty and Jerry over the desert to the seaside resort of Aqaba, followed by a visit to the spectacular, ancient city of Petra, where Betty and Jerry followed the trail of bedouins on camel. "I went through the two weeks, sober, clear eyed, and able to appreciate everything," Betty recalled. "I thought about other times when my schedule had been heavy, and I'd leaned on drugs and alcohol to keep me going, and I could not remember half of what had happened."

One year earlier, there was no way she could have made that trip. "Now I was physically well," she said. "I had some stamina, and I had been relieved of the obligation to keep up with whatever social drinking was being done by my companions. And I thought to myself, *Hey, I'm doing all right.*"

The Fords had barely unpacked from the Middle East trip when out-of-town guests started arriving in Palm Springs for Susan and Chuck's wedding. Clara Powell came, of course, but most of the guests, including many of the celebrities with whom they'd become friends, were people Betty had not seen since the intervention. She knew that even though Susan was the bride, many eyes would be on her, too.

"The wedding, I think, was very hard on her," Susan said, looking back. "She didn't even have a year of sobriety . . . and she told some friends of mine that until the moment I walked down the aisle, she never expected me to do it."

They were a handsome couple: Susan, blonde and fair, in a long-sleeved white lace gown with matching veil, and Chuck, the dark-haired, Secret Service agent with a thick moustache and charming smile, dressed in a suit and striped tie. Once the vows were said, the music commenced, and the drinks started flowing.

Betty made it through the reception, greeting their guests and family members with a smile, posing for photos, as waiters came by with trays of champagne. At times, she would go into the house, and Steve would follow her. It would be so easy for her to slip. He'd sit with her, holding her hand until she was ready to go out and mingle again. The day was all about Susan and Chuck, but at one point, Tony Orlando grabbed Betty and went up to the microphone. As he sang his famous "Tie a Yellow Ribbon," Betty laughed and danced right alongside him, just as she'd done at the 1976 convention.

The wedding was a milestone, and although she'd made it through without a hitch, there were times over the next few months when Betty would slip into periods of depression. She couldn't figure out why she was feeling so blue. Everything seemed to be going great in her life. What was missing?

"That first year of recovery, I just wanted to get my own life turned around," Betty said. "But always there was the mail." Those first two garbage bags full of mail that came when she was at Long Beach were only the beginning. Every day, there were more letters: "I need help." "Please help, how did you do it? Tell me the formula."

Ever since she first left Long Beach, the former first lady had balked at suggestions to share her story of recovery with others. She didn't want to preach. She didn't want to go around talking about herself. That's just not who she was.

On her sixty-first birthday, one year and a week after the family intervention, she received a call from her next-door neighbor and close friend, Nicky Firestone, that would change everything.

25

The Betty Ford Center

It was to be a birthday dinner for Betty—a special celebration of not only her birthday but also one year of sobriety. The Fords had invited Pat Benedict to stay for a few days at the house, to help celebrate the momentous occasion.

The afternoon of Betty's birthday party, Nicky Firestone called and said, regrettably, she and her husband would not be able to attend. "Leonard is in terrible shape," Nicky confided.

Leonard Firestone had struggled with alcoholism for years, and although he'd been sober for nearly a decade, the disease had struck back with a vengeance. The former ambassador was one of Betty and Jerry's closest friends, and on this night, which meant so much to Betty, he was too drunk to attend the party next door.

Pat went over to evaluate him. She found that he had been drinking for three or four days and was in perilous condition, with abnormally high blood pressure. A doctor was called, and between Pat and the doctor, they started giving him medication, beginning a detox process. Within forty-eight hours, an intervention was arranged with Dr. Pursch (who was now retired from the navy and had started his own rehabilitation center), Nicky, Leonard's son Brooks, Pat Benedict, and Jerry and Betty Ford.

Leonard was lying on the couch, as Pat Benedict rubbed his feet. "I loved that," Leonard recalled. "I thought she was doing it to be nice." The truth was, Pat was doing it to hold him on the couch so that he couldn't get up and get a drink, and so he'd be there when the others walked in to begin the intervention.

"He knew the minute we walked in what was going on," Nicky Firestone said, "because Betty had had her intervention the year before."

It was terribly emotional for all of them, but no one backed down. "It's relentless, but it's kind," Nicky said. "You don't scream at each other, but you don't give up. You keep hammering until the alcoholic gives in."

Once Leonard heard everyone tell him how his drinking had hurt each of them, he agreed he had a problem and said he'd be willing to go to AA. But Betty knew AA alone wouldn't be enough. She understood the denial that was going through his mind; she'd been in the same place just one year earlier.

"No, no, no, Leonard," Betty said. "You're going to go to treatment."

President Ford stood strong too. "You're my best friend, Leonard," he said, "and I'm not going to let you lie over here and die."

Finally, realizing he had no choice, Leonard agreed to be admitted to Dr. Pursch's treatment center and spend four weeks in rehab.

"It was really beautiful how it all came together," Caroline Coventry reflected. "Mrs. Ford had come full circle. She had recovered enough to acknowledge things in this way, and she and President Ford were working as a team."

But what was also occurring, in the year since Betty's intervention, was the way people were beginning to view alcoholism.

At first, Leonard Firestone was ashamed that he hadn't been able to control his drinking. "It was my second go after nine years of sobriety," he said. But when he got to Pursch's treatment center and had to cancel some business appointments and a golf match, he told everyone, "I'm at rehab. I'm doing the same thing Betty Ford did."

Around the time that Firestone went into treatment, President Ford went to his doctor and said he felt like he needed to lose about ten pounds. The doctor said, "That's easy. Either give up your nightly martini or give up your butter pecan ice cream." That was a no-brainer for Jerry Ford. He loved his ice cream. He had never been much of a drinker, and now, with his best friend and his wife not drinking, he realized he didn't need it either. He stopped drinking and from that day forward, never touched alcohol again.

When Leonard Firestone came out of treatment, people noticed something different about him: he seemed to exude an inner peace that hadn't been there before. Walter Annenberg, a former ambassador to Britain, billionaire publisher, and philanthropist, was a close friend to the Fords as well as the Firestones. Annenberg found the change in Leonard so striking and so positive, he asked him bluntly, "What did they give you in treatment? What is it that you have found?"

"I found I was allergic to alcohol," Leonard said. "You might say I've got a busted filter. I used to be able to drink, but I can't drink anymore, so I've learned to let go." But beyond the physical enlightenment, he'd found there was a spiritual factor as well. "I've learned I needed love and understanding and help from counseling and a higher power."

Walter Annenberg had seen the change in their mutual friend Betty, and now, seeing the dramatic change in Leonard, he had an idea. "You and Betty should put your heads together to come up with a plan for starting an alcoholic treatment center."

As soon as Leonard hung up the phone, he called Betty, filled with excitement.

"You know," he said, "we've got this disease—it's almost killed us both—and yet we have the means and the influence to help turn this around. We could help a lot more people to address addiction in their lives. Let's talk about starting a treatment center."

At first, Betty wasn't so sure about being involved—she was only a year sober herself. What did she know about starting a treatment center?

"Mom was a bit reluctant to jump right into that so soon," Mike Ford recalled, but Leonard wouldn't give up.

One of the things they'd both learned in treatment was that you have to give it away to keep it. In other words, you have to help others—by giving them your knowledge, your emotion, your compassion—in order to keep it for yourself.

You have to give it away to keep it.

Betty couldn't forget how being honest and forthright about her breast cancer and mastectomy had helped thousands of women and had undoubtedly saved thousands of lives. She realized that perhaps her personal battle with alcoholism and addiction could do the same thing.

It was as if the stars had aligned, and every challenge, every success she'd had in her life had brought her to this moment. "With my recovery, and Leonard's recovery, and Walter Annenberg's awed response to Leonard's serenity," she recalled, "everything changed."

And then, Mike Ford recalled, "She got fired up! I mean, really, she got really fired up!"

"That was a huge moment," observed Caroline Coventry. "Mr. Firestone was such a gentle, wonderful man, and he and Mrs. Ford had this special bond; I think they kept each other sober. And when they decided to join forces, it was a beautiful thing."

Both Leonard and Betty served on the board of the Eisenhower Medical Center, and their vision was to have a stand-alone facility on the same property. In fact, Dr. Joe Cruse had been trying to start a treatment center in the Palm Springs–Rancho Mirage area known as the Coachella Valley for years, but he hadn't had much luck. Sixteen years earlier, he had seen golf course communities with little cottages around them, with a central pod, and he had a vision for a treatment center based upon that configuration. He had even put together slides of how it would look, but he couldn't get the financial backing for it.

As a successful businessman, Leonard Firestone knew they'd need to prove the necessity for such a facility, so the first step was to develop a Chemical Dependency Recovery Hospital (CDRH) Task Force, on which Betty and Leonard were cochairs.

Bob Hope's wife, Dolores, had also witnessed Betty's remarkable transformation, and as a board member of the hospital, she knew the issue well.

"We were having a problem at Eisenhower because we were getting alcoholic patients, and under the provisions of an acute-care hospital, we weren't really supposed to take them in," Mrs. Hope explained. Nationwide, the common practice was that alcoholics were given four or five days' inpatient treatment in an acute-care facility and then released. It wasn't uncommon for someone to stay sober for a few weeks and then start drinking again. Hospitals weren't equipped to deal with this revolving door of alcoholics, and often they wouldn't admit them unless they had some other illness or symptoms such as chest pain or a stomach disorder that the physicians knew how to treat.

Betty and Leonard traveled around the country gathering information from other treatment centers and took the best ideas from each. Hazelden, in Center City, Minnesota, was the most well-known and respected treatment center, known for its "Minnesota Method" for treating addiction. It had started in 1949 in an old white farmhouse on the banks of a lake, where "gentlemen" could get away to address their "problem" of alcoholism by attending daily lectures based on the 12 steps of Alcoholics Anonymous, and sharing their stories with other men. Originally known as Hazel's Den for a former owner of the farm, its reputation grew and its mission expanded, eventually accepting women patients as well.

One thing that concerned Betty was that every place they went had far fewer female patients than male. She knew women were just as likely to become alcoholic as men, so why weren't more women coming forward?

Betty and Leonard developed a proposal for a residential facility that would "provide low-cost, comprehensive alcoholism services on the campus of the Eisenhower Medical Center, Rancho Mirage, California." The proposal noted that "alcoholism is our number one public health problem," and that ignorance about it needed to be addressed and managed as the "family and societal disease it is."

Leonard and Nicky Firestone immediately offered $500,000, which was matched by another $500,000 courtesy of friends Leon and Barbara Parma via their charitable trust, the McCallum Desert Foundation. With $1 million in pocket, Leonard and Betty set out to raise several million dollars more to turn their dream into a reality.

Caroline Coventry had been Betty's assistant for nearly two years—two years in which she'd been at Mrs. Ford's side almost constantly, through her downward spiral after leaving the White House, the trauma of the intervention and detox, the reckoning at Long Beach, and the stressful, tenuous first year of recovery. Emotionally, the experience had taken its toll on Caroline, and now it was time for her to move on.

"I don't think I realized until much later that I was there for a reason," Caroline said. "I was there for that transition in her life, and then when she began to get well, it had to be time for me to leave."

Caroline realized that Betty needed someone to come in fresh. Someone who didn't know the past. Hadn't experienced the trauma.

"If people could just see in hindsight, they'd say, 'Oh, that was a cinch, if I could have just seen it,'" Caroline reflected. "But you can't. You have to go through the pain before you can get to the beauty. You can't appreciate what you get in the end without going through the pain."

Shortly after Caroline left, Betty received an invitation to attend a party in New York at which Martha Graham was going to be presenting fashion designer Roy Halston Frowick—known simply as Halston—with an award. Betty had yet to replace Caroline, so she asked Penny Circle, a young secretary on President Ford's staff, to join her.

"Have you ever been to New York City?" Mrs. Ford asked Penny.

"No," she said. "I spent the first ten years of my life in North Dakota, and then I've been in California ever since."

Betty was excited to show Penny everything she loved about New York, and for Penny, it would be a jaw-dropping experience. They stayed at the Waldorf, one of the Big Apple's iconic hotels, and the party was to be held at Studio 54—the hottest nightclub in the city.

The evening began with a private dinner at Halston's contemporary townhouse at 101 East Sixty-Third Street. It was an intimate group that included Betty and Martha Graham, and two of Halston's favorite, and most famous, clients: Liza Minnelli and Elizabeth Taylor. The ladies were all dressed in exquisite Halston designs: Taylor in a sapphire dress that matched her eyes and Minnelli in a purple gown with a skin-bearing cutout from her throat to her ribs—but Betty stood out, looking positively regal in a pale-apricot gown adorned with swirling patterns of sequins. After dinner, the group headed over to Studio 54, and that's where the party really began.

"It was wall-to-wall celebrities," Penny recalled. The nightclub had become a magnet for New York's fashion designers, socialites, and celebrities from all over the world. Mick Jagger, Olivia Newton-John, Andy Warhol, and Michael Jackson all frequented the club, and in this era between the advent of the birth control pill and the ominous dawning of the AIDS epidemic, Studio 54 had become notorious for its hedonistic atmosphere of casual sex, booze, and open drug use. It was not the kind of place you'd expect to see the former first lady a year after she'd come out of rehab.

As soon as they arrived, Halston and his group were scuttled downstairs to a private room that was exclusively for very, *very* important persons: the VVIPs. It was a testament to Betty's strength and commitment to her sobriety that she was even able to be in a place like that, where all around her, people were drinking and using drugs. But, having just gone through the intervention with Leonard Firestone, she was more determined than ever not to backslide. She danced and mingled, savoring the experience, completely sober.

Chris Chase, the writer who had helped Betty with her book, was there that night, too, and at one point, she and Penny went into the ladies' room together. There was a row of sinks, and all along the counter were rows and rows of white powder, arranged very delicately and precisely into straight lines.

"What's all this powder?" Penny asked Chris. She'd never seen or heard of such a thing. Chris explained that it was cocaine, and she'd be better off ignoring it.

That night, when they got back to the Waldorf, Betty and Penny were laughing and talking about the evening, and Penny told Mrs. Ford about the lines of powder in the bathroom.

"What did you do?" Betty asked.

"I just sucked in a breath and then blew it all away!" Penny said.

Betty's eyes widened. "Oh no! You didn't!"

Penny started laughing. "No, I didn't. I'm just kidding." Betty burst out laughing. It had been a wonderful night. A milestone indeed.

Shortly after the trip to New York, Betty hired a new assistant named Marion Evans, who had worked in Delaware governor Pete du Pont's office. Around that same time, some members of the Republican Party were strongly encouraging Jerry Ford to take another run for president in 1980. If he entered the race, he'd need to hire additional staff, so Marion convinced her friend Ann Cullen, a former colleague in Governor du Pont's office, to move out to Rancho Mirage, with the expectation that Ann could get a position working on the campaign.

Jerry put together a task force, and while he was seriously considering it, Betty had grave concerns.

"My new life was precious to me, and I was glad to be done with
politics," she said. But she had always been a dutiful wife, and she told
Jerry she would support him in whatever he decided.

In June 1980, Jerry announced that he was not going to run. There
were numerous reasons, but in the back of his mind, he was deeply
concerned about what it might do to Betty. They had been through too
much to risk going backward.

"Betty's recovery was never talked about," he said, "but if I had run,
and in the process it had interfered with her recovery, I would never
have forgiven myself."

Meanwhile, Ann Cullen had been doing small projects for the
Fords—such as going through all their photo albums from the White
House and identifying people in the pictures—while Marion had fallen
in love with one of the Secret Service agents and was planning to get
married and move back east.

"There I was," Ann recalled. "Mrs. Ford wasn't sure I was the right
person to replace Marion, but we agreed to try it for thirty days."

The job was undefined other than "you name it, I did it," Ann
recalled. "There were invitations every day asking Mrs. Ford to speak
and do things, requests for autographs, all kinds of stuff that needed
responses. I wrote her speeches. I did all of her scheduling. I traveled
with her when she went on events. I traveled with them when the two
of them went together. I took the dogs to the vet. I did her hair when we
were on the road. It was a little bit of everything."

It was a perfect match. Ann Cullen would be Betty's personal assistant for the next seventeen years.

Jerry and Betty flew to Detroit for the Republican National Convention in mid-July to support Ronald Reagan as the uncontested Republican nominee. The former film actor and California governor had not
yet chosen his running mate, and as soon as the Fords arrived, Reagan
called Jerry for a meeting. Reagan handed Ford a peace pipe and asked
if he'd consider running with him on the ticket as vice president. Jerry
agreed to consider it.

Meanwhile, as the Ford and Reagan camps were negotiating, an
ERA march had been organized to demonstrate against the Republi-

cans, who were planning to drop support of the amendment in their platform. Betty had known about the march, and because the marchers had been asked to wear white, she had specifically packed a white dress because she wanted to be a part of it.

"I can't tell you how many Republicans came to try and talk me out of it," she recalled. "They said it wouldn't reflect well on the party if I marched." She was upset with the party because the GOP had been the first to support the ERA.

Finally, Jerry asked her not to go. "As a favor to me," he pleaded.

"He didn't *tell* me not to," Betty said, but his sentiment was strong enough that she did not march.

As eleven thousand men and women marched in solidarity, carrying placards that said "Wake Up GOP It's 1980" and chanting, "Hey, hey, what do you say? Ratify the ERA!" Betty stood at the window of her suite at the Renaissance Center Hotel and "watched the parade go by, a dutiful wife and a disappointed feminist in one quivering package."

In the end, Jerry Ford declined Reagan's offer, George H. W. Bush was selected to run with Reagan on the Republican ticket, and Betty breathed a sigh of relief.

It was a turning point for Gerald Ford as well.

"I really saw a change in him," Mike Ford recalled. "He said, 'You know, this woman has been faithfully by my side for thirty-five years and loved me and cared for me and raised these kids and done all these things for me, made many sacrifices for me. It's my time to encourage her in her passion to do something of great public service.' So that's when he started getting real involved in fund-raising."

With Betty's public image and Leonard Firestone's connection to wealthy circles, "They were a pretty dynamic duo," Ann Cullen said. "They had a lot of friends they could hit up" to fund the treatment center, and Betty wasn't shy about asking for money. One time Betty and Jerry went with a group of friends on someone's private jet to Las Vegas to see a show, and on the way back—after the others had downed a few drinks—Betty got commitments for pledges written on cocktail napkins.

"It got to the point people didn't want to sit next to me at dinner parties," Betty recalled with a laugh. "They knew I'd be slipping them an envelope before the night was over."

She'd also seen how much money her husband got paid to give speeches, and, despite the well-known fact that she abhorred speaking in public, she started accepting paid speaking gigs. Every single dime went to fund the treatment center.

The fund-raising was moving along well, and the task force had come to the conclusion that it could maintain quality recovery at about one-third the cost of what was being charged in acute-care hospitals. One major hurdle loomed: there was no licensing in the state of California for the type of facility they were proposing. That meant they had to get a bill introduced in the legislature. Having a husband who was the former president of the United States suddenly came in very handy.

President Ford contacted Governor Jerry Brown and members of the state legislature, and managed to get the bill through in thirty days. But that was only the beginning. For the next year, Betty and Leonard practically commuted back and forth to Sacramento—meeting with state officials, and other people who were running different kinds of treatment centers—to establish a set of rules and regulations for a chemical dependency recovery hospital. It was tiring and tedious. Firestone felt like he was banging his head against a bureaucracy. "We know we can provide quality care in a noninstitutional setting at a low cost. What's the problem?" he argued.

Finally, they got the regulations approved. Meanwhile, they'd been tenaciously seeking donations, and, by the third anniversary of Betty's sobriety—less than two years since the idea was sparked by Walter Annenberg—they'd raised $3 million.

The board of the Eisenhower Medical Center had offered several acres on the southeast portion of its campus. Throughout the fundraising and bureaucratic process, they'd been calling the facility the Chemical Dependency Treatment Center at Eisenhower Medical Center. But Dr. Joe Cruse, who was heavily involved with the planning and development, knew this was so important that it needed, and deserved, a better name. He'd been giving it a lot of thought, and one day, when he and Leonard were driving back to the desert from Los Angeles, Cruse asked, "Do you think we could use her name on it?"

Leonard thought it was a great idea. Brilliant. "Let's ask her."

"Absolutely not," Betty said. "I'm too new in recovery. I don't think it's smart for me, I don't think it's smart for the center." In the back of her mind, she was also thinking, *I'll never be able to drink again.*

In addition, Betty was concerned about how it might affect the rest of the family. The last thing she wanted was to burden them with one more thing they'd never signed on for. But the answer was unanimous. "We're proud of you, Mom," they said. "Go for it."

It took some work, but eventually President Ford and Leonard Firestone convinced her that if she put her name on the center, it would greatly benefit their cause and serve as a beacon to give women the access they needed to get help.

In October 1981, Betty Ford, Leonard Firestone, and Dr. Joe Cruse simultaneously dug their shovels into the sand on the southeast corner of the Eisenhower Medical Center grounds, and construction of the Betty Ford Center began.

From the moment Betty agreed to put her name on the center, she took full ownership. "It was a hectic sobriety I was going through while the center was being built," she said. "I was a recovering alcoholic who wanted to have a say in every decision, to have her finger in every pie. My perfectionist spirit coming to the fore again."

"She bossed that construction crew around," Ann Cullen remembered. "She was there every day, rain or shine, hard hat on, in muck boots, saying, 'No, that's not supposed to be like that.'"

Betty did the decorating, she chose the fabrics, the furniture, the rugs, the artwork, the lamps. Every paint color had to have her approval. Colors were vital. They had to be colors that would make people feel welcome. The week before opening, she realized there weren't soap dishes in the patients' rooms, so she went to Kmart, Secret Service agents in tow, to buy soap dishes.

But most important was the staff. Both Betty and Leonard knew that if they were to have a first-class facility, they needed to recruit top-notch professionals. Dr. Cruse had agreed to be the medical director, and he and Betty went around the country searching for people who understood what they were trying to do. Throughout their travels, they found that in many cities, the vast majority of beds for substance-abuse treatment were in psychiatric hospitals; and most medical professionals received little to no training in the field of addiction. It was astonishing to her, and only reinforced her knowledge that what she was doing was for a greater cause—something much bigger than herself.

A year after breaking ground, the vision that had been hatched between two best friends, both recovering alcoholics, was now standing in existence. The administration building called Firestone was at the center of the campus, with curving paths that led to three twenty-bed residential halls. Betty insisted that there not be any private rooms—she had realized how important it was to have roommates, and for no patient to be treated more special than any other because of wealth or stature. Most rooms had two beds, but in each residence hall, there was one room with four beds, just like the one Betty had stayed in for her treatment. The rooms were not luxurious but had a feeling of warmth.

If you didn't know it was a treatment facility, you might think you were walking through the grounds of a country club. There was nothing institutional about the Betty Ford Center. Everywhere you looked, you saw grass, flowers, and palm trees, with the beautiful desert mountains rising up behind the contemporary stucco structures. It was an oasis of calm, peace, and serenity.

Betty insisted on one more thing: unlike other treatment centers, where the vast majority of patients were men, at the Betty Ford Center, 50 percent of the beds were to be for women. Although women were just as likely as men to be alcoholics, they were far less likely to seek treatment. And when they sought treatment, most often, they were treated through mental health programs. She was determined to change that.

On October 3, 1982, Vice President George H. W. Bush and his wife, Barbara, arrived in Rancho Mirage to join hundreds of VIPs at the dedication ceremony. It was a glamorous affair, filled with emotional tributes to Betty Ford and her courage. Vice President Bush recalled the day that Betty admitted she was an alcoholic after entering Long Beach Naval Hospital. "And then," he said, "Betty being Betty, set out to help others."

When President Ford took to the podium, he struggled to contain the depths of the emotion he was feeling.

"It's not easy to properly and in good taste express the feelings of the entire family," he said. He spoke of that unforgettable day when everyone had gathered for the intervention and the courage Betty showed throughout her recovery. And now to be standing there in the completed Betty Ford Center, "what a tribute to you, Betty, and our dear, dear friend Len."

President Ford turned to Betty, who was seated behind him on the dais, smiling with admiration. As he looked into her eyes, his voice cracked with emotion. "We're proud of you, Mom."

There was no mistaking the deep love and shared intimacy between the man and the woman on the stage, and it moved many in the audience to tears as well.

Finally, it was Betty's turn. She walked up to the podium, her graceful dancer's gait back once again, now that she was free of drugs and alcohol, her smile sparkling just as bright as her eyes.

She thanked her family for their "tough love"—the love to "let me see my problem." "This was a desert, you know," Betty said as she looked out into the audience of so many friends who had witnessed and supported her journey. "A pile of sand out here. But we've made it come alive. And it's even going to be more alive with those people who come here for help. Because there is a way for them. And there is a new life for them. We don't ever have to give up."

The day after the dedication, four patients entered treatment: two men and two women. Before long, all sixty beds were filled.

Because of Betty's experience at the naval hospital—"blame the navy," she quipped—she was determined that the Betty Ford Center would not become a place only for the rich and famous. It had to be for everyone.

From the beginning, Betty was there almost every day. She had an office, but you were more likely to find her chatting with some patients at the coffee bar or walking around with a garbage bag, picking up any litter that happened to be around.

Once a month, she gave a lecture to the group of patients. She'd walk into the auditorium, stand at the podium, and look out at the audience of people from all walks of life—truck drivers, housewives, actors, and musicians—who were here because they were at the end of their rope.

"Hello. I'm Betty, and I'm an alcoholic."

"Hello, Betty," the audience would respond in unison.

And for the next hour, she'd share her story, straight from the heart, offering proof that if she could overcome her addiction, so could they.

If Betty Ford could do it, so can you.

26

Betty Ford, the Legacy

With the opening of the Betty Ford Center, Betty Ford, the woman, became the face of alcohol and drug addiction treatment. She had always been so relatable, and now the center that bore her name was attracting people from all walks of life—housewives, pilots, grandmothers, business executives—ordinary people who wanted to get well. Dr. Cruse had been right. Betty's name made all the difference in the world. But it was Betty Ford herself who connected with individuals.

"Mrs. Ford had a way of talking about the joy of recovering and helping people see that if you take these steps, you can have this too," recalled longtime staff member Jerry Moe. "She'd show them that this is not as complicated as people make it out to be."

In December 1983, fourteen months after the Betty Ford Center opened its doors, Elizabeth Taylor was confronted by her family with an intervention. The glamorous screen legend was fifty-one years old, and, like Betty, she had become addicted to pills and was combining them with alcohol. There was only one place to go.

"It's an experience unlike any other I've known," Taylor wrote in her diary during her first week of treatment at BFC. "There are people here just like me, who are suffering just like me, who hurt inside and out, just like me. Nobody wants anything from anybody else, except to share and help. It's probably the first time since I was nine that nobody's wanted to exploit me."

BFC adhered to a strict privacy policy—to this day, no one representing the center will confirm or deny the names of any patients, past or present—but after some paparazzi using ultralong telephoto lenses caught pictures of Elizabeth Taylor on the grounds, the actress felt cornered into making a statement.

Betty remembered that night in Studio 54 four years earlier, sitting with Taylor and Liza Minnelli, watching soberly as everyone around her was drinking and snorting cocaine. She wasn't in a position then to offer advice, but now, after all she'd learned, she was able to counsel her famous friend.

"Betty Ford and I discussed what it would be like to go public," Taylor recalled. Betty knew how terrifying it was, but she convinced Elizabeth that she would be better for it—when the world was watching, it was an incentive to stay sober—and that there was no shame in getting help. That day, Elizabeth Taylor became the first celebrity to reveal having treatment at the Betty Ford Center. And when she emerged from therapy seven weeks later, eleven pounds lighter, glowing with her newfound sobriety, word spread quickly throughout the Hollywood community.

Less than a year later, the cycle of drugs and alcohol caught up with Liza Minnelli, too. One night, after a particularly bad binge, Liza's half sister, Lorna Luft, corralled Liza onto a private jet, and they flew straight from New York to Palm Springs. At the urging of Taylor and Luft, Liza checked into the Betty Ford Center first thing the next morning.

Like many who struggle with addiction, Liza would relapse, and when she did, Betty was quick to offer encouragement. She wrote caring, personal letters, and sent reading material to help the entertainer stay on track. After a stay at Hazelden in Minnesota, Liza wrote Betty to thank her for her letter, which, she said, "not only helped me, but several other very worthwhile women who were in a lot of pain at the time. Thank you for caring about me."

When actress Ali MacGraw entered treatment at BFC in July 1986, she was surprised to find that Betty Ford was very much in evidence on campus.

"She had her finger on every aspect of it, and she knew, from firsthand experience, the best way to go through this," MacGraw said. "Just being there, seeing her speak, feeling her absolute one-on-one attention to each of us as we spoke to her was inspiring, moving, life changing."

The shame of addiction was being lifted to the point that going into treatment at the Betty Ford Center started to be seen almost as a status symbol. In Hollywood, a joke started going around that "You're nothing unless you've been to Betty Ford."

But those who went through treatment knew it was no joke. Betty Ford was changing, and saving, lives. Country singer Johnny Cash credited Betty for giving him "a new hold on life," and singer Stevie Nicks of Fleetwood Mac said that hearing Betty tell her own story made her need to fix herself even stronger. "Talk about being famous," Nicks said. "God, if Betty Ford can come through this, I can come through it, too."

Years later, Stevie Nicks returned to BFC to speak at an alumni event, and when she saw Betty there, much older and quite fragile at the time, the singer and songwriter took the opportunity to express her gratitude. She actually got down on one knee, and said, "If it were not for you, Betty Ford, I would be dead. Absolutely. So, all the songs that I have written since I was here, I dedicate to you. All the songs, and all the poems, and the shows, and all the amazing things I got to do between 1985 and now, is because of you."

Mary Tyler Moore remembered how sad she'd felt for then–First Lady Betty Ford when she'd struggled to say her few short lines while filming the episode of *The Mary Tyler Moore Show*, but eight years later, Mary turned to the Betty Ford Center to treat her own addiction to alcohol.

"Now, here we were in a role reversal," Moore wrote in her memoir. "She was extending the helpful hand to me, and while at first I felt like an errant schoolgirl, as I identified with her story and digested her almost brutal honesty, I was able to grow emotionally. Those five weeks at the center transformed my life."

Betty would hear similar sentiments over and over again, with thousands of people telling her how she had saved their lives. But every time, she refused to take credit.

"No, no, no," she'd say. "We provided the tools, but you're the one that did the work."

The media attention that rock stars and Hollywood actors brought to the Betty Ford Center certainly contributed to its reputation as the international gold standard for chemical dependency treatment, but, in reality, celebrities have always made up less than 1 percent of its patients. Around 99 percent are average men and women, ranging in age from eighteen to eighty-eight. Whether it was a housewife from Topeka, Kansas, with an addiction to prescription drugs, a head of state from a foreign country abusing alcohol, an airline pilot combining pills and booze, or a world-famous rock star battling a variety of demons, Betty Ford treated everyone the same.

Geoff Mason had a heady job as executive vice president of NBC Sports, in which he traveled all over the world on an extremely liberal expense account. He'd managed to rise to the top of his profession while maintaining a "vodka high," but eventually, he drifted into complete and total dependence on alcohol.

"I had become a serious black-out drinker," he said.

Ironically, Mason had been in Moscow in 1977 doing a pre-survey for NBC's planned coverage of the 1980 Olympics and had met Betty Ford when she was there covering the Bolshoi Ballet. He'd seen the obvious signs of her tragic addiction, had followed her recovery, and in 1983, when he finally hit rock bottom, he realized there was only one place for him to go.

After checking himself into the Betty Ford Center, Mason emerged seven weeks later, a sober, changed man. As it turned out, that day happened to be the one-year anniversary celebration of the Betty Ford Center. At the gala dinner that night, he introduced himself to Betty, and told her how great he felt, and what a terrific, life-changing experience his time at BFC had been.

"She took me into a corner and we talked for half an hour," Mason recalled. She wanted to know his story, and all about him. During the conversation, Betty got an idea.

"You know," she said, "I'd like to organize a network of support, so that when people like you go home, you have people you can call on, people we can connect you with, who have had the same experience, to help ease you into the world of AA. I'd like to think an alumni project could be the legacy of our work here."

She paused and looked Geoff Mason right in the eye, and asked, "Would you like to help me get that started?"

"Now what was I going to say?" Mason recalled with a laugh. "That

I've got this big television job and don't have time to take on a project like that?"

Instead, he said, "I'd be honored." Over the next two decades, Mason worked tirelessly to create alumni chapters throughout America and in other countries, and in the process, he and Betty Ford developed an extraordinary friendship.

Throughout the years, Betty would appear every so often on the cable TV talk show *Larry King Live*. King would have her on for a full hour, and at the end of the program, the host would invite people to call in with questions. By the end of the show, the phone lines at the Betty Ford Center would be jammed with people calling about treatment for themselves or loved ones. The center would be 100 percent full for the next one and a half years.

Betty recognized that holidays could be especially tough for patients in treatment, so she made sure that at Thanksgiving, there was turkey and all the trimmings, and then during Hanukkah and Christmas, the halls were decorated with garlands, lights, menorahs, and Christmas trees. Every Memorial Day, there was a big barbecue for all the patients who happened to be there at that time. Picnic tables were decorated with red, white, and blue tablecloths, with the staff dishing out potato salad and corn on the cob, while Betty Ford herself poured lemonade and iced tea. But the biggest surprise for the patients was always when they walked over to the big grill and saw that the tall blond-haired man flipping hamburgers and hot dogs was Gerald R. Ford, the thirty-eighth president of the United States.

"President Ford was so proud of her," observed Jerry Moe. "He always took a step back and let Mrs. Ford take the lead."

Betty's passion and dedication to the center never wavered. For years, she was on the BFC campus almost every day, but she kept her priorities in perspective. "I don't give one hundred percent of my time to the recovery of others," she told the *Los Angeles Times*. "I give one hundred percent to my own recovery, and my own recovery involves being well and being drug free in order to help other people as a role model."

Beyond being a role model for people struggling with alcohol and drug addiction, Betty Ford continued to commit herself to issues that needed attention. In the early 1980s thousands of people were dying of AIDS, and because the majority of victims were gay men, tremendous fear and stigma surrounded the disease. In 1985, less than two years after her stay at the Betty Ford Center, Elizabeth Taylor took on the role as chair of the first major AIDS benefit, and started telephoning friends in Hollywood, asking for donations and participation. She was shocked when most of them declined or simply didn't return her calls. But when she called Betty Ford, there was no hesitation.

"She stepped forward and promised to be there when others refused," Taylor said.

"Mrs. Ford had quite a few gay friends," Ann Cullen pointed out, "and I think she was horrified about how the gay community was being treated with regard to this disease. In her mind, it was just another disease that needed to have the stigma removed, and so, there she was."

When actor Rock Hudson announced in 1985 that he was being treated for AIDS, Hollywood's elite turned out for Taylor's event, packing the ballroom at the Bonaventure Hotel in Los Angeles. That night, Liz Taylor presented Betty Ford with the first AIDS Project Commitment to Life Award.

"I watched her at the Betty Ford clinic in Palm Springs," Taylor told the audience. "She comes every week . . . She is proof. She is courage. She is commitment. She is one angel that has never feared to tread."

Every single one of the 2,500 people in the room rose in a standing ovation as Betty walked onstage to accept the award. She still got stage fright—especially in front of a crowd like this—but she stepped up to the microphone and graciously accepted the honor.

"Tonight is about conquering fear, and it's about saving lives," she said. She talked about how the public's attitude toward alcoholism and cancer had changed, adding, "attitudes toward AIDS can change as well."

In 1983, Larry Buendorf, the Secret Service agent who had grabbed the gun from Squeaky Fromme during the assassination attempt on President Ford, was asked if he would take over the Ford detail.

"I was very pleased that I was selected, because I had a great deal of respect for both of them," Larry said.

When he first arrived in Rancho Mirage, he went in to meet with President Ford, and then Mrs. Ford came in. She walked right up to Larry, gave him a hug, and said, "We're so happy to have you with us again."

They chatted for a while, and then Betty began to leave. Before she got to the door, she turned around and said, "Larry, you know, we don't have any female Secret Service agents on our detail."

"That's all she had to say," Larry recalled. "I got the message." He made some calls, and from that point forward, the Ford protective detail always had at least one female agent.

In 1992, the Betty Ford Center celebrated its tenth anniversary. Since opening its doors, the BFC had helped more than fifteen thousand men and women struggling with drug and alcohol addiction. Liza Minnelli and Whoopi Goldberg donated performances for the gala fundraiser, and tickets sold out almost immediately.

"I would do anything for the Betty Ford Center," Liza told the audience, "because like so many people, it did indeed save my life."

It was a spectacular evening, a tribute to both Betty and Leonard Firestone, for their vision that had helped so many people. What Betty didn't know was that, at the same time, one of her own children was struggling with the demons of addiction.

The Ford children had all gone on with their lives and were scattered around the country. Betty was thrilled to be a grandmother—a sober, loving "Gramma" to five granddaughters—two from Susan and Chuck, and three from Mike and Gayle. Jack was living in San Diego and had married a lovely woman named Juliann, while Steve wound up as an actor in Hollywood. He'd had a recurring role on the daytime soap opera *The Young and the Restless,* followed by some movie roles, and was currently hosting *Secret Service*, a popular television show that reenacted real Secret Service cases. Best of all, Steve had fallen in love and was engaged to be married the following summer.

The invitations were sent out—it was to be a June wedding in Santa Monica—but fourteen weeks before the wedding, Steve called his parents from Toronto, where he was shooting the television series.

"Mom, Dad," he said, "I need to come home. There's something I need to tell you."

Steve sat down with his parents in their living room in Rancho

Mirage—the same room where the family had staged the intervention with Betty fifteen years earlier—and told them he was struggling with alcoholism.

Betty and Jerry were both shocked. They'd never seen any signs that Steve had a problem. Sure, he drank beer or a glass of wine when the family was all together, but they'd never seen him out of control.

"Oh, Steve, no you're not," Betty said. "You can't be an alcoholic." She, of all people, should know. For the past ten years, she'd worked with addicts on a daily basis. She'd know if her own son had a problem.

Steve was embarrassed and ashamed. He struggled to tell his mother and father—the two people he admired and respected more than anyone in the world—how he had a habit of binge drinking and womanizing while he was on the road.

Betty listened, but she still wasn't convinced that her son's drinking made him what she'd call an alcoholic. In that moment, she was just a mother trying to understand something that didn't make sense.

Finally, Steve said, "Mom, wait a second. Listen to what I'm telling you: I'm turning myself in. For goodness sakes, you're Betty Ford."

They talked for a long while. Steve shared more and more details of things he'd done that made him deeply ashamed, all because one drink would lead to another and another.

"You raised me to be a better man than this," Steve said.

There were tears and hugs, and eventually Betty realized that her son did have a problem. Not only was he asking for help, he needed it.

Ironically, being treated at the Betty Ford Center was not an option for Steve because of its standard policy that spouses or family members of staff and employees could not be admitted—there was just too much emotional stuff that needed to be addressed. Betty was able to set up appointments for Steve to be evaluated by some of the counselors and doctors at the center, though, and they, in turn, made recommendations for treatment at another facility, along with the option that Steve begin attending AA meetings.

It was extremely painful for everyone, but Steve knew he had to get well before he could commit to marriage. The wedding had to be called off and letters of explanation sent to all the invited guests.

"Mom was wonderful during that time," Steve recalled. "One of the most important things she gave me was a little book called *A Day at a*

Time." Often, when Steve visited his parents in Rancho Mirage, he had seen his mother at the kitchen table with a box of these same books, signing each one. "She had probably signed thousands, which she gave to patients at the center, but I never imagined I was going to need one," he said.

A Day at a Time had a page for each day of the year, and for every day, there was a message of reflection, a prayer, and a short phrase to remember. When Betty handed Steve the book, she said, "I read mine every day."

Inside the palm-sized book, she had written:

Dear Steve . . . Enjoy your life. I love you and think you are truly sincere in your search. It works if you work it.
    Love, Mom

Steve began attending 12-step meetings—ninety in ninety days— and, with the love and support of his mother and father, began the long, satisfying road of recovery.

From the moment of its inception, the Betty Ford Center was Betty's primary focus, but ever since leaving the White House, she had continued to speak out for women's rights and breast cancer awareness. The deadline to pass the Equal Rights Amendment had been set for June 1982, and in the year leading up to it, Betty had agreed to be the national honorary chair of the ERA Countdown Campaign alongside actor Alan Alda. She traveled around the country rallying support in the fifteen states that had yet to ratify the amendment. Just three more states were needed in order for it to pass, but in the end, it couldn't be done, and the ERA did not become law.

In the seven years since she had come forward with her own breast cancer diagnosis, more women were being diagnosed with the disease than ever before, and finding it in earlier stages was leading to higher survival rates. For Susan G. Komen, who was just thirty-three when she got the devastating diagnosis of breast cancer, the outlook was not good. With her sister Nancy Brinker's encouragement, Suzy fought it with everything she had.

"Every time they'd give her a new therapy," Brinker recalled, "Suzy would say, 'If Betty Ford could do this, I can do it.' Betty was a beacon of hope for us."

When Suzy died just twenty months after her diagnosis, her sister vowed to find a cure and started the Susan G. Komen Breast Cancer Foundation. It was just getting off the ground in 1982, when Nancy contacted Betty Ford and asked if she'd be willing to participate in their inaugural fund-raising event in Dallas, at a women's polo tournament. They wanted to present Betty with the first annual Susan G. Komen Award.

Betty didn't hesitate. "I'm delighted to help," she said. "But I don't have to ride a horse, do I?"

"Quite honestly," Nancy Brinker recalled, "if I'd said yes, I think she would have given it a try."

The event was a big success, and from that point on, Betty Ford was a steadfast supporter of Nancy Brinker's mission. When Nancy herself became a breast cancer patient, Betty Ford was the first person who called her in the hospital.

"She told me to take one day at a time and take care of myself and have faith," Nancy recalled. "Not to be afraid to be aggressive with this disease, because it was an aggressive disease."

That phone call meant so much to Nancy as she went through her treatment. "To have someone I knew, who was rock steady in her spirituality, really helped me. Just the way she related to people, she never judged you. She did not judge you."

Nancy Brinker became a cancer survivor, and Susan G. Komen for the Cure would become the largest donor to breast cancer research and breast cancer funding in the world. Every year the organization honors individuals who have committed their life to engaging in public awareness of breast cancer with an award in Betty Ford's name.

In 1984, Betty hosted a conference at the Gerald R. Ford Presidential Library and Museum in Grand Rapids to examine the role of first lady. During the conference, Betty and Rosalynn Carter realized that the interests they championed—Betty, with substance abuse; and Mrs. Carter, with mental health issues—were connected. In talking, they found they had a lot of common ground. Over the next ten years, they worked on numerous projects together and formed a close friendship.

In 1994, Mrs. Carter and Mrs. Ford showed a joint front as they traveled to Washington and testified before Congress, encouraging the inclusion of mental health and substance abuse treatment benefits in the national health care reform plan. "She rounded up the Republicans, and I rounded up the Democrats," Rosalynn Carter recalled, as they pleaded the case that spending money for treatment actually saved taxpayer dollars in the long run. "Our political differences never entered into it at all."

Two former first ladies, whose husbands had been fierce political rivals, showing that it was possible to find common ground and work toward the greater good.

As the years went by, Betty was honored with hundreds of awards for her tireless work to help others and make positive changes. In 1991 she was shocked when she got a call from the White House notifying her that President George H. W. Bush had chosen her, as one of ten people that year, to receive the Presidential Medal of Freedom. It was the nation's highest civilian award, the same award she had urged her husband to present to her role model Martha Graham fifteen years earlier— an award she'd never sought and never imagined she would ever do anything worthy of being its recipient.

Now seventy-three years old, she was back at the White House, with Jerry beaming proudly in the front row.

"Her courage and candor have inspired millions of Americans to restore their health, protect their dignity, and shape full lives for themselves," President Bush said. *Millions of Americans.* She, Betty Ford, had made an impact on millions of American lives. It was difficult to fathom, and impossible to quantify, the magnitude of her contributions to society.

Eight years later, the Congressional Gold Medal, the highest award bestowed by the legislative branch of the US government, was presented jointly to President and Mrs. Ford. At the formal ceremony in the US Capitol Rotunda, President Bill Clinton praised President Ford for his decades of leadership in Congress and for the tough decisions he had to make in an effort to heal the country after Richard Nixon's resignation.

Then President Clinton turned to Betty. "Perhaps no first lady in our history, with the possible exception of Eleanor Roosevelt, has touched so many of us in such a personal way. Because I lost my mother to breast cancer, Betty Ford is a heroine to me. Because my family has been victimized by alcoholism, and I know what it's like to see good, fine people stare into the abyss of their own personal despair, I will be forever grateful to the Betty Ford Center—and for the millions of other people whose lives have literally been turned around and often saved . . . You gave us a gift, and we thank you."

As they grew older, both Betty and Jerry continued to work on behalf of causes that were important to them, but most important, always, was their family. They had the house in Rancho Mirage, and a couple of years after leaving the White House, they'd built a large home—big enough for all the children, spouses, and increasing numbers of grandchildren, to gather at Christmas and over Fourth of July—in Beaver Creek, Colorado, next door to their best friend Leonard Firestone.

Jerry Ford passed along his love for swimming to his grandchildren— he'd stand at the edge of the pool saying, "Show me your breaststroke"— and almost from the time each of them could walk, he had them on skis. Skiers at Beaver Creek would do a double take when they'd see a man who looked just like former president Jerry Ford walking to the ski school, carrying five pairs of skis on his shoulders, with five little girls trailing behind him.

Whenever the family was all together, there'd be competitive games of Pictionary and Balderdash, with Betty leading one team and Jerry the other. "Grandpa used to spell out curse words in front of us," Susan's daughter Heather Vance Devers recalled with a laugh, "long after we were all teenagers."

There were always lively debates about politics and current events, and even the grandchildren were expected to have an opinion. "It was an open platform," Susan's other daughter, Tyne Vance Berlanga, said. "This conservative Republican family had raised five confident, headstrong granddaughters who weren't afraid to stand up to our much older uncles with differing opinions. There were definitely some right leaners and some left leaners."

Betty loved to sit back and let the conversation play out. "She always encouraged us to speak up and say what we felt," Tyne said. But if she felt like her granddaughters were getting ganged up on, Betty would step in.

"There wasn't a stronger voice at the table than Gramma's," Tyne said. And no one respected or adored their grandmother more than their grandfather.

"Grandpa always referred to Gramma as his bride," Heather recalled. "I'd be sitting with him, and Gramma would walk into the room, and he'd say, 'Look how beautiful my bride looks this evening. Isn't she beautiful?'"

As the years ticked by, age began to take its toll, but the romance never faded. The grandchildren would remember seeing their grandparents sitting together on the sofa watching television, their hands clasped together like courting teenagers.

By 2006, President Ford had suffered a series of minor strokes and had congestive heart failure. That summer, as he approached his ninety-third birthday, everyone was concerned that perhaps going to Beaver Creek wasn't a good idea, because of the high altitude. Jerry wouldn't hear of it. He and Betty were going to their beloved Colorado, just as they'd done every summer for more than forty years.

They celebrated the Fourth of July—watching the parade go by from Sheika and Pepi Gramshammer's second-floor balcony in Vail—and were surrounded by friends and family ten days later as Gerald R. Ford celebrated his birthday.

Shortly thereafter, President Ford's health began failing rapidly. His heart wasn't going to hold out much longer. When Susan and her second husband, Vaden Bales, came to visit, the family was facing two options. It was time to bring in hospice, or there was a chance the president's life could be prolonged with surgery. A doctor from the Mayo Clinic had successfully performed aortic valve replacements in elderly patients using a new procedure, and he was optimistic that President Ford was a good candidate.

The family discussed it, and finally, President Ford said, "I'm inclined to proceed with the surgery." Then, turning to Betty, he asked, "What do you think, Mother?"

Betty looked at her husband, his once strong, muscular body now weakened by age. She knew the risks of surgery in someone his age, and yet, if they did nothing, she was going to lose him very soon.

"I'll support whatever you want to do, dear," she said.

Despite the risks and pain that would come with the surgery, President Ford decided he wanted to go forward with it.

"Our quick weekend changed drastically in forty-eight hours," Susan said. The plan was for Susan to fly with her parents from Eagle Vail Airport on a plane provided by the Mayo Clinic, to Rochester, Minnesota, two days later.

The next day, as they were getting organized, Betty began complaining of horrible pains in her legs. When the nurse examined her, she said, "Mrs. Ford, you need to get down to Denver right away. If you don't get down to a lower elevation and get the circulation back in your legs, they're going to have to be amputated."

"I can't go to Denver," Betty said. "I've got to go to Mayo tomorrow with Jerry."

By evening, Betty was in such pain, she could hardly move.

"Mom, I'm taking you to Denver. We're going now," Susan said. "Vaden will fly with Dad to Mayo."

After staying overnight in Denver, Betty had stabilized, but it was determined that she'd developed a blood clot, and she, too, needed surgery. By this time, President Ford was at Mayo, getting ready to have heart surgery. No one wanted them to be apart. If one of them died, the other needed to be there. Their love affair couldn't end this way.

So, after a whirlwind of phone calls—it helped to have Secret Service agents with the ability to make spur-of-the-moment logistical changes—Betty and Susan were on a plane from Denver to Rochester so that Betty and Jerry could have their surgeries in the same hospital.

Ultimately, the doctors determined that President Ford could not survive the surgery, so instead, they inserted a pacemaker and a couple of stents to alleviate some of his symptoms.

For ten days, the former president and first lady were in the Mayo Clinic, although the public never knew that Betty was also a patient. Both of them completed their treatments and, finally, were able to go home. Then came the crushing news: the Mayo doctors told them that because of the altitude, they couldn't return to Beaver Creek. Not now, not ever again. They'd seen the mountains of Colorado for the last time, and now they were headed back to their home in the desert.

The next few months were tough for everyone as they began to face the inevitable. Susan and Ann Cullen went through the house in Beaver Creek, clearing through all the belongings that had been accumulated over the course of Jerry and Betty's life together—nearly sixty years of memories—so that the house could be put up for sale. Mike, Jack, Steve, and Susan, and all the grandchildren picked out the things that meant the most to them, and the rest would either go to the Gerald R. Ford Presidential Library or be sold.

In the weeks leading up to Christmas, it was clear that President Ford was not going to be on this earth much longer. It was a matter of days or weeks. Betty spent every waking hour by her husband's side, often just sitting and holding his hand, stroking his forehead, and bringing whatever he needed. It seemed odd to be in the desert for Christmas, but Betty tried to make it as festive as possible—decorating with lights and garlands, hanging stockings, and playing Christmas music throughout the house. She knew it would be her last Christmas with her husband, and she wanted it to be as special as it always had been.

The Secret Service agents who had been with the Fords had grown close to them, and they knew what a difficult time this was. One evening, they had a surprise for Mrs. Ford.

"Come on out and look," they said.

They'd taken dozens of strands of little white lights and carefully wrapped them around each branch of the big olive tree at the front of the house. It was magical, and Betty loved it.

On December 26, 2006, at six forty-five in the evening, Betty was at Jerry's side, in their home, when he took his last breath.

"He had been kind of in and out of consciousness for several days," Susan said. "But he waited. I am truly convinced that he chose not to die on Christmas Day because Christmas was so special to us."

Jerry and Betty had spent fifty-eight Christmases together, and now Betty could not imagine life without him. He had been everything to her, and she to him. All she really wanted to do was grieve quietly, surrounded by her children and grandchildren, but she knew that wasn't possible.

For every sitting president, and every former president, there is a formal funeral plan in place, so that when the president dies—whether it be sudden and unexpected, or, as in this case, after a steady, predictable decline—the state funeral can move forward in an orderly manner. Greg Willard, who had been President Ford's aide in the White House and had stayed for a short while postpresidency, had been designated President and Mrs. Ford's personal representative for the state funeral. Over the past several years, he had worked closely with both President and Mrs. Ford on the myriad of details, adding their wishes and personal touches to the military's seven-page standard state funeral template, and overseeing what eventually became the final 538-page funeral plan.

Several hours after the president's death, Greg arrived at the Fords' home and sat down with Mrs. Ford in the living room for the discussion they'd both dreaded: implementing the funeral plan.

After reminiscing for a while, Betty managed a smile and said, "Well, I think you and I have a little bit of work to do, don't we? What do we need to do?"

Greg took her hand and said, "You don't need to do anything, Mrs. Ford. The plan we developed with the president can go exactly as planned, with a single exception: we'll need to stay at Blair House one extra day."

He explained that if they followed the plan and the original timeline of events, the National Day of Mourning and the service at Washington National Cathedral would fall on New Year's Day, which, obviously, wasn't appropriate.

"We can simply extend one additional day to the lying-in-state period at the Capitol Rotunda, and then have the National Day of Mourning and services on January 2."

With weary eyes, Betty nodded. "Yes, that will be lovely. It's what needs to be done. He would be pleased for you to do that for him."

Within minutes, the world learned of the plans for America's farewells to Gerald R. Ford, the thirty-eighth president of the United States.

President George W. Bush declared a thirty-day period of national mourning and decreed that January 2, 2007, would be a National Day of Mourning. Flags across America were lowered to half-staff.

The solemn dignity of a presidential state funeral had occurred only five times in the previous sixty years: John F. Kennedy in 1963, Herbert Hoover in 1964, Dwight D. Eisenhower in 1969, Lyndon Johnson in 1973, and Ronald Reagan in 2004. For the next six days, President Ford's casket would be accompanied by an armed forces honor guard as the state funeral went from Palm Desert to Washington, DC, and finally to Grand Rapids.

On Friday, December 28, thousands of people lined the streets, holding signs and waving flags as the funeral motorcade passed through Palm Desert. Friends from all over the West, including many from Vail and Beaver Creek, came to pay their respects at the private visitation at St. Margaret's Episcopal Church, which the Fords had attended since moving there in 1977.

Betty sat on a stool near the casket and personally greeted everyone as they filed by to pay their respects. She was genuinely comforted and strengthened by the outpouring of love from so many people who had traveled from near and far during this holiday period. But at the same time, it was apparent to those around her that she was already physically spent.

That night, back at the house, it became evident to everyone that Betty was not well. She had developed a deep, nagging cough, and now, on top of that, she had a high fever. Everyone was worried about how she was going to hold up the next day, much less get through the rest of the week.

Meanwhile, nearly 57,000 people streamed through St. Margaret's Friday night and Saturday morning, some waiting up to four hours for a few moments to pay their respects to the former president who had, along with Betty, become pillars of this close-knit community.

Betty arose early Saturday, December 29, and prepared for what would be a long, grueling day, filled with motorcades and military ceremonies steeped in tradition. It was all in tribute to her husband, and although she felt terrible, she was determined to stand by his side—the devoted wife she had been for fifty-eight years.

President George W. Bush had sent one of the presidential aircraft to Palm Springs the day before to transport President Ford's body, and the Ford family, back to Washington, DC, for the services there. There was a military ceremony at Palm Springs International Airport as the flag-draped casket was uploaded onto the blue-and-white Boeing 747, followed by a long, somber flight to Andrews Air Force Base.

Knowing that Mrs. Ford was ill, President Bush had sent some of the White House medical personnel to monitor her condition, and on the flight, they determined she had a severe lung infection. Amid the grief of losing their father, Susan and her brothers were now deeply worried about their mother.

It was dark when the plane touched down in Washington around five thirty that evening, and as everyone stepped off the aircraft, the biting cold cut like a knife. Betty stood, shivering, through another military ceremony as the president's casket was off-loaded into a hearse, and then she and the rest of the family and staff piled into a string of cars for a motorcade through the streets of the nation's capital. There was a planned stop, just for a moment, at the National World War II Memorial—a ceremonial pause in mutual tribute to President Ford and his fellow World War II veterans. Sitting in the back of her limousine, Betty was surprised, and deeply touched, to see thousands of mourners and a large group of female naval officers—graduates of the US Naval Academy—who had spontaneously come in uniform to the memorial to say goodbye, and thank you, to her husband for being the first president to admit women to the academy. As the hearse pulled to a stop, the female officers drew their hands to their foreheads in simultaneous salute. Dabbing her eyes with a tissue, Betty nodded and waved. It was an unexpected and poignant tribute, one she knew Jerry would have appreciated.

When the motorcade arrived at the US Capitol, the casket was carried by military honor guard up the east steps of the US House of Representatives and through Statuary Hall, in a symbolic tribute to President Ford's twenty-five years in Congress, before being placed in the rotunda on the Lincoln Catafalque. The state funeral proceeded with heartfelt eulogies recalling the touchstones of President Ford's life, from combat in the Pacific, to a career he cherished in Congress, to a vice presidency and presidency he did not seek.

Being there brought back memories for each of Betty and Jerry's children of those many Saturdays playing hide-and-seek through the big statues, getting lost in the maze of underground tunnels, and the requisite thank-you notes typed to Mother.

For Betty, this was where her life had changed course. Growing up in Grand Rapids with dreams of being a dancer, she'd forsaken her own goals when she married Gerald R. Ford Jr., and together they'd moved to Washington. "If I hadn't been married to my husband," she had said, "I never would have had the voice that I did . . . Being married to him was probably the biggest decision I made and the best decision I made."

The memories of her life with Jerry flashed through her mind, like a roller-coaster ride with dozens of twists and turns, accentuated by moments of extreme highs and lows. All those years as the dutiful congressman's wife; the unimaginable events that catapulted them into the White House; the outpouring of love following her openness about her breast cancer battle; speaking up for women's rights and the ERA; the devastating defeat of the '76 presidential campaign; returning to testify to Congress on behalf of Americans battling alcoholism and substance abuse. They had supported each other—always striving to follow the 70 percent rule to give more than you receive—and it had been a wonderful life together.

When the eulogies were finished, Betty got up out of her seat and walked to the casket. She clutched her hands together and placed them on the flag, and quietly bowed her head in prayer. Standing nearby, David Kennerly could hardly contain his emotions as he snapped a photo of the intimate goodbye.

It had been a grueling day that began before dawn in California, but finally, the public events were over, and the family was taken to Blair House, where they'd spend the next three nights.

The next day, thousands upon thousands of people lined up, waiting for hours in the cold to pass by the flag-draped casket in the rotunda as President Ford lay in state. Bill Livingood, the sergeant at arms of the House of Representatives at the time, recalled the tremendous outpouring: "There were so many people—even at eleven o'clock at night, the lines were still way toward the White House—so we extended the hours."

Even more impressive to him was the decorum of President and

Mrs. Ford's children. For as long as President Ford lay in the rotunda, either Susan, Steve, Mike, or Jack—and sometimes two or three of them at a time—stood at the entrance to personally thank each and every person who walked through the door.

"I had never seen that before," Livingood said. "It was a class act. It spoke volumes about that family."

On New Year's Day, Betty stayed at Blair House and received guests all day—ambassadors from the countries President Ford had visited during his presidency; President and Mrs. George W. Bush; former presidents George H. W. Bush, Bill Clinton, and Jimmy Carter, and their wives; Lynda and Luci Johnson; Happy Rockefeller, the widow of President Ford's vice president, Nelson Rockefeller; and many others.

Through it all, the doctors were giving Betty multiple antibiotics, but she was running on fumes. Everyone tried to convince her to forgo some of the planned events and get some rest. "But that was not in her," Susan said. "She would suit up and show up."

By Tuesday, January 2, the National Day of Mourning, however, Betty's condition had deteriorated even further, and everyone was concerned about how she was going to manage another long day. By sheer will and determination, she stood out in the shivering cold as her husband's casket was brought down the Senate steps of the Capitol, and then took her place in the limousine for the ride to the National Cathedral. The plan was for all the children and grandchildren to walk in a processional to their seats, and then for Betty to be escorted by President George W. Bush down the long central aisle to her seat in the front row. But those around her concluded that there simply was no way she was going to be able to walk the length of the cathedral—more than five hundred feet—in her severely weakened state, so a wheelchair had been arranged.

When the time came for her entrance, she turned to President George W. Bush and curtly motioned away the wheelchair. "I can do this!" she said emphatically. Then Betty hooked her left arm through his right arm and said, "Mr. President, if you please."

Suddenly the giant main doors of the cathedral swung open, and, arm in arm, the two of them walked the entire way to the front row.

* * *

After the services, it was back onto the presidential aircraft, with the family and the casket, to fly to Grand Rapids. There President Ford would have his final resting place on the grounds of the Gerald R. Ford Presidential Museum. As the plane approached Ann Arbor, Michigan, the pilot dropped to an altitude of just eight hundred feet and tipped the wings over the University of Michigan football stadium in an airborne salute. Looking out the window, through glassy eyes, Betty couldn't help but smile.

When they arrived in Grand Rapids, there was yet another military ceremony at the airport with the University of Michigan Marching Band present and then a motorcade to transport President Ford's body to the presidential museum that bore his name for a public viewing prior to the services the next day. As the motorcade turned onto Pearl Street, there was a stunning sight: lining the street on both sides, ten and fifteen deep, were men, young and old, aged fifteen to eighty-five, all of them Eagle Scouts in uniform, standing in solemn salute. The family had encouraged Eagle Scouts to attend and had been told earlier that week that several dozen might participate. Instead, more than 470 Eagle Scouts answered the call, coming from all over the Midwest to pay tribute to the only president who had earned the badge of Eagle Scout. As the motorcade passed by the group, an agent in the Secret Service follow-up vehicle was amazed. "I've been in thousands of motorcades, but I've never seen anything like that gathering of Eagle Scouts—remarkable!"

Betty woke up the morning of January 3, 2007, in Grand Rapids, the day of the final services and interment, and realized she simply had no more energy to continue. Sitting in her suite at the Amway Grand Plaza Hotel, she said with a deep sigh, "I just don't think I can make it any further."

Susan held her hand and tried to reassure her that everyone would understand.

About that time, Lilian Fisher, her best friend from kindergarten and dance school, arrived. Within minutes, the two childhood friends were laughing and telling stories.

"It was like watching a flat tire inflate," Susan recalled.

Lilian finally said, "You can do this, Betty. I know you can!"

Betty nodded, and to the sheer and utter surprise of her family, she announced that she was going to participate after all. At eighty-eight years old, Betty Bloomer Ford still had the will of a dancer, and on this final curtain call for her husband, she was determined to be there, center stage.

There was a final church service at Grace Episcopal Church—the same church in which she and Jerry had been married—and then, finally, the flag-draped casket was brought to its final resting place, at the north end of the Gerald R. Ford Presidential Museum, to be entombed in a grassy hillside on the banks of the Grand River.

As dusk fell, the family gathered around "Mother," clutching together with overwhelming sadness, wiping away tears through one last twenty-one-gun salute, followed by the roaring flyover by a group of twenty-one F-15 fighter jets in the missing-man formation, and the final playing of "Taps." Bundled in a fur coat, her lips turning blue from the cold, Betty watched as the military honor guard raised the flag from the top of the casket, and, with white-gloved hands, folded it with calculated precision into a tight triangle. Then the officer in charge of the honor guard turned and solemnly handed the flag to President Ford's longtime friend and advisor Dick Cheney, who was currently the vice president of the United States.

Vice President Cheney walked over to Betty, and as he handed her the flag, he said, "On behalf of the president of the United States and a grateful nation, please accept this flag as a symbol of our appreciation for President Ford's honorable and faithful service to the United States of America."

Betty clutched the flag in her hands and, closing her eyes, lifted it to touch her cheek.

The state funeral tradition is that the widow of a former president is flown back to her residence on a smaller military aircraft. However, because Betty was so ill, President Bush ordered one of the presidential 747s to fly her and the family back to Palm Springs on January 4. Just before landing, Mrs. Ford made a personal request.

"After we land, can we arrange for the crew to be out on the tarmac? I want to thank them."

As her request was passed through the aircraft, the reaction was universal. *How does she do this?* The woman seated in the presidential compartment was seriously ill; she'd just buried her husband after six days of grueling public pomp and circumstance; and yet she was now insisting on taking the time to personally thank each and every crew member.

Greg Willard and Special Agent Todd Matanich accompanied Betty from her motorcade vehicle to the now-empty house on Sand Dune Road. Ever since Vice President Cheney had handed her the flag from the casket, it had barely left her hands, and now she clutched it tightly to her chest as they walked to the front door.

"I think I'd like to lie down for a while," Betty said.

"That's a good idea, Mrs. Ford," Greg said as he helped her to the bedroom.

She sat down on the bed, looked down at the flag in her hands, and began to weep.

They sat quietly for a few minutes, and then Betty turned and said, "Thank you for everything, Greg. It all went so beautifully. Just like he had wanted."

"It's been an honor," he replied. "Now, Mrs. Ford, you need to rest."

He walked into the hallway and softly closed the door behind him.

For the first time since Jerry had died, Betty was alone. She didn't have him, in body, but she felt his presence, and a sense of comfort, in that triangular-shaped flag. She held it against her face, and laid it on the pillow next to hers, in the space where Jerry had slept up until he was moved to a hospital bed in the den. As she lay down, she looked out the window and saw the sparkling white lights on the branches of the olive tree. Closing her eyes, she said a prayer, and finally fell into a deep sleep.

For the next four and a half years, the white lights remained on the olive tree—"So when he looks down," Betty said, "he'll know I'm okay"— and the flag stayed on the pillow next to hers, a constant reminder of the man she'd loved.

* * *

Betty continued to serve as chairman emeritus of the Betty Ford Center, and she relished time with her grandchildren and great-grandchildren.

"She was always very interested in our lives," Heather Vance Devers said. "What we were doing, who we were dating. And she loved *Dancing with the Stars*."

But nothing was the same after Jerry died. The question Betty continued to ask herself was, "Why am I still here?"

"I just want to go see my boyfriend," she'd say. "That's all I want to do."

On July 8, 2011, Betty got her wish.

AFTERWORD

On July 14, 2011—what would have been President Ford's ninety-eighth birthday—Elizabeth Anne Bloomer Ford was laid to rest in the tomb alongside her husband, near the Gerald R. Ford Presidential Museum in Grand Rapids. As family and friends mourned the woman they loved and admired, amid the grief there was joy, for no one doubted that Jerry and Betty were together again—laughing, holding hands—and, if there are beds in heaven, they were sharing one.

For the previous four and a half years, Betty had slept with Jerry's folded casket flag next to her, on his pillow, but as she neared the end of her life, she had to consider what should be done with it once she was gone.

Shortly before President Ford died, he learned that the United States Navy was going to name its next aircraft carrier, CVN 78, the USS *Gerald R. Ford*. It would be the first in a new class of nuclear-powered carriers, and even though he would never see the ship built to completion, President Ford wrote that it was a source of "indescribable pride and humility to know that an aircraft carrier bearing my name may be permanently associated with the valor and patriotism of the men and women of the United States Navy."

Betty, knowing that Jerry had always been fiercely proud of his service as a lieutenant commander in the US Navy, directed that the flag's final home was to be on the USS *Gerald R. Ford*.

"Mother's decision about the flag was characteristically firm," Susan recalled. "She gave us specific instructions about the flag—very specific."

As the ship's sponsor, Susan was integrally involved in the eleven-year shipbuilding and commissioning process, and it was an emotional moment when she unveiled the still-folded flag, now encased in a wood-and-glass frame etched with her dad's vice presidential and presidential seals, and presented it to the commanding officer, Captain John Meier.

"On behalf of Mother," Susan said, "I hereby entrust the flag of President Gerald R. Ford to you, and the ship's future captains, to remain at all times aboard the ship until such time as she is decommissioned."

The USS *Gerald R. Ford* was commissioned in July 2017, and while the 2,600 sailors who live aboard the ship have a keen sense of President Ford's legacy, Betty Ford's healing spirit is among them too. Ironically, it was at the Long Beach Naval Hospital where Betty learned, in those life-changing four weeks of treatment after her intervention, that sailors are not immune to alcoholism, drug abuse, or mental health issues. So, inside the medical unit of this floating city is a tranquil space filled with inspirational books, behind a door with a plaque that says:

Betty Ford Counseling and Assistance Center
This Is a Place Where You Can Go, That You Can Feel Safe and
Look Inside Yourself and Discover Yourself.
—*Betty Ford*

It is impossible to quantify Betty Ford's legacy or to overstate it. So many things we take for granted come as a direct result of her candor and courage.

For any woman diagnosed with breast cancer today, her chances of survival—especially if it is detected early—are infinitely greater than in 1974 when Betty Ford received that devastating news. Betty made it okay to talk publicly about breasts and cancer—and by encouraging that conversation, and then working tirelessly to keep it going, funding for research, education, and care has grown exponentially. Each year, hundreds of thousands of people participate in the Susan G. Komen Race for

the Cure; doctors now ask, "Have you had your annual mammogram?";
and cancer is no longer something that's spoken about in hushed voices.
At Betty's funeral in Grand Rapids, historian Richard Norton Smith
remarked, "Where women's health issues are concerned, American history is divided into two unequal periods: Before Betty and After Betty."

The same can be said about treatment for alcoholism and drug
addiction. More than a hundred thousand people have been treated at
the Betty Ford Center since its inception in 1982, and it remains the
only treatment facility in the world that has an equal number of beds for
women as for men. The reason for the center's success and world-class
reputation came from Betty's philosophy that "at the Betty Ford Center,
we do it right the first time." Over the years, people tried to convince her
to set up Betty Ford Centers all over the world—New York, Paris, even
Saudi Arabia—but, in all cases, she was adamantly against it.

"We do one thing, and we do it really well," she'd say. "If you have
centers all over the place, how do you control the quality?" It was her
name on the center, and she wasn't willing to risk sacrificing the reputation they'd worked so hard to build.

"You can't be all things to all people," she said. "So we're going to
focus on alcoholism and drug addiction. We're going to focus on family
and children. And we'll feel good about that."

In 1975, when Betty began championing the Equal Rights Amendment, women's wages were less than 60 percent of men's. By 2017, women,
on average, were earning 80 percent of what men earn—an increase, for
sure, though still far from equal.

It is astonishing that the issues Betty Ford brought into the national
conversation in the 1970s and 1980s are just as relevant today. Women
are still marching for equal rights and equal pay; breast cancer still claims
tens of thousands of lives each year; and addiction to opioid drugs has
become a national crisis.

According to the US Department of Health and Human Services, in
2016 an estimated 11.5 *million* people in the United States misused *prescription* opioid pain relievers, and more than 17,000 died as a result of
overdosing on *commonly prescribed opioids*. Millions of people get prescriptions for opioids—from their doctors—to treat chronic pain. One
in four misuse the drugs. And of those people, 5 percent will transition
to heroin. The problem is systemic, with plenty of blame to go around.

But the staggering reality is that there are countless people just like Betty Ford, who become addicted to legal drugs prescribed by their physician. And month after month, the doctors continue renewing prescriptions for drugs that are known to be addictive.

President and Mrs. Ford never expected or required their children to follow in their footsteps, and none has entered politics. Three of the Ford children serve as trustees of the Gerald R. Ford Presidential Foundation, and while Jack has chosen to remain out of the public eye, Susan, Steve, and Mike continue to work on behalf of causes that Betty Ford cared about so deeply.

Susan worked alongside her mother to help launch National Breast Cancer Awareness Month in 1984 and remains a vocal advocate for women's health issues. She has been an active member of the board of directors of the Betty Ford Center since 1992 and succeeded her mother as chairman of the board from 2005 to 2010. In 2014 the Betty Ford Center merged with the Minnesota-based Hazelden Foundation, and Susan currently serves on the board of what is now known as the Hazelden Betty Ford Foundation.

Steve Ford has proudly remained sober for more than twenty-five years, and finds tremendous satisfaction mentoring young men battling addiction and speaking to groups all over the United States about his personal recovery journey.

Mike Ford continued his work in the ministry and found his "calling" working with college students. During his thirty-six-year career in administration at Wake Forest University, his primary focus was on the personal and holistic development of students to become enlightened and contributing leaders and citizens.

The merger between the Betty Ford Center and Hazelden created the nation's largest nonprofit addiction treatment provider, but, staying true to Betty's wishes, there remains only one inpatient Betty Ford Center. Despite the change in management, Betty Ford's aura permeates the campus in Rancho Mirage. Framed portraits of her hang on the walls, along with the artwork she handpicked and placed, while her philosophy and encouraging words are etched into plaques throughout the facility. Patients entering Firestone Hall see these words emblazoned on the wall:

"Anyone and everyone can escape the hell that addiction has created for them and their families if they dare to take that first big step—reaching out for, and accepting, help."

Throughout the writing of this book, I felt Betty's unmistakable guidance every step of the way. I never knew Betty Ford, but knowing what I know now, there is little doubt in my mind that she orchestrated this entire process.

The first time I met Susan Ford Bales was at her home in Tulsa, Oklahoma. For several hours she shared with me her memories of growing up as Betty Ford's daughter. It was late afternoon when she walked me outside to my car, and as we stopped in the courtyard to say good-bye, a single yellow butterfly appeared out of nowhere and flew in a figure eight around the two of us.

Two days later, I was back home in California and happened to go out for breakfast after a morning doctor's appointment. It was my first time at Theresa & Johnny's Comfort Food in San Rafael, and I was stunned when the waitress appeared before me wearing the restaurant's "uniform": a black T-shirt etched with David Kennerly's photo of Betty Ford dancing on the Cabinet Room table. On the back it proclaimed, "Breakfast That Will Make You Want to Dance!"

While conducting interviews at the Betty Ford Center, I contacted the new owners of the former Ford residence on Sand Dune Road in Rancho Mirage, and they graciously allowed me to tour the home. As I stepped outside the door from the living room and onto the patio facing the golf course, I kid you not, a single yellow butterfly arose from the bushes and fluttered above my head.

Most of my writing was done on my laptop while sitting at the head of my dining room table, surrounded by books and yellow legal pads filled with notes, facing a large window overlooking San Francisco Bay. Inevitably, there would be those times when the words just wouldn't come; when I couldn't figure out exactly how to bring Betty to life on the page. I'd pause and look up from the screen, and so many times—so many times—there would be a single butterfly—sometimes yellow, sometimes a bright-orange monarch, but always a single butterfly—peering in as if to say, "Keep going. You've got this. One day at a time."

There is a remarkable sense of serenity at the Betty Ford Center. The purple desert mountains stand guard like giant arms protecting the campus with a gentle grace. If there comes a time when you happen to be a patient walking along the winding palm tree–lined paths, struggling on your own journey, don't be surprised if you happen to see a single butterfly fluttering its wings like a graceful dancer, hovering just overhead.

ACKNOWLEDGMENTS

First and foremost, I must acknowledge and thank Susan Ford Bales, who gave so freely of her time and memories. Not only did she meet with me on several occasions, answering questions and reminiscing for hours at a time, but she also responded graciously to countless emails and phone calls about minute details and highly personal family matters, and then read multiple versions of the manuscript, offering corrections for accuracy. Not once did she request I remove anything. I admire her integrity and commitment to her parents' legacies, and I am honored to call her a friend.

Additionally, Susan connected me to dozens of people whose differing perspectives provided deeper insight into her mother's life—from aunts and cousins to longtime family friends. Two who were especially helpful, and to whom I am indebted, are Greg Willard and Caroline Coventry Morgan.

Greg, who is the embodiment of diplomacy, shared poignant memories of his special relationship with the Ford family in multiple interviews, spent innumerable hours reviewing several versions of the manuscript, and provided on-point suggestions for clarity and accuracy. His assistance and friendship are priceless.

Caroline Coventry Morgan's contribution is, I hope, evident in the story. We spent two days together in Santa Fe—two days and evenings filled with tears and laughter, as she shared her own deeply personal side of Betty Ford's story—and another treasured friendship developed.

David Hume Kennerly's contributions also cannot be overstated. From our first meeting at his home—which, as you can imagine, is like a museum—he was generous with his time and candid memories of Betty Ford. Even though, to this day, he respectfully refers to her as "Mrs. Ford," you get a sense of the special bond they shared from the mischievous expression on her face in that fantastic photograph we chose for the jacket cover.

It was important to me that all four of the Ford children have a voice in this story, and I am grateful to Steve, Mike, and Jack, for their cooperation and willingness to share humorous anecdotes, as well as deeply personal moments. Susan's daughters Tyne Berlanga and Heather Devers helped me see Betty Ford as Gramma, while relatives Greg Ford, Linda Ford Burba, and Bonnie Bloomer Baker provided insight into Betty's earlier years.

I am grateful to Ann Cullen, Nancy Chirdon Forster, Penny Circle, Sheila Weidenfeld, and Jan Hart, each of whom worked with Betty Ford at different times in her life and gave generously of their time to provide their unique perspectives.

It is a testament to Betty Ford herself that so many people agreed, and indeed were eager, to share their memories of this incredible woman. It was an honor to speak with Vice President Dick Cheney and Secretary Donald Rumsfeld; First Lady Rosalynn Carter graciously met with me at the Carter Center in Atlanta; Tom Brokaw, Andrea Mitchell, Ali Mac-Graw, Geoff Mason, and Nancy Brinker each spent considerable time with me by telephone. In Vail, I had the wonderful opportunity to reminisce with the incomparable Sheika Gramshammer in Pepi's Restaurant. Many thanks to Dr. Joseph Cruse, Linda and John Galvin, Ann Lewis, Toto Fisher, Joan Secchia, Barbara Yardley Appleby, Bay Innamorati, board members of the Mary Free Bed Rehabilitation Hospital, Lorna Luft, and Lynette Williams Thomas for their memorable contributions.

The staffs of the Gerald R. Ford Presidential Museum in Grand Rapids and the Ford Library in Ann Arbor were invaluable. I am grateful to Elaine Didier, Don Holloway, Jamie Draper, Geir Gundersen, Stacy Davis, and Elizabeth Druga for their knowledge and assistance every step of the way. At the Gerald R. Ford Presidential Foundation, I am thankful to Joe and Donna Calvaruso, Marty Allen, Hank and Liesel Meijer, David and Judy Frey, and Bob and Judy Hooker for their support of this project from the beginning. Special thanks to Bob and Nancy Sellers for their hospitality in Harbor Springs and the introduction to their Michigan friends that set everything in motion.

One of the highlights during my research was visiting the Betty Ford Center in Rancho Mirage. The staff is truly amazing and it's easy to understand why the Hazelden Betty Ford Foundation continues to be the gold standard in addiction recovery. I am incredibly grateful to Laurie Skochil, Mark Mishek, Jerry Moe, Dr. Marv Seppala, Jim Steinhagen, Mark Baumgartner, Neil Gussardo, Jerry McDonald, Joan Clark, Carolyn Friend, and the anonymous patient who gave me a tour of her room.

It was important to me to visit the Fords' former residences and it was wonderful to find that the current owners are keenly aware and proud of the historical significance of their homes. Thanks to the Lloyd and Bailey families in Alexandria, and to John McIlwee and Bill Damaschke in Rancho Mirage, who graciously allowed me to tour their residences.

Many thanks to former Secret Service agents Larry Buendorf, Dick Keiser, Dick Hartwig, Bob Alberi, Jerry Bechtle, Ron Johnston, Bob Innamorati, and Paul Masto, all of whom spoke to me with great discretion and the utmost admiration for President and Mrs. Ford.

This is now my fifth book with Gallery Books, and the team there has become like family. My editor, Mitchell Ivers, is simply the best and I'm so honored he brought me this project. Huge thanks to the trailblazing team of Jennifer Bergstrom, Jennifer Robinson, Aimee Bell, and Jennifer Long for their passion and enthusiasm, and to Hannah Brown, Abby Zidle, Diana Velasquez, Mackenzie Hickey, Anabel Jimenez, Alexandre Su, Caroline Pallotta, and Jaime Putorti for their behind-the-scenes efforts that contributed to this beautiful book.

Thanks to Kayla Tucker, my research assistant who helped with tasks big and small, and to Josie Freedman, my agent at ICM, who shares a passion for this story. I am grateful to my parents, Wyman and Gay Harris, and my sister, Stephanie Ryder, for their love and encouragement, and to Meg Crofton and my (almost) daily walking partner Mary Potuznik for their friendship and wisdom.

And finally, to Cooper, Connor, Abby, and Clint: I can't imagine life without you. I am blessed.

NOTES

Abbreviations Used in the Notes

ATTH	Gerald R. Ford, *A Time to Heal: The Autobiography of Gerald R. Ford* (New York: Harper & Row, 1979).
BAGA	Betty Ford with Chris Chase, *Betty: A Glad Awakening* (New York: Doubleday, 1987).
TTOML	Betty Ford with Chris Chase, *The Times of My Life* (New York: Harper & Row, 1978).

Prologue

xii *"It's time"*: Susan Ford Bales, in discussion with author, February 17, 2017.

xii *"Dad," she pleaded, "you need to come home immediately"*: *BAGA*, 14.

xii *"This is not going to be pleasant"*: ibid., 17.

xii *"No," Dr. Pursch responded. "It never is"*: ibid.

xii *"scared to death"*: Caroline Coventry Morgan, in discussion with author, February 27, 2017.

xiii *"After you've buried somebody"*: *BAGA*, 14.

xiii *"the boys"*: Susan Ford Bales, discussion, February 17, 2017.

xiii *"Mom, you need to stop"*: ibid.; also *BAGA*, 11.

xiii *"Well, I am stopping"*: Susan Ford Bales, discussion, February 17, 2017.

xiv What a bunch of pips: *BAGA*, 10; also Morgan, discussion, May 20, 2017.

xiv *"You're all a bunch of monsters . . . never come back!"*: *BAGA*, 11.

xiv *"Mike! Gayle!"*: Michael Ford, discussion with author, October 26, 2017.

xiv *"Mother . . . sit down"*: *BAGA*, 19.

xv *"This is Dr. Joe Pursch"*: Morgan, discussion, May 19, 2017.

xv *"almost like a doll"*: BAGA, 19.

xv *"Mrs. Ford, you don't have to be alarmed"*: ibid.

xv *"Mike, you start"*: Michael Ford, discussion, October 26, 2017.

xv *"Mom," he said, "being the oldest"*: ibid.; also BAGA, 18.

xvi *"Mother," Gayle began, "you know we've been married"*: BAGA, 19.

xvi *"There were so many times"*: ibid., 18; also Jack Ford, in discussion with author, February 17, 2018.

xvi *"Betty, we love you"*: Steve Ford, in discussion with author, November 23, 2016.

xvi *"Mom, do you remember that weekend"*: ibid.

xvii He's got some nerve: BAGA, 22.

xvii *"Mom, when I was little"*: BAGA, 20; also Susan Ford Bales, discussion, February 17, 2017.

xvii *"We love you, Betty . . . we love you"*: Steve Ford, discussion, November 23, 2016.

PART 1: BETTY FORD, DANCER

1: The Bloomer Girl

3 *"Mother always said I'd popped out of a bottle of champagne"*: TTOML, 6.

3 *William S. Bloomer had accepted a job*: "Notes of the Rubber Trade," *India Rubber Review* (June 15, 1918): 374, https://babel.hathitrust.org/cgi/pt?id=nyp.33433108137906;view=1up;seq=380.

4 *The house at 1410 Josephine Street*: Department of Commerce, Bureau of the Census, *Fourteenth Census of the United States, State Compendium: Colorado*, 1920 Population, Denver, CO, District 0247, www2.census.gov/library/publications/decennial/1920/state-compendium/06229686v1-7ch05.pdf, 4B.

4 *taking a position at the Quaker City Rubber Company*: "Bloomer with Quaker City," Personals of the Rubber Trade, *Rubber Age and Tire News* 7, no. 1 (April 10, 1920): 24, https://books.google.com/books?id=w7Y7AQAAMAAJ&pg=PA10&lpg=PA10&dq=%22The+Rubber+Age+and+Tire+News%22+%22April+10,+1920%22&source=bl&ots=yEerrATo02&sig=jyi2_WkeMKsrOnCN9vLS5slI-rM&hl=en&sa=X&ved=0ahUKEwj0zray0q_aAhUCyYMKHWbRCiEQ6AEIJzAA#v=onepage&q=%22The%20Rubber%20Age%20and%20Tire%20News%22%20%22April%2010%2C%201920%22&f=false.

5 *"filled with light"*: TTOML, 8.

5 *Hortense's cousin Charlotte Neahr Irwin*: Bonnie Bloomer Baker, in discussion with author, July 13, 2017; also Department of Commerce, Bureau of the Census, *Fourteenth Census of the United States, State Compendium: Michigan*, 1920 Population, Grand Rapids City, Kent County, MI, Ward 3, www2.census.gov/library/publications/decennial/1920/state-compendium/06229686v20-25ch1.pdf, 19A.

5 *rent a lakeside cottage for $10 a week*: *Michigan Summer Resorts: A Guide to the Summering Places in the Lake and River Region of the State of Michigan* (Detroit: Pere Marquette Railway Company, 1913), 37.

5 *"Please do not feed this child"*: TTOML, 7.

6 *"He was a great fisherman"*: ibid.

6 *"terrible tomboy"*: ibid., 9.

6 *"Oh, dear Betty . . . don't you realize?"*: Lynn Minton, "Betty Ford Talks About Her Mother," *McCall's*, May 1976.

7 *"You sound just like a horse"*: TTOML, 10.

7 *Spankings in the household were rare*: Minton, "Betty Ford Talks About Her Mother."

7 *"every phase of dance art"*: Calla Travis Graded System of Dance Instruction Loose Notes, Kay Clark Grand Rapids Dance Collection, box 1, folder 29, Grand Rapids Public Library, Grand Rapids, MI.

8 *"Ladies! . . . You sit with your legs crossed!"*: Ann Lewis, in discussion with author, October 29, 2016.

8 *"I signed up for everything"*: TTOML, 17.

8 *"She was pretty"*: Lilian Fisher, interview by Richard Norton Smith, February 27, 2012, transcript, Oral History Project, Gerald R. Ford Presidential Foundation, Grand Rapids, MI, 2, https://geraldrfordfoundation.org/centennial-docs/oral history/wp-content/uploads/2013/05/Lilian-Fisher-.pdf.

8 *"There was no kind of dance"*: TTOML, 17.

9 *Betty cleverly realized*: ibid.

9 *She would bring in a phonograph*: ibid., 14.

10 *Some committed suicide*: Fisher, interview, 4.

10 *would be no more household help*: TTOML, 16.

11 *"Twenty-five, ninety-five. Third-floor sportswear"*: ibid., 18.

11 *"Talk about personality . . . She was one hell of a gal"*: Barbara Boorn, "Betty's Blooming as First Lady No Surprise to Grand Rapids Friends," *Accent*, June 1976, 18.

11 *Betty earned $3 a week*: TTOML, 18.

11 *"she could come down the stairs"*: Boorn, "Betty's Blooming," 14.

11 *the girls liked her, the boys liked her*: Lewis, discussion, October 29, 2016.

11 *"She was very popular"*: Fisher, interview, 3.

11 *"I would set my cap for somebody"*: TTOML, 19.

12 *"You're no gentleman"*: ibid., 36.

12 *"You'll meet a tall, dark stranger"*: Jean Libman Block, "The Betty Ford No One Knows," *Good Housekeeping*, May 1974.

12 *"You will be meeting kings and queens"*: ibid., also TTOML, ix.

13 *wheeling up*: ibid., 21.

13 *"waving and yelling and showing off"*: ibid.

13 *"Shh!" . . . "Just calm down"*: ibid.

13 *"What's happened?"*: ibid.

13 *"They had to take your father"*: ibid.

13 *"efforts to revive him were of no avail"*: Obituary, *Grand Rapids* (MI) *Press*, July 19, 1934.

14 *he had been unemployed*: ibid.

14 *"He'd gone through the Depression and lost everything"*: Biography: This Week, "Betty Ford: One Day at a Time."

14 *her father had been an alcoholic*: TTOML, 286; also Biography: This Week, "Betty Ford: One Day at a Time," featuring Betty Ford, President Gerald Ford, the Ford

children, Gloria Steinem, aired October 4, 1998, on CBS, copy provided to author courtesy of GRF Library, 2003-NLF-010-025.

14 *"It was rougher for everybody after that"*: TTOML, 22.

14 *"how independent a woman can be if she needs to be"*: Betty Ford: The Real Deal (MacNeil/Lehrer Productions, PBS Home Video, 2009, 60:00), DVD.

15 *"beautiful"*: Minton, "Betty Ford Talks About Her Mother," 76.

15 *"I told her what I wanted to"*: ibid.

15 *"did sort of a sloppy job . . . If you don't do it well, don't do it at all"*: ibid.

15 *"We had black patent tap shoes"*: Edith "Toto" Fisher, in discussion with author, November 20, 2016.

16 *That year, Miss Travis invited*: Kay DeFreest (name appears as Mrs. Collins C. Clark), interview by Thomas F. Soapes, January 28, 1980, Oral History Interview, Gerald R. Ford Presidential Library, Ann Arbor, MI, March 3, 2017, www .fordlibrarymuseum.gov/library/document/0268/38-0268-f-1536968.pdf.

2: The Martha Graham of Grand Rapids

17 *Martha Hill, Doris Humphrey, Louis Horst*: personal scrapbooks and mementoes, Betty Ford Personal Papers Collection, viewed by author at Gerald R. Ford Presidential Library, Ann Arbor, MI, October 26, 2016.

17 *"born to dance"*: Mrs. Ford's Remarks, Bennington Arts Center Dedication, May 22, 1976, Frances K. Pullen Files, box 1, Gerald R. Ford Presidential Library, Ann Arbor, MI.

18 *"We breathed, we ate, we slept—nothing but dance"*: ibid.

18 *Betty, despite having ten years of dance experience, landed in group one*: personal scrapbooks and mementoes, Betty Ford Personal Papers Collection, Gerald R. Ford Presidential Library, Ann Arbor, MI.

18 *Breakfast was at seven fifteen*: ibid.

18 *"Martha Graham Technique"*: Betty Ford personal memos from Bennington College, Betty Ford Personal Papers Collection, viewed by author at Gerald R. Ford Presidential Library, Ann Arbor, MI, October 26, 2016.

18 *In between classes*: Mrs. Ford's Remarks, Bennington Arts Center Dedication, May 22, 1976.

18 *"Bennington Campus Seethes with Women Who Jump in Odd Fashion"*: TTOML, 26.

19 *"ecstasy"*: ibid., 23.

19 *"worshipped her as a goddess"*: ibid., 24.

19 *"a beautiful instrument"*: ibid.

20 *"grabbed Martha's hand, and blurted out"*: ibid., 26.

20 *"colorful"*: ibid.

21 *"straight from the sticks"*: ibid., 28.

21 *"This is a waste of time, I'm not going to make it"*: Block, "Betty Ford No One Knows," 139.

21 *"I'll see you"*: ibid.

21 *"Come into my office"*: TTOML, 28.

21 *"pretty heavy"*: ibid., 29.

21 *She cut out all his columns*: personal scrapbooks, Betty Ford Personal Papers Col-

lection, viewed by author at Gerald R. Ford Presidential Library, Ann Arbor, MI, October 25, 2016.

21 *"You've got ability"*: TTOML, 30.

22 *"You can't carouse and be a dancer too"*: ibid.

22 *"had arrived"*: ibid., 31.

22 *"sixteen-year-old girl with her first beau"*: ibid., 34.

22 *"come home for six months"*: ibid., 31.

23 *"part of a training of a dancer"*: Anna Kisselgoff, "A Martha Graham Student Comes Back," *New York Times* online, June 12, 1975.

23 *"I'm going home for six months"*: TTOML, 32.

23 *"I think it's a wise thing for you to do"*: ibid.

23 *"Where Fortunate Children Spend Summer at Play"*: "Parents Find Good Training Is Helpful," *Rhinelander Daily News*, September 4, 1930.

23 *"a happy and safe out-of-doors vacation for the growing girl"*: *Bryn Afon: A Camp for Girls* brochure, personal scrapbooks, Betty Ford Personal Papers Collection, viewed by author at Gerald R. Ford Presidential Library, Ann Arbor, MI, October 27, 2016.

24 *"You took the train"*: Lewis, discussion, October 29, 2016.

24 *"She was fun"*: ibid.

24 *Grand Rapids Concert Dance Group*: Boorn, "Betty's Blooming," 15.

24 *"Martha Graham of Grand Rapids"*: TTOML, 33.

25 *"wild friends"*: ibid., 34.

25 *"I won't talk to you now"*: ibid.

25 *"That's all right"*: ibid.

26 *"typically a generous-natured man"*: ibid., 37.

26 *"there were always boys lined up for her"*: *Betty Ford: The Real Deal.*

26 *"wined and dined by the local bachelors"*: TTOML, 36.

27 *"the five-year misunderstanding"*: ibid., 39.

3: The Five-Year Misunderstanding

28 *an agent with the Northwestern National Insurance Company*: Ignazio Messina, "Betty Ford lived in Area with 1st Spouse," *Toledo (OH) Blade*, July 11, 2011.

28 *"demonstrator"*: ibid.

28 *"She was spectacular looking"*: ibid.

28 *"We moved around, pillar to post"*: TTOML, 39.

29 *"Bill Warren was very ambitious"*: DeFreest, interview, 3.

30 *"Why don't you come down here, and we'll go somewhere to eat?"*: TTOML, 41.

30 *"a little backup"*: DeFreest, interview, 3.

30 *"the things that made our dating so amusing, made the marriage difficult"*: TTOML, 41.

30 *"He can do what he wants with his life . . . this is not for me"*: TTOML, 42.

30 *"I'm sending your things to your family's house"*: ibid.

30 *"Bill has taken ill"*: ibid.

31 What am I doing here when I no longer love this man?: ibid.

31 This must be my cross: ibid.

32 *He was physically and emotionally abusive*: James Cannon, *Gerald R. Ford: An Honorable Life* (Ann Arbor: University of Michigan Press, 2013), 41.

32 *she called him Junior, or Junie*: ibid., 42.

33 *Gerald would take the boys camping*: ATTH, 45.

33 *"I'm Leslie King, your father"*: ibid., 47.

33 *"Now, you buy yourself something"*: ibid., 48.

34 *"a carefree, well-to-do man"*: ibid.

34 *Jerry lay in bed, sobbing, turning to prayer*: Cannon, *Gerald R. Ford*, 47.

35 *"Have you ever been a model?"*: James Cannon, *Time and Chance: Gerald Ford's Appointment with History* (Ann Arbor: University of Michigan Press, 1994), 28.

35 *the two of them appeared in a six-page spread*: *Look*, March 12, 1940, accessed online at www.fordlibrarymuseum.gov/library/document/selected/Look.pdf.

35 *"After his mother, I was the first important woman"*: Cannon, *Time and Chance*, 29.

35 *"The end of our relationship caused me real anguish"*: ATTH, 57.

36 *"as much action as I'd ever hoped to see"*: ibid., 58.

4: A Courtship and a Campaign

37 *"Who's around that a bachelor my age can date?"*: ATTH, 62.

37 *The two had been friends*: Gordon L. Olson, *"In the Name of All Marys . . ."*: A History of the Mary Free Bed Guild and the Mary Free Bed Hospital and Rehabilitation Center* (Grand Rapids, MI: Mary Free Bed Guild, 1991), 53; also in *TTOML*, 46. Note that in *TTOML*, Betty incorrectly spells Peggy's last name as Newman.

37 *"How about Betty Warren?"*: ATTH, 62.

38 *"She's getting a divorce"*: ibid.

38 *"Well, would you give her a call?"*: ibid.

38 *"Hello, Betty"*: The pursuant conversation was re-created from ATTH, 62–63; also TTOML, 46.

39 *"I can't say love at first sight"*: *Biography: This Week*, "Betty Ford: One Day at a Time."

39 *"quite shocked"*: TTOML, 47.

39 *Betty was officially and legally divorced*: Jerald F. terHorst, "The Makings of Gerald Ford—V: Betty Ford Athletic Too," *Charleston* (WV) *Gazette*, August 29, 1974.

39 *"plunked himself down on the couch"*: TTOML, 47.

39 *"I don't know about you guys"*: ibid.

40 *"What are your intentions"*: ibid.

40 *"I'm very interested"*: ibid.

40 *"Fine . . . I just wanted to find out"*: ibid.

40 *"pretty nervy"*: ibid., 48.

40 *"I wondered if I was going to ruin everything"*: ibid., 47.

40 *Jerry wasn't very demonstrative*: Betty Ford, interview by James Cannon, April 30, 1990, James M. Cannon Research Interviews and Notes, 1989–1994, box 1, Gerald R. Ford Presidential Library, Ann Arbor, MI.

40 *"Betty just lit me up"*: Douglas Brinkley, *Gerald R. Ford* (New York: Times Books, 2007), 13.

40 *"knew darn well he would have a good time"*: TTOML, 50.

40 *"silly"*: ibid.

41 *"To the light of my life"*: ibid.

41 *Bradshaw Crandell*: note that in *TTOML*, Crandell is spelled incorrectly as Crandel, 51–52.

41 *"If you think I'm going to call him up"*: ibid., 51.

41 *"Darling, what a surprise!"*: ibid., 52.

42 *"At the same time, she was staking out a prior claim"*: ibid.

42 *Betty and Jerry had been writing to each other daily*: ATTH, 65.

42 *"did you by any chance get a letter"*: TTOML, 53.

43 *"It was our big Saturday bash"*: ibid., 48.

43 *"I'd like to marry you"*: ATTH, 65.

43 *"He didn't tell me he loved me"*: TTOML, 53.

43 *"We can't get married until next fall"*: ibid., 54; also ATTH, 65.

43 *"A fall wedding will be fine"*: ATTH, 65.

44 *"Bets darling, Your letter just arrived"*: Hortense Bloomer Godwin to Betty Bloomer Warren, letter, April 9, 1948, Gerald and Betty Ford Special Materials Collection, box B2, folder "Godwin, Hortense," Gerald R. Ford Presidential Library, Ann Arbor, MI.

44 *"it wasn't that he didn't trust her"*: TerHorst, "Makings of Gerald Ford."

44 *"I'm going to run for Congress"*: TTOML, 54.

44 *She didn't know what running for Congress meant*: ibid., 55.

45 Only old men go to Congress: ibid.

45 *"it was wild"*: ibid.

45 *"campaigning furiously"*: ibid.

45 *"He took to campaigning like a starving man to a roast-beef dinner"*: ibid.

45 *"I've never been in politics"*: ibid., 56.

46 *"most particularly because of Jerry's character"*: DeFreest, interview, 5.

46 *"There was no pretense there"*: ibid.

46 *"It was exhilarating to be in a race like that"*: TTOML, 57.

46 *"We worked our tails off"*: Cannon, *Gerald R. Ford*, 70.

46 *"Like fire and water"*: TerHorst, "Makings of Gerald Ford," 1, 5A.

46 *"What do you think about me marrying Betty?"*: ibid.

46 *"Well, I've known Betty"*: ibid.

46 *"What do you think about Jerry and me?"*: ibid.

46 *"Well, Betty," Jack said, "if you can accept"*: ibid.

47 *"You won't have to worry about other women"*: TTOML, 57.

47 *"I loved him for that"*: Betty Ford, interview with James Cannon.

47 *"because it was fall . . . we couldn't miss a Saturday football game"*: TTOML, 9.

48 *It was four o'clock, and Jerry had yet to appear*: Bonnie Bloomer Baker, discussion, November 11, 2016.

48 *"growing more livid by the moment"*: TTOML, 58.

48 *"gave him the devil"*: ibid., 59.

48 *"whooping it up"*: ibid., 60.

48 *"The thing wasn't over till midnight"*: ibid.
49 *"Oh, Betty . . . I won't be home for dinner tonight"*: ibid., 61; also *ATTH*, 67.
49 *"Like every woman"*: Betty Ford, interview with James Cannon.

PART 2: BETTY FORD, WASHINGTON WOMAN

5: A Congressman's Wife

53 *"Dear Betty: Your mother is sick"*: Arthur Godwin to Betty Ford, letter, November 18, 1948, Gerald and Betty Ford Special Materials Collection, box B2, folder "Godwin, Arthur," Gerald R. Ford Presidential Library, Ann Arbor, MI.
54 *"She's gone, honey"*: TTOML, 62.
54 *"holding on to one another"*: ibid.
54 *"She would not have wanted to live a restricted life"*: ibid., 63.
54 *"I believe there's a meaning for everyone's coming into this world"*: ibid.
55 *was not a political animal"*: Biography: This Week, "Betty Ford: One Day at a Time."
56 *"We were all new together"*: TTOML, 65.
56 *"Lyndon . . . I want you to meet this young couple"*: ibid., 66.
56 *"Where were you last night?"*: ibid., 64.
57 *"adjustment"*: ibid., 68.
57 *"Oh, Mrs. Truman, it's so nice of you to have us"*: ibid., 66.
58 *"Heavens, it's you who are nice to come out in such terrible weather"*: ibid.
58 *"with that, she went straight to my heart"*: ibid.
58 *"He was nice and fat"*: ibid., 72.
58 *"the most wonderful news of all"*: William "Bill" Bloomer to Betty Ford, letter, April 28, 1950, Gerald and Betty Ford Special Materials Collection, box B2, folder "Bloomer, William," Gerald R. Ford Presidential Library, Ann Arbor, MI.
58 *"Clara was like an angel that came into our lives"*: TTOML, 69.
59 *She and her husband, Raymond, had no children of their own*: Susan Ford Bales, discussion, October 6, 2016.
59 *wearing a uniform of a white dress, always freshly cleaned and pressed*: ibid.
59 *"just beginning to giggle and grr"*: TTOML, 73.
59 *"That's right, talk to your dad"*: ibid.
59 *"What's new? . . . What book should I read?"*: ibid., 65.
60 *"If I acted smart, and looked smart"*: BAGA, 35.
60 *"She was terribly nervous"*: Boorn, "Betty's Blooming," 118.
60 *"a small act of courage"*: TTOML, 65.
61 *There were strict rules for residents*: United States Department of the Interior, National Park Service, "National Register of Historic Places Registration Form," Parkfairfax Historic District, City of Alexandria, Virginia, December 14, 1998, available at www.dhr.virginia.gov/registers/Cities/Alexandria/100-0151_Parkfairfax _HD_1999_Final_Nomination.pdf.
62 *"Let me fix you something to eat"*: TTOML, 75.
62 *"All I want," she said, "is a martini and a sandwich"*: ibid.
62 *"Once I took him to visit somebody"*: ibid., 78.

62 *"wall to wall with tricycles and wagons and toys"*: Betty Ford, interview.

62 *"If you are going to run for Congress"*: ibid.

62 They bought a plot for a token $10: "President Ford: The House," Clover College Park Civic Association online, www.clovercollegepark.com, accessed February 10, 2017.

65 *"surrounded by empty lots and mounds of red Virginia clay"*: TTOML, 79.

65 *"to go out in cowboy hats and discover snakes"*: ibid., 80.

65 *"dear little pink-wrapped bundle"*: ibid.

65 *"My seat in the House seemed safe"*: ATTH, 71.

65 *"I dreamed of becoming Speaker of the House"*: ibid.

65 *"the tiniest bit sorry"*: TTOML, 82.

66 *"so swollen and sweaty"*: ibid., 90.

67 *"not because the birth was so imminent"*: ibid.

6: Wife and Mother

68 *"I don't know how many times I went to Mount Vernon"*: TTOML, 63.

69 *"I know it's legal"*: ATTH, 70.

69 *"I saw that I would have to grow . . . being left behind"*: Boorn, "Betty's Blooming," 18.

69 *"begging and borrowing from museums and friends"*: TTOML, 93.

69 *"shake up the Republican wives"*: ibid., 122.

69 *"If anybody asks you to do anything"*: ibid.

70 *"the busy wife of a congressman"*: Bet Hart, "How Does She Dress So Well and Not Spend a Fortune?," *Ladies' Home Journal*, April 1961, 76.

70 *"the party in power . . . you have to convince on legislation"*: TTOML, 98.

70 His office happened to be across the hall from John F. Kennedy's: President Gerald R. Ford, foreword to *President John F. Kennedy Assassination Report of the Warren Commission,* signed limited ed. (Nashville: FlatSigned Press, 2004), *iii*.

71 *"The Kennedy White House was much more sophisticated"*: TTOML, 98.

71 *"I don't know how Mrs. Kennedy ever got the ladies"*: ibid.

71 Details about the Mount Vernon dinner: Clint Hill with Lisa McCubbin, *Mrs. Kennedy and Me* (New York: Gallery Books, 2012), 94–98.

71 *"It took you back in time"*: TTOML, 100.

72 *"Of course, they outranked the Johnsons"*: ibid.

72 *"Being a housewife seems to me a much tougher job"*: Cokie Roberts, "Eulogy by Cokie Roberts" (Betty Ford Memorial Service, Palm Desert, CA, July 12, 2011, transcript available at Gerald R. Ford Presidential Foundation online), https://geraldrfordfoundation.org/eulogy-by-cokie-roberts.

72 *"All of us were always rushing"*: Block, "Betty Ford Nobody Knows," 140.

72 *"I remember her . . . screaming at her ankles"*: TTOML, 92.

73 *"You got up, you got dressed, and we went to church on Sunday"*: Susan Ford Bales, discussion, October 6, 2016.

73 *"Dad was always home for Sunday-night dinner"*: ibid.

73 *"I know that the children looked forward"*: ATTH, 72.

73 *"Our house was chaos"*: Susan Ford Bales, discussion, October 6, 2016.

73 *"truth test"*: ibid.

73 *"you can forget about order"*: TTOML, 92.

74 *"Jack, give Mike your gladiator helmet!"*: Charles Peterson, "The First Family and Christmas Memories," *Washington Post, Parade*, December 21, 1975; corroborated by Jack Ford, email message to author, April 3, 2018.

74 *There was a joke*: Susan Ford Bales, discussion, October 6, 2016.

74 *"Mom was able to deal with the blood"*: Steve Ford, discussion, November 23, 2016.

74 *"They'd take my roller skates"*: Susan Ford Bales, discussion, October 6, 2016.

74 *"I put in three years' hard time"*: TTOML, 95.

74 *"I got a modicum of respect for this minor talent"*: ibid.

74 *"Their bodies aren't made to do that"*: Susan Ford Bales, discussion, October 6, 2016.

74 *"Be a giraffe"*: ibid.

75 *"When you have a pool in your backyard"*: ibid.

75 *"We are not lifeguards"*: ibid.

75 *"One of my strongest memories"*: Steve Ford, discussion, November 23, 2016.

76 *"We had rabbits, hamsters, gerbils—you name it, we had it"*: Susan Ford Bales, discussion, October 6, 2016.

76 *"At the time, I guess it was legal"*: Steve Ford, discussion, November 23, 2016.

76 *"It would bite you every time you got near it"*: ibid.

76 *"I'll never forget"*: ibid.

76 *"But Mother ended up"*: Susan Ford Bales, discussion, October 6, 2016.

76 *"Clara helped dig the grave"*: TTOML, 93.

77 *"He called to say"*: Michael Ford, discussion, October 26, 2017.

77 *"The first thing he would make us do"*: Susan Ford Bales, discussion, October 6, 2016; also Steve Ford, discussion, November 23, 2016.

77 *"Dear Mom, you're the greatest"*: Steve Ford, discussion, November 23, 2016.

77 *"Okay. You're free to go"*: ibid.; corroborated by Susan Ford Bales, discussion, October 6, 2016.

77 *"We'd ride them back and forth"*: Susan Ford Bales, discussion, October 6, 2016.

78 *"They would take all of the things"*: Anne Holkeboer, interview by Richard Norton Smith, August 8, 2008, Oral History Project, Gerald R. Ford Presidential Foundation, Grand Rapids, MI, 13, https://geraldrfordfoundation.org/centennial-docs/oralhistory/wp-content/uploads/2013/05/Anne-Holkeboer.pdf.

78 *"How grown up you are"*: Steve Ford, discussion, November 23, 2016.

78 *"She ran our house"*: Susan Ford Bales, discussion, October 6, 2016.

78 *"Don't expect me to bail you out of this"*: ibid.

78 *"They were not rescuers"*: ibid.

78 *"Wait until your father gets home"*: Kenneth Gross, "Mrs. Gerald Ford Is Reluctant First Lady," *Madison* (WI) *Capital Times*, August 14, 1974.

79 *"Dad would always come home"*: Susan Ford Bales, discussion, October 6, 2016.

79 *"It put a strain on the marriage"*: TTOML, 126.

79 *"I'd have my five o'clock drink"*: BAGA, 34.

80 *"Dad and Mom would always have an evening drink"*: Michael Ford, interview

by Richard Norton Smith, May 2, 2011, Oral History Project, Gerald R. Ford Presidential Foundation, Grand Rapids, MI, 5, https://geraldrfordfoundation .org/centennial-docs/oralhistory/wp-content/uploads/2015/11/Mike-Ford .pdf.

7: A Second Mother

81 *"She was my mom when my mom wasn't home"*: Susan Ford Bales, discussion, October 6, 2016.

81 *"We embraced her that way"*: Steve Ford, discussion, November 23, 2016.

81 *"I really didn't have a chance to nurse"*: TTOML, 134.

82 *"You loved it"*: Susan Ford Bales, discussion, October 6, 2016.

82 *"She and I used to laugh about everything"*: TTOML, 136.

82 *"She was wonderful"*: Michael Ford, discussion, October 26, 2017.

82 *"Now, Steve Ford"*: Steve Ford, discussion, November 23, 2016.

83 *"My mom made the best meatloaf"*: Susan Ford Bales, discussion, October 6, 2016.

83 *"Clara was a mainstay"*: ATTH, 71.

83 *"we'd all pile into Mom and Dad's bed"*: Susan Ford Bales, discussion, October 6, 2016; corroborated by Michael Ford, discussion, October 26, 2017; and Steve Ford, discussion, November 23, 2016.

83 *"It was 'wrasslin' "*: Susan Ford Bales, discussion, October 6, 2016.

83 *"Swing low, sweet chariot"*: ibid.

83 *"She was an incredible woman"*: ibid.

83 *"Whatever void needed to be filled"*: Lynette Williams Thomas, in discussion with author, September 22, 2017.

84 *"It wasn't punishment"*: Susan Ford Bales, discussion, October 6, 2016.

84 *"And she knew everything"*: Steve Ford, discussion, November 23, 2016.

84 *"Steve Ford"*: ibid.

84 *"She got really mad at me"*: ibid.

84 *"But," she wrote, "in a way, she was their mother"*: TTOML, 134.

84 *"All of us loved her"*: ATTH, 71.

84 *"He seemed so much brighter"*: TTOML, 114.

84 *"The news was crushing"*: ibid., 102.

85 *"seemed to move through a haze of pomp"*: ibid.

85 *"There weren't many tears"*: ibid.

86 *"Up until that moment"*: ibid., 104.

86 *"Jerry attended meetings religiously"*: ibid., 106.

86 *"Beyond a reasonable doubt"*: ATTH, 76.

86 *"I would imagine that Jerry knows"*: TTOML, 106.

87 *"Some of my fondest memories were spending summers at Ottawa Beach"*: Carol Steves, "Once-Rebellious Jack Ford Plays Host to Republicans," *Detroit Free Press*, August 4, 1996.

88 *"I'm taking you to the emergency room"*: ATTH, 83.

88 *"I knew exactly how that happened"*: DeFreest (name appears as Mrs. Collins C. Clark), interview, 22.

88 *"put her in a soft collar"*: ATTH, 83.

88 *"The first time the hospital attendants took me"*: TTOML, 118.

89 *"Clara was indispensable"*: ATTH, 83.

89 *"Don't let the pain start"*: BAGA, 35.

89 *In the 1960s, there were no warning labels*: Dr. Marvin Seppala, chief medical officer, Hazelden Betty Ford Foundation, in discussion with author, September 28, 2017.

89 *"Mother's Little Helpers"*: Deborah Frazier, " 'Mother's Little Helper': Valium: Most Abused Drug in Nation," *Eau Claire* (WI) *Leader Telegram*, May 11, 1977.

89 *"If I became minority leader"*: ATTH, 77.

90 *"Go for it, Dad"*: ibid.

8: "Mom's Really Upset; You Need to Go Fix It"

91 *"he was wonderful"*: Dorothy Marks, "Physical, Psychological and Emotional Changes Seen in Betty Ford," Women's News Service, May 17, 1974.

91 *"Dad had tunnel vision"*: BAGA, 148.

92 *"the wife of Minority Leader Gerald R. Ford"*: ibid., 35.

92 *"I couldn't accept that people liked me for myself"*: ibid.

92 *"What are you doing here?"*: TTOML, 123.

92 *"were going through adolescence"*: Marks, "Physical, Psychological and Emotional Changes."

92 *"I hated feeling crippled"*: BAGA, 35.

93 *"We kids took advantage of that"*: Steve Ford, discussion, November 23, 2016.

93 *"a doormat to the kids"*: BAGA, 35.

93 *"Jack's the son with whom I've crossed swords most often"*: TTOML, 114; corroborated by Jack Ford, discussion, February 17, 2018.

93 *"Mom's really upset"*: Susan Ford Bales, discussion, September 24, 2017.

93 *"It's okay, Mom"*: ibid.

93 *"That's it!"*: ibid.; also mentioned in TTOML, 124, and BAGA, 36.

94 What does she mean?: Susan Ford Bales, discussion, September 24, 2017.

94 *"whole ungrateful family"*: BAGA, 36.

94 *"I need to get hold of my dad"*: Michael Ford, discussion, October 26, 2017.

94 *"Let me go talk to Mother"*: Susan Ford Bales, discussion, September 24, 2017.

94 *"Mrs. Ford, it's Clara"*: ibid.

94 *"Dad went up with Mom"*: ibid.

94 *"Your momma is sick"*: ibid.

95 *"I'd been too busy"*: BAGA, 36.

95 *"the problem that has no name"*: Betty Friedan, *The Feminine Mystique* (New York: W. W. Norton, 1963), 63.

95 *"We can no longer ignore"*: ibid., 22.

95 *"I saw no reason to discuss my drinking"*: BAGA, 37.

95 *"I had to step in"*: Michael Ford, discussion, October 26, 2017.

96 *"I think most of my family"*: Jack Ford, discussion, February 17, 2018.

96 *"No doubt that my role"*: Steve Ford, discussion, January 16, 2018.

9: The Nixon White House

97 "terribly wrong": TTOML, 127.

97 "I just wasn't the Bionic Woman": ibid.

97 "You won't have Nixon to kick around anymore": Jason Schwartz, "The Last Press Conference," Richard Nixon Foundation online, last modified November 14, 2017, www.nixonfoundation.org/2017/11/55-years-ago-last-press-conference.

98 "That, and by the time she got four kids": Susan Ford Bales, discussion, October 6, 2016.

98 "zooming down the slopes": ATTH, 94.

98 "Come on out to Vail": Randy Wyrick, "Jerry and Betty Focused the World on Vail," Vail (CO) Daily, December 25, 2016.

99 "It was amazing": Susan Ford Bales, discussion, October 6, 2016.

99 "I, Richard Milhous Nixon": "President Richard Nixon's First Inaugural Address," January 20, 1969 (Richard Nixon Foundation online, video, 17:38), www.nixon foundation.org/1969/01/president-richard-nixons-first-inaugural-address.

100 "the week that changed the world": Clint Hill with Lisa McCubbin, Five Presidents: My Extraordinary Journey with Eisenhower, Kennedy, Johnson, Nixon, and Ford (New York: Gallery Books, 2016), 384.

100 "the chance to visit China was a rare opportunity indeed": ATTH, 97.

100 "I don't give a damn": ibid., 96.

100 "third-rate burglary": ibid., 94.

100 "an inept effort at God knows what": TTOML, 142.

101 "The Chinese are likely to feed you anything": ibid., 140.

101 "trying to choke down sea slugs": ibid.

101 "The people were enthralled by us": ibid.

101 "Jerry and I thought President Nixon": ibid., 139.

102 he logged 138,000 miles: ATTH, 99.

102 had attended college: Terry Ryan, "Son of Vice President Designate Not the Competitive Type," Nashua (NH) Telegraph, November 9, 1973.

102 "Come sit up here": Susan Ford Bales, discussion, October 6, 2016.

102 "I can remember it to this day!": ibid.

103 "You know, a boy did that to me once": ibid.

103 "God, I'd have loved to have seen that!": ibid.

103 "Now, if you have any questions": ibid.

103 "I think I took the same box": ibid.

103 "Mother would come to all my games": Steve Ford, discussion, November 23, 2016.

103 "Mom!" he hissed. "What are you doing?" . . . "She was just a great mother that way": ibid.

103 "We lived it": ibid.

104 "baby girl": Susan Ford Bales, discussion, October 6, 2016.

104 "the Golubin twins": ibid.

104 "We all got in": ibid.

104 "Susan would come up, and we used to sew": TTOML, 135.

105 "We agreed that I would run": ATTH, 99.

105 *"still active enough to practice law"*: ibid.

105 *"He promised me he would retire"*: TTOML, 142.

10: A Five-Dollar Bet

107 *"Let us think about it"*: ATTH, 104.

107 *"splendid cap"*: ibid.

107 *"What about your promise?"*: implied conversation, ibid.

108 *"That's the best part"*: ibid.

108 *"But it is highly unlikely Nixon would choose me"*: ibid.

108 *"We've talked about it and agreed"*: ibid.

108 *"Has your husband told you to get your hair done?"*: TTOML, 146.

108 *"No . . . I just had it done yesterday"*: ibid.

108 *"Has your husband told you to go out and get a new dress?"*: ibid.

109 *"blood oath"*: Thomas M. DeFrank, *Write It When I'm Gone: Remarkable Off-the-Record Conversations with Gerald R. Ford* (New York: G. P. Putnam's Sons, 2007), 10.

109 *"I drew the Gerald Ford straw"* . . . *"He did not seem like a guy who was waiting by the phone"*: David Kennerly, in discussion with author, March 30, 2017.

110 *"Mom, do you think President Nixon"*: Susan Ford Bales, discussion, March 8, 2017.

110 *"No, Susan, honestly I don't"*: ibid.; also TTOML, 145.

110 *"Well, I think it's going to be him"*: Susan Ford Bales, discussion, March 8, 2017.

110 *"All right . . . You're on"*: ibid.

110 *It was just before six thirty*: ATTH, 106.

111 *"What's happening, Dad?"*: Susan Ford Bales, discussion, March 8, 2017.

111 *"Do you know who it is, dear?"*: ibid.

111 *"The only thing I know"*: ibid.; also ATTH, 106.

111 *"Does Dad know who it's going to be?"*: the scene on pages 111 to 113 was pieced together from information in TTOML (146–47); ATTH (106); Susan Ford Bales, discussion, March 8, 2017; corroborated by Steve Ford and Michael Ford, discussions.

114 *"a mad dash"*: TTOML, 147.

114 *"Distinguished guests and my fellow Americans"*: "Nixon Announces New Vice President," October 13, 1973 (C-Span online, video, 12:35), www.c-span.org/video/?153731-1/nixon-announces-vice-president.

114 *"Here's Betty"*: ibid.

114 *"Not yet"*: ibid.

115 *"They told me to sit with you"*: TTOML, 147.

115 *"Oh, yes, of course"*: ibid.

115 *"Come on, Jerry"*: Jerry Bechtle, in discussion with author, October 30, 2017.

115 *"Jerry . . . I'd like you to meet Jerry Bechtle"*: ibid.

115 *"Nice to meet you"*: ibid.

115 *"No, Jerry, you tell him when it's time to leave"*: ibid.

116 *"I wasn't convinced that"*: Susan Ford Bales, discussion, October 6, 2016.

116 *"What are you doing?!"*: Steve Ford, discussion, November 23, 2016.

116 *"It's funny now, but we were scared to death"*: ibid.

11: Betty Ford, Second Lady

117 *"You couldn't move"*: TTOML, 149.

117 *"May [God] answer you in time of trouble"*: ATTH, 112.

118 *"I am a Ford—not a Lincoln"*: ibid.

119 *"You better tell the vice president"*: Bechtle, discussion, October 30, 2017.

120 *"All right . . . how much?"*: ibid.

120 *"With all the communications"*: ibid.

120 *"My God . . . the house cost only thirty-five thousand"*: ibid.

120 *"We jokingly referred to it"*: Susan Ford Bales, discussion, October 6, 2016.

121 *"For all of us, it was fun for about ten and a half seconds"*: ibid.

121 *"Get down there as fast as you can"*: TTOML, 152.

121 *"I have no doubt whatsoever that the president is not guilty"* . . . *"What about the drug scene around school?"*: The Dick Cavett Show, featuring Vice President Gerald Ford and the Ford family, aired January 10, 1974, on ABC Late Night (Gerald R. Ford Vice-Presidential Papers: Audiotapes, 1973–74, AV82-14-R4, Gerald R. Ford Presidential Library, Ann Arbor, MI).

122 *"I was never so glad"*: TTOML, 152.

122 *"a thoughtful, pretty woman"*: Marks, "Physical, Psychological and Emotional Changes."

123 *"I like to think of myself as a feminist"*: ibid.

123 *How do you feel about the Supreme Court's ruling"*: TTOML, 151.

123 *"I agree with the Supreme Court's ruling"*: ibid.

123 *"some high school girls who are forced to marry"*: Kandy Stroud, "Betty Ford Becomes Instant First Lady," Times-Sun (West Newton, PA), August 18, 1974.

123 *"Maybe I shouldn't have said it"*: ibid.

123 *"basically got hammered"*: Kennerly, discussion, March 30, 2017.

124 *"Ten o'clock. We'll see you then"*: TTOML, 146.

124 *purchased a third-floor, three-bedroom, $50,000 condo*: "Ford loved Vail, and it was mutual," Denver Post, December 26, 2006.

124 *"In fact, I learned how to ski"*: Kennerly, discussion, March 30, 2017.

124 *"I'd go up on the chairlift"*: Dick Cavett Show, January 10, 1974.

125 *"They were so warm and friendly"*: Kennerly, discussion, March 30, 2017.

125 *"No, no, I hope not"*: ibid.

125 *"It was our last private Christmas"*: Susan Ford Bales, discussion, October 6, 2016.

126 *"Pick Out Your Curtains, Betty"*: TTOML, 152.

126 *"I was so excited for the weekend"*: Susan Ford Bales, discussion, October 6, 2016.

126 *"Just go talk to the agents"*: ibid.

126 *"Daddy is ruining my life!"*: ibid.

127 *"I honestly did not know"*: Bob Innamorati, discussion, July 21, 2017.

127 *"We've got tickets to see a concert"*: ibid.; also Susan Ford Bales, discussion, October 6, 2016.

127 *"Unfortunately, everything you do"*: ibid.

127 *"They were shutting down my social life"*: Susan Ford Bales, discussion, October 6, 2016.

127 *"Mike is marrying a lovely girl"*: Betty Ford to Mary Lou Logan, letter, May 16, 1974, courtesy of the Logan family; used with permission.

127 *Susan wasn't happy about sharing it*: Susan Ford Bales, discussion, October 6, 2016.

127 *"Somebody up there has been looking out for me for years"*: TTOML, 155.

128 *"really worried"*: Rosalynn Carter, in discussion with author, June 14, 2017.

128 *"everything begins an hour earlier than it actually does"*: ibid.

129 *a long, yellow knit dress she had borrowed from Nancy Howe*: Marks, "Physical, Psychological and Emotional Changes," https://www.newspapers.com/news page/53620695/.

129 *"really quite beautiful"*: Kandy Stroud, "She Likes Being Second Lady," *Women's Wear Daily, Shreveport* (LA) *Times*, April 19, 1974.

129 *"I'd rather not talk about that"*: ibid.

129 *"Now I'm down to a size eight"*: Marks, "Physical, Psychological and Emotional Changes."

129 *"What do you think is the role of a political wife?"*: Stroud, "She Likes Being Second Lady."

129 *"I think we have to be supportive"* . . . *"sharp as a tack"*: ibid.

130 *"Do you ever become accustomed to this?"* . . . *"Twenty-five years"*: ibid.

130 *"we were late everywhere we went that day"* . . . *"No, I don't know them at all"*: Rosalynn Carter, *First Lady from Plains* (Boston: Houghton Mifflin, 1984), 100; also Carter, discussion, June 14, 2017.

131 *"Can't I just thank the mayor and sit down?"* . . . *"I've learned to roll with the punches"*: Marks, "Physical, Psychological and Emotional Changes"; also Louise Sweeney (staff correspondent of the *Christian Science Monitor*), "Mrs. Gerald Ford Talks About Her Role as Second Lady," *Daily Messenger* (Canandaigua, NY), May 2, 1974.

132 *"Mrs. Ford, are you on something?"*: Carter, *First Lady from Plains*, 100; also Carter, discussion, June 14, 2017.

132 *"Well, I do take Valium every day"*: Stroud, "She Likes Being Second Lady."

132 *"Valium, three times a day"*: ibid.

132 *"any blemish on the public's image"*: Carter, *First Lady from Plains*, 100.

132 *Betty didn't realize that she had created a stir*: Carter, discussion, June 14, 2017.

132 *In 1974 Valium was by far the most prescribed drug*: Cheryl Pilate, "Valium Becoming Socially Accepted Crutch, Just Like Double Martini," *Colorado Springs* (CO) *Gazette Telegraph*, July 18, 1976.

132 *"a dope addict"*: Stroud, "Betty Ford Becomes Instant First Lady."

133 *"I'm candid"*: ibid.

133 *"My parents thought if you had the agents"* . . . *"before anyone could recognize me"*: Susan Ford Bales, discussion, October 6, 2016.

134 *"The process was like undergoing a physical exam in public view"*: ATTH, 110.

135 *"the* National Enquirer *was going to write a piece"*: Kennerly, discussion, March 30, 2017.

135 *"I didn't know she was married before!"*: ibid.

135 *"Well, yeah, nobody does"*: ibid.

135 *"So, essentially it drove a stake"*: ibid.

135 *"I think this is when my relationship with her got stronger"*: ibid.

135 *"I wasn't thrilled about it at the time"*: Steve Ford, discussion, November 23, 2016.

12: The Unthinkable Happens

138 *When Betty toured the house for the first time*: Betty Monkman, interview by Richard Norton Smith, November 17, 2009, Oral History Project, Gerald R. Ford Presidential Foundation, Grand Rapids, MI, n.p., https://geraldrfordfoundation.org/centennial-docs/oralhistory/wp-content/uploads/2009/11/Betty-Monkman.pdf.

138 *"It was far more expensive"*: ATTH, 7.

138 *"I want to alert you that things are deteriorating"*: ibid., 2.

139 *"was that Nixon could agree"*: ibid., 4.

139 *"Throughout my political life"*: ibid., 5.

139 *"I want some time to think, Al"*: ibid., 4.

139 *"That was really important to him"*: Michael Ford, interview, 12.

139 *"The exercise at this moment, I felt, was ridiculous"*: ATTH, 7.

140 *"Her eyes widened in disbelief"*: ibid., 9.

140 *"dumbfounded"*: ibid.

140 *"My God, this is going to change our whole life"*: ibid.

140 *"Neither she nor her husband were emotionally prepared to ascend to the White House"*: David Kennerly, discussion, March 30, 2017.

140 *"You should not get involved"*: ATTH, 10.

140 *"I really think he got a lot of strength from her"*: Michael Ford, interview, 12.

140 *"God give us strength"* . . . *"and He shall direct thy paths"*: ATTH, 10.

141 *"right now I am quite involved"*: Betty Ford to Mary Lou Logan, letter, August 2, 1974, courtesy of the Logan family; used with permission.

141 *"I didn't see it"*: TTOML, 2.

141 *"Every time you went in and out"*: Steve Ford, discussion, November 23, 2016.

141 *"Nixon is going to announce his resignation"*: ATTH, 29.

141 *"Up until then"*: TTOML, 2.

142 *"dragging a U-Haul"*: ibid.

142 *"Here I was working with all these guys"*: Steve Ford, discussion, November 23, 2016.

142 *"I was numb"*: TTOML, 2.

142 *"[S]he was not particularly well"*: Michael Ford, interview, 12.

143 *"People were crying"*: TTOML, 3.

144 *"My heavens, they've even rolled out the red carpet"*: ibid.; also ATTH, 39.

144 *"The moment was terribly painful"* . . . *"Goodbye, Mr. President"*: ATTH, 39.

144 *What does he think he has won?*: Clint Hill, in discussion with author, August 9, 2017.

144 *"We couldn't help but feel sorry"*: Kennerly, *Extraordinary Circumstances*, 25.

145 *"We can do it. We're ready"*: ATTH, 40.

145 *"Most presidents get nominated"*: Kennerly, *Extraordinary Circumstances*, 26.

145 *"At that historic moment"*: ATTH, 40.

146 *"Mr. Vice President, are you prepared to take the oath of office"*: ibid.

146 *"The words cut through me"*: TTOML, 4.

146 *"Ladies and gentlemen, the president of the United States"*: "Gerald Ford Sworn in as President of the United States," August 9, 1974 (C-Span online, video, 11:32), www.c-span.org/video/?320430-1/gerald-ford-sworn-president-united-states.

146 *"Mr. Chief Justice, my dear friends, my fellow Americans"*: ibid.

147 *"Way to go, Jerry!"*: Kennerly, *Extraordinary Circumstances*, 28.

147 *"The morning had begun with tears"*: TTOML, 159.

147 *"Jerry, something's wrong here"*: Steve Ford, discussion, November 23, 2016.

147 *"She had a fantastic sense of humor"*: Kennerly, discussion, March 30, 2017.

147 *"David, I want you to stay after everyone else leaves"* . . . *"glad to have me as an advocate for them in the White House"*: ibid.

149 *"David Kennerly, call the operator"* . . . *"you are there for a lot of very personal moments"*: ibid.

PART 3: BETTY FORD, FIRST LADY

151 *"Okay, I'll move to the White House"*: TTOML, 158.

13: The Ford White House

153 *"Mrs. Ford, we are just wondering"*: TTOML, 162; also Susan Ford Bales, discussion, October 6, 2016.

153 *"What state dinner?"*: ibid.

153 *"King Hussein is coming on the sixteenth"*: ibid.

154 *"Why don't you go ask a few members"*: Sheila Rabb Weidenfeld, in discussion with author, December 8, 2016.

154 *"Literally ten months earlier"*: Steve Ford, discussion, November 23, 2016.

155 *"I guess we should send them to Goodwill"*: DeFrank, *Write It When I'm Gone*, 43.

155 *"Jerry, I think some of this stuff may be a little important now"*: ibid.

155 *"depressing"*: Susan Ford Bales, discussion, October 6, 2016.

155 *"It was Pepto-Bismol pink"*: ibid.

156 *"Susan has always wanted a brass bed"*: ibid.

156 *"Oh, a brass bed really doesn't fit the era"*: ibid.

156 *"If you have a brass bed in storage"*: ibid.

156 *"Jerry and I have shared the same bed"*: ibid.

156 *"Clem Conger's taste was impeccable"*: TTOML, 175.

157 *"She didn't want to have the presidency make her something she wasn't"*: Dick Hartwig, in discussion with author, September 15, 2016.

157 *"I really don't consider it my house"*: Associated Press, "First Lady Gets Tour of the White House," *Daily News-Record* (Harrisonburg, VA), August 14, 1974.

157 *"People started saying I was disgraceful"*: TTOML, 157.

158 *"Fords Bring Dancing Back to White House"*: United Press International, "Ford Brings Dancing Back to White House," *Holland* (MI) *Evening Sentinel*, August 17, 1974.

158 *"It was one of the liveliest parties in the executive mansion"*: ibid.

158 *"It's a very strange feeling"*: TTOML, 165.

158 *"Passkey"... "Panda"*: Hill, discussion, August 9, 2017.

159 *"Crown"*: ibid.

159 *"a very traumatic experience"*: TTOML, 165.

159 *"The day the Fords came into the White House"... "It was so refreshing"*: Robert Alberi, in discussion with author, March 21, 2017.

160 Dear _____ ... they appreciate the effort you made to convey your opinions: First Lady Correspondence file, box FL-5-1, 10/74–12/74, Gerald R. Ford Presidential Library, Ann Arbor, MI.

161 *"that is not the group you want to hang out with"*: Steve Ford, discussion, November 23, 2016.

161 *The press focused on the aftermath*: Patricia J. Matson, interview by Donna Lehman, January 16, 2015, Oral History Project, Gerald R. Ford Presidential Foundation, 2, https://geraldrfordfoundation.org/centennial-docs/oralhistory/wp-content/uploads/2016/12/Patricia-J.-Matson.pdf.

161 *Wearing a tailored shirtdress in a warm butter yellow*: "First Lady Press Conference," September 4, 1974, NPC film 1211-128-75, Gerald R. Ford Presidential Library, Ann Arbor, MI; copy provided to author courtesy of GRF Library.

162 *"At least my checkbook has to balance"... "Bonnie, I hoped you were keeping it for me!"*: ibid.

162 *"I'm all for babies"... "But they definitely do not like it and it is not used"*: Susan Peterson, CBS News, September 8, 1974, Gerald R. Ford Presidential Library, Ann Arbor, MI, WHCA F757; Mrs. Ford composite tape 1974. Copy provided to author courtesy of GRF Library.

163 Ford Kids Probably Tried Pot, *The Brownsville Herald* (TX), September 8, 1974, https://www.newspapers.com/image/23530305.

163 *"she is like champagne"*: Myra McPherson, "The Blooming of Betty Ford," *McCall's*, September 1975.

163 *"Betty Ford, in the first month of her stay"*: Sally Quinn, "Betty Ford: Speaking Out Without Speaking Up," *Washington Post*, September 18, 1974.

163 *"They've asked me everything"*: McPherson, "Blooming of Betty Ford," 120.

164 *"And so, I went up there"*: Betty Monkman, interview, 12.

164 *"in the beginning"*: TTOML, 179.

164 *Privately, Betty was very spiritual*: Elizabeth Peer, Jane Whitmore, and Lisa Whitman, "Free Spirit in the White House, Woman of the Year," *Newsweek*, December 29, 1975.

165 *"I think Nixon has suffered enough"*: implied conversation, ATTH, 162.

165 *"she felt enormous sympathy for his family"*: ibid.

165 *"I'll support whatever you decide"*: ibid.

165 *one month after Gerald Ford took the oath*: ibid., 180.

166 We were all a little reluctant: Betty Ford to Mary Lou Logan, letter, September 12, 1974, courtesy of the Logan family; used with permission.

14: Going Public with Breast Cancer

167 *At one point, Betty commented*: TTOML, 236.

168 *"Come along with me"*: Sheila Weidenfeld, interview by Richard Norton Smith,

April 14, 2010, Oral History Project, Gerald R. Ford Presidential Foundation, 8, https://geraldrfordfoundation.org/centennial-docs/oralhistory/wp-content/up loads/2013/05/Sheila-Weidenfel.pdf.

168 *"There's something I need to tell you"* . . . *"It was devastating"*: Susan Ford Bales, discussion, October 6, 2016.

168 *"a woman's disease"*: ibid.

169 *"They want to operate immediately"* . . . *"they can't operate immediately"*: TTOML, 183.

169 *"I'm sure everything's going to turn out"*: ATTH, 190.

170 *"I want to go through my activities"*: TTOML, 183.

170 *"She was adamant about going public with it"*: Kennerly, discussion, March 30, 2017.

171 *"The purpose of the surgery"*: Office of the White House Press Secretary, "Statement by Ron Nessen," news release, September 27, 1974, Gerald R. Ford Presidential Library, Ann Arbor, MI, 1, www.fordlibrarymuseum.gov/library /document/0248/whpr19740927-006.pdf.

171 *"We were all scared to death"* . . . *"I need to talk about this"*: Michael Ford, discussion, October 26, 2017.

171 *"She showed no apprehension"*: ATTH, 190.

171 Dearest Mom: Gerald and Betty Ford Special Materials Collection, box B2, folder: "Ford, Gerald R," Gerald R. Ford Presidential Library, Ann Arbor, MI.

172 *"Here's one for* Women's Wear Daily*"*: United Press International, "Malignancy Verified: Mrs. Ford's Breast Removed," *Leader-Times* (Kittanning, PA), September 28, 1974.

172 *"She was the strong one, holding us all up"*: Susan Ford Bales, discussion, October 6, 2016.

172 *"No fear"*: David Kennerly, discussion, March 30, 2017.

172 *"Throughout this ordeal"*: Office of the White House Press Secretary, "The White House Press Conference of Dr. William Lukash . . ." news release, September 28, 1974, Gerald R. Ford Presidential Library, Ann Arbor, MI, 1, www.fordlibrary museum.gov/library/document/0248/whpr19740928-008.pdf.

172 *"We all sat around and prayed"*: Susan Ford Bales, discussion, October 6, 2016.

172 *"Go ahead and cry"*: ATTH, 191; also Cannon, *Gerald R. Ford*, 273.

172 *"Bob, I just don't know what I'd do"*: ibid.

173 *"How am I going to live the rest of my life without my mom?"*: Susan Ford Bales, discussion, October 6, 2016.

173 *In 1974 Betty Ford was one of more than ninety thousand women*: Nancy G. Brinker, *Promise Me: How a Sister's Love Launched the Global Movement to End Breast Cancer* (New York: Crown Archetype, 2010), 215.

173 *75 percent chance of surviving*: "Fact Sheet: Breast Cancer," National Institutes of Health online, last modified October 2010, https://report.nih.gov/nihfactsheets /Pdfs/BreastCancer(NCI).pdf; also Susan G. Komen Breast Cancer Foundation and information provided by Barbara Schwarz, founder of Oklahoma Project Woman.

173 *"Even before I was able to get up"*: TTOML, 186.

173 *"ringing off the hook"*: Frances Lewine, Associated Press, "Messages to First Lady 'Thrill' Her," *Oakland Tribune*, October 4, 1974.

174 *"One Sunday, I was sitting at home"* . . . *"People saw in Mrs. Ford a woman who was so relatable"*: Nancy Chirdon Forster, in discussion with author, August 22, 2017.

174 *"This was a revelation"*: Nancy Brinker, in discussion with author, October 16, 2017.

174 *"I will even go so far as to say"* . . . *"You're just a super lady"*: White House Social Office Central Files, box 24, "First Lady: Health," Gerald R. Ford Presidential Library, Ann Arbor, MI; samples of letters written to Betty Ford following her breast cancer surgery, viewed by author, October 24–27, 2016.

175 *"She had Dad walk into her hospital room"*: Susan Ford Bales, discussion, October 6, 2016.

175 *"Don't be silly"*: TTOML, 192.

175 Every time I look at these pills: ibid., 187.

176 *"Shh!"*: Hartwig, discussion, September 16, 2016.

176 *"What are you doing out here?"* . . . *"Here, catch!"*: ibid., TTOML, 188; also Kennerly, discussion, March 30, 2017.

177 *"Oh, Susan, it's beautiful"*: Susan Ford Bales, discussion, October 6, 2016.

177 *"When is it going to stop?"*: ibid.

177 *"I knew that if she died"*: ibid.

178 *"The people are a friendly middle-aged couple"*: David Hume Kennerly, *Shooter* (New York: Newsweek Books, 1979), 155–56.

178 *"We Love You, Betty"* and *"Welcome Home"*: photos from contact sheets, digital archive, "White House Photographs: October 11, 1974," Gerald R. Ford Presidential Library, Ann Arbor, MI.

178 *"I had no words for the joy I was feeling"*: TTOML, 191.

15: A Reluctant Role Model

179 *"Come on out on the balcony"*: TTOML, 192.

179 *"It was a fantastic anniversary"*: ibid.

180 *"From that moment on"*: Forster, discussion, August 22, 2017.

180 *"Neither of us had any idea"* . . . *"to get the first lady off the social page and onto the front page"*: Weidenfeld, discussion, December 8, 2016.

181 *"The Christmas parties started, and I didn't think they'd ever stop"*: TTOML, 199.

181 *"She was obviously in great pain"*: Sheila Rabb Weidenfeld, *First Lady's Lady: With the Fords at the White House* (New York: G. P. Putnam's Sons, 1979), 89.

182 *"Who skis?"* . . . *"mountain familiarization"*: Larry Buendorf, in discussion with author, November 11, 2016.

182 *"I guess I'll have to keep the drapes pulled"*: Weidenfeld, *First Lady's Lady*, 53.

183 *"I knew them before her dad became vice president"* . . . *"something she did not have to do"*: Barbara Yardley Manfuso Appleby, in discussion with author, August 1, 2017.

184 *"She was a mother I never had"*: Sheika Gramshammer, in discussion with author, November 10, 2016.

184 *"We were always included"* . . . *"Hey, yellow bird!"*: ibid.

184 *"We were concerned because you could spot him"*: Buendorf, discussion, November 10, 2016.

185 "Mrs. Ford Goes Shopping," Associated Press, *Southern Illinoisan* (Carbondale, IL), December 24, 1974.

185 *"Susan's mom came out and made a cup of tea"* . . . *"like I was part of the family"*: Appleby, discussion, August 1, 2017.

185 *"Hey, Dick,"* *the president said. "You guys did an excellent job"* . . . *"Yes, sir, Mr. President"*: Buendorf, discussion, November 10, 2016; also Richard Keiser, in discussion with author, July 20, 2017.

16: The First Lady Speaks Out

187 *"it had moral force"*: TTOML, 202.

187 *"legal inequities between sexes"*: ibid.

187 *"Before I sign this"* . . . *"I don't quite know how to respond to that"*: "Signing Ceremony Establishing a National Commission on the Observance of International Women's Year," January 9, 1975 (Gerald R. Ford Presidential Library online, video, 7:16), www.youtube.com/watch?time_continue=62&v=9-WDtJCa0Rc.

188 *"pillow talk at the end of the day"*: TTOML, 201.

188 *"are extremely well treated"*: Marlene Cimons, "First Lady Sticks to Her Guns on ERA," *Los Angeles Times,* February 18, 1975.

189 *"It just isn't right that we pay so much"*: ibid.

189 *"Frankly, I enjoy being a mother"*: Weidenfeld, *First Lady's Lady*, 90.

189 *"I'm going to stick . . . I'm not bothered by it"*: Cimons, "First Lady Sticks to Her Guns."

189 *"Betty Ford Is Trying to Press a Second-Rate Manhood on American Women"*: Weidenfeld, *First Lady's Lady*, 90.

190 *"Why don't I have any flags?"*: Hartwig, discussion, September 16, 2016.

190 *"We should make Mrs. Ford a flag"*: ibid.

190 *In bold white letters on top*: ibid.

190 *"She really got a kick out of it"*: ibid.

190 *Capraro, who had just gone into business*: Marji Kunz, "First Lady's Order Makes Capraro a Fashion Name," Lifestyle, *Salt Lake Tribune,* January 31, 1975.

191 *"Mr. Capraro? This is Betty Ford"* . . . *"Those are my designs!"*: ibid.

192 *"She loved helping someone new"*: Susan Ford Bales, discussion, October 6, 2016.

192 *"perfect model: size six"*: Kunz, "First Lady's Order."

192 *"We always had fun with Albert"*: Susan Ford Bales, discussion, October 6, 2016.

192 *"I called her the palace guard"*: Weidenfeld, discussion, December 8, 2016.

192 *"the only White House staffer"* . . . *"tickled"*: Betty Beale, "Nancy Howe Handles Key Role for First Lady," *Indianapolis Star*, October 6, 1974.

193 *"It's not a good time"*: Susan Ford Bales, discussion, October 18, 2017.

193 *"She interfered with our relationship"*: ibid.; also TTOML, 180.

193 *"Betty Ford's Best Friend"*: Frances Spatz Leighton, "New Job at the White House: Betty Ford's Best Friend," *Family Weekly,* March 2, 1975.

193 *"She was hysterical"*: Weidenfeld, discussion, December 8, 2016.

193 *"She is not my best friend!"*: Weidenfeld, *First Lady's Lady*, 90.

194 *"Oh, David!" she exclaimed. "We heard your helicopter was shot at!"*: David Kennerly, telephone discussion with author, November 17, 2017.

195 *"Cambodia is gone"*: ibid.

195 *"babylift"*: President's Speeches and Statements, box 7, folder "4/3/75—Opening Statement at Press Conference at San Diego, California," Gerald R. Ford Presidential Library, Ann Arbor, MI, available at www.fordlibrarymuseum.gov /library/document/0122/1252273.pdf.

195 *"I have directed that money"*: ibid.

196 *"Well, I didn't fire Nancy Howe"*: TTOML, 235.

196 *"It broke my heart"*: ibid.

197 *Tongsun Park would eventually be indicted*: Phil McCombs, "Tongsun Park's Club," *Washington Post*, October 16, 1977.

197 *"The South Vietnamese forces were inadequate"*: Kennerly, *Extraordinary Circumstances*, 73.

197 *"They were only nineteen and twenty-two"* . . . *"Yes. Yes, I will"*: Weidenfeld, *First Lady's Lady*, 129.

197 *"Schedule"*: ibid., 139.

198 *"there wasn't any time to come into a city and ask which way to the beauty salon"*: ibid.

198 *"My health is good and I'm having a ball!"*: United Press International, "Betty Says She 'Had a Ball,'" *Columbus* (NE) *Telegram*, June 4, 1975.

198 *"Be good"*: Susan Ford Bales, discussion, October 6, 2016.

198 *Susan nearly didn't have a date*: ibid.

200 *"I was willing to take on four more years"*: TTOML, 255.

200 *"She was my teacher"* . . . *"We're just good friends"*: Anna Kisselgoff, "Martha Graham Is Paid Tribute by Betty Ford," *New York Times*, June 13, 1975.

202 *"I had never met her before"* . . . *"Look"*: Arthur Unger, "Frankness and Informality Mark Betty Ford's Style as First Lady," *Grand Rapids* (MI) *Press*, August 12, 1975.

202 *"enthusiastic, excellent camera presence"* . . . *"So was she"*: Weidenfeld, *First Lady's Lady*, 162.

202 *"Elizabeth Ann Bloomer was her name"* . . . *"You know, everybody can't be perfect"*: Morley Safer, "The First Lady," *60 Minutes*, aired August 10, 1975, on CBS. Video provided to author by Gerald R. Ford Presidential Library, Ann Arbor, MI, WHCA-F388; also, Dick Cheney and Donald Rumsfeld, discussions with author, July 21, 2017.

206 *"Well?"* . . . *"thirty million votes!"*: Weidenfeld, *First Lady's Lady*, 172; also corroborated by Cheney, discussion, July 21, 2017, and Rumsfeld, discussion, July 21, 2017.

206 *"All hell broke loose"*: Matson, interview, 9.

206 *"Betty Ford said today"*: Weidenfeld, *First Lady's Lady*, 172.

206 *"My stock with the public did not go up"*: TTOML, 206.

207 *"Even though Mrs. Ford had said more"*: Unger, "Frankness and Informality Mark Betty Ford's Style."

207 *"I don't know which was more tasteless"* . . . *"I move Betty Ford be retained as first lady"*: "The First Lady," *60 Minutes*, viewer response, aired August 17, 1975, on CBS. Video provided to author by Gerald R. Ford Presidential Library, Ann Arbor, MI, WHCA F396.

207 *"I had a little trouble with Donald and Dick"*: TTOML.

207 *"We think Betty needs to lay low"*: Dick Cheney, in discussion with author, July 21, 2017.

207 *"If you want Betty to tone it down"*: ibid.

207 *"had long ceased to be perturbed by his wife's remarks"*: Mary Campbell, Associated Press, "Women Made Big Headlines in 1975," December 25, 1975.

207 Thank you for writing about my appearance: Weidenfeld, *First Lady's Lady*, 177.

208 *"the perfect letter"*: ibid., 170.

208 *"Keep Speaking Out, Betty"*: ibid.

209 *The reaction to Mrs. Ford's remarks*: ibid.

209 Dear Morley: ibid., 182.

17: Two Assassination Attempts

210 *"I think I have learned over the past months"*: Natalie Gittelson, "Is Betty Ford Too Frank?" *McCall's*, February 1976.

210 *"And while she acknowledged a loss of privacy"*: ibid.

210 *"Mrs. Ford, I have an emergency call from Mr. Keiser"*: Keiser, discussion, July 20, 2017.

210 *"Hello, Mrs. Ford. Not to worry"*: ibid.

211 *"But I had never worried about them"*: ATTH, 310.

211 *"Ernie, it's such a beautiful day"*: ibid.

211 *"Of course, Mr. President"*: ATTH, 310.

211 *"Suddenly he shoots across the street"*: ibid.

212 *"The pistol was loaded with four rounds"* . . . *"Well, I didn't think it would be very polite"*: Buendorf, discussion, November 10, 2016.

212 *"I remember Mom telling us"* . . . *"You know, that was a great thing about Mom and Dad"*: Steve Ford, discussion, November 23, 2016.

212 *"I'm so thankful you were there, Larry"*: Buendorf, discussion, November 10, 2016.

212 *"Everyone did the right thing"*: ibid.

212 *"It was very scary"*: TTOML, 236.

212 *"handshaking"* . . . *"I was appalled"*: Weidenfeld, discussion, December 6, 2016.

213 *"Move Pinafore to Angel with all possible speed"* . . . *"You tell her, Rummy"*: Hartwig, discussion, September 15, 2016.

214 *"Quite a few martinis were consumed on the flight back"*: Edward Epstein, "Ford Escaped 2 Assassination Attempts—Both in California," *San Francisco Chronicle*, December 27, 2006.

214 *"We had two televisions in there"*: Susan Ford Bales, discussion, February 17, 2017.

214 *"Shots were fired at your father"*: Steve Ford, discussion, November 23, 2016.

215 *"While many new opportunities are open to women"* . . . *"Freedom for women to be what they want"*: "First Lady Betty Ford's Remarks to the International Women's Conference," October 25, 1975. Video provided to author by Gerald R. Ford Presidential Library, Ann Arbor, MI.

216 *"They loved her"*: Weidenfeld, *First Lady's Lady*, 207.

216 *"The wife of a president could* never *do that"*: Weidenfeld, discussion, December 8, 2016.

217 *"she had trouble remembering her dialogue"*: Mary Tyler Moore, *Growing Up Again: Life, Loves, and Oh Yeah, Diabetes* (New York: St. Martin's Griffin, 2010), 67.

18: "Betty's Husband for President!"

219 *"Nineteen-seventy-six is a jumble in my head"*: TTOML, 255.

219 *"busy being president"*: Kennerly, discussion, March 30, 2017.

219 *"chaperone"*: Susan Ford Bales, discussion, October 6, 2016.

220 *"Oh, are you two girls getting excited"* . . . *"Of course, I got in trouble"*: ibid.

221 *"scatter blitz"*: Weidenfeld, discussion, December 8, 2016; also Joan Secchia, October 28, 2016.

221 *"Keep on talking for President Ford"*: ibid.

222 *"No tribute could be more spectacular"*: Weidenfeld, discussion, December 8, 2016.

222 *"most glamorous"*: TTOML, 225.

222 *"the social event of the century"*: ibid., 224.

223 *"You're* never *going to be ready"*: TTOML, 225.

223 *"Mrs. Ford wanted guests to have a good time"*: Matson, interview, 7.

223 *"Jack came flying in, still fiddling with his shirtfront"*: TTOML, 226.

223 *"I have one just like it at home"*: ibid.

223 *"We had violinists stationed along the paths"*: ibid., 225.

223 *The US Marine Band had a set list*: David G. Wright (saxophonist, US Marine Band), "When Protocol Was Trampled at the White House," *Washington Post*, Letters to the Editor, June 15, 2012.

224 *"If I hadn't kept mixing up"*: TTOML, 225.

224 *"Eat your hearts out, girls!"*: Patricia J. Matson interview by Donna Lehman, January 16, 2015, transcript, Oral History Interview, Gerald R. Ford Library, Ann Arbor, MI.

224 *"That gives you a sense of a certain playfulness"*: ibid.

224 *"Mrs. Ford used to be visited periodically"* . . . *"She didn't seem to be there"*: Forster, discussion, August 22, 2017.

225 *"looked exhausted and sounded as though she were having trouble* concentrating*"* . . . *"Where do you draw the line"*: Weidenfeld, discussion, December 8, 2016; also Weidenfeld, *First Lady's Lady*, 306.

226 *"We figured it was the medication"*: Forster, discussion, August 22, 2017.

226 *"I just think there's something wrong here* . . . *He didn't say 'It's none of your business'"*: ibid.

227 *"Is Mrs. Ford all right?"* . . . *"The pills are for her pinched nerve and arthritis"*: Weidenfeld, *First Lady's Lady*, 313.

228 *"Who would make a better president"*: Weidenfeld, *First Lady's Lady*, 303.

228 *"when her polls were just skyrocketing"*: Maria Downs, interview by Richard Norton Smith, June 18, 2009, Oral History Project, Gerald R. Ford Presidential Foundation, 25, https://geraldrfordfoundation.org/centennial-docs/oralhistory/wp-content/uploads/2013/05/Maria-Downs.pdf.

228 *Across the country*: Greg Willard, in discussion with author, November 17, 2017.

228 *"Coming into the convention"*: ibid.

229 *"Nothing was more important"* . . . *"As usual, she was right"*: ATTH, 405.

229 *"Suddenly,"* President Ford recalled, *"I felt her hand in mine"*: ibid.

230 *"It was something we as a family all came to embrace"*: Michael Ford, discussion, October 26, 2017.

230 *"We took that motor home from California"*: Steve Ford, discussion, November 23, 2016; also Weidenfeld, *First Lady's Lady*, 356.

231 *"Steve's mother"* . . . *"go and get your tape recorder"*: United Press International, "Betty, Steve Woo Calif. Vote," *Town Talk* (Alexandria, LA), October 20, 1976, 41.

231 *"I have something for you"*: TTOML, 265.

232 *"troubled, and they have been tough"*: Maury DeJonge, "Home Ground Never So Dear for the Fords," *Grand Rapids* (MI) *Press*, November 2, 1976.

232 *"we're going to make America great again"*: ibid., 2B.

232 *"I just want to say how absolutely"*: ibid.

19: Last Days in the White House

233 *"Here we go, Prez!"*: Willard, discussion, April 2, 2017.

234 *"there wasn't a darn thing that I could do"*: ATTH, 434.

234 *"Do you think we should wake him up?"* . . . *"Governor, I hope you know"*: Willard, discussion, April 2, 2017.

234 *"You know, I had the craziest thing"*: ibid.; also Susan Ford Bales, discussion, February 17, 2017.

234 *"Oh, Mother, you won't believe"*: ibid.

234 *"Okay, everyone, it's going to be a busy day"*: Willard, discussion, April 2, 2017.

235 *"Good night"*: ibid.

235 *"Oh, Mrs. Ford, I'm so sorry"*: ibid.

235 *"Now, you listen to me"*: ibid.

235 *"crying like a baby"* . . . *"She could have been despondent"*: ibid.

235 *"was a day when more than a few tears were shed"*: Kennerly, discussion, March 30, 2017.

235 *"I can't talk"* . . . *"I can't read the concession speech"*: ibid.

236 *"Of course I will"*: ibid.

236 *"It's perfectly obvious"* . . . *"Now let me call on the real spokesman"*: "President Ford Concession Speech," November 3, 1976 (C-Span online, video, 5:32), www.c-span.org/video/?153625-1/president-ford-concession-speech.

237 *"Don't show any emotion"*: Mary Murphy, "What Do You Do for an Encore," *New West*, November 21, 1977.

237 *"The president asked me to tell you"* . . . *"Signed Jerry Ford"*: "Ford Concession Speech," November 3, 1976.

238 All I have to do is get us all through: Murphy, "What Do You Do for an Encore."

238 *"People with low self-esteem crave reassurance"*: BAGA, 58.

239 *"We'll Miss You, Betty Ford"*: Judy Clabes, "We'll Miss You, Betty Ford," *Evansville* (IN) *Press*, January 1, 1977.

240 *"We walked by the Cabinet Room"* . . . *"I think that'll about wrap it up for this place"*: Kennerly, discussion, March 30, 2017.

240 *"We were all human beings"*: TTOML, 277.

241 *"I'm sure her thoughts are as deep"*: Carter, *First Lady from Plains*, xxi.

241 *"The food is so delicious there"*: ibid.

241 *"All our married life was being left there"*: TTOML, 278.

PART 4: BETTY FORD, AFTER THE WHITE HOUSE

243 *"Something has to be done about Mother"*: Susan Ford Bales, discussion, February 17, 2017.

20: *"Kiss Today Goodbye"*

245 *$375,000 house they leased*: David S. Smith, "Ford Reveals Final Home Site," *Desert Sun* (Palm Springs, CA), January 29, 1977, 1.

246 *"Office of the Thirty-Eighth President of the United States"*: Willard, discussion, April 2, 2017.

246 *"Those of us on the staff"*: ibid.

247 *"Mrs. Ford, a bunch of us have been talking"* . . . *"Well, then, let's get four tickets"*: ibid.

250 *"If today were the day you had to stop dancing"*: "What I Did for Love," music by Marvin Hamlisch, lyrics by Edward Kleban.

250 *"Kiss today goodbye"*: ibid.

250 *"Wasn't it wonderful, Jerry?"* . . . *"The choreography was marvelous!"*: Willard, discussion, April 2, 2017.

250 *"Follow-up—Venker. Passkey's ready"*: ibid.

251 Oh my God. That song . . . "What I Did for Love" *was* their *song*: ibid.

253 *"Greg, can you come down here to the house"*: ibid.

253 *"As you can see"* . . . *"You should be able to go home by early afternoon"*: ibid.

254 *"By late afternoon, she was clearly not well"* . . . *"keep her here overnight"*: ibid.

255 *"Tell us what you're* not *looking for"* . . . *"It just doesn't make sense"*: ibid.

256 *"something was not right"*: ibid.

21: A Downward Spiral

258 *"I had a long hallway"*: Dr. Joseph Cruse, in discussion with author, July 25, 2017.

259 *"I introduced myself"* . . . *"It was a genuine smile"*: Morgan, discussion, May 19, 2017.

259 What do you say when you are facing the former president's wife . . . *"There were good days and bad days"*: ibid.

260 *"a bad summer"*: Murphy, "What Do You Do for an Encore." *New West*, November 21, 1977.

260 *"Betty Ford looked five years older"*: ibid.

260 *"Poor darling"*: Gramshammer, discussion, November 10, 2016.

261 *"Fine, but we're not going to support you financially"*: Susan Ford Bales, discussion, February 17, 2017.

261 *"They went from a modest life"*: Morgan, discussion, May 19, 2017.

262 *"Betty going on and on and on"*: Chris Chase, interview by Richard Norton Smith, January 21, 2011, Oral History Project, Gerald R. Ford Presidential Foundation, https://geraldrfordfoundation.org/centennial-docs/oralhistory/wp-content/uploads/2013/05/Chris-Chase.pdf.

262 *"She always had iced tea"*: Morgan, discussion, May 19, 2017.

262 *"It was an art that she had perfected"* . . . *"Oh, Caroline, you're not fooling me"*: ibid.

263 *"Sometimes she would surprise you"* . . . *"they just couldn't tolerate being around her"*: ibid.

263 *"Wherever I went that fall"* . . . *"kind of a zombie"*: BAGA, 42.

263 *"She was painfully lonely"*: Morgan, discussion, May 19, 2017.

264 *"knew how to take care of her"*: ibid.

264 *"I was not a professional"*: BAGA, 41.

22: The Turning Point

265 *"That was her juggling act"* . . . *"They rarely quarreled"*: Morgan, discussion, May 19, 2017.

268 *"Caroline would come home and tell me"*: Susan Ford Bales, discussion, February 17, 2017.

268 *"Susan was really there for me"*: Morgan, discussion, May 19, 2017.

268 *"She would say her neck hurt"*: Susan Ford Bales, discussion, February 17, 2017.

269 *So Jerry would tell everyone*: BAGA, 42.

269 *"Dad and I covered for her"* . . . *"She was not a daytime drinker"*: Susan Ford Bales, discussion, February 17, 2017.

269 *"We wanted to carry on as if everything was fine"*: Michael Ford, discussion, October 26, 2017.

269 *"Eating with her was torturous"* . . . *"Just trying to make it"*: Morgan, discussion, May 19, 2017.

270 *"She was not in good shape"*: Tom Brokaw, in discussion with author, August 22, 2017.

270 *"We sat in the bedroom"*: Morgan, discussion, May 19, 2017.

270 *"The Wonderful World of Disney will not be presented"* . . . *"enduring popularity"*: *Betty Ford: Nutcracker at the Bolshoi Ballet*, aired December 14, 1977, on NBC. Video provided to author by Gerald R. Ford Presidential Library, Ann Arbor, MI, AV83-11-44 and AV83-11-45.

272 *"That was pretty bad, wasn't it?"*: Morgan, discussion, May 19, 2017.

272 *"Yeah, it was"*: ibid.

272 *"something of a disaster"* . . . *"sloe eyed and sleepy tongued"*: BAGA, 41.

272 *"And they were right"*: ibid.

273 *"Christmas vacation in Vail that year was utter hell"*: Morgan, discussion, May 19, 2017.

273 *"She was incoherent"*: BAGA, 8.

273 *"Caroline, can't you just get Mom dressed in the morning?"* . . . *"Mother's problem"*: Morgan, discussion, May 19, 2017.

273 *"We were up in Vail, there was a lot of good snow"*: BAGA, 8.

273 *"in second gear"* . . . *"increasingly difficult to lead a normal life"*: ibid., 22.

273 *"She was scared to death"*: Morgan, discussion, May 19, 2017; also Susan Ford Bales, discussion, February 17, 2017.

274 *"I understand what's wrong with you"*: ibid.

274 *"The agents warned me not to get involved"* . . . *"She had lived through all of that as a child"*: Morgan, discussion, May 19, 2017.

275 *"That was a rude awakening"* . . . *"I'll talk to Susan"*: ibid.

276 *"I didn't know anything about Alcoholics Anonymous"*: Susan Ford Bales, discussion, February 17, 2017.

276 *"You're talking about your mother, aren't you?"*: ibid.; also Cruse, discussion, July 25, 2017.

276 *"Yes. I just don't know what to do"*: ibid.

277 *The intervention technique had been developed*: "Johnson Model Intervention," Interventionsupport.com, accessed January 16, 2017, www.interventionsupport .com/intervention-techniques/johnson-model.

277 *"I knew she had a problem"*: Cruse, discussion, July 25, 2017.

277 *"Joe," he said, "can't you go do it by yourself?"*: ibid.

277 *"He didn't want to do it"*: ibid.

279 *"I did a little self-prescribing"*: BAGA, 166.

23: The Intervention and Treatment

280 *"We have to do something now"*: Susan Ford Bales, discussion, February 17, 2017.

280 *"You are all a bunch of monsters!"*: ibid.; also BAGA, 11.

280 *"I was devastated"*: ibid.

280 *"It was a big mistake"* . . . *"Don't worry, she's said that before"*: Cruse, discussion, July 25, 2017.

281 *"Boy, was I glad she was there"*: Susan Ford Bales, discussion, February 17, 2017.

281 *"Don't worry," Clara said, "Mother's fine"*: ibid.

281 *"Captain Pursch was quite a personality"*: Morgan, discussion, May 19, 2017.

281 *A Chicago native*: Allan Parachini and the *Los Angeles Times*, "The Navy Way to Beat the Bottle," *Washington Post*, March 13, 1979, www.washingtonpost .com/archive/lifestyle/1979/03/13/the-navy-way-to-beat-the-bottle/a42f6d85 -7d19-430c-9cea-4d19695918c4/?utm_term=.6809d34f4d26.

281 *"When I met Pat Benedict"*: BAGA, 14.

281 *"We've got to do this for Mother"*: ibid.

281 *"You felt very, very guilty"*: Morgan, discussion, May 19, 2017.

282 *"The doctors literally gave us a set of instructions"*: BAGA, 17.

282 *"We began to understand the nature of chemical dependence"*: ibid., 14.

282 *"It was so tense"*: Morgan, discussion, May 19, 2017.

282 *"No one had ever seen her cry like that before"*: ibid.

282 *"I had given my whole life to my family"*: Betty Ford, in *A Legacy of Hope*, Hazelden Betty Ford Foundation, YouTube, December 6, 2016, 53.39, www.youtube.com /watch?v=iNBKYQ1LM2c.

282 *"Mrs. Ford, are you willing to go into treatment?"*: BAGA, 23.

283 *"Betty, I have had a problem"*: ibid.

283 *"I got dressed and put myself together"*: ibid., 24.

283 *"sedated to the teeth"*: ibid.

284 *President Ford was stunned*: ibid., 42.

284 *"I was more concerned with the pills"*: ibid.

284 *"There were bottles and bottles and bottles"*: Susan Ford Bales, discussion, February 17, 2017.

284 *"I took out an entire grocery bag"*: Cruse, discussion, July 25, 2017.

284 *"It was like the family was a family once again"*: BAGA, 25.

284 *"It was horrible what that body went through"*: Morgan, discussion, May 19, 2017.

285 *"It was miserable"*: Susan Ford Bales, discussion, February 17, 2017.

285 *"I shook so much"*: BAGA, 26.

285 *"President Ford was very strong"*: Morgan, discussion, May 19, 2017.

285 *"Why does she keep throwing up?"* . . . *"celebrated in the kitchen with glasses of Cranapple juice"*: BAGA, 27.

286 *"I want her up and dressed and at that party"*: ibid., 28.

286 *"I marveled that I was able to eat"*: ibid.

286 *"It had been a brutal week"*: Morgan, discussion, May 19, 2017.

286 *"I believe you have to treat VIPs"*: BAGA, 46.

286 *"I almost turned right around"*: ibid.

286 *"She was a wreck"* . . . *"She had lost all her privacy"*: Morgan, discussion, May 19, 2017; also BAGA, 47.

287 *"Former First Lady Betty Ford was hospitalized"*: press release from Caroline Coventry Morgan, personal files.

288 *"Policies and Routine for Patients"*: information from Caroline Coventry Morgan, personal files related to Eisenhower Medical Center, alcohol rehabilitation treatment.

288 *"Six-Pack"*: BAGA, 53.

288 *"addicted to drugs and drink"*: ibid.

288 *"I was not a model patient"*: ibid, 48.

289 *"They had to clean the toilets"*: Morgan, discussion, May 19, 2017.

289 *"I could not say I was alcoholic"*: BAGA, 51.

289 *"not a quiver in her voice"*: Morgan, discussion, May 19, 2017.

289 *"The hand I held gave me strength and faith"*: ibid.

290 *"I wasn't convinced"*: Susan Ford Bales, discussion, February 17, 2017.

290 *"No, he didn't!* . . . *I'm the one that did all the work"*: ibid.

290 *"The whole family is so raw"* . . . *"When is it going to be my turn?"*: ibid.

290 *"For the first time"*: BAGA, 63–64.

291 *"I was so offended"*: Steve Ford, discussion, November 23, 2016.

291 *"Steve, this is exactly what your mother needs"*: ibid.

291 *"Her doctors would prescribe whatever she wanted"*: BAGA, 63.

291 *"I made the dumb statement"*: ibid.

291 *"Steve, is your mother an alcoholic?"*: Steve Ford, discussion, November 23, 2016.

291 *"I know that the problem exists"*: Myra McPherson and Donnie Radcliffe, "Betty Ford Says She Is Addicted to Alcohol," *Washington Post*, April 22, 1978, A5; also United Press International, "Son Says Drugs, Drink, Affected Mrs. Ford," April 15, 1978.

291 *Betty still had not admitted*: TTOML, 284.

291 *"She had begun to pull back"*: Cruse, discussion, July 25, 2017.

291 *"We are here because something"*: ibid.

292 *"If you're going to call me an alcoholic, I won't stand for it"*: Morgan, discussion, May 20, 2017.

292 *"So far, you have talked"*: BAGA, 53.

292 *"I don't want to embarrass my husband"* . . . *"he had to shock her"*: ibid., 54.

292 *"He knew that if she put it"*: Morgan, discussion, May 20, 2017.

292 *"I cried so hard my nose and ears were closed up"*: BAGA, 55.

293 *"Here is the statement from Mrs. Ford"*: Gerald Faris, "I'm Addicted to Alcohol—Betty Ford," *Los Angeles Times*, April 21, 1978.

293 *"she opened the door for* women *to seek treatment"*: Pat Benedict, in *A Legacy of Hope*, video.

293 *"To the laymen, it was just a statement"*: Morgan, discussion, May 20, 2017.

293 *"We've never had too much success"*: Faris, "I'm Addicted to Alcohol—Betty Ford."

293 *"Mrs. Ford is a gutsy lady"* . . . *"medications any of us would get"*: ibid.

293 *Barrett emphatically denied*: Bob Locke, Associated Press, "Betty Ford Says She's Hooked on Alcohol as Well as Medicine," April 21, 1978.

293 *"My drinking hasn't caused my folks any trouble"*: BAGA, 58.

294 *"I'm Betty, and I am an alcoholic"*: ibid.

294 *it would take more than two years*: ibid., 48.

294 *"We learned that alcoholism kind of comes in two ways"*: Morgan, discussion, May 20, 2017.

295 *"I was astonished at the amount of newspaper coverage"*: BAGA, 60.

295 *"People don't understand the mood swings"* . . . *"I could kill you for doing this to me!"*: ibid., 56.

295 *"She was so angry"* . . . *"I was a mess"*: Morgan, discussion, May 20, 2017.

296 *"Part of it was this is a family disease"*: Michael Ford, discussion, October 26, 2017.

296 *"No, I won't do it"*: BAGA, 61.

296 *"It was a crisis"*: ibid.

296 *"Mrs. Ford how do you feel"* . . . *"I know that she felt so vulnerable"*: Morgan, discussion, May 20, 2017.

297 *"Nobody had consulted me"* . . . *"It was a cruel intrusion"*: BAGA, 69–70.

297 *"What she has done is the most significant advance"*: Phyllis Battelle, "Betty Ford May Change Course of Million Lives," *Brownsville* (TX) *Herald*, May 8, 1978.

297 *"alcohol addiction is a physical disease, not a moral sin"*: ibid.

298 *"Betty Ford has earned the admiration"*: Associated Press, "Betty Ford Called Most Popular," *Philadelphia Inquirer*, May 25, 1978.

24: *Recovery*

299 *"Thousands of them"*: Morgan, discussion, May 19, 2017.

300 *"I was on a high"*: BAGA, 65.

300 *"You're not here to play former first lady"*: ibid.

300 *"Once in a while, during the first year of my sobriety"*: ibid., 69.

301 *"She must be drinking again"*: ibid., 70.

301 *"I know you were kidding"* . . . *"This was dangerous stuff"*: ibid., 71.

301 *"The evening went beautifully"*: ibid., 73.

302 *"The president was very supportive"*: Morgan, discussion, May 19, 2017.

302 *"There's been such a precipitous increase"*: Carol Kleiman, "Giving a Lift to the Face-Lift Business," *Chicago Tribune*, October 19, 1978.

303 *"Betty is supposed to be opposed to another campaign"* . . . *"Her manner and voice bore no resemblance"*: Myra MacPherson, "Betty Ford Night at the Waldorf," *Washington Post*, November 11, 1978.

304 *"It was a very rocky relationship"*: Susan Ford Bales, discussion, February 17, 2017.

304 *"It was a surprise for everybody"*: Alberi, discussion, March 21, 2017.

304 *"I hope you've thought about this"*: Susan Ford Bales, discussion, February 17, 2017.

304 *"I was throwing things back"*: ibid.

304 *"Susan was our youngest child"*: BAGA, 75.

304 *"There was no fondness there"*: Susan Ford Bales, discussion, February 17, 2017.

305 *"I liked alcohol"* . . . *"I went through the two weeks"*: BAGA, 74–76.

306 *"The wedding, I think, was very hard on her"*: Susan Ford Bales, discussion, February 17, 2017.

306 *"That first year of recovery"*: BAGA, 88.

25: The Betty Ford Center

308 *"Leonard is in terrible shape"*: BAGA, 79.

308 *"I loved that"*: ibid., 85.

309 *"He knew the minute we walked in"*: ibid., 86.

309 *"No, no, no, Leonard," Betty said. "You're going to go to treatment"*: ibid.

309 *"You're my best friend, Leonard"*: ibid.

309 *"It was really beautiful"*: Morgan, discussion, February 27, 2017.

309 *"It was my second go after nine years of sobriety"*: BAGA, 87.

309 *"That's easy. Either give up your nightly martini"*: Ann Cullen, in discussion with author, December 9, 2016.

310 *"What did they give you"* . . . *"You and Betty should put your heads together"*: BAGA, 90.

310 *"You know," he said, "we've got this disease"*: Michael Ford, discussion, October 26, 2017.

310 *"Mom was a bit reluctant"*: ibid.

310 One of the things: Morgan, discussion, May 20, 2017.

311 *"With my recovery, and Leonard's recovery"*: BAGA, 90.

311 *"She got fired up!"*: Michael Ford, discussion, October 26, 2017.

311 *"That was a huge moment"*: Morgan, discussion, May 20, 2017.

311 *"We were having a problem at Eisenhower"*: BAGA, 91.

311 Nationwide, the common practice: Cruse, discussion, July 25, 2017.

312 *"gentlemen"* . . . *"problem"*: "The History of Hazelden," Hazelden Betty Ford Foun-

dation online, accessed January 16, 2017, www.hazeldenbettyford.org/about-us
/mission/history/hazelden.

312 *"provide low-cost, comprehensive alcoholism services"*: proposal materials for "A
Recovery and Training Facility for Chemical Dependency," Betty Ford: Post–
White House Papers, Gerald R. Ford Presidential Library, Ann Arbor, MI.

313 *"I don't think I realized until much later"*: Morgan, discussion, May 20, 2017.

313 *"If people could just see in hindsight"*: ibid.

313 *"Have you ever been to New York City?" . . . "No, I didn't. I'm just kidding"*: Penny
Circle, in discussion with author, January 17, 2018.

315 *"My new life was precious to me"*: BAGA, 96.

315 *"Betty's recovery was never talked about"*: ibid.

315 *"There I was. Mrs. Ford wasn't sure"*: Cullen, discussion, December 9, 2016.

316 *"I can't tell you how many Republicans"*: BAGA, 97.

316 *"He didn't* tell *me not to"*: ibid.

316 *"Wake Up GOP"*: Associated Press, "ERA Supporters Rally," *Detroit Free Press*,
July 15, 1980.

316 *"watched the parade go by"*: BAGA, 97.

316 *"I really saw a change in him"*: Michael Ford, discussion, October 26, 2017.

316 *"They were a pretty dynamic duo"*: Cullen, discussion, December 9, 2016.

316 *One time Betty and Jerry*: Cruse, discussion, July 25, 2017.

316 *"It got to the point people didn't want to sit next to me"*: ibid.

317 *She'd also seen how much*: Cullen, discussion, December 9, 2016.

317 *"We know we can provide quality care"*: BAGA, 94.

317 *"Do you think we could use her name on it?"*: ibid., 95.

318 *"Absolutely not, I'm too new in recovery"*: John Schwarzlose, president, Betty Ford
Center, in *A Legacy of Hope*, video.

318 *I'll never be able to drink again*: BAGA, 95.

318 *"We're proud of you, Mom"*: Steve Ford, discussion, November 23, 2016.

318 *"It was a hectic sobriety"*: BAGA, 95.

318 *"She bossed that construction crew around"*: Cullen, discussion, December 9,
2016.

319 *"And then, Betty being Betty, set out to help others"*: "Bush Ends Visit to State,"
Eureka (CA) *Times Standard*, October 4, 1982.

319 *"It's not easy to properly and in good taste express the feelings"*: Betty Ford Center
footage provided to author by Gerald R. Ford Presidential Library, Ann Arbor,
MI, 2003-NLF-010-012.

320 *"tough love"*: ibid.

320 *"blame the navy"*: BAGA, 114.

321 *"Hello. I'm Betty"*: Jerry Moe, in discussion with author, March 28, 2017.

26: Betty Ford, the Legacy

322 *"Mrs. Ford had a way of talking"*: Moe, discussion, Betty Ford Center, Rancho
Mirage, CA, March 28, 2017.

322 *"It's an experience unlike any other I've known"*: John Duka, "Elizabeth Taylor:
Journal of a Recovery," *New York Times*, February 4, 1985, A16, https://times

machine.nytimes.com/timesmachine/1985/02/04/issue.html?action=click&
contentCollection=Archives&module=LedeAsset&region=ArchiveBody&pg
type=article.

323 *"Betty Ford and I discussed what it would be like to go public"*: ibid.

323 *"not only helped me, but several other very worthwhile women"*: Betty Ford Special
Letters, Box B3, Folder J-R, Gerald R. Ford Presidential Library, Ann Arbor, MI.

323 *"She had her finger on every aspect"*: Ali MacGraw, in discussion with author,
April 12, 2017.

324 *"You're nothing unless you've been to Betty Ford"*: P. J. Corkery, "Addiction à
L.A. Mode," *New Republic* online, July 7, 1985, https://newrepublic.com/article
/91735/betty-ford-center-addiction-elizabeth-taylor.

324 *"a new hold on life"*: Johnny Cash to Betty Ford, letter, February 15, 1984, Betty
Ford Special Letters, Box B1, Folder A-C, Gerald R. Ford Presidential Library,
Ann Arbor, MI.

324 *"Talk about being famous"* . . . *"All the songs, and all the poems, and the shows"*:
Judy Kurtz, "Stevie Nicks Remembers Betty Ford," *Hill*, July 11, 2011, http://the
hill.com/blogs/in-the-know/in-the-know/256247-judy-kurtz.

324 *"Now, here we were in a role reversal"*: Moore, *Growing Up Again*, 4.

324 *"No, no, no"*: Moe, discussion, March 28, 2017.

325 *celebrities have always made up less than 1 percent*: Mark Mishek, CEO, Hazelden
Betty Ford Foundation, in discussion with author, March 27, 2017.

325 *"President Ford was so proud of her"*: Moe, discussion, March 28, 2017.

325 *"I don't give one hundred percent"*: Beverly Beyette, "Betty Ford, On Reflection,"
Los Angeles Times, January 18, 1989.

326 *"She stepped forward"*: Pat Roeske, "AIDS Benefit L.A.-Style," *Washington Post*,
September 21, 1985.

326 *"Mrs. Ford had quite a few gay friends"*: Cullen, discussion, December 9, 2016.

326 *"I watched her at the Betty Ford clinic"*: Roeske, "AIDS Benefit L.A.-Style."

326 *"Tonight is about conquering fear"*: ibid.

327 *"I was very pleased that I was selected"* . . . *"I got the message"*: Buendorf, discussion, November 11, 2016.

327 *"I would do anything for the Betty Ford Center"*: Jamie Shoop Bray, "After 10 Years,
Betty Ford Center Is a Star in Rehab," *North Hills* (PA) *News Record*, November 6,
1992.

327 *"Gramma"*: Heather Devers, in discussion with author, February 17, 2017.

328 *"Mom, Dad"* . . . *"I read mine every day"*: Steve Ford, discussion, January 16,
2018.

329 Dear Steve . . . Enjoy your life: Steve Ford, email message to author, January 18,
2018.

330 *"Every time they'd give her a new therapy"*: Brinker, discussion, October 16, 2017.

330 *"I'm delighted to help"* . . . *"she would have given it a try"*: ibid.

331 *"She rounded up the Republicans"*: Carter, discussion, June 14, 2017.

331 *"Her courage and candor"*: President George H. W. Bush, "Remarks on Presenting the Presidential Medal of Freedom Awards," November 18, 1991, American
Presidency Project, University of California, Santa Barbara, www.presidency
.ucsb.edu/ws/?pid=20239.

332 *"Perhaps no first lady in our history"*: President Bill Clinton, "Remarks on Presenting the Congressional Gold Medal to Former President Gerald R. Ford and Former First Lady Betty Ford," October 27, 1999, American Presidency Project, University of California, Santa Barbara, www.presidency.ucsb.edu/ws/index.php?pid=56803&st=&st1.

332 *"Show me your breaststroke"*: Devers, discussion, February 17, 2017.

332 *"Grandpa used to spell"*: ibid.

333 *"It was an open platform"* . . . *"There wasn't a stronger voice"*: Tyne Vance Berlanga, in discussion with author, October 10, 2017.

333 *"Grandpa always referred to Gramma as his bride"*: Devers, discussion, February 17, 2017.

334 *"I'm inclined to proceed"* . . . *they were headed back to their home in the desert*: Susan Ford Bales and Vaden Bales, in discussion with author, February 17, 2017.

335 *"Come on out and look"*: Jan Hart, in discussion with author, March 27, 2017.

336 *"He had been kind of in and out"*: Susan Ford Bales, discussion, February 17, 2017.

336 *"Well, I think you and I have a little bit of work to do"* . . . *"If I hadn't been married"*: Willard, discussion and email message to author, February 2–4, 2018.

339 *David Kennerly could hardly contain his emotions*: Kennerly, discussion, March 30, 2017.

340 *"There were so many people"*: Wilson "Bill" Livingood, in discussion with author, December 8, 2016.

340 *"I had never seen that before"*: ibid.

340 *"But that was not in her"*: Susan Ford Bales, discussion, February 17, 2017.

341 *"I can do this"*: Willard, discussion, February 2, 2018.

341 *"I've been in thousands of motorcades"*: ibid.

341 *"I just don't think I can make it any further"*: ibid.; also Susan Ford Bales, telephone discussion with author, February 3, 2018.

342 *"It was like watching a flat tire inflate"*: Susan Ford Bales, ibid.

342 *"You can do this"*: ibid.

342 *"On behalf of the president"*: Willard, email message to author, February 4, 2018.

343 *"After we land"*: Willard, discussion, February 2, 2018.

343 How does she do this?: ibid.

343 *"I think I'd like to lay down for a while"* . . . *"It's been an honor"*: ibid., November 17, 2017.

344 *"So when he looks down"*: Hart, discussion, March 27, 2017.

344 *"She was always very interested"*: Devers, discussion, February 17, 2017.

344 *"Why am I still here?"*: ibid.

344 *"I just want to go see my boyfriend"*: ibid.

Afterword

345 *"indescribable pride and humility"*: President Gerald R. Ford to Greg Willard, letter, November 6, 2006.

346 *"Mother's decision about the flag"*: Susan Ford Bales and Greg Willard, discussions with author, February 4, 2018.

346 *"On behalf of Mother"*: ibid.

347 *"Where women's health issues are concerned"*: Richard Norton Smith, Betty Ford Funeral, Grand Rapids, MI, July 14, 2011 (C-Span online, video, 1:46:30), www.c-span.org/video/?300520-1/betty-ford-funeral.

347 *"at the Betty Ford Center"*: Moe, discussion, March 28, 2017.

347 *"We do one thing"* . . . *"You can't be all things to all people"*: ibid.

347 *According to the US Department of Health and Human Services . . . 5 percent will transition to heroin*: HHS.Gov/opioids.

348 *Susan worked alongside her mother*: Susan Ford Bales, discussion, January 16, 2018.

348 *Steve Ford has proudly remained sober*: Steve Ford, discussion, January 16, 2018.

348 *Mike Ford continued his work*: Michael Ford, discussion, October 26, 2017.

INDEX